The Operas of Giuseppe Verdi

Abramo Basevi

THE OPERAS OF
GIUSEPPE VERDI

ABRAMO BASEVI

Translated by Edward Schneider with Stefano Castelvecchi

Edited by Stefano Castelvecchi

The University of Chicago Press
Chicago and London

Abramo Basevi (1818–85) was a composer, music promoter, scholar and critic who played a major role in the cultural life of nineteenth-century Florence. He published extensively on music and philosophy and founded the periodical *L'armonia*, where his study of Verdi's operas first appeared. **Stefano Castelvecchi** is a lecturer in music at the University of Cambridge and a fellow of St John's College, Cambridge. He is the editor of critical editions of works by Rossini and Verdi and the author of *Sentimental Opera: Questions of Genre in the Age of Bourgeois Drama*. **Edward Schneider** studied music at Oxford and has translated several books on music and cooking. He was an editor at United Nations Headquarters.

The University of Chicago Press, Chicago 60637
The University of Chicago Press, Ltd., London
© 2013 by The University of Chicago
All rights reserved. Published 2013.
Printed in the United States of America

23 22 21 20 19 18 17 16 15 14   1 2 3 4 5

ISBN-13: 978-0-226-09491-5 (cloth)
ISBN-13: 978-0-226-09507-3 (e-book)
DOI: 10.7208/chicago/9780226095073.001.0001

Questo libro è stato tradotto grazie ad un contributo alla traduzione assegnato dal Ministero degli Affari Esteri italiano.

This book was translated thanks to the support of the Italian Ministry of Foreign Affairs.

Frontispiece: bust of Abramo Basevi, held at the Conservatorio di musica Luigi Cherubini, Florence; photograph from Album W/3 ("R. Istituto musicale di Firenze, Fotografie [1890–1910]"), Biblioteca del Conservatorio di musica Luigi Cherubini, reproduced with permission.

Library of Congress Cataloging-in-Publication Data

Basevi, Abramo, 1818–1885, author.
　[Studio sulle opere di Giuseppe Verdi. English]
　The operas of Giuseppe Verdi / Abramo Basevi; translated by Edward Schneider with Stefano Castelvecchi; edited by Stefano Castelvecchi.
　　　　pages cm
　"This book Abramo Basevi's Studio sulle opere di Giuseppe Verdi (A study of the operas of Giuseppe Verdi) was published in Florence in January 1859"—Editor's introduction.
　Includes bibliographical references and index.
　ISBN 978-0-226-09491-5 (cloth : alkaline paper)—ISBN 978-0-226-09507-3 (e-book)
1. Verdi, Giuseppe, 1813–1901. Operas.　I. Schneider, Edward, 1950–translator.
II. Castelvecchi, Stefano, 1960– editor, translator.　III. Title.
　ML410.V4B213 2013
　782.1092—dc23

　　　　　　　　　　　　　　　　　　　　　　　　　2013040476

♾ This paper meets the requirements of ANSI/NISO Z39.48–1992 (Permanence of Paper).

In memory of
Pierluigi Petrobelli (1932–2012)

CONTENTS

EDITOR'S INTRODUCTION

This Edition

Abramo Basevi's *Studio sulle opere di Giuseppe Verdi* (A study of the operas of Giuseppe Verdi) was published in Florence in January 1859, at the height of Verdi's career. Though early versions of its individual chapters had appeared as journal articles before being revised and collected into a book, they were clearly conceived from the outset as parts of a systematic study, and Basevi's was in fact the first detailed monograph on Verdi's operas ever to be published.[1] Basevi did not examine Verdi's first two operas—*Oberto, conte di San Bonifacio* (1839) and *Un giorno di regno* (1840)—which he saw simply as very early, tentative works, but he dedicated a chapter to each of the twenty that followed, from *Nabucco* (1842) to *Aroldo* (1857). Verdi's final six operas, from *Un ballo in maschera* to *Falstaff*, together with the later versions of *Macbeth* (1865) and *Simon Boccanegra* (1881), postdate the publication of the *Studio*, and Basevi never returned to it in order to update it (which he could have

---

1. Precedents include Benedetto Bermani's much earlier *Schizzi sulla vita e sulle opere del maestro Giuseppe Verdi (estratto dalla Gazzetta musicale di Milano)* (Milan: Ricordi, 1846), which, at thirty-five pages of main text, is no more than what its title candidly declares—a gathering of journalistic "sketches." A book published in the same year as Basevi's *Studio*, Niccola Marselli's *La ragione della musica moderna* (Naples: Detken, 1859), devotes considerable space to Verdi but is not dedicated exclusively to him, and does not come anywhere near Basevi's work in terms of either comprehensiveness or detailed discussion of Verdi's operas.

done in relation to the four new operas that were to appear within his lifetime, up to *Aida*).

Basevi's study of Verdi's operas is unique in a number of respects. Its author was not only a contemporary of Verdi's but also a particularly competent one—a trained musician, a scholar of phenomenal erudition, and someone with a remarkable grasp of the operatic repertoire, past and current. Moreover, as commentators have observed from very early on, his brand of opera criticism was unusual for its day, chiefly in terms of its degree of technical detail: whereas most other writers of the time were verbose and technically deficient—as a distinguished colleague would write on Basevi's death in 1885— this could not be said of Basevi, whose study of Verdi was already considered by many to be a model of music criticism.[2] Such technical detail—especially in relation to what Basevi called "forma"—is largely and understandably seen as the main reason for the "Basevi renaissance" in Verdi studies of the last few decades.[3] But the *Studio* also provides us with a window onto many aspects of operatic culture, and of culture more generally, in Verdi's Italy, and this in spite of those passages that today's reader is likely to find odd, to say the least—indeed, often because of them.

Such considerations help explain the unabating appeal of Basevi's *Studio* among those who wish to engage with Verdi's theater and its ambient culture, and it is hardly surprising that the book should continue to be a point of reference for Verdi scholars (it is mentioned or quoted myriad times even in studies published in only the last decade). A number of terms and concepts found in the work still have currency, or are at least the object of debate, in the scholarship on Verdi and on nineteenth-century Italian opera more generally. This seems especially true in the Anglo-American world, and indeed the main purpose of the present volume is to offer a translation of Basevi's *Studio* to the interested English-reading public.[4] Such a translation should be of use not only to students taking courses or writing dissertations on Verdi and Italian opera (and perhaps to more technically inclined operagoers) but also to

2. Alessandro Biaggi, "Del Dottore Abramo Basevi," *La nazione*, December 1, 1885, in *Catalogo Basevi*, li–liv, li, lii.

3. An important step in the critical revival of Basevi as a formalist is Harold Powers, "'La solita forma' and 'The Uses of Convention,'" *Acta musicologica* 59 (1987): 65–90.

4. Two chapters of Basevi's book have already appeared in English translation, the one on *Macbeth* (in a translation by Edward Schneider) in David Rosen and Andrew Porter, eds., *Verdi's Macbeth: A Sourcebook* (Cambridge: Cambridge University Press, 1984), 421–25; and the one on *Simon Boccanegra* (in a translation by Walter Grauberg) in Ian Bent, ed., *Music Analysis in the Nineteenth Century*, 2 vols. (Cambridge: Cambridge University Press, 1994), 2:200–212.

scholars who wish to resort to a ready English text for quotations or in order to check on their comprehension of the original: Basevi's language—technical, often stylistically ornate, and in places philosophical—can prove challenging even for those non-native scholars who have a good grasp of Italian (as indeed it sometimes does for native ones).

Basevi's Italian text of 1859 is widely available in a facsimile reprint from 1978 and in a modern edition from 2001.[5] This is one of the reasons for the decision to retain his somewhat idiosyncratic paragraphing in this English translation, in that it will allow readers who want to refer back to the Italian text to do so more readily. (And however peculiar that paragraphing may look today it will be found to have a logic of its own.) We have not attempted to bring Basevi's text up-to-date—a gargantuan task that would only overburden the translation and would anyway be out of place here. The footnotes rather provide references and additional information for the musical passages, historical figures and events, and sources (literary or otherwise) mentioned by Basevi, at times commenting on his analytic approach, lexical choices, and cultural allusions. It has been noted that, "in virtually all of Basevi's bibliographic references, he cites neither chapter nor verse, and he frequently neglects to give the titles of the works he cites"[6]—which was of course far from unusual at the time. I have attempted to trace as many as possible of the sources for his references and allusions. His "asides" alone would be sufficient evidence of an astonishing cultural compass, especially considering that he basically wrote the book in his late thirties (he finished it at forty): quite apart from his thorough knowledge of musical scores (to which we will return), his sources—many of them far from obvious, some downright obscure—range from ancient Greek and Latin to medieval and modern European languages, traversing music theory, literature, drama, historiography, political theory, aesthetics (and philosophy more generally), and much of the nascent field of musicology.

5. Abramo Basevi, *Studio sulle opere di Giuseppe Verdi* (Florence: Tofani, 1859; facsimile reprint, Bologna: Antiquae Musicae Italicae Studiosi, 1978). For the 2001 edition, see the entry *Piovano* in our list of bibliographic abbreviations. Piovano's edition is extremely useful in many ways (to which we will have frequent occasion to return), in spite of a number of typesetting errors (including the omission of words or sentences from Basevi's text).

6. Jesse Rosenberg, "Abramo Basevi: A Music Critic in Search of a Context," *Musical Quarterly* 86 (2002): 630–88, 634. Rosenberg's article is the most substantial attempt to outline Basevi's overall intellectual and cultural profile in a way that extends well beyond the customary focus on the *Studio* (which Rosenberg still considers at length).

Basevi

Abramo Basevi was born in 1818 in Livorno, then part of the Grand Duchy of Tuscany, into a prominent Jewish family (his father Emanuele served as chancellor of the city's "Università Israelitica," as the Jewish community was known).[7] He took a degree in medicine from the University of Pisa, but being of independent means was then able to devote himself chiefly to his favorite fields of study—music and philosophy. He studied composition under Pietro Romani in Florence, the city that would become the center of his activities, and in which he would die in 1885. It was there that two operas composed by Basevi in his twenties were staged, but while *Romilda ed Ezzelino* (to his own libretto, Teatro Alfieri, 1840) seems to have achieved at least a degree of critical success,[8] the failure of *Enrico Howard* (libretto by Francesco Guidi, Teatro alla Pergola, 1847) marked the end of his compositional career. By this time, Basevi's operatic endeavors, like those of many other Italian musicians of his generation, were becoming eclipsed by the success of a composer only five years his senior, as would be brought home to him with almost brutal directness when the fiasco of his *Enrico Howard* was immediately followed in the same season at the Pergola by an early revival of Verdi's *Macbeth*, a work that had premiered to great acclaim in the same theater a couple of months earlier.

Florence was at this time a flourishing center of many forms of musical activity, to all of which Basevi was to make important contributions. As we will see, he would rise to prominence in the musical life of the city (and beyond) not only through his work as a critic and scholar, but also by taking an active part in—and in many cases being the main engine for—the promotion of concerts, lectures, and composition competitions, the publication of journals and musical scores, the foundation of a musical society, and the establishment of the institution that would eventually become Florence's conservatory. As dizzying as the number, variety, and innovatory aspects of these activities might appear, from a distance they can all be seen to have been spurred by a common

---

7. The following overview of Basevi's life relies extensively on Antonio Addamiano, "La figura e il ruolo di Abramo Basevi nella vita musicale del secondo Ottocento a Firenze," in *Catalogo Basevi*, ix–xxxv; and Ugo Piovano, "Abramo Basevi e il suo tempo," in Piovano, 7–48.

8. On the basis of newspaper reports, Marcello De Angelis claims that *Romilda ed Ezzelino* was well received by both critics and spectators, whereas Piovano presents a more checkered picture. See Marcello De Angelis, *La musica del Granduca: Vita musicale e correnti critiche a Firenze, 1800–1855* (Florence: Vallecchi, 1978), 38; and Piovano, 14.

motivation—what Basevi saw as the much-needed betterment of Italy's musical culture and musical life.

In the nineteenth century, Florence was host to numerous music publishing houses, in 1840 becoming the first city in Italy to have a periodical specifically dedicated to music, the *Rivista musicale di Firenze*. It was in this journal that, in 1841–42, Basevi published his first articles, which—drawing on his scientific, philosophical, and musical competences—focused on aesthetics and on the physiology of hearing. Some sense of the intellectual temperament of the twenty-two-year-old Basevi may be gleaned from a glance at "Music from a Philosophical Point of View," which expounds a radically relativistic theory of music: as music does not imitate nature but is only a product of the human mind, musical taste is inevitably influenced by factors such as upbringing and habits, which accounts for the variety of taste to be found among different peoples. Thus, "there is no such thing as an absolute rule in music," and any norm about the beautiful in music will vary according to individual conditions, geography, and customs. Such relativism extends from the geographic axis to the historical: we should not renounce music that gives us pleasure "in order to follow the rules established by the ancients, as we certainly have no obligation to hear with our ancestors' ears."[9]

Basevi would later collaborate with the Florentine music publisher Giovanni Gualberto Guidi in the production of three important music periodicals, to which he contributed variously as founder, critic, editorial adviser, and director: the *Gazzetta musicale di Firenze* (1853–55); its successor, *L'armonia*, audaciously subtitled *Organo della riforma musicale in Italia* (1856–59); and *Boccherini* (1862–82), the official organ of the Società del Quartetto (on which more below). Basevi and Guidi also worked together on the publication of affordable pocket scores for study of the "classics" of chamber and orchestral music (but also of miniature full scores of operas, which Guidi is quite possibly the first to have printed).

This music publishing activity was inextricably bound up with that of promoting concerts. Since the 1830s, Florence had been an important center for the performance in Italy of what was coming to be called "musica classica"

9. "La musica considerata filosoficamente," *Rivista musicale*, August 16, September 1, 1841, reprinted in Giuseppe Mazzini, *Filosofia della musica, e Estetica musicale del primo Ottocento*, ed. Marcello De Angelis (Rimini and Florence: Guaraldi, 1977), 112–17, 115 ("[la] varietà del gusto musicale dei diversi popoli e delle diverse nazioni"), 116 ("mancanza di una norma assoluta in fatto di musica"), 117 ("onde seguire le regole stabilite dagli antichi; giacché noi non siamo sicuramente obbligati ad udire colle orecchie degli antenati").

(mostly orchestral and chamber music from beyond the Alps), through a lively concert life in both private and public venues, and through the establishment of the first philharmonic society in the peninsula. An idea of the major role Basevi would soon play in this and related phenomena can be gained from a list of the initiatives he helped found (and often fund): the concert series Mattinate Beethoveniane (from 1859), which in 1861 turned into the Società del Quartetto (the first of its kind in Italy, offering performances of instrumental music by Boccherini, Haydn, Mozart, Beethoven, Schumann, and Brahms); the Concorso Basevi, a competition for composers initially of string quartets (1861), then of quartets with piano, and finally of symphonies; the Concerti Popolari (from 1863), in which "musica classica" was performed by a large orchestra to wide audiences; series of lectures introducing Boccherini, Haydn, Mozart, Beethoven, and Mendelssohn in association with performances of their music (from 1864); and concerts of operatic music by composers such as Cimarosa, Spontini, Sacchini, Mayr, and Paer.[10]

In the years around 1860, during which Tuscany gradually became part of the new Kingdom of Italy, Florence laid the foundations of an independent Istituto Musicale (which eventually turned into today's Conservatorio Luigi Cherubini). Basevi was called on to participate in the committee that drew up the statutes and ordinances of the new institute, and later became a member of its board of directors. It was to this institution that he bequeathed his extraordinary collection of books, music manuscripts, and printed scores, which is still held there as the Fondo Basevi.[11] Indeed, many a graduate student will have heard Basevi's name in connection not with Verdi but with one of the important manuscripts from this collection. (The "Basevi Codex," for example, is an early sixteenth-century source for secular and sacred music.)

Concurrently with all these activities, Basevi kept up with his work as a critic and scholar: he published a plethora of articles,[12] and his book on Verdi—which within a year of publication had gained him an entry in Fétis's *Biographie universelle*—would be followed in the 1860s by two in which he

---

10. Much of this activity related to a perceived need to foster the production and consumption of instrumental music in Italy, where opera was predominant. The established opera composer Giovanni Pacini claimed to have been inspired to write string quartets, something he had never done before, by "the impulse given to chamber music" by Basevi. Giovanni Pacini, *Le mie memorie artistiche* (Florence: Guidi, 1865), 145 ("l'impulso dato alla musica da camera").

11. Of a planned catalog of the entire collection, only the volume for opera scores (manuscript and printed) has been published so far. See the entry *Catalogo Basevi* in our list of abbreviations.

12. For a list of Basevi's articles, see Piovano, 76–84.

developed his perception-based theory of harmony.[13] By 1867, he had abandoned all public activity connected with music (though he would continue to acquire scores for his personal library), thenceforth devoting himself chiefly to philosophical studies.[14]

Into the *Studio*

The *Studio sulle opere di Giuseppe Verdi* is largely a reworking of a number of articles Basevi had published in *L'armonia* between 1856 and 1858. (The book's preface was written afresh.) With very few exceptions, these articles were not ordinary journalistic material, but rather formed part of a more ambitious plan from the very beginning, appearing under the common title "Studio sulle opere di Giuseppe Verdi" followed by a progressive chapter number.[15] In turning his articles into a book, Basevi introduced changes with an eye to the overall shape of the work, eliminated references to specific singers' performances, and toned down some of his criticisms of Verdi.[16]

As we have seen, the man who conceived this wide-ranging study of Verdi's theater had given up on his own hopes of a career as an opera composer about a decade earlier. Though the book never refers explicitly to this personal background, it is hard not to read into a few of its passages a crypto-autobiographical component. The most notable example is found toward the very beginning of the book, where we read of young composers "falling suddenly into oblivion and abruptly and irrevocably losing all the fruits of the tremendous effort required merely to place a work before the public." Basevi was all too familiar with the case of at least one of these young musicians, condemned to "pitiable silence" and "perpetual banishment" from the operatic stage "after one or at the most two tries."[17] But it would be unfair to read his critical work as the fruit of composerly discontent or even animosity: Basevi

13. Abramo Basevi, *Introduzione ad un nuovo sistema d'armonia* (Florence: Tofani, 1862), and *Studi sull'armonia* (Florence: Guidi, 1865). See François-Joseph Fétis, *Biographie universelle des musiciens et bibliographie générale de la musique*, 8 vols., 2nd ed. (Paris: Firmin Didot, 1860–65), vol. 1 (1860), s.v. "Basevi (A.)." Of a projected concise outline of the history of music Basevi published only the first two volumes (under sixty pages each), covering the period from antiquity to Palestrina: *Compendio della storia della musica* (Florence: Guidi, 1865–66).

14. Basevi went on to publish three more books between 1871 and 1882, all of which deal with the principle to which he referred as "divination." See Rosenberg, "Abramo Basevi," 668–76.

15. The exceptions consist of four reviews, one of which was the only one of these writings to appear before 1857. See Piovano, 52–53.

16. For a number of significant original readings, see Piovano, passim.

17. See pp. 1–2 below. See also the final paragraph of chapter 11.

was ready to praise living composers of opera when he felt admiration for them (as he does often with Verdi, and always with his idol Meyerbeer), and indeed was commended by Fétis precisely for his evenhandedness.[18]

On the whole, Basevi's book can make for unusual reading from our point of view: it is easy to become impatient at the way he examines pieces blow by blow (and operas piece by piece), or at his many and often lengthy digressions, his moral asides, and even his occasional "composition lesson" to Verdi. But careful reading brings its rewards, some of which were already apparent to a contemporary of Basevi's who commented on the *Studio*: "Some found the book too methodical, too analytical, too detailed [. . .]. And so it proves [. . .] to those who read it only to read it. But the book needs, rather, to be studied."[19] And of course in our case there is the added element of historical distance, which will increase both the efforts and the rewards.

Basevi's digressions can contribute substantially to our piecing together, if not a systematic aesthetics (which is present only *per fragmenta*), at least a living, pragmatic poetics of music and opera—the author's own, and to some extent that of his environment. Aside from his discussion of technical terms (some of which he either coined or bestowed with special meaning), a number of his excursuses and asides come close to the field of aesthetics proper (for example, those on imitation in music and on the unity of the artwork, to name but two subjects).[20] For him, music is emphatically neither a determinate language (like verbal language) nor an imitative art (like the visual arts or literature). On the other hand, it is capable of relating in very concrete ways to its milieu. Basevi declares his historicist—or perhaps contextualist—stance from the very preface: "The relationship between music on the one hand and politics, philosophy, and industry on the other is so important that I have taken every opportunity to discuss it, to the extent that befits the nature of this book."[21] And so he has. We may smile at the long digression that provides a sketchy survey of the history of Western music, but we should acknowledge Basevi's effort to see developments in composition in relation to developments in society and politics, philosophy and religion.[22] Of a similar cast are

18. See Fétis, "Basevi," 262 ("Appréciateur impartial des ouvrages du compositeur Verdi").

19. Biaggi, "Del Dottore Abramo Basevi," lii ("Da alcuni quel libro venne giudicato troppo metodico, troppo analitico, troppo minuzioso [. . .]. E tale riesce [. . .] a chi lo legge per leggerlo. Ma quel libro invece, vuol essere studiato").

20. On imitation in music, see pp. 62–64 below. The book deals in more than one place with the question of unity and related topics, to which we will return.

21. See p. 10 below.

22. See pp. 127–32 below.

his specific attempts to locate Verdi's works in their (often most immediate) historical and cultural circumstances. Thus, we are invited to see *I Lombardi alla prima crociata* as emerging in the same context as Vincenzo Gioberti's book *Del primato morale e civile degli Italiani* (which was written at the same time), to see *Ernani* as a response to a Europe-wide revolutionary and libertarian drive that entails Hugo's romanticism and the July Revolution in Paris, and to see *La traviata* as part of a recent trend of moral decay in literature and in society at large.[23]

In a general sense, Basevi's views about the current state of opera are relatively clear. Moving from an initial position of skepticism toward Wagner, he had experienced a brief Wagnerian idyll, which by the late 1850s was spent.[24] In his view, the much-needed reform of Italian opera might draw inspiration not so much from Wagner as from Meyerbeer. As he explains in the book's final pages, the effects of German influence could give new life to Italian music and opera. Some "marrying" (*affratellamento*) of the two national traditions had been successfully accomplished at various points in the past, and Verdi had recently made a laudable yet unsuccessful attempt in that direction with *Simon Boccanegra*. Better results were being achieved by Meyerbeer, a German whose music had already been "tempered" by Italian music. (No mention here of the French component so important in Meyerbeer by this time.) In this, Basevi's views partly overlapped with those expressed in another book published in 1859, Niccola Marselli's *Ragione della musica moderna*. Marselli, a Hegelian, felt that the "Artist of the Future" was bound to be whoever could achieve a "synthesis" between the German and the Italian schools, which had found their greatest fulfillment in Meyerbeer and Verdi, respectively; he thought that *Boccanegra* marked a step in the direction of that "median point"—he could breathe in it "the air of Germany, while still remaining in Italy"—and urged Verdi to continue along that path.[25]

Also of interest are Basevi's remarks on a number of more specific topics: the necessity of balancing the claims of verisimilitude with those of operatic convention, for example, or the need for a composer occasionally to "betray"

23. See pp. 28, 44–45, and 191–95 below.

24. Between February and July 1856, Basevi published a three-part article on musical reform in Germany, had an exchange of letters with Wagner, and then published two sets of excerpts from *Oper und Drama* in Italian translation. His rapid disillusionment with Wagner is likely to be due to the composer's position on Meyerbeer and to his anti-Semitism. See Rosenberg, "Abramo Basevi," 643–46.

25. Marselli, *Ragione della musica moderna*, 101, 242 ("Io sento nel *Boccanegra* l'aura dell'Alemagna, rimanendo tuttavia in Italia"), 243.

the libretto—to transcend or bypass the strict meaning of the words when he can see more deeply than the poet into the nature of a dramatic situation.[26] These two examples alone give us some idea of what Basevi may have meant in calling for a full-fledged "poetics of opera"—one of several areas that the embryonic field of opera studies (and musicology more generally) was in need of developing, together with a "musical genealogy" (concerning the historical emergence and decay of melodies) and a "musical morphology."[27]

Of course the *Studio* does more that just hint at such a morphology, and we will return to this aspect of the book, one that has received a great deal of scholarly attention. But it is to be hoped that readers will not allow this focus on form (which is undeniable, though has perhaps been overemphasized in the past few decades) to blind them to the many critical insights that either grow out of it or are entirely independent of it. In the case of the duet for Macbeth and Lady Macbeth following the murder of King Duncan, for example, the legitimate interest in Basevi's label for the opening section (*tempo d'attacco*) should not divert our attention from his sensitive hearing of the passage in which an "almost *opera buffa*–like" melody, in association with the dramatic context and orchestration, manages to intensify "the horror of the scene [. . .] with a blood-red glow."[28] To be sure, many of Basevi's assessments will appear superseded in light of more recent scholarship. (We no longer take such a negative view, for example, of the reworking of *Lombardi* into *Jérusalem*, and today's critic would be hard put to argue that *La traviata* compares unfavorably with *I Lombardi*.) It should be no less interesting, however, for the reader to note the frequent instances of the opposite—the many cases in which Basevi's remarks and insights, especially in matters of detail, have been revived (whether consciously or not) by Verdi critics of the following 150-plus years.

In addition to the parts of Basevi's text that are difficult to comprehend for linguistic reasons, there are occasional passages that perplex us in other ways—passages that make the cultural distance between Basevi's world and ours especially evident—and steering clear of these passages, on account of their opacity or the unease they may cause, would show a curiously unhistorical approach.[29] A notorious example, and one with a proven potential to

26. See pp. 49–50 and 157 below.
27. See pp. 103, 113, and 247 below.
28. See p. 95 below.
29. This is one of the main contentions of Roger Parker's "'Insolite forme,' or Basevi's Garden Path," in *Leonora's Last Act: Essays in Verdian Discourse* (Princeton, NJ: Princeton

surprise modern readers, is that of Basevi's attack on *La traviata* on moral
grounds.[30] And yet if his attitude, however alien to us, is at all historically
significant, it may be so not because of its uniqueness but for the opposite
reason—that it is likely to be representative: it is hard to imagine that, in the
1850s, Basevi would have been the only member of the Florentine bourgeoisie
to condemn "free love" (and the apparent condoning of it by Verdi's opera).
These moments of "anthropological dissonance" can of course provide good
starting points for the work of the cultural historian, but our discomfort at
them—or indeed our attraction to them—should not distract us any more
than Basevi's "formalism" from his critical accomplishments. In the case in
point, rather more noteworthy than his moralism (and leaving aside his attempt to place *Traviata* within a broad literary trend that includes Stendhal,
Balzac, and George Sand) is that few people would have been able to discern
and articulate so precisely the complex of features that characterize this opera
and its modernity: its strong French associations (partly stemming from the
use of musical forms), as well as the constellation of traits that bring it very
close to the traditions of domestic tragedy and bourgeois drama (the association of pathos with "comic" elements such as private situations, a contemporary setting, and characters of a social condition similar to that of the spectators).[31] In the 1870s, a French biographer of Verdi would quote at considerable
length the passage in which Basevi discusses these issues of genre, calling him
"an Italian critic of excellent sense," and apparently finding nothing extraordinary in his moral censure.[32] Here too Basevi's assessment partly overlaps
with that of Marselli: the two critics sensed similar elements in *Traviata* (its
generic specificity and its connections with modern life and the literature and
drama that reflected it; its sympathy for the female protagonist and tolerance
toward a certain kind of amorous relationship), but attributed opposite value
to them. Marselli placed *La dame aux camélias* in a literary tradition (beginning with Prévost's *Manon Lescaut*) that had managed to turn seemingly

---

University Press, 1997), 42–60 (also published in Martin Chusid, ed., *Verdi's Middle Period
[1849–1859]: Source Studies, Analysis, and Performance Practice* [Chicago: University of Chicago
Press, 1997], 129–46).

    30. See chapter 17 below, esp. pp. 191–95 and 202–3.

    31. See esp. pp. 196–97 below.

    32. Arthur Pougin, *Verdi: Histoire anecdotique de sa vie et de ses oeuvres* (Paris: Calmann Lévy,
1886), 161–63, 161 ("un critique italien de grand sense"). The book originates in a series of
articles published in a French periodical, in which this passage already appears (*Le ménestrel*,
February 10, 1878, 81–83, 83).

lascivious women into objects of compassion; for him, Verdi, "artista mo-
dernissimo," was "the artist of our society, in that he gives musical expression
to modern drama."[33]

Basevi's "Critica Analitica"

A number of Basevi's remarks suggest that he basically thought of his book
as one written by a musician for the benefit of other musicians, albeit with an
eye to a broader readership. And indeed, despite the important role played by
factors such as dramaturgy, history, and aesthetics, the *Studio* keeps a strong
focus on the musical side of things. For all his interest in its theoretical and
historical aspects, Basevi had an intensely concrete, practical relationship
with music, as is clear from the nature of his musical references. One marvels
not just at the breadth of his knowledge, especially in relation to the Italian
and French operatic repertoires, but at his aural command of those repertoires, evident in his ability to recall passages analogous to those under discussion. (And readers inclined to pursue his references will soon discover for
themselves what I have only occasionally signaled in footnotes, namely, that
his parallels are often musically richer than he suggests—pertinent in ways
that go beyond the traits he explicitly mentions.)

As we have seen, the degree of technical specificity found in the *Studio* was
unusual for the time—something that has been noted by commentators from
its day to our own, and that was in a sense acknowledged by Basevi himself.[34]
In the preface, he observed that a book intended principally for "maestri"
would have to eschew impressionistic description in favor of "analytic criticism," later referring to his "method" as "analysis."[35] Basevi seems to have
used the term *analysis* largely in the way in which it is used by philosophers
(to refer to the breaking down of a complex whole into its elemental constitu-
ents—as is also shown by his opposing it to *synthesis*) and perhaps also by
grammarians (witness his "analisi" of the "discorso musicale" into "frasi"

33. Marselli, *Ragione della musica moderna*, 76, 79, 80 ("l'Artista della nostra Società poi che
dipinge coi suoni il Dramma moderno").

34. After a discussion of *parlanti* lasting several pages, for example, Basevi remarks that he
thought it useful to have examined a matter that had previously been given little attention (see
p. 37 below).

35. See pp. 8 ("critica analitica") and 103. Basevi's work is anthologized, and given very
serious consideration, in a relatively recent book on nineteenth-century music analysts—Bent,
ed., *Music Analysis*.

and "periodi").[36] And indeed his reader has to bear with a certain amount of tautological, left-to-right description (there is this, and then this, and then this . . .). It could be argued that the analysis is not purely linear and additive but also has a hierarchical dimension (smaller elements form phrases, phrases form periods, and so on to form entire pieces). The impression remains, however, of a predominantly paratactic process—and one almost entirely devoid of developmental aspects (an approach that is anyhow largely invited by the nature of the musical material).

Basevi's analytic practices could be said to reveal a quintessentially Italianate mind-set: his idea of form is clearly melody dominated[37] and indeed most often voice dominated.[38] But focus on the voice does not imply focus on the poetic text. In several cases, the clear impression is that the formal analysis proceeds directly from the musical score, without consideration of the libretto: Basevi at times ignores the formal makeup of the poetry, for example, or describes passages in the score as (more or less literally) "reprised" or "repeated," without distinguishing cases in which the musical material returns in association with the original words from those in which it is used to press on with new portions of text.[39]

Basevi could hardly be called an organicist in the most radical sense (he never suggests, for example, that everything in a piece—let alone in an opera—should germinate from a single seed). Still, ideas of organicism and unity clearly play an important part in his musical thinking. In the preface, he states that Giuseppe Carpani's book on Haydn "is sorely lacking in anything approaching *criticism proper*" (emphasis added) because Carpani's examination of the "organismo" of musical pieces is superficial; not long afterward

36. See, for example, Basevi's use of "discorso musicale" (or "discorso delle melodie") on pp. 134, 178, and 245.

37. Basevi's position can occasionally come across almost as a caricature of the Italian ideal of the primacy of melody, as when he discourages Verdi from adopting Rossinian pseudo-canonic techniques and claims that imitative counterpoint has been used by composers (especially the "ancient" Flemish ones) to conceal a lack of imagination—basically equating musical imagination with melodic inventiveness (see p. 19 below).

38. This is sometimes apparent from Basevi's measure counts (which are frequently not watertight anyway). When, for example, he states that the Terzetto–Finale terzo of *I Lombardi* concludes with *six* cadential measures (see p. 39 below), it is because he is counting only those that include music for the vocal parts, not the ensuing ones for the orchestra alone.

39. See, for example, Basevi's use of *repeat* and *reprise* on pp. 20 (in relation to Nabucco's delirium), 145 (the andantino "Fra' mortali ancora oppressa" from *Luisa Miller*'s first-act finale), and 190 (*Trovatore*, Finale ultimo). Needless to say, the relationship between music and the deployment of poetic material in a given musical setting is part of the composer's formal choices and warrants consideration in analysis.

he claims that, since musical pieces work as organisms, analytic criticism is
the form of inquiry that can lead us from their anatomy to their physiology.[40]
In the realm of opera, his brand of musical organicism certainly applies to
what he calls "pieces"—individual numbers or substantial movements within
multipartite numbers. In at least one case, his suggestion that any good piece
will display a degree of "unity"—a connection between "the various parts
of a musical edifice"—is phrased in terms of his favorite melodic-discourse
analysis; in another, his praise for what he calls the "structure" of a largo
comes at the end of a brief examination that manages to integrate aspects of
melody, texture, dynamics, harmony, and rhythm.[41]

If Basevi could be an organicist of sorts in relation to segments of an opera,
he believed that it was not possible to apply the same approach to an opera as
a whole—or at least not *yet* possible, for theatrical music was not sufficiently
developed. In no one opera could one find a specific *musical* idea that would
work as a unifying factor; for such a centripetal force, operatic music had to
rely on "the general concept behind the drama" (so that the much-discussed
tinta, an opera's overall musical "coloring" or "hue," is in a sense a by-product
of the drama's unity rather than music's main goal).[42] Yet some unity of conception was also the composer's business, as a number of passages in the *Studio* indicate. Not only is our perception of a piece influenced by the other
pieces in the same opera because of the necessary relationship between them;
more importantly, within an opera the composer should maintain continuity
in each character, consider the proportions between the dimensions of individual pieces and those of the "whole," and impart a degree of musical ho-
mogeneity—uniformity of musical conception and style.[43] It is perhaps worth
recalling that the conflicting drives we sense in Basevi—on the one hand the
relatively self-contained nature of the parts of a number opera and on the
other their interrelations within the opera as a whole—also characterize Verdi's own operatic conception and practice.[44]

The glossary that follows will allow us to examine Basevi's terminology
in the context of nineteenth-century usage in general, and this will often—
perhaps not surprisingly—lead us back to those specific matters of form for
which Basevi is most frequently mentioned. A few words on the nature of his

40. See pp. 7 and 8–9.
41. See pp. 154 and 156.
42. See p. 104.
43. See pp. 109, 211, 212–13, 215, and 217.
44. See Fabrizio Della Seta, *Italia e Francia nell'Ottocento* (Turin: EDT, 1993), 216–18.

"formalism" are perhaps in order here. Basevi was undoubtedly a formalist, if by that we mean that he valued a particular approach to music, one evident in his call for a "critica analitica," his continual recourse to formal criteria (and indeed to the word *forma*, however intended), and his frequent references to formal conventions. But he was *not* a formalist if the implication is (as sometimes seems to be the case) that he would have judged pieces in terms of their adherence to a formal "norm." In fact, on many occasions he showed himself to be far from disappointed by Verdi's divergence from established practice, often in fact commending the composer for it. In the book's first few chapters, for example, we are told that in *Nabucco* Verdi's avoidance of the usual wholesale repetition of a section "obeys dramatic truth" and his closing an act without the customary cadential passages demonstrates his "love of art"; that the third-act finale of *I Lombardi* does not have a stretta because Verdi attached greater importance to the effect on the audience than "to slavishly obeying an inveterate habit of composers"; and that the Terzetto finale of *Ernani* is "to be numbered among the most beautiful of pieces, also for a certain novelty of form."[45] Similar assertions are to be found in the articles in *L'armonia*: the cases in which Verdi did not use a stretta to close an act finale had scandalized old fogeys (*parrucconi*), and Solera's libretto for *I Lombardi* "displays such independence of form that it greatly helped Verdi to avoid the many commonplaces by which music had almost been rendered infertile."[46] Ironically, the man best known for his reference to the "solita forma" was one who, with regard to music, often used *solito* or equivalent terms in an ironic or derogatory way—as did Verdi himself on a number of occasions.[47]

Of course there are times when Basevi has no reservations whatsoever about Verdi's adherence to standard practice—or when he indeed complains about his divergence from it. (Perhaps the most notable case is that of some of the "novelties" in *Boccanegra*, of which he declared himself unable to see

45. See pp. 20, 40, and 54 below.

46. *L'armonia*, May 15, June 30, 1857 (Piovano, 379, 383: "mostra tale indipendenza nella forma, che non giovò poco al Verdi per evitare i tanti luoghi comuni, che avevano presso che isterilita la musica").

47. It is more generally true that the Italian adjective *solito* has both a more neutral sense (meaning simply "usual," "customary") and a more loaded one, as in "la solita storia" (the rough equivalent of "the same old story"). The frequently negative implications of Basevi's use of *solito* have already been noted by Rosenberg ("Abramo Basevi," 653). On Verdi's use of this and related terms, see Paolo Gallarati, "Oltre la 'solita forma': Morfologia ed ermeneutica nella critica verdiana," *Il saggiatore musicale* 16 (2009): 203–44, 220 (Verdi uses *formule solite, soliti modi, forma comune*, and *solite forme*).

the point.) But there is no contradiction here. Basevi saw the relationship between tradition and innovation as a dialectical one, as we noted earlier in relation to the delicate balance between convention and common sense: there is no doubt that art "is based on a degree of convention,"[48] but whenever necessary the demands of drama will take precedence over those of established patterns. Indeed, he expressed his "conviction" that there is no such thing as a form that is "proper" to music to the exclusion of other forms, and that "*any* musical form is apt when it responds well to the conception of the drama" (emphasis added).[49] On this matter too we need hardly note that Basevi's ideas chime with Verdi's.

Once again, then, Basevi's approach tends to be pragmatic and contextual, never suggesting that the formal practices he discusses form part of a prescriptive system. ("Normative" interpretations of Basevi may perhaps have been encouraged by the cultural climate of the 1980s, by which time speaking in terms of "norm" and "deviation" had become predominant through the success of metadisciplines such as linguistics and semiotics.) There are all the signs that we can comfortably use Basevi's *Studio* without invoking norms in any authoritarian sense.[50] And as we come to know more about his musical and cultural contexts, and to read his work in light of those contexts, we can acknowledge both his critical voice and his contribution to our understanding of Verdi's world.

48. See p. 157 below.

49. See Basevi's *L'armonia* article of July 15, 1857, in Piovano, 390–98, 397 ("ogni forma [è] acconcia quando risponda bene al concetto drammatico").

50. For a recent methodological reconsideration of Basevi, see Gallarati, "Oltre la 'solita forma.'"

GLOSSARY

The great philologist Gianfranco Contini once showed that Dante's sonnet "Tanto gentile e tanto onesta pare" is bound to be misunderstood by the many Italians who read it today: *gentile*, *onesto*, and *parere*—to look at only the poem's first line—meant something quite different seven centuries ago.[1] Preparing an English edition of Basevi's *Studio* necessarily entails consideration of the degree of "translation," of explication and reformulation, that its original text might require even for today's native speaker of Italian. While such a question occasionally arises in relation to ordinary parlance, it becomes especially pressing in the realm of technical vocabulary: Basevi's "staccato," "allegro," "preparazione," and "modulazione" (to mention just a few examples) do not, or not always, have the same meaning as their modern equivalents.[2] Needless to say, most of the time this is a straightforward matter of different linguistic contexts, Basevi simply using words as other nineteenth-century Italian writers would do. But in a few cases the difference relates to individual usage—what a linguist would call Basevi's "idiolect."

1. Gianfranco Contini, "Esercizio d'interpretazione sopra un sonetto di Dante" (1947), in *Varianti e altra linguistica: Una raccolta di saggi (1938–1968)* (Turin: Einaudi, 1970), 161–68.
2. Earlier studies of Basevi's vocabulary include Alessandro Roccatagliati, "Le forme dell'opera ottocentesca: Il caso Basevi," in *Le parole della musica, I: Studi sulla lingua della letteratura musicale in onore di Gianfranco Folena*, ed. Fiamma Nicolodi and Paolo Trovato (Florence: Olschki, 1994), 311–34; and Piovano, passim (esp. 61–64 and 97–100).

This glossary of technical terms has three main purposes: to explain the terms that have been retained in Italian in the translation, to clarify some of our choices of English equivalents, and even to assist readers (Italian or otherwise) of Basevi's original text. The definitions generally refer to nineteenth-century Italian practice; where Basevi's usage is particular to him, this has been noted. The following brief introduction to basic technical matters is intended to facilitate use of the glossary, and of the book more generally.

Italian opera traditionally distinguished between two fundamental types of poetic verse. One was *versi sciolti* (literally, "loose verse"), a free, irregular alternation of long and short lines (*endecasillabi* and *settenari*—basically eleven- and seven-syllable lines) with no stanzaic organization and only occasional rhyme. The other was *versi lirici* (lyrical verse), organized in stanzas characterized by regularity of poetic meter and rhyme structure. By the early eighteenth century, these two categories largely corresponded to two basic kinds of musical and dramatic treatment, the more speech-like *versi sciolti* being set as recitative that was dramatically "kinetic" (presenting situations and moving the action forward at a naturalistic pace), and *versi lirici* being set as musical numbers (predominantly solo arias at first) that were generally dramatically "static" (the fictional time represented on stage would slow down or stop entirely as action yielded to reflection or the expression of feelings).[3] In the second half of the eighteenth century, an ever greater amount of action was incorporated into the musical numbers, especially those involving more than one character—a process initially more perceptible in comic opera. In the various types of multipartite number discernible in Rossini's operas by the early 1810s (such as duets and act finali), kinetic and static sections alternated in a balanced and successful way, contributing to the establishment of formal practices whose influence would be felt in Italian opera for the following fifty or sixty years.[4]

The works by Verdi discussed in Basevi's book were, like all Italian operas of their time, still organized as number operas; the most visible development in segmentation had been the incorporation of virtually all recitatives into the numbers, most often at their beginning (see the first meaning of *scena* below). Multipartite pieces would often relate to Rossinian and post-Rossinian prac-

3. The terminological opposition *kinetic/static* is derived from Philip Gossett, "The 'candeur virginale' of *Tancredi*," *Musical Times* 112, no. 1538 (April 1971): 326–29.
    4. See ibid.; and Philip Gossett, "Verdi, Ghislanzoni, and *Aida*: The Uses of Convention," *Critical Inquiry* 1 (1974): 291–334.

tice, focusing on two main static sections, the cantabile/largo and the concluding cabaletta/stretta, each of them often preceded and prepared for by a kinetic one—respectively, the *primo tempo/tempo d'attacco* and the *tempo di mezzo*. (On these terms and their various equivalents, see the entries below.) Within a number, then, *versi sciolti* would be used for the recitative passages but could also appear in kinetic sections such as *tempi di mezzo*. Verdi's autograph manuscripts generally make the segmentation into numbers clear, as was common practice at the time. (Individual portions of an autograph score would be sent on to copyists while the composer was working on others, and it was essential that their overall sequence remained unambiguous throughout this process.) But that original segmentation (and the formal choices it implies) is virtually always obfuscated in early printed editions (mostly vocal scores): for practical and commercial reasons, publishers would slice up the operatic acts further, producing smaller units and introducing more titles and sequential numbers. Basevi never makes reference to any numbering, but his segmentation into pieces, and even his wording for their titles, is often in line with that of the published sources: in many cases, what he calls a "cavatina" (or "duetto" or "terzetto") is in the composer's plan not an independent number but part of a larger one (such as an *introduzione* or a finale).[5] Critical editions attempt to restore composers' numbering and titles, and it is to these that the footnotes to our translation will refer whenever possible.

allegro. As well as retaining its general sense (a fast tempo), this term was often used as an equivalent of *cabaletta*.

ansietà (effetto di). Basevi's "ansietà" is less anxiety than anticipation, eagerness, or yearning. He discusses the effect at length in chapter 7, though a better sense of what he means may be gained from an earlier article in *L'armonia* (October 14, 1857), where he says that the *ansietà* induced in us by musical devices is analogous to what we feel "when we see two fast horses approach the end of a race almost side by side"—that is, whenever we desire to see a fast resolution to a situation.[6]

---

5. It should be noted that the two systems are far from mutually exclusive, this being perhaps most obvious in the use of "amphibious" titles. A publisher could carve out of the original numbers some smaller ones but then give them titles such as "Cavatina nell'Introduzione" or "Seguito del Finale," thus alluding to the composer's larger subdivisions. Conversely, a composer, though writing a given section as part of a larger number, could in a private letter refer to it as, say, "cavatina nell'introduzione," thus conceding to it a degree of formal autonomy.

6. The passage is transcribed in Piovano, 197 n. 193.

appendice. As used by Basevi, this term denotes an extended melodic period following a completed melodic period (such as a "lyric prototype": see chapter 3, n. 35, below) but preceding the cadential passages. In one of the articles in *L'armonia* Basevi had written of "a sort of coda or appendix, not to be confused with the usual final, cadential phrases."[7]

attacco. 1: See *tempo d'attacco*. 2: Basevi and his contemporaries sometimes apply *attacco* (in expressions such as *frase d'attacco*) to transitions or codas (a usage relating to *attaccare* in the sense of "connecting" or "appending," rather than "beginning," as in *tempo d'attacco*).

cabaletta, stretta. These terms were commonly used to refer to the final movement of a multipartite number. Dramatically static, this movement was often lively in tempo and rhythmically energetic. In the context of arias and duets, Basevi clearly prefers to use *cabaletta* or its equivalent, *allegro* (which elsewhere of course has the general meaning of fast tempo); within larger ensembles (three or more voices, *introduzioni*, finali) he will rather use *stretta*. In its basic form, a cabaletta involves two statements of a complete, tonally closed melodic period (the two statements being connected by a transition and followed by concluding material). *Cabaletta* appears to have initially designated that main melodic period per se (Basevi himself occasionally seeming to refer to it as "cabaletta" or "allegro").

cantabile. 1: Basevi often refers to a passage as "cantabile" in the general, still current sense of the term ("singable," characterized by a smooth, legato line), sometimes lifting the word directly from the performance direction provided by Verdi for the passage in question. 2: Basevi at times uses *cantabile* as a general term for any sung passage that is not recitative or *parlante* (a usage found in other writers of the time) or, perhaps more precisely, for all static sections—including cabalettas, whose character is often far from cantabile in sense 1 above. In at least one case, Basevi sets up a dichotomy between an opera's cantabili and its "ancillary" parts (*parti accessorie*). 3: Scholars use *cantabile* to refer specifically to the first of two important static sections of a multipartite number. Usually slow in tempo, a cantabile will often be the first formal section of a "double aria"; in multipartite ensembles such as grand duets and finali, it tends to be prepared for by a kinetic section (see *tempo d'attacco*). Rather than *cantabile*, Basevi and many of his contemporaries will often use terms such as *andante* or *adagio* for this formal section (which in the case of finali can have other names,

---

7. Piovano, 385.

such as *largo* or *largo concertato*); their application of *cantabile* to such a section is often likely to be simply a by-product of the use of the word in senses 1 and 2 above.

cavatina. In nineteenth-century Italian practice, this term generally denoted the first aria sung by a particular character in an opera. It was more rarely used with the meaning that had prevailed in the eighteenth century, that of a short, one-section aria, which is the way Basevi uses the term in relation to "Oh de' verd'anni miei" (N. 10 of *Ernani*). The term *cavatina* can be applied to an independent number or to a part of a larger one (as in, for example, "cavatina nell'introduzione").

colorito. See *tinta*.

concertato, largo. Together with phrases such as *largo concertato* or *pezzo concertato*, these form a cluster of terms with partly overlapping meanings. All of them could be used to refer to a formal cantabile section in a large ensemble such as a finale (thus, a static passage in slow tempo involving many voices). Technically, *concertato* refers to *any* passage sung by a number of characters (and possibly the chorus) who have independent parts at least some of the time. *Largo* can of course denote a tempo in general; like *adagio* and *andante*, it can also be used to define the cantabile section in any kind of number.

di forza. Basevi uses the expression in very few places, always with reference to passages in which Verdi gives the vocal part the performance instruction "con forza" ("with strength, with force") or "tutta forza" ("full strength").

di getto, di un sol getto. These expressions—generally meaning "straight off," "in a single sweep," "in a single casting"—were used in musical contexts to refer to melodies, pieces, or even entire operas that give the impression of having been written in a single outburst of inspiration.[8] Basevi uses these phrases (as well as "tutto d'un getto") with specific reference to musical periods that present little or no regularity (melodic repetition or parallelism)—periods that he found especially apt for depicting natural declamation or expressing passion. He also states that to deserve the appellation "di getto" an irregular succession of notes must show the cohesion of a single musical idea.

8. See, for example, Lichtenthal, 1:296 (s.v. *getto*); *Ammaestramenti*, 159, 255; and *Copia-lettere*, 220–21.

discorso, periodo, frase, mezza frase (frasetta, membretto). Like many writers on music since the eighteenth century, Basevi uses the vocabulary of grammarians to define the syntactic units of music. He may be inconsistent in deciding precisely what constitutes a *frase* or a *periodo*, but he is fairly consistent with regard to the hierarchical order: several *frasi* form a *periodo* (as in standard use), several *periodi* form a *discorso*, and a long piece can contain more than one *discorso* (though *discorso* can also be used as a general term, to refer to the way music proceeds). In referring to units smaller than the phrase, he writes variously of *frasette* (small phrases), *mezze frasi* (half phrases), and *membretti* (small units or motifs).

di slancio. See *slancio*.

duettino, terzettino. These diminutive terms were applied to pieces for two or three characters of a lesser formal scope than the respective *duetto* or *terzetto*, generally having one static section only.

economico. A term used to describe a melodic unit consisting of two halves that are identical or almost identical (rather than simply symmetrical, as in ordinary periodic phrasing). An economic period, for example, is formed by the first two phrases of "Di quell'amor" in N. 2 of *Traviata*. *Procedimento economico-musicale* refers to the relative compositional procedure. This usage of *economico* was coined by Basevi (as he implies on p. 22), who treats it as a technical term (it is italicized and indexed in the *Studio*).

effetto di ansietà. See *ansietà*.

effetto di sonorità. See *sonorità*.

forma variata. See *variato*.

frase, mezza frase, frasetta. See *discorso*.

getto. See *di getto*.

introduzione. The title usually given to the first sung piece in a nineteenth-century Italian opera. It is N. 1 of the opera even if preceded by a *sinfonia* (as the latter is not usually numbered), but N. 2 if preceded by a numbered orchestral piece such as a *preludio*. *Introduzioni* are often multisectional (including, for example, choruses, passages of *scena*-like or *parlante* dialogue, cavatinas for the leading characters, and strettas), at times vying in scope with act finali.

largo (largo concertato). See *concertato*.

melodramma. Not to be confused with cognate terms (such as the English *melodrama* and the French *mélodrame*), the Italian *melodramma* can be used to mean "opera" generally. In Basevi, it more often means specifically "libretto" (a drama to be set to music)—a frequent usage in the nineteenth century. Today, the term is also used with more specific reference to nineteenth-century Italian operas of post-Rossinian generations (by which time the eighteenth-century definitions *opera seria* and *opera buffa* were losing their grip).

membretto. See *discorso*.

modulazione. See *transizione*.

mossa. Basevi uses this term (which in general usage can mean "start," "initial impulse") to refer to the opening musical gesture of a piece or section. It does not translate well into *incipit*, as Basevi applies it to anything from the smallest motif to an entire melodic phrase or longer passage.

motivo. This term was generally used by Basevi and his contemporaries—as to some extent it is today—not so much in the sense of "motif" as in that of a more extended idea, self-contained and with a recognizable physiognomy (a "tune")—often a "main melodic idea" or (the most frequent translation below) a "theme."

parlante. Though sometimes used as a synonym for the performance direction "parlando" (in a speaking manner), the noun *parlante* refers to a compositional technique, a specific texture in which the orchestra carries a continuous (often repeating) melodic discourse while, "floating" on top of it, the vocal parts interject syllabically in a more irregular manner. Melodically, the voices can declaim as "speakingly" as in a recitative (though of course constrained by the orchestra's regular pace and harmonies), or they can "sing along with" stretches of the orchestral melody to a greater or lesser extent. Basevi uses the term often and discusses it at length in chapter 2, where he introduces his terminology for the spectrum of *parlante* textures (*armonico-misto-melodico*), a terminology that has been widely adopted since.

periodo. See *discorso*.

pertichino. A vocal number can include secondary interventions by voices other than those of its main character(s); in theatrical jargon, these interventions, or the characters singing them, were known as *pertichini*. *Pertichini* do not change the basic nature of a number; thus, N. 3 of *Traviata* (Violetta's "Ah forse lui") is still fundamentally a solo number (and is indeed labeled "Aria") in spite of the presence of a second voice (Alfredo's, during the cabaletta).

pezzo. Basevi uses the term with reference not only to pieces in the stricter sense (musical numbers) but also to sections thereof that are relatively

self-contained; where the meaning seems clear we have retained his terminology and employed "piece."

pezzo concertato. See *concertato.*

preludio. See *sinfonia.*

preparazione. Basevi occasionally uses this term in its standard technical
sense relating to part writing (as in the English *preparation*). But he more
frequently uses it in another way (which he treats as a technical coinage,
italicizing it, and indexing it at the end of the book)—to refer to the process
by which a secondary musical element, often of little or no appeal in itself,
is used to predispose the listener to the arrival or return of another, more
important one (which will thus become more desired or acquire greater
relief, eventually giving more pleasure).

primo tempo. See *tempo d'attacco.*

procedimento economico-musicale. See *economico.*

quadro musicale. Basevi treats this phrase ("musical picture") as a technical term (often italicizing it), though its meaning is somewhat elusive. He
explains that the historical development of musical numbers, or at least of
their static sections, has allowed music to create more autonomous "pictures" (within the limits of musical depiction, which is by its nature indeterminate)—something that was exploited more fully by Meyerbeer than
by Verdi. For Basevi the term clearly refers not only to tableaux and other
static passages but also to longer, integrated scene–complexes.

racconto. The Italian for "narration," in opera this term denotes a narrative
sung by a character or the chorus. It can form an independent number or
be part of a larger one.

ritmo. This term could be used not only in the usual sense (analogous to
that of the English *rhythm*) but also with reference to large-scale proportions (see, for example, Lichtenthal's use of "qualità ritmica").[9] Basevi's
description of the *brindisi* of *Traviata* ("Libiamo ne' lieti calici") as being
in "an unusual rhythm," for instance, refers to the melody's odd measure
count.

ritmo staccato. See *staccato.*

romanza. A solo song, generally consisting of one static movement in moderate tempo. A standard model, deriving from the French *romance*, is
strophic or modified strophic in form (often setting two stanzas: Basevi
applies the term to three such pieces in *Traviata*). In many examples, the

9. See Lichtenthal, 2:118 (s.v. *periodologia*).

last part of each stanza shifts from the minor mode to the major, either relative or parallel (as in Violetta's "Ah forse lui" in N. 3 of *Traviata*). The label *romanza* was gradually extended to songs or arias that, though not strophic, displayed at least some of the features often associated with the genre—a single movement, moderate tempo, minor-major mode shift, lyrical character, narrative content, or "realistic" nature (portraying a piece performed and heard as a song by characters on stage). This usage is often found in Basevi, in a number of cases following Verdi's explicit titling (one example being "O vecchio cor, che batti" in *I due Foscari*).

scatto (scatti). See *staccato*.

scena. As well as retaining its various earlier meanings (see below), in the context of nineteenth-century Italian opera *scena* came to denote a passage of obbligato recitative or arioso, generally opening a number before the formal piece proper (so that the number would be called "Scena ed Aria," "Scena e Duetto," etc.). *Scena* would occasionally be extended to refer to an entire number (a singer's *gran scena*, for example, would often include sections of both recitative/arioso and aria). The other meanings of *scena* are as follows: the theatrical stage; the setting in which a portion of an opera takes place, especially with reference to the scenery (librettos would list the changes of *scena* from, say, a hall in a palace to a forest or a piazza); a segment of the libretto demarcated by the entrance or exit of one or more characters (as in "act 1, scene 2"); and, perhaps more informally, a dramatic situation (for example, "the scene in which Alfredo insults Violetta publicly").

sinfonia. In Basevi's time, this term was used to refer both to symphonies and to full-scale operatic overtures (such as that of Verdi's *Luisa Miller*). Verdi often gave his operas a shorter orchestral introduction, called a *preludio*.

slancio. Basevi uses *slancio* (meaning "élan, impetuousness, momentum") not only with reference to passages in which a vocal part bears the performance instruction "con slancio" (or analogous ones, such as "con impeto"), but also when, in the absence of such performance directions, he discerns a similarly vehement, propulsive quality in the vocal melody. He often labels a melodic segment "frase di *slancio*" or "periodo di *slancio*" (the latter a term he suggests is his own) to indicate a quality that is compositional before being performative. He writes of the predilection of contemporary audiences for this melodic thrust, which he treats as a quintessential trait of Verdi's music, especially in the composer's first period; indeed, Basevi credits Verdi with creating the extreme variety of this vocal manner (what he calls "grande *slancio*"). Though he sometimes mentions the impetus of a given passage with apparent approbation, he seems to have wearied of *di slancio* melodic periods (occasionally referring to them as "usual" [*soliti*]), and regarded their absence in *Rigoletto* as an auspicious sign within Verdi's stylistic development.[10]

sonorità (effetto di). Basevi's "sonority effect" occurs when the music's impression on the listener derives largely or exclusively from the intensity of the sound (e.g., when melodies are doubled in unison or octaves, trumpets are used, or singers "shout"). While acknowledging its impact, Basevi sees it often as an easy concession to the unrefined taste of audiences. The effect was already in fashion when Verdi made his debut, and it is to his credit that, after his first manner, he resorted less and less to it, and generally with good reason.

staccato, a scatti, a scatto. As well as using *staccato* in its standard sense (and for related styles of vocal delivery), Basevi often uses this term to define a quality he claims is characteristic of Verdi's music and contributes to its brusque energy. One or more features seem to lend a piece or passage the overall quality Basevi calls "staccato," "ritmo staccato," "a scatto," or "a scatti" ("jerky," "in fits and starts"): not only (occasionally even not at all) the written or implied rests between individual notes (staccato proper), but also rests between small portions of the melody (which chop it up), and rests in unnatural positions (within words, or between a dissonant note and its resolution); in some cases a role may be played by other rhythmic factors (such as the added sense of urgency created by the unexpectedly short notes for the main accented syllables of "Il ma-le-*det*-to non ha fra-*tel*-li" in the Coro di Leviti of *Nabucco*).

stretta. See *cabaletta*.

tempo d'attacco. Where the first static movement (cantabile/largo) of a multipartite piece is preceded by an opening, generally kinetic movement (as is frequently the case in duets and ensembles and occasionally in arias),

---

10. The characteristics of this manner of vocal writing are discussed by Gilles De Van in *Verdi's Theater: Creating Drama through Music*, trans. Gilda Roberts (Chicago: University of Chicago Press, 1998), 120–27. See also Roccatagliati, "Le forme dell'opera ottocentesca," 326–27. In an earlier article in *L'armonia* (June 30, 1857), Basevi had written that *di slancio* passages call for great vocal richness (*lusso*); he had also explicitly stated that they are "a concession to the dubious taste of the audience," and commended Verdi for dispensing with them in his later operas (see Piovano, 386).

musicologists often refer to the latter as the *tempo d'attacco*. Basevi seems to be the only nineteenth-century writer on opera to use the phrase: he uses it twice in the *Studio*, both times with reference to duets—one being the famous passage in which he claims that the *tempo d'attacco* is the first movement of "the usual form" (*la solita forma*) of duets. A much more common definition at the time would have been *primo tempo*. Neither phrase is likely to have been perceived as designating a particular *type* of movement—both being fairly neutral ways of saying "opening movement"; indeed, *primo tempo* could also be used by Basevi and his contemporaries to refer to the cantabile of a double aria (see *cantabile* sense 3), which is perhaps one of the reasons for the fortune of Basevi's *tempo d'attacco* in the musicology of the past few decades.

tempo di mezzo. As suggested by the name ("middle section"), this is, in multipartite numbers, a transitional, kinetic section between the two main static ones of cantabile/largo and cabaletta/stretta. Its action often entails an unexpected dramatic turn that functions as a trigger for the excited expression of the concluding section. Basevi is not the only nineteenth-century writer on opera to use the phrase in this sense, and does so often in the *Studio*.

terzettino. See *duettino, terzettino*.

terzetto. Italian usage largely distinguished between *trio*, meaning a composition for three parts (most often instrumental), and *terzetto*, meaning one specifically for three vocal parts.

terzine vuote. Meaning "empty" (or "broken") triplets, this is Basevi's own term for a triplet pattern, generally accompanimental, in which one of the three notes is missing. The pattern is usually note-rest-note (though in one case Basevi uses the phrase for the pattern rest-note-note).

tinta, colorito. Like other Italian critics and composers of the nineteenth century (including Verdi), Basevi writes of an opera's *tinta* or *colorito*—an overall "hue" or "coloring" that is related to the drama and depends on specific musical elements (such as motifs, harmonies, rhythms, timbres). Though not necessarily perceived consciously by the spectator, a musical *tinta* helps create an opera's unique character.

transizione. Basevi generally uses *transizione* to refer to a modulation (a change of key) and *modulazione* for any change of harmony, whether or not it entails a modulation (usages already recorded by Lichtenthal). Our translation uses the English terms in their current sense.

unisono. To indicate that two or more voices are simultaneously singing the same line Basevi uses the term *unisono*, whether the singing is in unison or in octaves (in the *Studio* he uses *ottava* only with reference to the melodic interval); we have employed the translation "unison" in all cases, as the meaning is always clear.

variato, forma variata. Throughout the book, Basevi makes (generally polemical) reference to what he calls the "old form" and "most ancient practice" by which the opening theme of a section of a duet (often a cabaletta) is presented by each of the two characters in turn, and a third time by the two together. He opposes it to the (traditionally less common) practice by which the two characters are assigned different melodic material, calling the resulting sections "varied" or in "varied form."

zoppo. Meaning "lame" or "limping," this term is used by Basevi to describe a melodic phrase or period of irregular length (five, seven, or nine measures). This use of *zoppo* is based on a well-established tradition, the Greek word *skazon* (limping) having long been applied to "irrational" rhythms in classical poetry.

EDITORIAL NOTE

Whenever an opera is already available in a critical edition, we adopt the numbering and titles of individual pieces, as well as measure numbers, from that edition. (The reader conversant with the repertoire might at times be taken aback by quotations such as "Ah forse lui"—rather than the more familiar "Ah forse è lui"—from the critical edition of *La traviata*.) In the titles of musical pieces we use "N." to mean "number" (as in "N. 6, Scena ed Aria"), a standard abbreviation found in much specialized literature and in critical editions such as those of Rossini, Bellini, Donizetti, Meyerbeer—and of course Verdi. In the case of operas for which there is not (or not yet) a critical edition, we have resorted to primary sources or widely available standard scores.

The textual incipits provided by Basevi have, like his other quotations from characters' words, generally been amended in accordance with our chosen main sources (silently, signaling only a few major variants), in order to avoid the confusion that might arise from a conflict between main text and footnotes, and to facilitate the job of the reader who will be keeping an eye on one of those sources. Thus, Basevi's "Nò, forme d'un angiolo" has been amended to "No! forme d'angelo," the version found in *WGV*'s edition of *Giovanna d'Arco*. (The kind of reader who is interested in such text-critical matters as Basevi's variant readings—whether resulting from errors on his part or reflecting the nature of the sources available to him—is one who will be able to resort to the original Italian, and would anyway want to do so.) Where textual incipits for the musical passages under discussion are not provided by Basevi,

and cannot be deduced from the titles in our footnotes, they have been added
to the main text in square brackets.

Where Basevi's tempo indications differ from those in our main sources,
on the other hand, they have not been amended. In many cases the differences
are small ("andante agitato" in place of "andante mosso"), in some less so
("adagio" rather than "andante"), but it is generally clear which passage he
is referring to. Moreover, Basevi's diverse use of terminology would make
amendment of this sort difficult: his "allegro," for example, might designate
a section in that tempo, but also a section in a different tempo that still serves
the function of a cabaletta or stretta.

Names of people have been editorially adjusted into now-standard forms
(for example, "Palestrina" in place of Basevi's "il Pierluigi" or "Josquin des
Prez" for his Italianized "Jusquino del Prato"). Historical variants in the spell-
ing of names of people or places have also been standardized (thus, Jommelli,
Mayr, Paer, Pergolesi, Steffani, and Senigallia, rather than Basevi's Jomelli,
Mayer, Paër, Pergolese, Stefani, Sinigaglia). Where first names are missing (or
represented only by initials) in the original Italian, these have been integrated
silently, as in the case of the many music critics Basevi lists in his preface.
In addition to the usual typographic modernization (for example, removing
Basevi's italics from the names of real-life people), we have introduced a mod-
icum of orthographic modernization when quoting from old sources (so that,
for example, Giovanni Battista Doni's "perfettione" and "soprauanzano"
have become "perfezione" and "sopravanzano").

For many of the Italian technical terms found in the main text (either allowed to stand from Basevi's original or provided in square brackets following
their translation) the reader may resort to the relevant entries in the glossary.

All translations in the footnotes are mine unless otherwise noted.

BIBLIOGRAPHIC ABBREVIATIONS

Ammaestramenti	Carlo Ritorni. *Ammaestramenti alla composizione d'ogni poema e d'ogni opera appartenente alla musica.* Milan: Pirola, 1841.
Budden	Julian Budden. *The Operas of Verdi.* Rev. ed. 3 vols. Oxford: Clarendon, 1992.
Catalogo Basevi	Antonio Addamiano and Jania Sarno. *Catalogo del Fondo Basevi nella Biblioteca del Conservatorio "Luigi Cherubini" di Firenze: Musica vocale—Opere teatrali manoscritte e a stampa.* Rome: Torre d'Orfeo, 1994.
Copialettere	*I copialettere di Giuseppe Verdi.* Edited by Gaetano Cesari and Alessandro Luzio. Milan: Stucchi Ceretti, 1913. Facsimile reprint, Bologna: Forni, 1968.
EC	*Edizione critica delle opere di Gioachino Rossini.* General editor Philip Gossett (1979–2005), Ilaria Narici (2006–). Pesaro: Fondazione Rossini, 1979–.
ECB	*Edizione critica delle opere di Vincenzo Bellini.* General editors Fabrizio Della Seta, Alessandro Roccatagliati, and Luca Zoppelli. Milan: Ricordi, 2003–.
EN	*Edizione nazionale delle opere di Gaetano Donizetti* (until 2001 *Edizione critica delle opere di Gaetano Donizetti*). General editors Gabriele Dotto and Roger Parker. Milan: Ricordi, 1991–.

ERO   *Early Romantic Opera: Bellini, Rossini, Meyerbeer, Donizetti and Grand Opéra in Paris*. Edited by Philip Gossett and Charles Rosen. New York: Garland, 1978–83.

GGA   *Christoph Willibald Gluck: Sämtliche Werke*. General editor G. Croll. Kassel: Bärenreiter, 1951–.

Grove   *The New Grove Dictionary of Music and Musicians*. Edited by Stanley Sadie. 29 vols. 2nd ed. London: Macmillan, 2001.

HW   *Joseph Haydn: Werke*. Edited by the Joseph Haydn-Institut, Cologne. Munich: Henle, 1958–.

IOB   *Italian Opera, 1640–1770: Major Unpublished Works in a Central Baroque and Early Classical Tradition*. Edited by Howard Mayer Brown. New York: Garland, 1977–84.

IOG   *Italian Opera, 1810–1840: Printed Editions of Complete Operas and Excerpts by the Contemporaries of Rossini, Bellini, and Donizetti*. Edited by Philip Gossett. New York: Garland, 1985–91.

Lichtenthal Pietro [Peter] Lichtenthal. *Dizionario e bibliografia della musica*. 4 vols. Milan: Fontana, 1826.

MWA   *Giacomo Meyerbeer Werkausgabe*. General editor Jürgen Selk. Munich: Ricordi, 2010–.

NMA   *Wolfgang Amadeus Mozart: Neue Ausgabe sämtlicher Werke*. Edited by the Internationale Stiftung Mozarteum Salzburg. Kassel: Bärenreiter, 1955–.

PaWV   Wolfram Ensslin. *Chronologisch-thematisches Verzeichnis der Werke Ferdinando Paërs: Die Opern*. Hildesheim: Olms, 2004.

Phillips-Matz Mary Jane Phillips-Matz. *Verdi: A Biography*. Oxford: Oxford University Press, 1993.

Piovano   Abramo Basevi. *Studio sulle opere di Giuseppe Verdi (1859)*. Edited by Ugo Piovano. Milan: Rugginenti, 2001.

Studio   Abramo Basevi. *Studio sulle opere di Giuseppe Verdi*. Florence: Tofani, 1859.

SW   *Richard Wagner: Sämtliche Werke*. Edited by Carl Dahlhaus et al. Mainz: B. Schott's Söhne, 1970–.

WGR   *Works of/Opere di Gioachino Rossini*. General editor Philip Gossett. Kassel: Bärenreiter, 2007–.

WGV   *The Works of/Le Opere di Giuseppe Verdi*. General editor Philip Gossett. Chicago: University of Chicago Press; Milan: Ricordi, 1983–.

ACKNOWLEDGMENTS

It is a pleasure to acknowledge my debt to the many people who have contributed in various ways to the preparation of this book.

For providing information or materials, heartfelt thanks are due to Patrick Boyde, Davide Daolmi, Paolo Fabbri, Andreas Giger, Helen Greenwald, Isabella Gualandri, David Kimbell, Roberta Marvin, Ugo Piovano, Michael Reeve, Federica Riva, Alberto Rizzuti, Jürgen Selk, and Marco Uvietta.

I should like to express my gratitude to the Press's referees, all of whom have been happy to have their names disclosed: Roger Parker made a number of useful comments on the first draft of the translation, while Philip Gossett and Francesco Izzo read the (quasi) final product, offering a great many valuable suggestions. On a more informal basis, Fabrizio Della Seta has been extremely generous with time and advice.

I am indebted to Laura Davey for her support—as always—in all matters editorial, practical, and personal.

Kathleen Hansell, former music editor at the Press, commissioned the book many years ago and waited patiently for it to materialize, providing expert technical input and words of wisdom throughout. She was succeeded at the Press by Marta Tonegutti, a no less supportive editor who has seen the book through to completion. Thanks are also due to the other members of staff at the Press involved in the editing and production of the book.

This edition is dedicated with affection and gratitude to the memory of the Verdi scholar Pierluigi Petrobelli, who will be sorely missed by many as a mentor, a colleague, and a man.

S.C.

The Operas of Giuseppe Verdi

PREFACE

My principal aim in publishing this study of Verdi's operas in book form has been to raise the standing of musical criticism in Italy as far as I am able. And this because I believe that critics have a duty to exert a good influence on the taste of the public and on composers themselves—which will promote the advancement of art.

But I do not presume to be able to achieve this unless the many Italian critics who are so much more equal to the task than I am work toward the same goal. To show that there is no dearth of extremely able music critics in our fair land, I shall name some of those who during Verdi's reign have stood out for their deep wisdom, extensive and well-founded knowledge, or exquisite taste. The following names come immediately to mind: Alberto Mazzuccato, Raimondo Boucheron, Pietro Alfieri, Luigi Ferdinando Casamorata, Carlo Andrea Gambini, Ermanno Picchi, Luigi Picchianti, Pietro Torrigiani, Ruggero Manna, Vincenzo Meini, Geremia Vitali, Raffaele Foresi, Felice Romani, Olimpo Mariotti, Angelo Catalani, Francesco D'Arcais, Giuseppe Staffa, Ferdinando Taglioni, Giuseppe Rovani, Girolamo Alessandro Biaggi—and many others I omit for the sake of brevity.[1]

---

1. Most of the critics named here were also musicians active as composers, performers, teachers, and administrators; they arguably represent the first generation to practice a technically oriented brand of music criticism in Italian periodicals. Among the few exceptions are two notable men of letters: the successful librettist Felice Romani and the writer Giuseppe Rovani.

These fine writers, however, have made the mistake of limiting their activities to critical articles destined only for newspapers. As a result, they have
not sought to give their work the breadth, the structure, or the format that
would make it more useful and important, and that would salvage it from the
oblivion awaiting even the finest things printed in periodicals.

It is also difficult to understand the willingness of even the ablest and most
erudite to go out of their way to hide their strengths, lowering themselves to
the level of the less competent.

This modesty, or rather this indifference to their own strengths, has encouraged other, totally inadequate journalists not merely to compete, but,
profiting by the timidity of their betters, impudently to seize the scepter and
set themselves up as legislators and judges, brazenly spreading among the
public the falsest and most ruinous notions about art.

Alas, the damage caused by this state of criticism is reflected in the work of
many composers, who—with neither hesitation nor shame in the face of good
criticism, seeing its brief life in the newspapers—heed nothing but the cheers
of the crowd, a few even duping it with a charlatan's chicanery.

Music critics must therefore rise from their torpor and assume the authority through which they can ensure that music will be more highly honored in
Italy than it is today.

In France, Castil-Blaze set about remedying the ill, not so much restoring as creating musical criticism, and paving the way for more able judges.
And today that country boasts an august company of fine and influential
critics, among them Paul Scudo, Hector Berlioz, Adrien de La Fage, Joseph
D'Ortigue, Pier Angelo Fiorentino, and many others. Belgium is graced with
the celebrated and indefatigable François-Joseph Fétis, director of the re-
nowned Brussels Conservatory.[2] I shall not even speak of Germany, as there
more than anywhere else musical criticism is held in high esteem and wields
great power.

---

2. Castil-Blaze (François-Henri-Joseph Blaze), who contributed to the founding of *La
France musicale*, may not have "created" French musical criticism but is certainly an important
exponent of its more technically informed trend, which includes the critics listed by Basevi; all
of them (with the exception of Fiorentino) were at least trained in composition if not actually
active as composers, while some of them (La Fage, d'Ortigue) were music researchers in a
more modern sense. François-Joseph Fétis, the founder of the *Revue musicale*, is best known for
his monumental *Biographie universelle des musiciens et bibliographie générale de la musique*, first
published in eight volumes between 1835 and 1844. That Basevi names him separately as the
foremost critic in Belgium should not obscure the fact that Fétis, who spent a good deal of his
professional life in Paris, was an equally central figure in French music criticism.

In Italy, we lack only determination—and faith in our own strengths and in their efficacy. As a result, the misconception that only the deaf would be unable to offer judgment on matters musical is permitted to run rampant. All the inept critics of the journalistic marketplace struggle to bolster this folly, and defend it by repeating continuously, with a thousand voices, that erudite and expert musicians have always waged war on talented beginners, who, in spite of them, and supported only by the public, have been victorious, and to the extent that they have forced their elderly adversaries to bow their heads in defeat.

It is true that jealousy often holds sway among those who profess the same art, but we must not therefore assume that all the judgments tendered by the expert are motivated by that vice. At the same time, it is true that trained musicians can at times be too strict, even intolerant, in their criticism of certain faults about which a great part of the public does not care. But such criticism, though without value for the public, is most important to the composer. There are those who, as proof of the utter uselessness of musical criticism, point to the great Rossini, who, many claim, invariably mocked the observations of the scholars and the knowledgeable. This is completely false. Some of the criticisms leveled at Rossini (I do not speak here of those inspired by jealousy) continue to be true—so much so that he splendidly acknowledged them with his magical masterpiece *Guillaume Tell*. Yes indeed: had Rossini listened to the advice of his fanatical admirers, he would never have advanced a step beyond *Tancredi*—and where would his frenetic claque be now? The skilled critics, on the other hand, have not changed their opinion, and think today what they thought at the time of *Tancredi*. When that opera winged its way from triumph to triumph throughout Europe, they appeared maliciously severe; today, when the public's taste has changed, they are considered rather to be blindly indulgent. But just criticism endures unaltered, and with the passing of time ultimately wins complete vindication.[3] Those who oppose fine and legitimate musical criticism should consider impartially that the so-called old fogeys who might once have taken the liberty of some carping censure

3. Composed when Rossini was not yet twenty-one, the *opera seria Tancredi* (Venice: Teatro La Fenice, 1813) marks the beginning of his European fame; *Guillaume Tell* (Paris: Opéra, 1829) is the work that concludes his career as opera composer, at thirty-seven. At the time of the publication of Basevi's book, Rossini, thirty years into his retirement from the stage, was still revered by many as the greatest living opera composer. Basevi had recently published an introduction to *Guillaume Tell* as an article in *L'armonia* (April 28, 1858); the essay would later appear in a printed score of the opera (Florence: Guidi, 1860): see Piovano, 107 n. 29.

of a few of Rossini's early works still had in their mind's ear the music of Gluck, Handel, Haydn, Mozart, Beethoven, Cherubini, Spontini, et al. It is no wonder that they should have proved a little fastidious! For all that, even the severest of his critics have always admitted the great Rossini's fertile genius.

Criticism by those who understand the art, even when extremely severe, is of more value to the composer than all the praises of the ignorant.

The natural judges on the subject of music are those who have been initiated into the mysteries of that art. Yet the laity too may judge, so long as they do not exceed certain limits. But always bear in mind that, while it is *possible* for a musician to err in his judgments, error is *probable* in a stranger to the art of music.

There is no doubt that the appreciation of musical beauty requires an ear trained by frequent hearing of a variety of music that has been deemed beautiful by the unanimous and enduring consent of the learned. One cause of errors of judgment in respect of musical beauty is the ease with which it can be confused with the beauty in fashion. In this respect music is similar to styles in dress or accessories: by virtue of habit, we all see beauty in things that in other times would have been thought ugly and ridiculous. The principal cause of this is that, when we repeatedly see a beautiful person wearing certain clothes and accessories, we unconsciously credit the style of the clothing with the pleasure we take in the individual's personal beauty and grace: we are tricked into thinking that the fashion is the source of that beauty, while in fact it is only its repository. There is a similar phenomenon in music, where fickle fashion rules with a firm hand: certain melodies, cadences, rhythms, and so forth come to seem pleasant and graceful simply because some singer or instrumentalist employs them frequently; as a result, we accept them more readily. And wherever he finds these musical features the inexpert listener, deceived by habit and by fashion, thinks he is in the presence of true beauty. It is a hard job even for the learned critic to free himself from the prejudices of his time—to say nothing of the ordinary listener!

One way to make musical criticism effective would without question be to transfer it from newspapers to books, in accordance with the ideas expressed by Gioberti in his *Rinnovamento*, where he writes that "only books can foster firm, broad, profound learning: newspapers vulgarize it, shred it, and sell it off by retail."[4]

---

4. The philosopher and politician Vincenzo Gioberti was a prominent figure of the Risorgimento. In *Del rinnovamento civile d'Italia* (Paris and Turin: Bocca, 1851), he had advocated a number of deep social and political reforms. The passage quoted by Basevi is on p. 472.

I maintain that critical books specifically about the works that constitute the artistic life of a single famous musician are completely lacking in Italy. Two books might seem to belie this: Carpani's *Le haydine* and Baini's *Memorie storico-critiche della vita e delle opere di Giovanni Pierluigi da Palestrina*.[5]

Carpani's book contains very valuable observations and wise counsels about art, much erudition, and a good many anecdotes, but the work is sorely lacking in anything approaching criticism proper. It examines the structure [*organismo*] of the musical pieces only superficially. For confirmation of my words, read, for example, the tenth letter, which discusses in detail the great Haydn's *Creation*. In that marvelous passage representing the creation of light, Carpani sees nothing but a unison, an ever-diminishing piano, and a "burst of the full orchestra in the resonant key of C major, replete with all possible sonority." Then, giving full rein to his imagination, he goes on to describe the effect on the listener's feelings, and says that "it struck each listener so strongly that it seemed that a thousand beacons had appeared all at once in the dark abyss of a deep cavern, or that, breaking over a cliff, the sun itself had suddenly materialized, bathing all in its rays, its great sphere filling every cranny." This is all well and good, but it does not explain the chief source of this piece's fine effect—that is, the transition from the minor mode, which induces sadness, to the major, which cheers and revives.

Baini's *Memorie storico-critiche* is a work of much greater value, and one that does high honor to Italy. But here too the bibliographic, historical, and biographical sides stand out, while the criticism is too general—though always worthy of its excellent author. Writing of the "seventh style," in which he places the famous Pope Marcellus Mass, Baini summarizes thus:[6]

> Who would believe it if he saw the hand of the blessed Fra Angelico of Fiesole applied to the "Judgment" in the Sistine Chapel at the Vatican, or that of Michelangelo applied to a miniature of a beetle or a butterfly or a leaf on the title page of a book in our apostolic chapel? Yet this is the case here. The pen

---

5. The librettist Giuseppe Carpani had in 1812 published *Le haydine, ovvero Lettere su la vita e le opere del celebre maestro Giuseppe Haydn*, the work notoriously plagiarized by Stendhal in his *Lettres* [. . .] *sur le célèbre compositeur Joseph Haydn* (Paris, 1814). Giuseppe Baini's *Memorie* (2 vols. [Rome, 1828]) is a pioneering monograph on Palestrina.

6. Baini had classified Palestrina's works according to ten different styles, the seventh style being represented by one work only, the *Missa Papae Marcelli* (*Mass of Pope Marcellus* [*II*]), published in 1567), usually celebrated for the transparency of its musical setting (allowing the liturgical text to shine through). What Basevi quotes here with understandable irony is the entirety of Baini's "description" of the seventh style. See Baini, *Memorie*, 2:423–31, esp. 428.

of Palestrina, faithful imitator of nature's most delicate forms in his earlier style, adopts the gigantic seventh style, and, with hitherto unimagined simplicity, clarity, naturalness, nobility, grandeur, and sublimity, writes the Pope Marcellus Mass. This is Palestrina's only work in this style, and by virtue of its uniqueness it is in a class with the *Iliad*.

The reader is told nothing more of this musical *Iliad*. Yet precisely because the music is so unfamiliar to us it deserved a detailed analysis that would have shown us clearly its distinctive characteristics and its individual qualities.

Not long ago, there appeared outside Italy two books intended as analytic studies of the works of a single composer. One is by Lenz—*Beethoven et ses trois styles*—and the other is by Oulibicheff and covers the life and works of the great Mozart.[7] Here and there in Lenz's book are some worthwhile analyses and useful general observations, expressed with verve, but many passages are merely poetic, and at times less poetic than strange and bizarre. For the rest, only the sonatas are considered in detail; only in the "Critical, Chronological and Anecdotal Catalog" is there any mention of the other important works.

Oulibicheff's *Biographie de Mozart* is a substantial work that cost the author ten years of study and research. This book contains a most praiseworthy and instructive analysis of the principal works of Mozart; it seems to me, however, that considering the music together with the vocal texts can confuse the reader who truly wishes to become acquainted with the organic aspect of the music. When the instrumental compositions are examined, their individual forms are not given the attention they deserve, and, in descriptive passages, the fanciful—a nearly universal defect of musical criticism—reigns at times too firmly.

Because music comes into being in a concrete, individual way[8] each time it takes form in a composition, and in this individual form functions as an organism, the type of criticism I deem necessary above all is analytic criticism—the

---

7. Wilhelm von Lenz, *Beethoven et ses trois styles: Analyses des sonates de piano suivies de l'essai d'un catalogue critique chronologique et anecdotique de l'oeuvre de Beethoven*, 2 vols. (St. Petersburg, 1852); Aleksandr Ulïbïshev (Oulibicheff), *Nouvelle biographie de Mozart, suivie d'un aperçu sur l'histoire générale de la musique et de l'analyse des principales oeuvres de Mozart*, 3 vols. (Moscow, 1843).

8. Our periphrasis is an attempt to render Basevi's "viene ad individuarsi," a phrase with philosophical connotations that suggests at once "coming into concrete existence" and "acquiring specific, individual characteristics."

only type that, as a form of inquiry into music's "anatomy," can lead us to the study of its "physiology."

I have rejected the aid of poetical descriptions of the music's effect on our emotions because I consider them useful only in writings aimed also at a nonmusical readership. But for musicians, to whom this book is addressed, I thought it more useful, for example, to attach a name to the kind of effects I call "of anticipation" [*ansietà*]—thus more vividly highlighting the musical organism that gives rise to them—than to pen a marvelously colorful description of the impression one receives from hearing the magnificent finale of *Norma*, which contains such an effect.[9]

I began this study of Verdi's operas in the Florentine journal *L'armonia* without a preestablished order in mind, and without the intention of making it into a book.[10] But encouraged by a number of notable people, I have ventured to assemble the articles, rearrange them, make major additions and alterations, and offer the whole in its present form to the public.

I have not included Verdi's first two operas, *Oberto, conte di San Bonifacio* and *Un giorno di regno*, as these are only early, tentative works.[11] I have examined the remaining operas in the manner I consider most advantageous to musicians—who can absorb them and strive to fertilize them with their own imagination in order to create similar works. To that end, musicians must be aware of the minutest details and must carefully consider their functions, in the manner of those who need to gather all the material necessary for their purposes. Thus, those who consider certain detailed analyses to be superfluous are mistaken; indeed, I regret not having been able to take my analysis further. But for all this, I have not entirely rejected synthesis, to which I have resorted whenever I saw it as the crowning of my analysis.

I decided to organize this study chronologically, for this must be considered the most logical and natural order for any intellectual endeavor.

9. On Basevi's "effetto di ansietà" and the passage in *Norma*, see pp. 86–88 below. See also the glossary, s.v. *ansietà*.

10. Yet Basevi must have thought in terms of an overall project from the earliest stages, as he gave each article in *L'armonia* the common title "Studio sulle opere di Giuseppe Verdi" followed by an ordinal number. See also Piovano, 51–52.

11. *Oberto* and *Un giorno di regno* were premiered at Milan's Teatro alla Scala in 1839 and 1840, respectively; whereas the first opera had some success, the second (a comic work) was a resounding fiasco. For Basevi, Verdi's real career begins with the triumph of *Nabucco*—a point of view shared by the operatic marketplace ever since: Verdi's two earliest operas are seldom produced.

I have come to discern four "manners" in the style of Verdi's writing, but these are not so clearly differentiated among the operas I examine as to permit me to make use of them as main divisions of the book.

The relationship between music on the one hand and politics, philosophy, and industry on the other is so important that I have taken every opportunity to discuss it, to the extent that befits the nature of this book.

I have illustrated my observations with many examples, some of them from little-studied operas, with the main intent of enticing the reader to study numerous composers who, to the great detriment of art, are completely neglected.

In any event, I offer this book to the public not as a perfect model of criticism but rather as a starting point for those more capable than I, so that they might better treat this or some other subject matter. I flatter myself to think that, however indirectly, I am contributing to Italian criticism's achievement of the significance it needs if it is to halt the decay of music among us.

Convinced of the thousand imperfections of this study of mine, I welcome, not merely with pleasure but with gratitude, any criticism that may be offered by those who are meticulous and expert in this field.

Florence, January 3, 1859

NABUCODONOSOR

Nabucodonosor was first performed at Milan's Teatro alla Scala in March 1842.[1]

Its reception was rapturous; the experts judged it worthy of a great master. Its majestic nature, its solemn cast, and a certain frankness and naturalness immediately made listeners think of Rossini—and kind Fame soon inspired hope that that composer's genius would be revived in the young man from Busseto.

With *Nabucodonosor* Verdi met one of the most stringent requirements that capricious fate imposes on young composers: the immediate demand for an opera worthy of comparison with those of the most skilled composers of fashion, on pain of falling suddenly into oblivion and abruptly and irrevocably losing all the fruits of the tremendous effort required merely to place a work before the public. And who knows how many artists are in this way condemned to pitiable silence, artists who otherwise, given further opportunities to try their strengths, might grow into the most illustrious and solid bastions of art?

---

1. The practice of abbreviating this title as *Nabucco* began early in the opera's history and was adopted by Verdi himself. The critical edition, by Roger Parker, was published as *WGV* I/3 (1988).

But which of today's impresarios does not take fright and condemn to perpetual banishment any composer who, after one or at the most two tries, falls
short of fully achieving the required success? Thus, not what is good but only
what is outstanding makes the grade. The exorbitant cost of operatic performances excuses the avarice of the impresarios, but not their lack of sagacity.

The shipwreck of *Un giorno di regno* had caused the pleasant voyage of
Oberto, conte di San Bonifacio to be forgotten, and had stripped Verdi of the
chance to venture once again onto the stormy seas of the theater. Still, he
hopefully accepted Solera's libretto of *Nabucodonosor*, which had been rejected by Nicolai.[2] He set it to music in his spare time, and only to give vent
to his ardent imagination. If Verdi had not had the luck to find someone who
would vouch for him financially with a certain impresario,[3] this score might
still languish in the portfolio of an obscure organist from Busseto.

Here briefly is how Solera framed the plot of his libretto. Nabucodonosor,
King of Babylon and conqueror of the Hebrews,[4] having broken into the Holy
Temple, is about to order a massacre. But seeing that his own daughter, Fenena, has fallen into the hands of the high priest, Zaccaria, and is threatened
with death, he suspends his cruel command. But Ismaele—son[5] of Sedecia,
the King of Jerusalem—loves Fenena and rescues her from this peril, returning her safely to her father. Nabucodonosor looses every restraint from his
brutal vengeance. Meanwhile, Abigaille, a slave (thought to be the firstborn
daughter of Nabucodonosor), fired by envy of Fenena, hatred of the Jews,
and boundless ambition, spreads rumors in Babylon of the death of the king
and prepares to ascend the throne. But Nabucodonosor arrives unexpectedly and, possessed by insane pride, proclaims that he must now be wor-
shipped not merely as a king but as a god. A thunderbolt immediately falls,
dashing his crown to the ground and stupefying him. Her nerve restored, Abigaille picks up the crown and sets it on her own head. Nabucodonosor, practi-
cally insane, can now rule his kingdom only through Abigaille, who forces him
to sign a death sentence for all the Jews. But when he realizes that Fenena is

2. The composer Otto Nicolai had indeed given up on Temistocle Solera's libretto, and
Bartolomeo Merelli, who was then managing the Teatro alla Scala, offered it to Verdi. Solera
had already collaborated with Verdi on the reworking of the libretto of *Oberto* and after *Nabucco*
would provide him with the librettos for *I Lombardi alla prima crociata*, *Giovanna d'Arco*, and
Attila.

3. On the possibility that Merelli received a subvention or a guarantee against loss for *Nabucco*, see Phillips-Matz, 113–14.

4. Nebuchadrezzar (Nebuchadnezzar) II (d. 562 BCE).

5. The libretto has rather "nipote" (nephew).

among them, he wishes to rescind it. He pleads in vain with Abigaille, then threatens to reveal her true station. She remains firm in her resolve, and responds to Nabucodonosor's threats by tearing to shreds the paper declaring her a slave. At this pass the poor father turns to the Almighty. He begs forgiveness of the God he has offended and thus all at once recovers his reason, his daughter, and his kingdom.

This libretto is by no means lacking in vehement, noble, grand feelings and in touching scenes, all well adapted to the new dramatic character of today's music. And Verdi found in it material congenial to his talent for depicting strong passions and events that inspire universal admiration and devotion.

To set this subject appropriately requires majestic music. However fertile his invention, no artist can find everything he needs within his own imagination; he needs to borrow a great deal from his artistic forebears. Thus, Verdi wisely looked mainly to the great Rossini, master of all in the majestic style, and took as his model the marvelous music of the new version of *Mosè*[6] and of *Guillaume Tell*. In those operas, for the reason mentioned above, Rossini too makes use of his predecessors' techniques, although he always develops and handles them in accord with his own talents. Certainly he owes no small debt to Haydn: it is sufficient in that connection to consider the lovely ensemble from *The Creation* "By thee with bliss."[7]

The grave, solemn character that inspires devotion and calm is well suited to music and renders it fit for association with words and topics concerning our relations with our Creator. This sort of music may be said to possess a sacred *colorito*.

There are some who believe it impossible to achieve this sacred *colorito* without using the ancient tonality of plainchant,[8] which survived—albeit with modification—through the time when Monteverdi boldly participated in the

---

6. Rossini reworked his three-act *azione tragico-sacra Mosè in Egitto* (Naples: Teatro San Carlo, 1818; libretto by Andrea Leone Tottola) into the four-act *opéra Moïse et Pharaon* (Paris: Opéra, 1827; libretto by Luigi Balocchi and Étienne de Jouy). Basevi's expression "*Nuovo Mosè*" refers to the latter version, which in turn circulated in an Italian translation by Calisto Bassi with the simple title *Mosè*. Basevi owned a printed vocal score of this Italian adaptation (Milan: Lucca, pl. no. 10040 [1857], *Catalogo Basevi* 230), a score that in various places refers to the opera as "Il nuovo Mosè."

7. Basevi cites the incipit in an Italian translation ("Dell'alta tua bontade"). See Joseph Haydn, *Die Schöpfung*, ed. Annette Oppermann, *HW* XXVIII/3 (2008), N. 12b, Chor ("Von deiner Güt'"/"By thee with bliss").

8. Basevi's phrase is "l'antica tonalità del *canto fermo*": here *canto fermo* means not "cantus firmus" but "plainchant" (a now obsolete usage), and the "tonality" in question is rather what in current musical parlance would be called "modality." We use the English *tonality*, however, in

establishment of modern tonality. Before Monteverdi, music proceeded with greater calm and was thus much better suited to represent the tranquility appropriate to spiritual contemplation of holy matters. In those days changes of harmony [*modulazioni*] were few, and the harmonic interval of the tritone—generator of every natural modulation [*transizione*]—was held in such horror as to be called *diabolus in musica*;[9] it was never used without precautions that robbed it of nearly all its effectiveness. Now, the mind is troubled by changes of harmony and modulations that are too remote and frequent; for this reason our music is truly incompatible with the gentle quietude of spirit that Palestrina could coax so skillfully from his magical notes. Thus, one can easily understand the enthusiasm of Paer (as related by Baini) when, in the Sistine Chapel, he first heard the music of the great Palestrina. "This," exclaimed Paer, "is the divine music for which I have searched so long—which I could not myself conceive yet trusted could be discovered by a new Apollo."[10] Still, it cannot be denied that, as a result of the music of our time—not wrongly called by Fétis the period of "pluritonic" tonality[11]—and of continual bombardment by many, extremely strange changes of harmony and modulations, ancient tonality no longer has the same effect on our emotions: in time, once the charm of novelty had worn off, it would come to seem too cold and dull. Therefore, I wish not to blame but rather to commend the best modern composers who, when writing sacred music, have availed themselves of all the new achievements in musical art—and even of its dramatic character, so successfully used first by Cherubini.

Although music associated with things sacred must possess a certain hue, it must change somewhat when destined for the stage rather than for the church. This distinction has been accepted by the finest composers, and it is surely a reasonable one: theatergoers are not gathered for prayer; the music

order to preserve Basevi's terminological opposition between "antica tonalità" and "moderna tonalità" within the same paragraph—an opposition found in other nineteenth-century writers.

9. On *transizione* and *modulazione*, see the glossary. In this passage, Basevi's term for the tritone is the disused *quinta falsa* (false fifth).

10. Ferdinando Paer is one of the central figures in the generation of Italian opera composers emerging around 1800.

11. Fétis viewed the history of Western harmony in four main phases. The third was that of his "ordre pluritonique," the developed system of modulation found in Mozart and Rossini, which in his view "represented the culmination and perfection of *tonalité moderne*." Brian Hyer, "Tonality," in *The Cambridge History of Western Music Theory*, ed. Thomas Christensen (Cambridge: Cambridge University Press, 2002), 726–52, esp. 747–48.

should not be devout, although to sustain the illusion it is proper that it be marked by a certain solemnity.

Let us now examine in order the pieces that make up *Nabucodonosor*, offering as we go along the comments we think most fit.

In the *sinfonia*, Verdi adopted for the most part the old Rossinian form, using several themes from the opera but in no logical order. The piece therefore turns out a meaningless mosaic.[12]

The *introduzione*[13] immediately seizes your attention through a broad and majestic manner that is entirely Rossinian; its melodies, however, contain nothing of great novelty.

The aria of Zaccaria (bass) follows.[14] It is particularly notable for its majesty, and we cannot imagine a better way to represent the character of a great high priest, full of eminence. For this majestic character to be fully effective, it must express at once devotion, admiration, and gravity. Some confuse the slow succession of long-held notes with the majestic;[15] they do not understand that this technique makes it easy to lapse into the pompous, the heavy, the affected, the colorless, and so forth. A truly majestic melody should not lose but rather gain in effect when performed by many voices. Now, as certain graces, embellishments, and so forth are clearly out of place in choruses, the majestic must derive its beauty from simplicity. Note that there are some choruses of magical effect whose melodies lose all their force and vigor when performed by a single voice. For that reason, these melodies cannot merit the name *majestic*: their effect lies principally in their powerful sonority [*sonorità*]. A big sound produces an effect that we must not leave unexamined. It consists of giving the notes the strength and tenacity that hold them together even

12. The *sinfonia* of *Nabucco* is indeed of the potpourri type that presents musical materials from the rest of the opera. Less obvious is why Basevi deems it largely in "the old Rossinian form." True, there is an element reminiscent of the "Rossini crescendo"—an eight-measure phrase taking us from tonic to dominant and back played three times in a row, the orchestration gaining in sonority and brilliance at each repetition. But Rossini's crescendos are also characterized by their structural work on a higher level: the archetypical Rossini overture is in sonata form without development, and the three-phrase crescendo concludes each statement of the secondary thematic material, thus reinforcing the different harmonic goals of exposition and recapitulation. The overture to *Nabucco* is not in that form, and its three-phrase crescendo articulates the same D major in both of its occurrences (mm. 155–78, 246–69)—as it does in the passage of the opera where it originates (mm. 300–323 and 396–419 of N. 4, the finale of the opera's first part). On the Rossinian archetype, see Philip Gossett, "The Overtures of Rossini," *19th-Century Music* 3, no. 1 (July 1979): 3–31.

13. N. 1, Introduzione ("Gli arredi festivi").

14. N. 2, Recitativo ("Sperate, o figli!") [e] Cavatina Zaccaria ("D'Egitto là sui lidi").

15. Basevi's phrase is "note *tonde*," indicating more specifically whole notes.

without true support or mutual attraction: without its sonority, the same melody would, so to speak, liquify and lose all its consistency. The andante "D'Egitto là sui lidi" is truly majestic, and there is a very fine effect of contrasting sonorities [*contrapposto*] where the chorus repeats Zaccaria's first phrase in unison. This is not a new effect; it is found, for example, in the aria "Bell'ardir" from Donizetti's *Marino Faliero*.[16]

While Verdi has found models for majesty in the music of Rossini, he has nonetheless shown great ingenuity in transplanting to his arias a quality Rossini used mostly in choruses, such as "Aux chants joyeux qui retentissent" from the first act of *Guillaume Tell*.[17] Nor was Mercadante ignored, although Verdi was able to steer clear of the rocks into which Mercadante often crashed. Only once did Mercadante succeed in truly achieving the majestic: in the aria from *La vestale* "Versate amare lagrime," which, however, sometimes totters on the verge of the pompous and stiff.[18] The cabaletta of Zaccaria's aria ["Come notte a sol fulgente"] is an early fruit of Verdi's impetuous talent, which in some ways resembles Rossini's, as seen in Assur's aria "Que' Numi furenti" from *Semiramide*—except that what is a constant attitude in Verdi was born in Rossini of a specific opportunity.[19] To add energy to this cabaletta Verdi again made use of the contrast of the chorus, which repeats a portion of the melody in unison.

A *terzettino* for Fenena, Abigaille (sopranos), and Ismaele (tenor)[20] contains a noteworthy section in the allegro that precedes the andante, where Abi-

16. In Donizetti's opera (Paris: Théâtre Italien, 1835), the Scena ("Finì la festa di Leoni?") ed Aria [Faliero] ("Bello ardir di congiurati") concludes the second act: this particular example may have occurred to Basevi because, as in Zaccaria's aria, the effect is used in association with a cantabile section, in C major, for bass and chorus.

17. This is the concluding section (mm. 419ff.) of the opera's first number (Introduction "Quel jour serein le ciel présage!"). Basevi refers to its opening line using the Italian translation ("Alziamo insieme il canto") found in the miniature score that would soon be published with his own preface (Florence: Guidi, 1860).

18. Scena ("Ah il foco . . . è spento") ed Aria Metello ("Versate amare lagrime") from the second act of Saverio Mercadante's *La vestale* (Naples: Teatro San Carlo, 1840). *IOG* 22 (1986) contains a facsimile of the vocal score printed by Ricordi in Milan in 1840.

19. "Que' Numi furenti" is the cabaletta of N. 12, Scena ("Il dì già cade"), Coro ("Ah! la sorte ci tradì"), e Aria Assur ("Deh . . . ti ferma . . . ti placa . . . perdona . . ."), from the second act of Rossini's *Semiramide* (Venice: Teatro La Fenice, 1823). The critical edition of the opera, by Philip Gossett and Alberto Zedda, is published as *EC* I/34 (2001).

20. N. 3, Recitativo ("Fenena! Oh mia diletta!") e Terzettino ("Io t'amava! . . ."). Verdi's (and Basevi's) use of the diminutive *terzettino* refers to the piece's formal scope: the *terzetto* proper (beginning at m. 84) is in one section only (andante).

gaille sings "Prode guerrier, etc."[21] There is great passion, energy, and pride in this declamatory singing; here Verdi sought to emulate the grandiloquence of the music of the last century—but without lapsing into the exaggeration that makes it ridiculous to us. The andante contains an agreeable theme, but it grows weaker when Fenena introduces a new melody.

In the chorus that begins the first finale, the scene of terror and agitation is aptly expressed—first by means of repeating the same phrase in various keys, then with certain little chromatic phrases.[22] The accompaniment is dominated by a triplet figure well suited to depicting the disquietude of the characters.[23]

The march accompanying Nabucodonosor's entrance is slick, but too tranquil and not really appropriate to military fierceness.

The andante of the first finale is notable.[24] It is a sextet with chorus that is praiseworthy in its variety: in fifty-eight measures, six main musical ideas unfold, not counting the cadential passage. By contrast, the composers in fashion when Verdi came on the scene seem to have taken pleasure in long-windedness, developing ideas made of numerous phrases and melodic periods, counting mostly on the sonority effect [*effetto della sonorità*]. In the *pezzo concertato* "Vicino a chi s'adora" in Mercadante's *Il giuramento* there are approximately ninety measures containing only three main ideas;[25] and in the celebrated largo in the first [second] finale of *Saffo*, Pacini wrote one hundred measures with but two dominant ideas.[26] Verdi had the shrewdness to search further back and take Rossini as his guide. In the first-act quartet of the new

21. Though Basevi's description is somewhat confusing vis-à-vis what appears in the score, he must be referring to the allegro of mm. 61–75 (from "Qual Dio vi salva? . . .").

22. The choral passage "Lo vedeste?" opens N. 4, Finale parte prima.

23. Basevi terms these triplets, which comprise three equal notes, "terzine semplici" (plain triplets) to distinguish them from his "terzine vuote" (empty triplets), those with the pattern note-rest-note.

24. "Tremin gl'insani del mio furore . . . ," mm. 169–227.

25. "Vicino a chi s'adora" is the quartet within the *introduzione* of Saverio Mercadante's *Giuramento* (Milan: Teatro alla Scala, 1837). *IOG* 18 (1986) contains a facsimile of the vocal score printed by Ricordi in Milan in 1837.

26. Giovanni Pacini's *Saffo* (Naples: Teatro San Carlo, 1840) is divided into three acts—or "parts"—in early sources, including the vocal score printed by Ricordi in 1841–42 (facsimile in *IOG* 36 [1986]) and owned by Basevi (see *Catalogo Basevi*, 207–8). Basevi's "finale primo" (first finale) obviously refers to what these early sources call "Finale secondo" (the finale of part 2), which indeed contains a largo of over one hundred measures for all seven characters and chorus ("Ai mortali, o crudo, ai numi"). There are good reasons for Basevi's misnomer: the tripartition creates a rather brief part 1 (basically two numbers only), whose "finale" brings on stage only two characters (and the chorus), so that the "real" first finale can be perceived to be that of part 2. Importantly, Pacini himself would later treat *Saffo* as though it were in two acts (see Gossett's introduction to *IOG* 36 [1986]).

version of *Mosè*, which begins "Dieu de la paix," the tempo changes three times in some thirty measures—measures also rich in variety.[27] And in the largo of the first-act finale of the same work there are forty-four measures with a single central idea: but with what miraculous variety is it repeated! Also, Verdi has made much use of the effect of chiaroscuro—the contrast between loud and soft. In this piece, look at the section where Abigaille sings a number of solo phrases and you will find some of these dynamic contrasts [*stacchi*] that make a great dramatic effect.[28] At the same time, note the melody—brusque, impetuous, and savage even in its agile ornaments. Here you find a clear manifestation of the inborn character of the Verdian genius. The stretta of this first finale[29] is modeled, with regard to its form, on that of the celebrated third finale of the new version of *Mosè*,[30] and it does justice to its model.

The second act opens with an aria for Abigaille.[31] The andante is of the kind much used by Donizetti and Bellini, in that little instrumental motifs used to accompany one of the aria's melodic periods turn it into a sort of small-scale *parlante* passage.[32] The melody is lovely and is adorned with *fioriture* that attest to Rossini's influence on Verdi's first musical ventures. The cabaletta ["Salgo già del trono aurato"] is in the most usual form, but has a *slancio* that is truly Verdian.

Zaccaria's prayer[33] is stately, but its melodic periods are none too well connected.

---

27. This is the quartet with chorus from *Moïse et Pharaon*'s N. 1, Introduction ("Dieu puissant, du joug de l'impie"), Quatuor et Choeur ("Dieu de la paix, Dieu de la guerre"). Basevi quotes the incipit of this section as "Dio della pace," a reading also found in the early Italian translation of the French libretto published anonymously in Rome in 1827 as *Mosè e Faraone*, though he is more likely to have simply been translating directly from the original French. (The 1827 libretto is reproduced in *Mosè in Egitto, Moïse et Pharaon*, ed. Emilio Sala [Pesaro: Fondazione Rossini, 2008], 457–506.) The incipit reads "Dio! possente in pace e in guerra" in the vocal score owned by Basevi (see n. 6 above), reflecting the more widespread Italian version by Calisto Bassi. Basevi writes here of changes in "tempo," which in Italian can refer either to meter or (as in the English use of *tempo*) to speed; in the passage in question, the brief subsections present changes in both meter and tempo.

28. See *Nabucodonosor*, N. 4, Finale parte prima, mm. 194ff.

29. At mm. 257ff. ("Mio furor, non più costretto").

30. At the words "Redoublez d'amour et de zèle."

31. N. 5, Scena ("Ben io t'invenni") ed Aria Abigaille ("Anch'io dischiuso un giorno").

32. See mm. 106–9 ("Piangeva all'altrui pianto").

33. N. 6, Recitativo ("Vieni, o Levita!") e Preghiera ("Tu sul labbro").

Among the trademarks of Verdi's style is the use of staccato rhythms—
jerky, convulsive rhythms that strongly shake the listener; this kind of rhythm
is employed in the chorus of Levites.[34]

In the canon quartet Verdi once again paid homage to Rossini.[35] It is said
that Piccinni was the first to bring canon into the theater.[36] We would not be
wrong to state unequivocally that with this piece Verdi should be the last:
nothing is more inimical to scenic effect than canon. Let us leave canons and
fugues to the contrapuntists; nor should we take the example of the ancients,
particularly the Flemish, who knew no other way of making music speak.
With such artifices they sought mainly to disguise and conceal the poverty of
their imagination. And that this *was* truly poor—or rather that melody did not
enjoy the favor of the ancient masters—is seen in the fact that even the finest
composers before the creation of opera did not disdain to use in their masses,
motets, etc. the melodies of popular songs (even indecent ones), madrigals,
and so forth. Thus, old masses bear such titles as "Baciatemi o cara," "O Ve-
nere bella," "Che fa oggi il mio sole," and so on. Even the great Palestrina followed the custom and wrote a mass on "Io mi son giovinetta" and another on
"L'homme armé"—this latter a very popular song that provided the theme
of sacred compositions by the finest masters, including Josquin des Prez,
Pierre de La Rue, Johannes Tinctoris, Cristóbal de Morales, and many others. It should be added that, in a dedication to Pope Gregory XIII, Palestrina
confessed to this sinful practice.[37] The likes of Bach, Handel, and Cherubini
may have shown themselves to be masters of the art of fugue, but they never

34. N. 7, Coro di Leviti ("Che si vuol?"). On Basevi's use of *staccato*, see the glossary;
the staccato rhythms in this number are obviously those of the allegro ("Il maledetto non ha
fratelli," mm. 15ff.).

35. Basevi's "*quartetto a canone*" is the section "S'appressan gl'istanti" (mm. 65–127) of
N. 8, Finale seconda parte ("Ma qual sorge tumulto!"). Rossini had provided influential models
for the writing of slow sections of operatic ensembles as "canons"—successions of imitative entries for the voices involved (more aptly called *falso canone* or pseudocanon, since the imitation
is not usually strict). Basevi calls this section "quartetto" (Abigaille, Fenena, Ismaele, Nabucco),
as one would in a case like this, in which the fifth soloist (Zaccaria) sings with the chorus; the
first printed vocal score (Milan: Ricordi, 1842), on the other hand, labels the section "Canone a
5 voci," in that the line of Zaccaria and the chorus (in unison/octaves) does provide a fifth entry
to the pseudocanon.

36. Basevi may have found this claim in Fétis, whose sentence he echoes: *La musique mise
à la portée de tout le monde*, 3rd ed. (Paris: Brandus, 1847), 142 ("Piccini est le premier qui ait
introduit les canons au théâtre"). The composer Niccolò Piccinni was a prominent figure in
Italian and French opera of the second half of the eighteenth century.

37. This is the dedication of his fourth book of motets, printed in Rome in 1583–84.

managed to give it any expressiveness other than the purely mechanical one born of hearing the same musical idea presented by different voices, at different pitches, and in different guises. Canons and fugues are useful academic exercises, nothing more. To temper the boredom generated by canon, Verdi employed the sonority effect [*effetto di sonorità*] in this piece, giving the chorus a final repeat of the theme in unison.

The mad scene of Nabucodonosor (baritone), which closes the second act, is extremely well conceived dramatically.[38] The initial ten-measure period is cast in a single sweep [*di getto*], without symmetry of phrases, or repetition, or imitation—a manner fitting for declamation, and for passion, which does not adapt easily to certain regular, obviously studied procedures. After this allegro period, a little adagio phrase follows[39]—symmetrical and regular, with a lovely melody—and then another ten-measure allegro period with an energetic melody, with which the aria ends. Then, rather than reprising the whole aria as usual, Verdi obeys dramatic truth by repeating nothing but the adagio, adding three measures to complete the melodic period.[40] After this, the piece finishes with five measures of a sort of obbligato recitative for Zaccaria and Abigaille. To end an act without the usual cadential passages shows the composer's love of art, for he risks a lack of applause at the fall of the curtain. The brief adagio of this aria is particularly notable, as it makes a fine contrast [*contrapposto*] between the two allegros. Verdi often made shrewd use of effects of contrast; he identified the most propitious times for them—such as when the audience has the strongest need for powerful emotions. Contrast makes a profound impression because it finds our senses in repose and at their most receptive. Psychological contrasts operate in the same way as their physical

38. See mm. 202ff. ("Chi mi toglie il regio scettro?"). Basevi refers to this passage as an "aria del delirio," though it is of course not an aria in the formal sense (an independent closed number) but rather the concluding section of the second finale (N. 8). Its fluid, unusual design (a typical operatic expression of madness) would make it hard even to label it as an "aria nel finale": in the 1842 vocal score, the entire portion of the finale that follows the canon is entitled "scena e delirio—finale II."

39. Mm. 214–18 (for which the primary sources show a mixture of andante and adagio markings).

40. Basevi's "aria" ("the aria ends" and "the whole aria") refers to the complete, tonally closed melodic period from the anacrusis to m. 204 to the downbeat of m. 229, though by this point Verdi has not yet even set the entire poetic text—and that text suggests a degree of formal openness, a suggestion to which Verdi has already responded abundantly (see the text's "quatrain" structure in relation to his setting). Basevi's description may betray a desire for formal regularization.

counterparts. For instance, a hand previously immersed in cold water will be more sensitive to warm water: the effect of the contrast is to make this seem extremely hot. In a sense, contrast is an artificial means of increasing sensitivity—or rather of compensating for its deficiency. Contrast was in great fashion in literature before much use of it was made in music. Mercadante and Pacini in their operas, written shortly before the advent of Verdi, were the first to avail themselves of this effect. Mercadante in particular often used it well: the rapid transition from fortissimo to pianissimo in the andante of the *pezzo concertato* toward the end of act 2 of *La vestale* is of magical effect.[41] As everyone knows, there are various kinds of contrasts. They consist mostly in the opposition of soft and loud, of slow and quick, and of solo and tutti, and in variety of rhythms, meters, keys, orchestration, and so forth. Most sensibly, Verdi has done his best to avoid one kind of contrast, one often embraced by particularly mediocre and careless composers: the contrast achieved by the juxtaposition of tedious music with enjoyable music. The tedious never changes its nature; rather it has the effect of rendering anything in its vicinity tiresome. Thus the pleasant, instead of acquiring greater prominence, loses it through proximity to the tedious.

This short discussion of contrast brings me to look briefly at a completely different device, one nevertheless used to the same end of increasing the enjoyability of music, a device we shall call "preparation." There are some melodic periods, themes, and indeed whole pieces of music that are not in themselves overly attractive—or not attractive at all—but that serve admirably to create a frame of mind and prepare the listener better to enjoy another melody, phrase, etc. These preparations do not induce the element of surprise; unlike contrasts, they are not founded on the effect of the unexpected or the sudden. Instead, they give a foretaste of something we are about to hear, to temper in some way its excessively brusque appearance—something that occurs especially, though not exclusively, at the return of a previously heard musical idea, melodic period, or phrase. The aim of preparations is to make us eager, as that of contrasts is to surprise us. Many and various are the ways of achieving the desired end, and they depend on the taste and ability of the composer. Meyerbeer, who handled contrasts with great skill, proved brilliant in preparations; his music is full of them. See, for example, with what great

---

41. See the opening of the andante sostenuto "Fatal dì! . . . La tetra luce" in the opera's Finale secondo (p. 154 of the score reproduced in *IOG* 22 [1986]).

effect the return of the theme of the children's chorus is prepared for in the fourth finale of *Le prophète*.[42] Verdi, on the other hand, took no great account of preparations, perhaps because they are incompatible with the nature of his brusque, impetuous, rustic talent.

The third act begins with a chorus, preceded and followed by the march of Nabucodonosor.[43] Note in this chorus a procedure used often by Verdi, one that may appropriately be named "musical economy" [*procedimento economico-musicale*]: the first two melodic periods of this chorus each comprise two identical phrases (disregarding one simple ornamental appoggiatura). Note that in saying "identical" I am drawing a distinction between these and the *similar* phrases that ordinarily make up the majority of melodic periods. The two effects are different: in the "economical" procedure, each phrase seems to be followed by the same punctuation mark, either a comma or a period, so that the effect is of simple repetition, whereas in the usual procedure the first phrase seems to end with a comma and the second with a period; thus, they lack equality, one being the necessary complement of the other. Donizetti used the economical technique on a number of occasions. See, for example, the stretta of the second finale of *Lucia* where the chorus enters in ⁶⁄₈ meter on the words "Esci, fuggi."[44] Bellini too provides an example in the first finale of *I Capuleti e i Montecchi* on the text "Se ogni speme è a noi rapita."[45] Neither Donizetti nor Bellini invented this procedure; it is found in Rossini and Paer, and also in Cimarosa. It is not only melodic periods that can be constructed economically but also phrases, half phrases, and so forth. Now, economy must not be confused with poverty; in music, as in all other things, unnecessary luxury, uncalled-for variety, and means disproportionate to the end are abominations to be avoided—and all the more so in that this fine art, because it exists in time, puts our memory to the test. Memory must not be overtaxed, lest it grow unable to grasp the overall musical idea. I will say more: that in music blind prodigality is a sign not of richness but of a mad and warped imagination, for—music being an art of creation—it takes very little

42. See Giacomo Meyerbeer, *Le prophète*, ed. Matthias Brzoska et al., *MWA* I/14 (2011), N. 24b, Choeur d'enfants et Choeur général ("Le voilà, le Roi Prophète!"), mm. 70ff.

43. N. 9, Introduzione parte terza ("È l'Assiria una regina").

44. *Lucia di Lammermoor* (Naples: Teatro San Carlo, 1835), N. 5, Finale atto secondo ("Per te d'immenso giubilo"). Gabriele Dotto and Roger Parker's critical edition of the opera is in preparation for *EN*.

45. Vincenzo Bellini, *I Capuleti e i Montecchi* (Venice: Teatro La Fenice, 1830), ed. Claudio Toscani, *ECB* 6 (2003). "Se ogni speme è a noi rapita" is at mm. 483ff. of [N. 6], Finale dell'atto primo ("Lieta notte, avventurosa").

effort for a composer to combine diverse notes, rhythms, meters, and tempos. Of course, like any good thing, economy must not be abused: at times variety is called for—as in those melodies, of which we have made mention, that are entirely *di getto*.

The duet for Nabucodonosor and Abigaille follows.[46] Note the short and lively *parlante* gracefully inserted in the midst of the recitative;[47] this makes for attractive and effective variety, and avoids the long *parlanti* so much used by other composers in order to get through any text that hampers them. In a fine example of another kind of economy, Verdi brought back the orchestral motif of the *parlante* later in the duet, to create the soprano's first melodic period in the cabaletta.[48] In the andante, the baritone has a very dramatic line with sixteen measures almost all in one sweep [*di un sol getto*].[49] The soprano's answer has another theme in a different rhythm and key; then the two voices sing together in duet until the cadence. This varied form [*forma variata*] is not new but was little used before, when it was considered desirable to hear the same melody three times: first sung once by each singer and then by the two together. In the allegro[50] there is a fine contrast between the pathos of the baritone and the soprano's lively and energetic part.

The chorus "Va pensiero" is a grand aria sung by all the choral parts together.[51] In this piece we encounter Rossinian majesty. Toward the end, when the second phrase of the first melodic period is repeated on the way to the cadence, the orchestration, now charmingly decorated, produces a fine effect.[52]

The act ends with the prophesy of Zaccaria, majestic and at times in the style of Mercadante in its harmonies, modulations, and certain modes of

46. N. 10, Scena ("Eccelsa donna") e Duetto [Abigaille e Nabucco] ("Donna chi sei?").
47. See mm. 69–76 ("Egro giacevi . . .").
48. The motif returns at mm. 239ff., this time Abigaille joining in fully ("invan mi chiedi pace").
49. See mm. 150ff. ("Oh di qual'onta aggravasi").
50. The cabaletta "Deh perdona" (mm. 222ff.).
51. N. 11, Coro ("Va pensiero") e Profezia ("Oh chi piange? . . ."). This description of "Va pensiero" as an aria (through much of the piece all choral parts intone the same melodic line) is one often attributed to Rossini. The attribution is found in a study of Verdi by Carlo Gatti (1931), who, as Pierluigi Petrobelli noted, does not provide a source for it: Pierluigi Petrobelli, "From Rossini's *Mosè* to Verdi's *Nabucco*" (1967), in his *Music in the Theater: Essays on Verdi and Other Composers* (Princeton, NJ: Princeton University Press, 1994), 8–33, 33 n. 30. There is a possibility that Gatti, whether wilfully or not, ascribed to Rossini a phrase that is genuinely Basevi's. (Rossini, incidentally, was still alive in 1859, when the description appeared in Basevi's *Studio*.)
52. At mm. 41ff.

expression.[53] The arrival of B major is pleasing, and the echoes [of Zaccaria's phrases] by the chorus in unison produce an effect of sonority [*effetto di sonorità*] much cherished by audiences.

In Nabucodonosor's aria opening act 4, the largo ["Dio di Giuda!"] does not stand out; there, the orchestral writing turns the third melodic period into a kind of *parlante*, such as Bellini often used and as we noted in the andante of the soprano aria in act 2.[54] The cabaletta ["Cadran, cadranno i perfidi"] leaves the realm of the ordinary by virtue of some changes in the usual distribution of the phrases and melodic periods between the chorus and the orchestra. Instead of two identical repetitions of the cabaletta, the first time through it is heard only in part: the orchestra plays the first melodic period, and the chorus sings the second; this forms a sort of very lengthy ritornello. After this, the baritone alone repeats with slight variations the first and second melodic periods; then the unison chorus sings half of the second phrase of the first period, which the baritone then completes. A final ten-measure period, sung by the baritone with choral interjections, completes the cabaletta, which is followed by a ten-measure cadential passage where the baritone and the chorus sing together. It is clear that the singularity lies in the ritornello alone.[55] Note that the *mossa* of the cabaletta is repeated intact to form the first half phrase, in accordance with the system of "musical economy."[56] Similar repetition is found often in the music of various composers; you may even trace it as far back as Pergolesi and find it in the aria "Se cerca, se dice" from *L'olimpiade*.[57]

The funeral march is of little importance, as are Fenena's prayer ["Oh dischiuso è il firmamento!"] and the hymn ["Immenso Jeovha"].

---

53. The Profezia proper begins at "Del futuro nel buio discerno . . ." (mm. 65ff.).

54. N. 12, Scena ("Son pur queste mie membra?") e Aria di Nabucco ("Dio di Giuda!"): the *parlante*-like passage described by Basevi is at mm. 122ff.

55. Basevi tends to understate this cabaletta's originality (which cannot be discussed in detail here): what is not "singular" is presumably the structure of the cabaletta's main body (mm. 177–96, i.e., excluding the opening "ritornello" and the coda and cadential passages that follow), in that it presents an extended version (A A' B B' A') of the well-established lyric prototype (see chapter 3, n. 35, below).

56. The *mossa* here is the first half of m. 161, with its anacrusis. On Basevi's "musical economy," see pp. 22–23 above, and the glossary, s.v. *economico*.

57. Giovanni Battista Pergolesi, *L'olimpiade* (Rome: Teatro di Tordinona, carnival 1735). Pergolesi's setting of Megacle's second-act aria "Se cerca, se dice" is one of the most celebrated of the eighteenth century (see *IOB* 34 [1979], 245–56), and indeed similarly opens with two identical motifs.

Abigaille's final scene ["Su me . . . morente . . ."] is very dramatic in some places, but by this time the action has already ceased to be of interest as the plot is fully unraveled. Because of this, the scene is generally cut in performance.[58]

Glancing now across this opera as a whole, we can easily see that Verdi was keeping very close to Rossini: indeed, in its majesty this music seems to be a reaction against the style of Donizetti. But the forms of the numbers, the shape of the melodies, and—most of all—the dramatic inflection show signs of Donizetti's influence, an influence that, as we shall see, grows stronger and stronger in the operas to come and leads Verdi to his "second manner." While Verdi strove to approach Bellinian pathos, his melodies, by their very nature, made this impossible. Like those of Rossini, Verdi's melodies are basically consonant, whereas Bellini's are rather dissonant, dominated by passing notes, suspensions, appoggiaturas, sevenths, tritones, and so forth, not so much as ornaments but as essential parts of the melody. You may see a clear example of this in *Il pirata*, on the text "Per te di vane lagrime."[59]

Because they are firmly founded on the roots of the chords [*basso fondamentale*], consonant melodies have a vigor that is lacking in the dissonant sort—which are, however, more touching, and make more of an impression through the anticipation [*ansietà*] generated by our yearning for the resolution of dissonance.

Verdi's melodies clearly flow from a rich stream, and provide good testimony to the luminous talents of this composer. When these melodies suggest a given continuation, the composer does not inconsiderately provide a contrary one, as so often happens in those stunted melodies that, without order or proportion, trickle drop by drop from the feeble imagination of so many musicians who defy nature in their obsessive determination to compose.

58. The march, prayer, hymn, and final scene discussed in this paragraph are all part of N. 13, Finale ultimo ("Va! La palma del martirio"). The designations used by Basevi (*marcia funebre, preghiera, inno, scena finale*) are all found in the vocal score of 1842. On the cut of Abigaille's death scene, see *WGV* I/3, introduction, xviii.

59. *Il pirata* (Milan: Teatro alla Scala, 1827). The passage in question is the opening of the cabaletta of N. 2, Cavatina Gualtiero "Nel furor delle tempeste" (see *ERO* 1 [1983], act 1, fol. 54).

2

I LOMBARDI ALLA PRIMA CROCIATA

Once Verdi was catapulted to fame with his fine *Nabucodonosor*, the doors of every theater were quickly opened to him—including Milan's La Scala, which eagerly awaited the newly commissioned opera *I Lombardi alla prima crociata*.[1]

Solera took the plot of the new opera from Grossi's poem of the same title.[2] Here is a summary of the libretto: Pagano and Arvino, sons of Folco, lord of Rò, are passionately in love with Viclinda; Arvino is the luckier and weds her. In a fit of jealousy, Pagano wounds his brother and flees. After a time, he returns to Milan, seemingly penitent, and is pardoned. But he contemplates a horrible vengeance, and, conspiring with a group of cutthroats who set fire to Arvino's house, he breaks into Viclinda's chamber. There he murders a man he takes to be his brother and kidnaps his beloved. He later finds Arvino unharmed and asks whose blood has been shed. He learns with horror that he has killed his own father. Utterly overcome with remorse for his horrible misdeed, he flees to Palestine, there to lead a life of penitence

1. The critical edition of the opera, by David Kimbell, will appear as *WGV* I/4. I am grateful to Professor Kimbell for allowing me access to his preliminary score and critical commentary in advance of publication.

2. Tommaso Grossi's epic poem, published in 1826, had been extraordinarily successful.

as a hermit. Some years later, Arvino is leading the Lombard troops to the conquest of Jerusalem. Near Antioch, his daughter Giselda is captured by the enemy and brought before Acciano, tyrant of the city. Acciano's son Oronte is much taken with the prisoner and she with him. Meanwhile, Arvino meets Pagano, whom he does not recognize, and receives his advice and assistance in recovering his lost daughter. Antioch is taken by stealth, and Pagano leads Arvino to the place where Giselda is being held captive. Believing Oronte to have been killed in the battle, she deliriously curses the mission of the crusaders. But Oronte has merely been wounded, and, as soon as he is able, he disguises himself as a Lombard and follows the trail of his beloved Giselda. The lovers flee, but they are followed, and Oronte receives another, more serious wound that obliges him to convalesce in a grotto. There the lovers meet Pagano; he baptizes Oronte, who wishes to embrace Christianity. Oronte dies, and the grief-stricken Giselda is comforted by a vision in which she sees the man she so dearly loved on earth safe in heaven. Pagano then hurries off to the conquest of Jerusalem and, first to scale the walls of the Holy City, sustains a mortal wound. Before dying, however, he reveals his identity to Arvino, who embraces him lovingly and forgives him.

Notwithstanding certain implausibilies and inconsistencies—even absurdities—this libretto contains moving scenes and sublime emotions that served as inspiration for Verdi's music.

The opera was first performed in February 1843.

Its success was complete, and it moved the audience even more than *Nabucodonosor*.

It must be remembered that at that time there was a vogue for religion, which completely imbued the philosophy of the day. Theology had invaded every area of knowledge, and, championed as the basis of civilization, Christianity was lent glowing splendor in the writings of certain brilliant authors. It was then that Gioberti wrote those eloquent pages that professed the civilizing power of Catholic philosophy united to the Italian spirit, and quickly ignited in our peninsula the great fire that only a few years later buried under its embers all who had stoked it.

In the music of *I Lombardi* Verdi reveals himself to have been inspired by the same enthusiasm for Christianity that Gioberti had exhibited in his *Primato morale e civile degl'Italiani*.[3]

---

3. Gioberti (see the preface, n. 4, above) started work on his *Primato* in 1842 and published it in the spring of 1843; the book is thus almost exactly contemporary with *I Lombardi*.

For that reason, while retaining in *I Lombardi* the sacred *colorito* of *Na-bucodonosor*, Verdi used it here with the added fire and vivacity that make it better suited to a subject that is more recent and that affects us more directly. In the music of *Nabucodonosor* you perceive a faith intensified by its antiquity, but in that of *I Lombardi* you admire timeless devotion. While the one moves you with the weighty authority of an old sage, the other sets you ablaze with youthful fervor. The youthfulness that breathes in the music of *I Lombardi* was skillfully reconciled with the gravity appropriate to holy matters. We may assert that no other opera so well embodies the "sacred-modern" character.

If you are curious to investigate the, so to speak, material and mechanical differences between the music of *Nabucodonosor* and that of *I Lombardi*, you may note in considering the main themes and melodies of the two works that the first contains a higher proportion of duple meters, slow tempos, and major keys. Perhaps it is because of these factors that *Nabucodonosor* has the greater majesty and grandeur we naturally associate with things ancient and wondrous.

A simple *preludio* takes the place of a *sinfonia*.

The introductory chorus begins over a lively and brilliant instrumental theme.[4] Its nimbleness recalls Donizetti in the chorus "L'inno della vittoria" from *Belisario*.[5] Note, however, that this easy manner, through frequent use, has become Verdi's own and one of the hallmarks of his genius. In Donizetti, as indeed in other modern and ancient composers, the nimbleness was, rather, occasional; an example is the chorus "Di giubilo di plauso" from Paer's *Sargino*.[6] After the lively theme come a few calmer measures that place the ensuing narrative ("Era Viclinda") in greater relief. This narrative, sung by the tenors and basses, gives you a taste of another characteristic of the Verdian genius: the brusque, the impetuous, and a certain gracelessness. The two staccato notes that close the first phrase and the second two half phrases of the first melodic period should be sufficient illustration. This introductory passage ends with a repetition of the first lively theme.

---

4. N. 1, Introduzione ("Oh nobile esempio!").

5. See, in the first act of Donizetti's *Belisario* (Venice: Teatro La Fenice, 1836), the Sortita di Giustiniano ("O Nume degli eserciti") e Coro ("L'inno della vittoria"), mm. 60ff.

6. See Ferdinando Paer's *dramma eroicomico Sargino, ossia L'allievo dell'amore* (Dresden: Kurfürstliches Theater, 1803), N. 18b, Coro con ballo ("Di giubilo e di plauso"): *PaWV*, 501.

The quartet "T'assale un fremito!"[7] begins with a melodic period made up of two three-measure phrases; this is extraordinary in Verdi, who always takes pleasure in binary symmetry. For the rest, this piece appears at first glance to be modeled on the similar "Tremin gl'insani" from *Nabucodonosor*.[8] There is a variety of musical ideas, although one phrase in "economical" form is most felicitously repeated three times in the course of the piece.[9] Moreover, note in Pagano's part a short melodic period with a most bizarre rhythm ["Pirro, intendesti"], a sharp departure from the rhythm of the rest; this returns twice, just as the part of Abigaille does in the above-mentioned piece from *Nabucodonosor*. The stretta ["All'empio, che infrange la santa promessa"] consists of a rather meager crescendo.

The *scena ed aria* for Pagano (baritone) is preceded by an offstage soprano chorus of religious character;[10] its rhythm is too uniform and hackneyed. This chorus ends in A major; then the C-major accompaniment of the andante of the next aria follows immediately. This brusque transition is startling, and strengthens the dramatic effect of the contrast between those praying to heaven and a man contemplating a horrible sin.[11] The melody of this andante ["Sciagurata! hai tu creduto"] has a thoroughly Bellinian *mossa* with that leap of a fourth toward the upper register so often used by that composer. This interval is indeed the most pleasing in all music and the easiest to sing—and thus to remember. The same *mossa* is found in the duet from *I puritani* "Il rival salvar tu devi."[12] In the final two measures of the first melodic period there is a *di slancio* passage with high-pitched, vibrant notes through which Verdi gave free rein to that manner of feeling of his that coincides with the taste of the audience. The second period, in G minor, is unusual in that it moves to a

---

7. This "quartet" is in fact a concertato section for five characters and chorus within the *introduzione* (andante, mm. 272–324). Basevi referred to it as a quintet both in the article on which this chapter is based (*L'armonia*, June 30, 1857; Piovano, 385) and later in the *Studio*.

8. This is the andante in *Nabucco*'s first finale, similarly praised by Basevi for the profusion of musical ideas (see p. 17 above).

9. See N. 1, Introduzione, mm. 278–81, 293–96, 311–14.

10. N. 2, Coro ("A te nell'ora infausta") ed Aria Pagano ("Sciagurata! hai tu creduto").

11. Chorus and aria are in fact separated by the recitative "Vergini! . . . il ciel per ora," but the effect described by Basevi obtains nonetheless: the recitative also concludes in A major, and the offstage chorus reprises its last phrase (though with different words) just before the aria's opening.

12. Vincenzo Bellini, *I puritani* (Paris: Théâtre Italien, 1835), [N. 8], Duetto [Riccardo e Giorgio] ("Il rival salvar tu devi"). All my references to the opera are based on the critical edition by Fabrizio Della Seta (*ECB* 10, forthcoming), whom I thank for providing me with the relevant information in advance of its publication.

distant key. As to form, this andante has one of the most common and simple: a first period of eight measures in two phrases, a second of four measures, and a repetition of the second phrase of the first period followed by another period as an "appendix" [*appendice*] and then immediately by the cadence.[13] In the *tempo di mezzo* there is a Verdian staccato chorus ["Niun periglio il nostro seno"]. The cabaletta ["O speranza di vendetta"] is modeled after "Come notte" from *Nabucodonosor*.[14]

The prayer "Salve, Maria" follows, sung by Giselda (soprano).[15] Its tranquility is well suited to the spirit of an ingenuous young girl. We might have said that the first two melodic periods were in one sweep [*d'un sol getto*] had they exhibited any cohesive force, but they are nothing more than a mere succession of notes not tied together in any way to form a musical idea; because of this flaw, the piece misses the mark for which every composer must aim. These melodic periods are adorned somewhat by their accompaniment, with playful figures in the clarinet and flute. Such caprices are remnants of a Gothic taste in art[16] and should be abandoned, as happened to the ritornellos that were heard at every turn in ancient operas as though to remind forgetful singers of the melody, and as also happened, even more logically, to the technique of having the instruments continue a melody begun by the voice, taking it out of the singer's mouth, almost as if to give him time to blow his nose or take a pinch of snuff. In some cases, to be sure, such an instrumental effect may prove expressive, but judging the proper time for it requires an extremely subtle philosophical mind. When the prayer reaches the melody "Vergine santa," the notes immediately acquire cohesive attraction and, with it, meaning. The tremolo on muted violins blends with the voice splendidly and increases its expressiveness; it causes a gentle quiver in the listener's soul that sweetly moves him, inclining him to ecstasy.

The quintet ["Mostro d'averno orribile"] of the first finale is majestic and energetic in its andante mosso.[17] There is a fine contrast where Pagano

13. As the first two four-measure phrases are similar, the basic melodic shape of this andante is an instance of the lyric prototype. See chapter 3, n. 35, below.

14. "Come notte" is the cabaletta (mm. 98ff.) in Zaccaria's cavatina "D'Egitto là sui lidi" (N. 2 of *Nabucodonosor*).

15. N. 3, Recitativo ("Tutta tremante ancor") ed Ave Maria ("Ave Maria!"). For reasons of censorship, the prayer had been turned into "Salve, Maria," the title given by Basevi.

16. In nineteenth-century Italian, the word *gotico* could be used to connote "antiquated" and "bizarre."

17. This is the slow concertato (mm. 57–116) of N. 4, [Scena ("Vieni! . . . già posa Arvino") e] Finale primo ("Ma gli sgherri han sparso il foco! . . .").

is from time to time heard alone dominating the ensemble, as called for by the dramatic context. Verdi also takes full advantage of the words "Farò col nome solo il cielo inorridir!" which are repeated many times in this quintet without ever cloying and indeed with a great effect of dramatic truth. This belies the accusation that music always distorts the text with too much repetition: where they are made in a suitable way, these repetitions do not impair but rather increase the effect the poet has tried to achieve. At measure 23[18] begins a melodic period of only a few notes and of a rather harmonic nature; it decreases gradually from fortissimo to piano with grave and solemn movement, a pattern Verdi has often enjoyed using. The shift to F major is also notable because Verdi forms what amounts to a new theme by making simple changes in Pagano's F-minor theme on the words "Farò col nome solo, etc." The stretta ["Va! sul capo ti grava l'Eterno"] is extremely noisy and none too happily conceived.

In the chorus of ambassadors that opens the second act,[19] the harmonic shifts are crude, as though to suggest the cruelty of the Muslims. The rhythm is staccato in a way seldom found in other composers. After a number of measures comes a new theme, constructed "economically" and with a different rhythm, vibrant and sung fortissimo; this forms an effective contrast, which is further strengthened by the alternation of stage band and orchestra. After a quiet repetition of the first rhythm, a very energetic final theme closes the piece.

The cavatina of Oronte (tenor)[20] is notable for its andante ["La mia letizia infondere"]. The melody is open, nicely inflected, and without vexing abstruseness; it is accompanied by the triplet motion that Verdi has often abused. For this he was reproved soundly—particularly as all the fledgling composers tried to imitate him. Still, beneath a clear and rhythmically simple melody, this triplet motion can make a gentle impression on the listener's emotions. Donizetti furnishes an example in the theme of "Di pescator ignobile" from *Lucrezia Borgia*.[21] Returning to our subject, I invite the reader's

18. Basevi is counting measures from the beginning of the concertato: his m. 23 is m. 79 of N. 4.

19. N. 5, Introduzione atto secondo–Coro di Turchi ("È dunque vero?").

20. N. 6, [Scena ("O madre mia, che fa colei?") e] Cavatina Oronte ("La mia letizia infondere").

21. See Donizetti, *Lucrezia Borgia* (Milan: Teatro alla Scala, 1833), N. 2, Romanza ("Com'è bello!"), Duetto [Lucrezia e Gennaro] ("Ciel! Che vegg'io?") e Finale primo ("Maffio Orsini, signora, son io"). "Di pescator ignobile" is at mm. 233ff. Roger Parker's critical edition of the opera is in preparation for *EN*.

attention to the section of the same andante—"Ir seco al cielo"—where there is an "economical" melodic period that requires forceful vocal production to generate the desired effect. This period contains in embryo the *slancio* that we will see later in other pieces and that became one of the characteristics of Verdi's first manner. The cabaletta ["Come poteva un angelo"], even though Verdi rewrote it, makes no great impression.[22]

Pagano's *scena* "Ma quando un suon terribile"[23] is solemn, but the melody is underdeveloped, and the two F-minor periods portend something grander and more important than what the subsequent section in F major provides.

The march of the crusaders is not very warlike; it is in fact rather brisk and in that sense not unsuited to hordes inflamed by a lust for combat.

There follows a *duettino* ["Sei tu l'uom della caverna?"] between Arvino (tenor) and Pagano,[24] handled as a musical dialogue: one character completes the musical idea begun by the other. This device must be used with restraint, and only when the scene involves two or more characters each intently interested in the words of the others. This also accords with real life: in an argument, one party, moved by passion, will interrupt the words of the other and tend to continue in much the same tone and with the same vocal inflections. Bellini made marvelous use of a similar kind of musical dialogue in the magnificent scene in *Norma* beginning "In mia mano alfin tu sei."[25] The same procedure does not seem quite so dramatic in the *terzetto* "Cruda sorte" in Rossini's *Ricciardo e Zoraide*; there the three characters are talking to themselves, and we therefore cannot understand how one character can continue the melody abandoned by another.[26] In the present *duettino*, too, this type of dialogue seems to me none too appropriate because the characters in the scene are not moved by strong passions for one another. Verdi did well not to continue this dialogue too long or too rigorously; he converts it into a *parlante*. The hymn of the crusaders with which this *duettino* ends is too vehement

22. Verdi wrote an alternative setting of the cabaletta text "Come poteva un angelo" for a later production (Senigallia, 1843). Published scores usually provide both versions.

23. N. 7, Scena ("E ancor silenzio!"), Marcia de' crociati, ed Inno ("Stolto Allhà!"); "Ma quando un suon terribile" is Pagano's *romanza* within the *scena* (mm. 41ff.).

24. This *duettino* is still within N. 7, as is the following hymn of the crusaders.

25. The passage opens the duet for Norma and Pollione that is part of N. 8, Finale dell'atto secondo, from Bellini's *Norma* (Milan: Teatro alla Scala, 1831). Here and in later references to pieces from this opera I adopt the numbering and titles from Philip Gossett's introduction to the facsimile of the autograph full score (*ERO* 4 [1983]).

26. See the opening lines of N. 5, Terzetto ("Cruda sorte!"), in act 1 of the opera (Naples: Teatro San Carlo, 1818). Printed score (2 vols. [Rome: Ratti & Cencetti, ca. 1828]) reproduced in *ERO* 10 (1980), 134.

and is more barbarous and fanatical than is appropriate to them. In this hymn the central idea is a melodic period made up of two identical phrases; it is repeated too many times and thus cloys. This excessive repetition is especially noticeable as it is not a common defect in Verdi, appearing only occasionally; in this he is unlike the majority of composers, who cherish their offspring like doting mothers, unable to abandon them even if they are ugly, monstrous, and painful to everyone else.

The chorus of slaves[27] is jocular, brilliant, capricious, and rather Paciniesque.[28] Here for the first time we encounter the time signature ⁶⁄₈—which does not appear at all in *Nabucodonosor*.

In the finale of this act,[29] Giselda's cantabile "Se vano è il pregare" is sweetly tuneful in its first melodic period, but in the second acquires a certain energy and vehemence that reveal the Verdian hand. Its form is among the simplest: it lacks the final "appendix" period and goes immediately into the cadential passage. There are some important things that should be pointed out in the soprano's allegro moderato ["No! . . . giusta causa"]. After an initial eight-measure period of declamatory melody with a rather routine rhythm, another period of four measures seems to conclude the musical idea; but suddenly a few percussive strokes of the orchestra and a slight exclamation by several characters and the chorus introduce a little phrase ending in a long rest. A più mosso ["I vinti sorgono"] ensues, with an initial eight-measure *di slancio* period followed by a more tranquil one of four measures. There is a brief halt, then immediately another eight-measure *di slancio* period, even more vehement than the first: neither Verdi nor any composer before him had ever approached such great forcefulness. Verdi, then, may be called the originator of these *grande slancio* melodic periods. It must be pointed out, however, that this invention was not something he remained long fond of; he did not employ it in the operas of his second manner. It was, then, in a moment of ingenuous sincerity that Verdi opened himself up to us, revealing his inner ardor unchecked. We were thus able to observe at its source the reason for the lasting appeal of Verdian melody—the forcefulness that meets so fully the current universal need for powerful emotions. After this second *di slancio* period, another melodic period completes the musical thought. In the repeti-

27. N. 8, Coro nell'harem ("La bella straniera").
28. The reference is to the operatic composer Giovanni Pacini.
29. N. 9, Finale secondo ("O madre, dal cielo").

tion of this cabaletta of sorts for the soprano, Verdi departs from the norm and, rather than repeating everything from the beginning, picks up from the tranquil period that preceded the second *di slancio* period.[30]

The third act opens with an extremely well-handled processional chorus, which has a religious character.[31] It recalls the bell chorus in *Guillaume Tell*[32] and the aria that, in Mendelssohn's *Saint Paul*, begins with the same words: "Jerusalem, Jerusalem."[33]

Before the andantino ["Oh belle, a questa misera"] of the duet for Giselda and Oronte,[34] note the brief *parlante* with its brisk, vivacious instrumentation, similar to that of the *parlante* in the *Nabucodonosor* duet for Abigaille and Nabucodonosor.[35]

Thus far we have seen Verdi to be very sparing in his use of *parlanti*—and wisely, for in so many passages of earlier operas, long, inconclusive *parlanti* impeded the cohesion required in the interests of drama. Who is not rankled by the long, long *parlanti* that precede and follow the magnificent andante of the quartet from Donizetti's *Lucia*?[36]

In *parlanti*, the theme is in the instrumental part rather than in the voice. Yet the composer must not neglect the singers to the extent that they will not hold the listener's attention. The melody of the accompaniment—save in cases where the composer wishes intentionally to direct the attention of the audience elsewhere—must pertain completely to the character who is singing so as to increase rather than to destroy his appeal, like the opulent royal vestments that add greater splendor to the authority of a ruler.

---

30. This "cabaletta of sorts" is in fact even more irregular than Basevi suggests: mm. 148ff. ("Che mai non furono") do pick up from 107ff., but the first time round the text was different ("A niuno sciogliere").

31. N. 10, Introduzione atto terzo ("Gerusalem! . . . Gerusalem! . . . la grande").

32. N. 8, Choeur ("Quelle sauvage harmonie"), which opens act 2 of Rossini's opera: at mm. 106ff., a chorus of shepherds (announced by an onstage bell) is heard from a distance, not unlike that of the pilgrims heard at the opening of act 3 of *I Lombardi*.

33. "Jerusalem, die du tödtest die Propheten" (soprano), in part 1 of the oratorio.

34. N. 11, Recitativo ("Dove sola m'inoltro?") e Duetto ("Teco io fuggo!").

35. N. 10, Scena ("Eccelsa donna") e Duetto [Abigaille e Nabucco] ("Donna chi sei?"), at mm. 69ff., 114ff. The passage in the duet in *I Lombardi* is at mm. 54ff., 89ff., and 101ff.

36. The andante in question is the celebrated concertato "Chi mi frena in tal momento" from *Lucia di Lammermoor*'s N. 6, Finale atto secondo ("Per te d'immenso giubilo"); this concertato is often referred to as a sextet (and used to be referred to as a *quartetto* in Italian, as by Basevi here).

Parlanti may be divided into three principal types. I shall call the first of them *parlante melodico*, for while the principal theme is presented in its entirety in the orchestra, the vocal part doubles it either in unison or at the third or sixth during some passages, sometimes at considerable length. An example of this kind of *parlante* is the *duettino* for Rustighello and Astolfo in act 2 of Donizetti's *Lucrezia Borgia*.[37] In some pieces it proves difficult to distinguish at first between *parlante melodico* and vocal melody accompanied by the orchestra in unison or at the third or sixth; but by carefully examining the parts one may discern whether the theme belongs principally to the voice or to the instruments. We come now to another order of *parlante*, which I think we may call *parlante armonico* inasmuch as the vocal part lacks a significant melody of its own but virtually forms a counterpoint to that of the accompaniment. In comic operas you will find many examples of this kind of *parlante*.[38] Where Figaro in Rossini's *Il barbiere di Siviglia* sings the words "Numero quindici, a mano manca," he uses no note other than D for a great many measures, while the orchestra plays its graceful theme.[39] Similar *parlanti* are found also in serious operas; one of these is in the duet that occasioned my observations on this point. In these cases the words must compensate for their unremarkable setting by their diverting, affecting, or otherwise important meaning; at the same time the accompaniment must not be allowed such predominance as will attract all the listener's attention, distracting it from the character who is singing.

It is good practice to write very brief *parlanti*, as Verdi did, and to alternate them with both simple and obbligato recitatives. As to expression, the instrumental part of a *parlante armonico* may depict the emotions of the character who sings or the general scene, or it may refer to some event unrelated to the character. There are many examples of the first, but I shall limit myself to

---

37. The *parlante* passage for Rustighello and Astolfo ("Qui che fai?")—variously called "recitativo," "scena," or "duettino" in different musical sources—is at mm. 74ff. of N. 4, Recitativo ("Addio, Gennaro") e Coro ("Non far motto") in act 1 of *Lucrezia Borgia*. The opera is in a prologue and two acts, but a number of sources refer to three acts (which is why Basevi places this passage in act 2).

38. Basevi's terms here—*opere buffe* and (a few lines below) *opere serie*—refer in this case to the opposition between comic and serious operas generally, not to the more specific genres of the eighteenth and early nineteenth centuries for which we reserve those terms today. This is made clear by his application of the latter to Verdi's *I Lombardi*.

39. See N. 4, Duetto ("All'idea di quel metallo"), mm. 152ff. The opera (Rome: Teatro Argentina, 1816) is now available in the critical edition by Patricia B. Brauner as *WGR* 2 (2008).

the duet of which we are speaking, where Giselda sings "Seguirti io voglio, etc." The orchestral theme very aptly expresses the joy mixed with worry that pervades the souls of the two lovers. This theme is interrupted by a recitative followed by a longish cantabile; the theme returns in a different key, and after another few measures of recitative it reappears in somewhat modified form. As an example of a *parlante armonico* where attention is not directed to the character who is singing, I must mention act 2, scene 4, of *I Lombardi*, where the instruments play the march of the crusaders.[40] Note that in such cases the vocal line should not have a melody like that played by the instruments, for that would be a contradiction (of a sort not always avoided even by the finest composers). *Parlante armonico* borders on *parlante melodico* and obbligato recitative, so it is not always easy to distinguish between them; for in *parlante armonico*, at times the vocal part imitates the instrumental part to a degree, while at other times the instrumental part does not have a very clear or well-developed theme.[41]

The third kind of *parlante* results from the union of the other two, yielding a *parlante misto* ["mixed"], but this is not the place to discuss this at length.

Similar to *parlanti* are pieces where instead of a solo voice there is a chorus that behaves in any of the ways we have noted for the vocal parts of *parlanti*. The chorus that opens the *introduzione* to *I Lombardi* is an example of this.

Because of the greater importance we now attach to the dramatic side of opera, *parlanti* must not dampen the action but enliven it; failing this, they are to be considered as less valuable than recitatives, even mediocre ones: there at least the words are intelligible.

The *parlante* in the duet between Giselda and Oronte has taken me too far afield, but I do not think it pointless to examine a subject that has been given neither much study nor much attention. Now, however, it is time to return to where we left off and examine the remainder of the piece. The andantino ["Oh belle, a questa misera"] has a sweet melody and is gently accompanied by a triplet pattern. This melody is richly harmonized; the first

40. See N. 7, mm. 11ff. Basevi deliberately uses generic terms ("istrumentazione," "istrumentale") as this march is played by a combination of orchestra and band (off stage, then on stage).

41. In other words, these borders are a matter of degree: a *parlante armonico* may gravitate either toward *parlante melodico* or toward obbligato recitative, depending on how much, respectively, its vocal part joins the main melody in the instruments or the instrumental part becomes less melodic.

four-measure phrase has eleven changes of harmony without the least abstruseness. Note that the tenor repeats the soprano's melody; here Verdi is
following the old duet form that he had abandoned in the other pieces we
have examined thus far. When the characters are motivated by the same feelings, we must not reject such repetition. The stretta ["Ah! vieni, sol morte
nostr'alme divida . . ."], on the other hand, is in an uncommon form, for it
consists of a single *di slancio* period sung by Giselda and repeated by Oronte;
this is interrupted by the cry of "All'armi" from an offstage chorus. After this,
the soprano and the tenor, in unison, sing a short phrase that continues the
interrupted musical idea in a most energetic—we may say Verdian—manner.
Then the cry of the chorus is heard again, followed by another brief, forceful
phrase that brings us quickly to a cadence that could not be simpler.

The chorus of crusaders and Arvino's aria offer little of note, except perhaps the staccato rhythm of the chorus, as one of the characteristics of the
Verdian genius.[42]

But now we come to the climactic piece of the opera, the celebrated *terzetto*, whose beauty surpasses that of any other piece previously written by
Verdi.[43] A violin solo prepares it. Verdi could not have chosen a fitter instrument than this, which is deservedly called the King of the Orchestra. The
indefinable vagueness born of the violin's inevitable uncertainty of intonation
makes it abler than other instruments to represent what is indistinct in the
depths of our soul; also, in its miraculous responsiveness, it is the most direct interpreter of the performer's feelings. Baillot observed that, because of
the rapport that develops between the violinist and his violin, a single instrument is not recognizable in the hands of another player.[44] It was easy to an-
ticipate that Italy—a country marked more than any other by a most delicate
way of feeling—would breathe life and vigor into the violin; this came about
through the efforts in instrument making of Amati, Stradivari, and Guarneri,
and, from the standpoint of technique and pedagogy, through the studies of
Corelli, Tartini, Pugnani, and others.

42. N. 12, Scena ("Che vid'io mai? . . .") ed Aria Arvino ("Si! . . . del Ciel che non
punisce"). This number includes the chorus of crusaders mentioned by Basevi ("Più d'uno
Pagano ha notato"), onto which is grafted the solo part for Arvino.

43. N. 13, Scena ("Qui posa il fianco! . . .") e Terzetto–Finale terzo ("Tu la madre mi
togliesti").

44. Pierre Baillot, French violinist and composer, published the successful violin method
L'art du violon (1834).

While the violin lends itself to the expression of all the player's most delicate emotions, it suits sad and melancholy feelings particularly well, for they
are characterized by the indistinctness that is also a part of the violin's expressiveness. For this reason, the violin solo suits the touching scene leading
to the aforementioned magnificent *terzetto*. With this same understanding,
Paer used a lovely violin solo in *Griselda* in the scene where Griselda loses
all hope for her love.[45] In Mayr's *Ginevra di Scozia* there is a violin solo in
the scene where Ginevra, slandered and condemned to death, gives vent to
her grief.[46] The violin solo conceived by Verdi unfolds with great grace up
to the moment when, in its quest for complexity, it becomes convoluted and
meaningless. In the recitative following this solo there are moments of apt
expression, notably where Pagano raises the baptismal water over the head
of Oronte and says, "L'acque sante, etc." Here the accompaniment pattern
consists of quick, wide-ranging arpeggios in the solo violin, representing the
rippling of the water.

The form of this *terzetto* may be compared with that of a grand aria, except
that, instead of a single voice, three voices, alternating or together, collaborate
in its development. The first, eight-measure period ["Qual voluttà trascorrere"][47] is sung by the tenor, and the second, also of eight measures, by the
soprano with a complementary part for the baritone. The tenor once again
dominates in a third, four-measure period, and after this the three voices join
in another four-measure period, with the soprano most prominent. An imitative passage for the baritone and the soprano occupies the fifth, four-measure
period, which prepares a fortissimo—another four-measure period that includes a unison of soprano and tenor and completes the musical idea. The
last two melodic periods are repeated, and the piece ends with six further
cadential measures. Fortissimos of this kind had become almost obligatory
in ensemble pieces after Mercadante and Pacini had gained great popularity
thanks to similar sonority effects [*effetti di sonorità*]. It may have been such

45. See Paer's *La virtù al cimento* (Parma: Teatro Ducale, 1798), N. 21b, Rondò Griselda
("Voi pur foste"): *PaWV*, 303. The opera is also known as *Griselda*.

46. Simon [Giovanni Simone] Mayr, *Ginevra di Scozia* (Trieste: Teatro Nuovo, 1801). See
the aria for Ginevra that concludes the first act ("Di mia morte s'hai desio").

47. Basevi implies that this is the beginning of the *terzetto* proper and that everything that
precedes it is a *scena* (indeed, a few lines above he refers to the baptism passage as a recitative).
Technically speaking, the opening of the Terzetto–Finale is rather at "Tu la madre mi togliesti"
(mm. 88ff.), where the libretto switches from recitative verse to lyrical verse, and Giselda's attempt at a grand melody (its second period is nipped in the bud by Pagano) marks the beginning
of a very fluid *tempo d'attacco*.

fortissimos that gave Verdi the idea for the *di slancio* melodic periods of which I have spoken. I believe that it was Rossini who awakened all composers with that magnificent rising tenor line in the trio from *Guillaume Tell*.[48] In this *terzetto* in *I Lombardi*, Verdi showed great flexibility with regard to the accompaniment; it is sometimes simple, sometimes complex, now in one rhythm, now in another. Another point of good effect is the entrance of the harp. The act ends without a stretta, Verdi thus showing how much greater importance he attached to keeping the listener's pleasure alive than to slavishly obeying an inveterate habit of composers.

The fourth act opens with a mediocre celestial chorus, followed by Giselda's vision, which is of no greater value.[49] Giselda's cabaletta ["Non fu sogno! . . ."] is brisk and pleasant; we hear one of the typical *di slancio* passages at "Scorre il fiume, etc."

The chorus of crusaders is very fine, and is modeled, rather wisely, after "Va pensiero" from *Nabucodonosor*.[50] Note the fourteen changes of harmony in the first phrase of this chorus, the result of a studied effort to avoid passing notes.

Then we hear the crusaders' hymn again.[51] After this comes an orchestral battle movement, made up of some of the themes earlier associated with the crusaders and with the Muslims, but with an infelicitous jumbled effect; these themes go back and forth between the orchestra and the stage band. I believe it would have been better and more logical to superimpose the different themes, as Meyerbeer did in the third act of *Les Huguenots*, where the litany and the "rataplan" are heard simultaneously.[52] A miserable *terzettino* ["Un breve istante"] for Giselda, Pagano, and Arvino follows immediately, and the

48. N. 11, Trio ("Quand l'Helvétie est un champ de supplices"), mm. 112–22 ("Mon père, tu m'as dû maudire!" etc.).

49. N. 14, Visione ("Componi, o cara vergine"; "Oh! di sembianze eteree").

50. The chorus "O Signore, dal tetto natio" opens the Finale ultimo, N. 15, and—as Basevi may be the first to have noticed—was indeed deliberately composed with an eye to the template of "Va pensiero." It is the most famous piece in *I Lombardi* and would before long be celebrated in Giuseppe Giusti's poem *Sant'Ambrogio* (1846).

51. The chorus "Guerra! guerra! S'impugni la spada" in this Finale is set to the music of the second act's Inno de' crociati ("Stolto Allhà! . . .").

52. In Meyerbeer's *Les Huguenots* (Paris: Opéra, 1836), the competing themes of the Catholic women and the Huguenot soldiers are first juxtaposed and then contrapuntally superimposed: N. 14, Couplets militaires des soldats huguenots ("Prenant son sabre de bataille"), Litanies des femmes catholiques ("Vierge Marie, soyez bénie"), [et] Morceau d'ensemble ("Profanes! impies!"). A facsimile of the full score printed by Schlesinger (Paris, [1836]) is reproduced in *ERO* 20. A critical edition of the opera, by Oliver Jakob, is in preparation for *MWA*.

opera ends with a hymn of victory ["Te lodiamo"], in which I find nothing worth mentioning.

It is clear from the briefest examination of *I Lombardi* that Verdi was seeking above all to avoid the damnable vices of negligence and carelessness in order to steer a course between two dangerous rocks obstructing the composer's path: boredom and impatience in the audience. Elsewhere I touched on how Verdi works to make his melodies appealing, attempting not so much to avoid boredom as to achieve pleasure. I still have not shown how Verdi protected himself against the impatience of the audience—a hazard far more dangerous because barely discernible. But before this explanation, I must note that I use the word *boredom* with reference to the cantabili,[53] to which the audience especially directs its attention; *impatience* applies to the remainder of the music that constitutes an opera. Verdi understood perfectly how little it is worth expending a tremendous effort on making a melody agreeable if the audience is irritated by what precedes it. The audience wants to get to the cantabili quickly; that desire is magnified when the music that precedes them is ugly and without appeal. That is how impatience is engendered, and when someone is burdened by impatience he will be exceedingly hard to please. Some think that by shortening the music between the cantabili they can avoid impatience; in a word, they believe that brevity is the entire remedy. But this is false, for great brevity is not always possible; the importance we attach today to drama makes it often necessary to develop the action to prevent it from becoming choppy and strangled. Without avoiding brevity where feasible, Verdi chose to deal with the audience's impatience by taking the greatest care in handling all of what we might call the ancillary parts of the score, either by making good use of the meaning of the text or by using *parlanti* that, to make them appealing, he constructed according to the same rules that increase the effect of cantabili. In short, Verdi has aimed to be conscientious; by this means he has acquired a distinction that many other composers—even when gifted with greater imagination—have been unable to attain or, following his success, to preserve.

53. It is quite likely that Basevi uses "*cantabili*" here to refer to all "*lyrical*" sections, as opposed to recitatives and *parlanti* (see the glossary, s.v. *cantabile*). This seems to be confirmed by his reference, later in the passage, to "ancillary" music.

3

ERNANI

With *Nabucodonosor* and *I Lombardi*, Verdi achieved such preeminence in Italy that he had little or nothing to fear from his rivals, whether young or old. Of them all, only Donizetti could have competed—and, I think, with sure success—if only his pliant genius, able to absorb and successfully employ every new technique it encountered, had not fought and been vanquished by a cruel illness that, alas, dimmed that shining mind that for so long had emitted such vibrant rays.[1]

One might have expected the religious tendencies we discussed earlier (although perhaps more apparent than real) to have discouraged the composer of *I Lombardi* from setting a nonsacred subject. But Verdi's instincts dictated that he try his hand at a secular plot.

The choice of subject was of the greatest moment, for this time success would be won chiefly through dramatic force and moving scenes. And while he could be plagued by no doubts about the new work's being widely performed, he could not be entirely confident about the staying power of the opera on which he was beginning work.

---

1. Basevi refers to the gradual loss of lucidity experienced by Donizetti in his last period, as a result of the syphilis from which he died in 1848.

Verdi had shown good sense in choosing Rossini as his guide for his two early "sacred" operas, but where was he to turn now for the guidance he needed? In this case, too, his wisdom served him well: without completely abandoning Rossini, he drew closer to Donizetti, from whom it had earlier appeared that he would live apart in perpetuity.

With his *Lucrezia Borgia* Donizetti had begun a revolution on the Italian stage that he later did not wish, or was unable, to see through—or rather that he did not recognize for the momentous event that it was. With that opera, theatrical music became associated with the strongest passions, those best understood and shared by all; it was the start of a realism for which music had never before had a more perfect and complete model. Rossini—surely influenced during his stay in Paris by the musico-dramatic school founded by Gluck and continued with success principally by Méhul, Cherubini, and Spontini—composed a masterpiece of dramatic truth: *Guillaume Tell*. But as is well known, its libretto is mediocre, so only occasionally could Rossini provide opportunities for the passionate operatic singing that no one before him had used with such power; one of these moments is the passage in act 3 where a tearful Tell says to his son, who is ready to offer himself as the target, "Jemmy, songe à ta mère!"[2] Donizetti did not face this problem when he chose the libretto of *Lucrezia Borgia*. It had been written with marvelous and effective novelty of genre by the prolific Felice Romani, who based it on Victor Hugo's play of the same title.[3] Since theatrical music derives its virtues from the drama it sets, it ought to resemble a sheer veil that obscures nothing of the drama over which it is draped. *Lucrezia* belongs to a group of plays with which Hugo aimed to mark a new step forward for dramatic art, one coinciding with the step taken by theatrical music: both aim first and foremost to stir the soul in the most powerful way by emancipating themselves from old restrictive artistic rules.

Following in Donizetti's footsteps, Verdi likewise took his subject from a play by Hugo, *Hernani*.[4] In his explanatory preface to the play, Hugo says his

2. See *Guillaume Tell*, N. 17-IV, [Récitatif] ("Je te bénis en répandant des larmes") [et Air Guillaume] ("Sois immobile, et vers la terre"), mm. 305ff. Basevi quotes in Italian ("Jemmy pensa a tua madre"), and indeed his criticism of the libretto of *Tell* is likely to be based on the bungled versions in which it was then known in Italy.

3. *Lucrèce Borgia*: the prose *drame* had first been staged at Paris's Théâtre de la Porte-Saint-Martin in February 1833 (the premiere of Donizetti's opera would follow only a few months later).

4. Hugo's *drame* was first staged at Paris's Comédie-Française in February 1830. It appeared in print as *Hernani; ou, L'honneur castillan* (Paris: Mame & Delaunay-Vallée, 1830). The critical edition of Verdi's *Ernani*, by Claudio Gallico, was published as *WGV* I/5 (1985).

intention was to bring about a revolution in dramatic art akin to the political and social revolution then seething in every mind—which shortly after this preface was written, in 1830, was translated into action on the streets of Paris.[5] Liberalism in art: that is what Victor Hugo aimed for.

Hugo found the restraints of classicism too burdensome. "Romanticism," he wrote, "so often poorly defined, is in essence nothing other than liberalism in literature."[6] Whether this freedom should rather be called license, and whether this license now jeopardizes the true advancement of art, is not my task at present to investigate. Suffice it to note that *Hernani* is a work of revolution, or rebellion, in dramatic art, and it is fitting that it should have joined forces with music at a time when feelings in general tended—though without any precise direction—toward exaggerated passions. Before too many years had passed, these were released in the great political upsurge that took place not only in Italy but virtually throughout Europe. Verdi, then, did not fail to respond to his times, and he put his mind to setting this secular drama to music.

Piave,[7] who was commissioned to convert Hugo's play to a libretto, arranged the action as follows. Ernani, alias Don Juan of Aragon, who with many of his friends has adopted the life of a bandit, falls in love with Elvira, niece and fiancée of the elderly Silva. She returns Ernani's love. Don Carlo, King of Spain, also loves Elvira, but she is loyal to Ernani and rejects all the ruler's offers of love. To free herself from his violent advances, she grabs his dagger, with which she threatens to stab herself. Don Carlo is about to call for his retainers when a furious Ernani appears. He tells the king how he hates him for having stripped him of his possessions and honors and for his father's murder of Ernani's own father. The two rivals draw their swords, but Elvira, armed with her dagger, places herself between them. At this, Silva arrives and, realizing that he has been dishonored, challenges each of the unknown rivals to single combat. He is stopped by the timely appearance of an esquire,

---

5. Hugo's play and its preface are considered a cornerstone of European romanticism. The reference is to the July Revolution of 1830.

6. "Le romantisme, tant de fois mal défini, n'est, à tout prendre, et c'est là sa définition réelle, que le *libéralisme* en littérature": Hugo, *Hernani*, ii.

7. The libretto for *Ernani* is the first written for Verdi by Francesco Maria Piave; it inaugurates the most fecund collaboration between the composer and any librettist, a collaboration that would last until *La forza del destino* (1862), also yielding *I due Foscari*, *Macbeth*, *Il corsaro*, *Stiffelio* (and its refashioning into *Aroldo*), *Rigoletto*, *La traviata*, and *Simon Boccanegra*.

who reveals the identity of the king, and the commotion subsides. Silva expedites his marriage to Elvira; all is in readiness when Ernani appears disguised as a pilgrim. Stricken by grief, he offers Silva the price on his own head as a wedding present. But faithful to the laws of hospitality, Silva conceals Ernani from the king's search party. Furious at not finding Ernani, the king resolves to take vengeance on Silva. Elvira manages to assuage the monarch's ire, and he takes her hostage. Left alone, Silva calls Ernani out of hiding and challenges him to a duel. But when Ernani learns that Elvira is with the king, he tells Silva of Don Carlo's love for her and asks a boon: that he be allowed to participate in the vengeance the furious old man is planning with his men. He swears that, if this boon is granted, he will slay himself whenever Silva commands it by sounding the horn that Ernani now gives him as an earnest of good faith. Silva agrees to the strange pact. Silva, Ernani, and many others gather in Aachen, in the catacombs containing the tomb of Charlemagne; there they plot to assassinate Don Carlo. Three cannon blasts announce Don Carlo's election as Emperor Charles V. The newly chosen emperor is alerted to the plot and, to the surprise of the conspirators, appears. But rather than punishing them, he pardons them all in a noble act of clemency inspired by the deeds of Charlemagne, of whom he has been reminded by his surroundings. Now completely reformed, he guides Elvira to Ernani's embrace and ordains that they should be man and wife. All is ready for the wedding, and the lovers are on the brink of the happiness they have so desired, when horn blasts announce to Ernani that he must kill himself. Silva then appears and offers him a dagger and a cup of poison. Ernani replies, "Let me taste at least the cup of love," but Silva is unmoved and insists that he die immediately. Elvira pleads for her husband in vain; Ernani is bound by his vow and plunges the blade into his breast.

This libretto contains many scenes [*quadri drammatici*] sure to move and keep in suspense any spectator who is more interested in experiencing strong emotions than in subjugating them to the constraints of good sense. Piave pulled himself through with no little ability, showing a good knowledge of dramatic effect. Nonetheless, imagine what an opera this would have been in the hands of a Felice Romani! The librettist of *Lucrezia Borgia* would have been a match for anyone else in Italy who might have tried his hand at such a plot. Romani's self-imposed silence after writing some 160 librettos without the least sign of flagging (indeed, his last works show that he completely understood—and was able where necessary to follow—the new directions in theatrical music) is a sad fact for opera, which has lost one of its most important sustainers.[8]

Ernani, as set by Verdi, was first performed in Venice in March 1844.[9] Before the year was out, it had been produced again in Venice as well as in Rome, Genoa, Florence (twice), Padua, Livorno, Senigallia, Brescia, Milan, Lucca, Bergamo, Cremona, Bologna, Treviso, and Trieste.[10] There are few other cases of such rapid dissemination of an opera. But it did not enjoy the same reception in all these places, and many listeners rather disliked it at first. This must be chiefly attributed to the abrupt change in direction between *I Lombardi* and *Ernani*.

The Florentine audience is among the most intelligent of our peninsula, as will be acknowledged by anyone who does not measure an audience's intelligence by the wealth of the theater it patronizes. Florence was the first city in Italy to appreciate the operas of Meyerbeer—and this is no small boast. Still, the first time *Ernani* was given at the Teatro alla Pergola—although it was performed by Frezzolini, Poggi, De Bassini, and Miral[11]—it did not have the best of fortune. The *Rivista di Firenze*, though always friendly to Verdi, wrote on July 2, 1844, of the public's coldness toward *Ernani*, and tried to explain this by denouncing the music as *not popular* in nature.[12] That explanation is incorrect, and in the same paper the same author could write on March 27, 1847, still speaking of *Ernani*, that "a flattering reception always awaited this work, which has emerged as Verdi's most *popular* to date." The Florentine audience was indifferent not because it could not recognize the value of this score but because it needed to consider its judgment.

But let us now say something about the numbers that make up this opera.

8. Felice Romani—whose librettos include those for Bellini's *Sonnambula* and *Norma* and Donizetti's *Elisir d'amore*—was one of the most successful librettists of the nineteenth century. Ninety librettos are known to have been written by Romani, for thirty-four different composers. See Alessandro Roccatagliati, "Romani, (Giuseppe) Felice," in *Grove*, vol. 21.

9. The venue was the Teatro La Fenice.

10. Basevi is accurate in the productions he enumerates, though the list would be even more impressive if it included the dozen he missed. See Marcello Conati, "Observations on the Early Reviews of Verdi's *Ernani*," in *"Ernani" Yesterday and Today*, ed. Pierluigi Petrobelli (Parma: Istituto di Studi Verdiani, 1989), 211–79, esp. 268–79 ("Appendix II: First Performances of *Ernani* 1844–1846").

11. Erminia Frezzolini (soprano, Elvira), Antonio Poggi (tenor, Ernani), Achille De Bassini (baritone, Don Carlo), Giuseppe Miral (bass, Silva).

12. Basevi himself italicizes both "*non popolare*" and "*popolare*" (in the next sentence), to emphasize the paradoxical contrast.

The very brief *preludio* contains two melodies, one referring to Ernani's oath to kill himself, and another that we hear later when Ernani is about to marry Elvira.[13] These represent the two cornerstones of the plot.

The introductory chorus is notable for its lovely variety, and for a fine chiaroscuro effect when, after a fortissimo on the words "beviam! beviam!" a pianissimo follows on "nel vin, nel vin."[14]

In the andante of the following cavatina for Ernani (tenor), there is nothing of note in the first melodic period;[15] but observe the modulations and rhythmic contrast of the third melodic period, declamatory and *di forza*, which leads to the reprise of the main theme on the words "S'ella m'è tolta."[16] The chorus "Quando notte il cielo copra" possesses that brusque character unique to Verdi; the cabaletta ["O tu, che l'alma adora"] is clear and nimble, but contains nothing unusual.

The cavatina for Elvira (soprano) has an andante in triplet motion;[17] because of certain remarkable leaps, its beautiful melody smacks somewhat of German music, specifically dance music. We also find here a period of the type I termed *di slancio* (on the words "per antri e lande inospite") and, in the fourth melodic period, an ornate accompaniment rich in Bellinian instrumentation.[18] The cabaletta ["Tutto sprezzo che d'Ernani"] is extremely graceful.

In the ensuing duet for Carlo and Elvira,[19] Verdi has followed that varied form [*forma variata*] he used in *Nabucodonosor*. A *terzetto* serves as cabaletta to this duet; it gains its effect solely through the use of unison writing and vocal display.[20]

---

13. Preludio, mm. 1ff. and 9ff.

14. N. 1, Introduzione ("Evviva! beviam!"), mm. 81ff.

15. N. 2, Recitativo ("Mercé, diletti amici") e Cavatina Ernani ("Come rugiada al cespite").

16. Indeed, the harmonic and rhythmic shift noted by Basevi at "Il vecchio Silva stendere" (mm. 27–31) is compounded by the speed with which the lines of the libretto are delivered, which accelerates to twice that of the opening. Basevi's description "declamato e di forza" is lifted more or less literally from Verdi's performance directions in the tenor part ("declamato" at m. 27, "con forza" at m. 30).

17. N. 3, [Scena] ("Sorta è la notte") [e] Cavatina Elvira ("Ernani! . . . Ernani, involami"). The cantabile that opens the cavatina proper is actually marked "Andantino piuttosto vivo."

18. A probable reference to mm. 50–53.

19. N. 4, Scena ("Fa che a me venga, . . . e tosto"), Duetto, indi Terzetto ("Qui mi trasse amor possente").

20. Because of the unexpected entrance of Ernani ("Tra quei fidi io pur qui sto!" mm. 127ff.), the number turns from a duet into a *terzetto*—a model found in Italian opera at least since Rossini. The cabaletta proper is launched by Ernani and Elvira in octaves, which Basevi terms, as usual, "unisono" ("Me conosci . . ."/"No, crudeli," mm. 153ff.).

The cavatina for Silva (bass) follows; this is curtailed to a mere andante that is as cold musically as it is dramatically.[21]

The adagio ["Vedi come il buon vegliardo"] of the first finale is a very noteworthy piece. The situation itself is an important one: it is where Silva is told that it is the king he has unknowingly challenged to a duel. Verdi conveys this solemn moment with great mastery. It begins without orchestral accompaniment when the king, speaking *sotto voce* to his squire Riccardo, mocks old Silva's surprise; he alternates with the others, who are astonished at the events. After thirteen measures, the orchestra enters, accompanying a majestic melody ["M'odi, Elvira" / "Tua per sempre"]; the change is so effective that one feels one's heart swell. The music is in keeping with the nature of the situation—even if it is not entirely apt for the words Piave has put into the mouths of Elvira and Ernani. In this piece, then, Verdi was more logical than Piave.

This would seem an opportune moment to make an important observation about scrupulous observance of the meaning of the text. There are deep pitfalls here for any composer who—by nature or education—is not capable of the level-headed criticism required to judge whether the librettist has correctly expressed the dramatic situation in harmony with the natural processes of the human heart. Absent this ability, the composer's music will often compound the blunders of the librettist. In the present adagio, Verdi was fully intent on the true nature of the scene—rather than on every detail of its poetic realization—and he heeded only the words that suited him, paying little mind to the rest. Nor did he allow a misconceived obedience to the librettist to deter him from following the right path, as indicated by the strength of his artistic convictions. It might have been desirable, however, for Verdi to have requested the librettist to change the words at some points, particularly in the parts of Elvira and Ernani, which contrast too sharply with the composer's music. I should like the reader to ponder this observation well, in order to be persuaded that the composer must not always be blamed when words and music do not agree: the mistake sometimes lies with the librettist, who, not having understood the dramatic effect, may have been unable to express it properly in his verse. It has been suggested that Verdi not infrequently writes the music before he has received the words. This procedure

21. What Basevi calls Silva's "cavatina" is not a number in its own right but rather the first lyrical section of N. 5, Finale primo ("Che mai vegg'io!"; "Infelice! e tu credevi"). On the later insertion of a cabaletta for Silva ("Infin che un brando vindice") to follow this andante, see *WGV* I/5, introduction, xxi–xxii.

must not be condemned out of hand in all cases, as it sometimes has been. We might well deride the composer were he indifferent to the librettist's text, but not when—having been moved by a dramatic situation and having already created the ideal music for it—he then asks the librettist to give poetic form to the ideas surging through his mind. Casti wrote a libretto lampooning composers who want "music first and then the words,"[22] but this should not offend those who work as Verdi does. Casti makes his composer say:

> Messrs Poets, you are mad.
> Friend, think: whoever
> do you believe wants to pay attention
> to your words?
> Today, music—music is what is wanted.
>
> THE POET
> But surely music must serve
> to express the feelings, one way or another.
>
> THE COMPOSER
> That's what is excellent about my music:
> it can accommodate anything equally well.[23]

Today, in fact, few composers write their music before having seen the words, but many rather run the risk of two equally damaging extremes: either they do not pay the least attention to the meaning of the text, or else they follow it too slavishly. Composers should avoid with equal caution both of these excesses, which are so contrary to the development of theatrical music. If the librettist has expressed the situation well, the composer has only to set the poetry suitably, but when the librettist has failed in his job, the composer may create music appropriate to the situation without binding himself to the poetry before him and have this altered subsequently to adapt it to his music.

22. Basevi's wording is literally the title of the piece under discussion, *Prima la musica e poi le parole* by the important librettist Giovanni Battista Casti. The one-act libretto was set by Salieri for a performance at Vienna's imperial residence of Schönbrunn (1786).

23. *Prima la musica*, scene 1: "IL MAESTRO: Voi signori poeti siete matti. / Amico, persuadetevi: chi mai / Credete che dar voglia attenzïone / Alle vostre parole? / Musica in oggi, musica ci vuole. / IL POETA: Ma pure questa musica conviene / Ch'esprima il sentimento, o male o bene. / IL MAESTRO: La mia musica ha questo d'eccellente, / Che può adattarsi a tutto egregiamente."

The stretta of this finale ["Io tuo fido?"] is less than felicitous. In the allegro [assai] agitato, Ernani's minor-mode theme, which is repeated by Elvira, is not at all well suited to the words; moreover, the melody is none too agreeable. When the section in the major mode begins, there is an utterly expressionless crescendo with trumpet calls; in both its manner of proceeding and its rhythm it slavishly imitates the stretta of the *introduzione* of *I Lombardi*.[24] If the diminuendo and general pause that precede the reprise of the crescendo yield no pleasant effect, at least they constitute something original and novel.

In the *introduzione* to the second act,[25] the galop with chorus is quite vivacious and graceful. This piece contains a second musical idea ["Quale fior che le aiuole giocondi"], in the dominant and in a rhythm different from the first but very heavy. Verdi seems to have included it with the aim of better setting off the first idea, but it lacks the qualities that would have made it an effective "preparation."[26] In that first musical idea, note the second phrase of the second melodic period, with its ingenious use of contrary motion between the principal melody and the bass.[27]

The *terzetto* for Elvira, Ernani, and Silva[28] contains a pleasant theme for the tenor. Later, the imitation between the bass and the soprano seems old-fashioned and is inappropriate. The tenor's minor-mode reprise of the *mossa* of his melody makes for a good effect; for the rest, this *terzetto*[29] has nothing singular to offer.

In the *duettino* section for tenor and soprano, Verdi made an effort to be both poignant and delicate, but he lapsed into affectation as his talents are not inclined to gentleness or delicacy. Aware that the piece ["Ah morir potessi adesso!"] was becoming enfeebled, he inserted at the beginning of the seventeenth measure a forte that ends, *morendo*, at the nineteenth, forming a phrase

---

24. Compare this crescendo (mm. 182ff.) with that in *I Lombardi*, N. 1, Preludio ed Introduzione ("Oh nobile esempio!"), mm. 375ff.

25. N. 6, Introduzione ("Esultiamo! . . . Letizia ne inondi").

26. See pp. 21–22 above; and the glossary, s.v. *preparazione*.

27. See mm. 44ff.

28. N. 7, Recitativo ("Jago, qui tosto il pellegrin adduci") e Terzetto ("Oro, quant'oro ogn'avido").

29. N. 7 is an extended *terzetto*, in which the opening and concluding trio portions frame a central part for Ernani and Elvira alone; Basevi's "this *terzetto*" here probably refers to the opening trio only, as he immediately proceeds to discuss the central "duettino." The "pleasant theme for the tenor" is at the opening of the *terzetto* proper ("Oro, quant'oro ogn'avido," mm. 57ff.), the "imitation" at mm. 73ff. ("Ohimè, si perde il misero!"), and the "minor-mode repetition" at mm. 77ff. ("Li miei dispersi fuggono").

that is at odds with the feeling sought for in the piece.[30] Beyond that, the musical discourse in this andantino proceeds with variety but without coherence. In short, Verdi fought against himself, but in vain. The stretta of the *terzetto* for Elvira, Ernani, and Silva now follows ["No . . . vendetta più tremenda"]. It is forceful and dramatic; the part the soprano and the tenor sing twice in unison is somewhat trite, although not without effect.

In the aria for Carlo (baritone)[31] the andante mosso is notable for certain passages where the notes must be sung most energetically, since the voice is competing with the trumpet—first on the words "se resistermi potrai," then on "la vendetta del tuo re" and elsewhere. Silva's *pertichino* ("No, de' Silva il disonore") is a felicitous idea through which the aria nearly becomes a duet. The cabaletta ["Vieni meco, sol di rose"] contradicts the andante mosso as it requires a completely different vocal timbre. Composers must take care to shun this sort of thing in order to avoid a situation where the performer who sings one section well must necessarily sing the other badly. And indeed, a singer who can give an effective rendition of this andante mosso, which is all force and vocal energy, will not be suited to performing the cabaletta, all sweetness and love.

The second act ends with a duet for Ernani and Silva.[32] It is in the form of a dialogue and is treated mostly as *parlante melodico*.[33] Later, when Silva says, "O rabbia," this becomes *parlante armonico* for a few measures. The theme Verdi chose to symbolize Ernani's vow to slay himself when he hears Silva's horn blast ["nel momento in che Ernani vorrai spento"] is too somber, and is at odds with Ernani's frank, fair, and sincere nature. Of no great moment is the *a 2* in which they invoke heaven's wrath against the traitor ["Iddio ne ascolti"]. The stretta ["In arcione, in arcion, cavalieri"]—in which the cho-rus too takes part, echoing the song of Ernani and Silva phrase by phrase—has a warlike character and aptly expresses the anger that inflames every breast. The staccato passage ["chi resister s'attenti, pria cada"] pushing forward and building to a fortissimo produces a fine effect.

30. The reference is probably to mm. 179–81, though at m. 179 there is not a forte (if not in the harp part) but rather a sudden tutti.

31. N. 8, Scena ("Cugino, a che munito") ed Aria Carlo ("Lo vedremo, o veglio audace").

32. N. 9, [Recitativo] ("Vigili pure il ciel sempre su te") e Duetto Ernani e Silva ("A te . . . scegli . . . seguimi").

33. The description applies to the opening section of the duet, especially at mm. 31–51.

At the beginning of the third act is a cavatina for Carlo.[34] The andante con moto unfolds according to the usual form, aside from the presence in the "appendix" [*appendice*] of a short, *di forza* melodic period that, serving as a *di slancio* period, vitalizes the piece at this point.[35]

The conspiracy scene[36] begins with a *parlante misto*, alternating with an obbligato recitative; while not lacking in mysterious character, it is none too well expressed. The unison statement "Si ridesti il Leon di Castiglia" is forceful and energetic. Nothing more invites our consideration until the famous septet ["Oh sommo Carlo"],[37] in which Charles V, standing before the tomb of Charlemagne, feels his soul soar to the apogee of virtue and extends his clemency to the conspirators. At this point the drama contains a scene that attains the sublime, and that can never fail to be profoundly moving; for the veneration of tombs is instilled in the human heart, and if we do honor to the bodies of the departed, how much more must we honor the minds of those who have shed luster on the human race? Moreover, clemency is a virtue that distinguishes us from beasts, with whom we *do* share anger and vengeance. Clemency is a sublime gift that in every time and place inspires awe and respect. And in this final scene the cult of tombs and the sublimity of pardon are combined to touch us deeply. Verdi was able to rise to the level of the drama, and wrote one of those pages that will certainly never be forgotten. As soon as "Oh sommo Carlo" begins, no compassionate and nobly inclined soul will remain impassive to the music, which so skillfully interprets these most noble of feelings. The second melodic period of this adagio, Carlo's "Perdono a tutti," is declamatory. Such simplicity is a trait that approaches the sublime, for any emphasis, any sophistication, and even any studied attempt to please the ear would have been out of place here, and would have marred the moment in which the composer had no other task but to reach into the soul of the spectator and move him effectively. Then the fortissimo "A Carlo Quinto sia gloria ed onor" is of magical effect, although it is nothing but the commonest of major cadences. From this we learn that even the simplest things, used properly, may produce the greatest, most stupendous effects. With slight alterations, the first portion of the piece is then repeated by all in

---

34. N. 10, Scena Carlo ("È questo il loco? . . ."; "Oh de' verd'anni miei").

35. In this case, "la forma solita" refers to the common melodic pattern A A' B A"—what musicologists of the last fifty years or so have called the "lyric prototype" (together with the variant A A' B C); Basevi's short melodic period is at mm. 89–92.

36. N. 11, Congiura ("*Ad augusta!* Chi va là?").

37. N. 12, Finale terzo ("Qual rumore!"; "Oh sommo Carlo"); the "settimino" is at mm. 99ff.

harmony, in major mode, and fortissimo, accompanied by a continuously moving bass. The baritone then continues with the second phrase in the minor, accompanied at intervals by the other characters and by the chorus. Soon, another musical thought begins: Carlo initiates its first phrase, and Elvira and Ernani complete it in unison. Carlo then begins the second phrase, which is likewise finished by the tenor and the soprano; a second period of four measures yields a forte, a fortissimo, and a *morendo* of beautiful effect, concluding the second idea. Note in the fortissimo a most pleasing example of contrary motion. The second idea is then repeated in its entirety, and with a simple cadence the act ends, and along with it one of the most beautiful pieces Verdi has written—one of the most beautiful in all of music.

The last act begins with a ball and chorus.[38] The orchestral theme, over which the chorus sings in a sort of *parlante armonico*, is graceful; its rhythm and certain melodic leaps give it a rather foreign flavor. While differing in tempo, it recalls a theme in the overture to Weber's *Oberon*, that drawn from Reiza's second-act aria.[39]

The Terzetto finale for Elvira, Ernani, and Silva[40] is also to be numbered among the most beautiful of pieces, also for a certain novelty of form. There are ninety-five measures of andante mosso in ¾ time,[41] forming ten melodic periods, and then a short cadential passage; these elements follow one after another, sometimes repeated, with or without modification; because of the effective way in which they are connected, they form a single musical thought of marvelous variety. The melody first alternates between the soprano and the bass, then passes to the tenor, at times in unison with the soprano; next, it is continued by the bass, sometimes together with the soprano or the tenor; finally, all three together conclude the *terzetto*. To maintain a certain unity in all this variety, Verdi gives the bass the phrase "È vano, o donna, il piangere," which is appositely reiterated several times, and which stands out to great theatrical effect. There is also a rich variety of harmonies in this piece; various keys are employed, to the ear's delight, and the listener is not repelled even by the nine changes of harmony that occur in the first four measures. Adopting

---

38. N. 13, Festa da ballo ("Oh come felici gioiscon gli sposi!").

39. In this finale, the theme is first heard at mm. 9ff. Compare, in Weber's *Oberon* (London: Covent Garden, 1826), the theme from the concluding Presto con fuoco of Reiza's recitative and aria N. 13 ("Ocean! thou mighty monster"), at the words "Quick, quick for a signal," which is also found in the overture's second group.

40. N. 14, Scena ("Cessaro i suoni, disparì ogni face") e Terzetto finale ("Solingo, errante e misero").

41. This is the andante assai mosso "Ferma . . . crudele, estinguere" (mm. 147ff.).

a single musical idea that, divided into several phrases and melodic periods, can be associated with more than one character is a good concept, but one that must not be abused, for the listener's musical memory is limited: it does not pay to fatigue it by forcing it to remember more than it can. Moreover, the composer should not insist on variety at the expense of the desirable unity of the whole. Examples of variety of the sort mentioned above are found also among the older composers: the great Sacchini provides a notable one in the second-act trio of his *Oedipe*.[42]

At certain important points in this opera, Verdi deliberately used rhythms whose musical accent is not in its natural place within the measure. To some degree, this makes a melody resemble German music. Modern Italians have an instinctive feel for musical accent—there are none among us who lack this. I say "modern" Italians because the music of the ancients shows that they did not possess this sense. Indeed, they repeated their melodies, varying their position within the measure each time. An example is the aria "Fortunati miei martiri" from one of Alessandro Scarlatti's cantatas.[43] Nor did Pergolesi respect musical accent. Look at the duet "Lo conosco a quegli occhietti" from *La serva padrona*, where the second syllable of "occhietti" falls on the second quarter of a common-time measure.[44] The musical accent falls naturally at the beginning of the measure and, in common time, in the middle as well. In Germany this accent is but scantly heeded, either because they do not feel it the way we do or for whatever other reasons there may be. I choose from a thousand examples the ⁶⁄₈ allegro that Ännchen sings in act 3 of Weber's *Der Freischütz*, where for several measures the accent is forcibly placed on the third eighth instead of the fourth.[45] This is not to say that the contrast between natural and artificial accents—which we may call "counteraccentuation"— will not sometimes cause much pleasure; it is this sort of pleasure that Verdi sought in some passages of *Ernani* by using certain odd rhythms. I should

42. Basevi's "*Edipo*" refers to Sacchini's *Oedipe à Colone* (Versailles, 1786). See the opening of N. 13, Trio "O bonté secourable et chère."

43. The aria is from Alessandro Scarlatti's cantata for soprano and continuo "Và pur lungi da me," and indeed opens by setting the words "Fortunati miei martiri" twice in two different metric positions. For different purposes, Basevi would later use the opening of this aria as a musical example in his *Introduzione ad un nuovo sistema d'armonia*.

44. The two *intermezzi* that make up Pergolesi's *La serva padrona* (Naples: Teatro San Bartolomeo, 1733) have been considered a model for comic opera ever since the eighteenth century. The duet cited by Basevi is in the first *intermezzo*.

45. N. 13, Romanze ("Einst träumte meiner sel'gen Base") und Arie ("Trübe Augen"): the passage in question is the opening phrase of Ännchen's Arie. Weber's "romantische Oper" was first performed at Berlin's Schauspielhaus in 1821.

detain the reader too long if I tried to indicate all these places; I shall limit myself to noting the example just discussed—the phrase "È vano, o donna, il piangere" in the final *terzetto*—where "È vano" is repeated with an accent on the second quarter, which does not normally carry such an accent.[46]

I shall make another observation on the melodies of this opera: they are composed for the most part of ascending patterns of notes. This signals a vigor that Verdi certainly possessed—especially since, as noted by Grétry, ascending phrases are characteristic of the young and descending ones of weary spirits.[47] One illustration will serve: the cabaletta, "Tutto sprezzo," of Elvira's cavatina.

46. See N. 14, m. 173 and passim.
47. "Les compositeurs à la fleur de l'âge, se servent souvent de phrases ascendantes, tandis que ceux qui sont fatigués font le contraire." André-Ernest-Modeste Grétry, *Mémoires; ou, Essais sur la musique* (1789), 2nd ed., 3 vols. (Paris: Imprimerie de la République, Pluviôse, an V [1797]), 1:236n. Grétry (1741–1813) was one of the foremost composers of eighteenth-century *opéras comiques*.

4

I DUE FOSCARI

If the least doubt remained in the mind of any Italian about the identity of the composer destined to inherit the legacy of Donizetti and Bellini in the musical world, surely it was completely dispelled by the success of *Ernani*. After this, Italy almost unanimously acknowledged Verdi as the worthy successor to those masters. But the composer still had several operas to write before he was similarly recognized throughout Europe.

Considering that, had Verdi not come on the scene, a modern-day Lamartine would have been able to refer—perhaps more justly—to musical Italy as "the land of the dead,"[1] we must not merely admire but also offer thanks to his genius, which has made the name of Italy resound gloriously in the artistic world over nearly the entire surface of the globe. And the miracle seems greater still given the multitude of composers who vied with Verdi on the path

---

1. The French author Alphonse de Lamartine (1790–1869) was often quoted—as by Basevi here—for having called Italy the "land of the dead": he apparently never used the expression verbatim, though in a poem he had lamented the decline of Italy, the "land of the past," and referred to contemporary Italians as "human dust." *Le dernier chant du pèlerinage d'Harold* (Paris: Dondey-Dupré, 1825), 56 ("terre du passé"), 59 ("poussière humaine").

that led him to such heights. Between 1842 and 1857 no fewer than 641 new operas were staged in Italy. Here is a breakdown of these by year:[2]

Year	Number of Operas	Year	Number of Operas
1842	42	1850	27
1843	53	1851	60
1844	35	1852	60
1845	32	1853	52
1846	36	1854	44
1847	29	1855	53
1848*	14	1856	40
1849†	. . .	1857	64‡

* Political events having affected nearly all the theatrical and music periodicals, I have been unable to identify new operas produced after mid-July.
† For the reason given in the preceding note, I must leave the number of operas blank. In this year Verdi gave his *Luisa Miller*.
‡ In 1858, thirty-one new operas had already been given by the end of September.

The majority of these works are the first or at most the second attempts of young musicians; from this you can guess the extraordinary number of composers there are. Notwithstanding this abundance of operas and composers, Italy has never before been so impoverished because never before has she possessed only a single composer. In saying "a single" composer, I mean not that there are no others of merit, but simply that only one is able today to satisfy the musical taste of audiences—not only of Italy but of the world. The great Rossini, though a colossus, had his emulators, who shared popular favor with him. Verdi, on the other hand, has not thus far had a single rival who could overshadow him. Yet other composers too have written fine operas, though not as successful as his. Mercadante and Pacini, who continued to write, composed operas that certainly contain much that is praiseworthy. Among new composers, many may boast of resounding successes—that is, of applause and curtain calls—but their works have a swift and inexorable enemy: time. Petrella, however, has struggled on for many years, with varying

2. The three notes at the bottom of the table are Basevi's own.

fortune, in many theaters of this peninsula—and that is saying not a little. But the composer we must certainly not omit is Teodulo Mabellini. Anyone who cares to examine his sacred compositions, such as the Responses and the Requiem, will easily see this excellent musician's great knowledge and fine talent. I could spend time on other composers; perhaps I shall do this on another occasion.[3]

One of the causes of this musical decadence in Italy is the ignorance of musicians—who generally know little more than how to read and who certainly have no love for the study of the musical classics. Hence, they are without the erudition that is indispensable for anyone who wishes to advance rather than backslide in his art. A proof of this ignorance is the existence of many self-styled "theatrical" journals, those literary rags that don judicial robes without understanding an iota of the art on which they presume to pronounce. Many believe that anyone can talk about music, as though a commentator on that art required nothing but good taste. This is false. Certainly, without good taste one can judge neither music nor painting nor any other fine art, but great knowledge is also required, and long practice in the art one has undertaken to discuss. It is told of Apelles that he once exhibited a painting that many passersby examined with interest. Among them was a cobbler, who noticed a defect in the shoe buckle of one of the painted figures. Apelles did not take this criticism amiss but thanked the cobbler for his advice. The artisan then grew bolder and added that he thought there was another defect, in the leg. To this, Apelles replied, "Cobbler, stick to the shoe."[4] The same might be said to many journalists. Two or three music periodicals are laudable exceptions, but they reap little or no fruit, for they are neither read nor valued—even, it is sad to say, by musicians, who, owing to their unlettered minds, are unable (I speak here of most, but not of all) to understand anything but the

3. The composers named in this paragraph were all active in the 1840s and 1850s—that is, in the phase of Verdi's career discussed in Basevi's book. Mercadante and Pacini were prominent operatic composers of an earlier generation (both, like Rossini and Donizetti, were born in the 1790s and had their operatic debut in the 1810s). Errico Petrella was of the same age as Verdi (who had little time for his music) and one of the most performed composers of the period. Mabellini, only a few years younger than Verdi, was a rather less successful operatic composer; as a conductor, he would later collaborate in the Concerti Popolari organized by Basevi in Florence (1863–80).

4. The anecdote about the celebrated Greek painter Apelles (fourth century BCE) is found in Pliny the Elder (first century CE), who claims that Apelles's sentence "a shoemaker should not judge above the sandal" ("ne supra crepidam sutor iudicaret") became a proverb in its own right (*Naturalis historia*, 35.85). A related English proverb is of course "Let the cobbler stick to his last."

miserable, stupid articles spouted by the ignoramuses. Because of this, music papers cannot bloom and flourish in Italy, the land of music, but are barely able to survive.

If it pleased heaven that we should have only the ignorance of the journalists to lament, we would be happy enough. But an entirely different spectacle looms, one that makes us blush for ill-fortuned Italy. I reveal our ailment in the hope that the sickness may thus more easily find its remedy. Today, a great number of these theatrical journals simply carry out a vile commerce in praise and censure, a trade some ply under the hypocrite's cloak and others brazenly, in broad daylight. Unprincipled vagabonds prostitute their pens to satisfy human vanity and malice. Many people, perhaps too naive, will not believe it possible that in today's sermonizing world—not at night, not in remote villages, but in broad daylight, in our capital cities—the press, an instrument of civilization, is being used as a barbarous weapon to molest and slander individuals under the pretext of criticism, with the sole aim of extorting cash from them. Nor will these people be willing to believe that the same press is used to celebrate and glorify—to raise to near divinity—those who have paid the price levied in this new, no less terrible species of banditry.

If the writing in vogue is the mirror of a civilization, we must weep for Italy, and all the more because this journalistic corruption is found in no other country to the degree it is here.

But let us return to our subject, leaving to others the task of wiping out this new plague that is come among us, spreading daily, and claiming ever more fresh victims.

The success of *Ernani* encouraged Verdi to continue on his path of secular drama, and Piave was commissioned to prepare a new libretto. He wrote *I due Foscari*, taking the concept and the plot from a tragedy by Byron.[5] In this he displayed but little acumen. In a letter to Murray, Byron had confessed that this play was too simple and thus unable to move the spectator.[6] Moreover, it is expansive emotions that lend themselves particularly well to music, and this work is dominated by the opposite sort, such as suspicion, terror, fraudulence, and concealment. Without for a moment meaning to detract from Byron's reputation, it is reasonable to consider this tragedy a middling work, unequal to the genius of its author. Jeffrey summed it up in these words: "This

---

5. The critical edition of the opera, by Andreas Giger, will appear as vol. I/6 of *WGV*. I am grateful to Professor Giger and to the University of Chicago Press for allowing me access to a preliminary version of the score in advance of publication.

6. The London publisher John Murray had issued Byron's tragedy *The Two Foscari* in 1821.

work depends entirely on feelings so unique to a single person, so bizarre, so eccentric that they excite no sympathy."[7] Yet there are some notable scenes, and we cannot remain silent about the magnificent final scene—but none of this suffices to save the tragedy.

Here is an outline of Piave's libretto. Jacopo Foscari, son of the doge Francesco, has returned to Venice from exile but has been banished anew on the suspicion of the Council of Ten. He is forbidden from taking with him his wife Lucrezia and his children, in order to exacerbate a sentence that, as an act of mercy, had replaced the death to which he had originally been condemned. The terrorized doge does not dare defend or plead for his son. On leaving, Jacopo dies, news of his death reaching the doge at the same time as proof of his innocence. The doge had treated his son harshly to please the Ten, and they now force him to abdicate on the pretext that, enfeebled by age and intense grief, he requires rest and quiet. Just as he gives up the dogal insignia, a bell signals the election of a new doge. At this, Francesco can no longer control his anger and grief, and, overwhelmed by fierce anguish, he falls dead.

This libretto contains nothing but the continuous whining of the doge, Jacopo, and Lucrezia; it lacks the variety of emotions that helps increase the appeal of any dramatic composition.

Undaunted by the libretto's problems, and confident in his own powers, Verdi approached the task eagerly; in a few months the score was ready, and in November 1844 it was performed in Rome at the Teatro Argentina.

The reception of the first performance was none too encouraging, but later, without really stirring up enthusiasm, the work came to enjoy higher standing and greater appreciation. Repeated on other stages, *I due Foscari* always achieved a success that, if not like that of *Ernani*, was nonetheless solid and enduring.

The opening chorus, "Silenzio, mistero," is well fashioned;[8] its *mossa* aptly depicts the cautious and suspicious behavior of the Council of Ten, as required by the text. Note also that when the principal theme returns it is accompanied and adorned in a different and richer fashion—especially by a lovely movement in the bass. The musical idea that characterizes this chorus is alluded to several times in the course of the opera, and very judiciously, whenever the council comes on stage; this gives the work the general *colorito*

---

7. The literary critic Francis Jeffrey had written of Byron's *Foscari*: "The interest is founded upon feelings so peculiar or overstrained, as to engage no sympathy" (*Edinburgh Review*, February 1822, 413–52, 435).

8. N. 2, Introduzione ("Silenzio, mistero"). The opera's N. 1 is the orchestral Preludio.

and the unity that are desirable in any composition. Linking a musical idea to a particular scene or character is not a new procedure; it was used ingeniously by Meyerbeer, then distorted into exaggeration by Wagner.

The cavatina for Jacopo (tenor), which follows, begins with a sad eleven-measure introduction in G minor, which fittingly returns in the third act when Jacopo appears before departing for his exile.[9] After a short recitative, the orchestra claims our attention with some attractive imitative music in preparation for the text "Brezza del mar natio." Its principal effect lies in the flute, which plays a sort of tremolo with two rapidly alternating notes. This tremolo alternates with responses in the strings, later reinforced, always gently, by the woodwinds. Such imitation affords an opportunity for some general observations.

It is useful to remember that the true goal of music is not imitation, which is sometimes used only as an aid to give greater determination,[10] if not greater power, to the language of music. By making music approach an everyday definite language, physical imitation distances it from the indeterminate, universal, spiritual form of expression that is music's signal virtue. In instrumental music the artifice of imitation may be used with restraint, but it must be shunned in vocal music, where it usually makes for ridiculous exaggeration.

We can compare the contrast between instrumental and vocal music with that between mime and declamation to demonstrate that, just as it would be absurd and ridiculous to accompany declamation with the somewhat exaggerated gestures a mime has to use (lacking a text with which to express the ideas easily), it is contrary to every sound artistic precept and to good sense (not to mention effect) to translate into sounds the words being sung—as though the meaning of the words could ever happen to be less clear than that of a group of notes.

In vocal music, melody can often be analogous to declamation, in its vocal inflections and in pitch, and also with regard to rhythm, as when it is used to express vehement anger, grief, sobbing, and so forth. But it is not reasonable in these cases to say that the goal of the music is to imitate speech. The analogy should be seen as a simple coincidence, born of the fact that music and speech possess the same means of expression, though in different de-

9. N. 3, Scena ("Qui ti rimani alquanto") [ed] Aria Jacopo ("Dal più remoto esiglio"). Compare the opening of this number with that of N. 13, Scena ("Donna infelice") ed Aria Jacopo ("All'infelice veglio").

10. Basevi uses the verb *determinare*, in opposition to the following sentence's "indeterminato"—for him one of the main attributes of music.

grees. Declamation and music must not contradict each other, though they should not be confused to the point of meriting Julius Caesar's reproof to an orator: "You're speaking too much if you're singing, and singing too much if you're speaking."[11] Nor must physical imitation be confused with expression. In Haydn's *Creation*, when the music goes into the major with a fortissimo at the words "and there was Light," the intention is not to imitate light, but rather to arouse the sense of fulfillment or surprise that is a part of one's reaction to an unexpected burst of light.[12] Thus too in *Les Huguenots*, when in the quarrel chorus between the Catholic and Protestant women Meyerbeer uses dissonances of the major and minor second to describe their chatter, we cannot accuse him of translating the words into music, for the chatter results from the sound of the words, not from their meaning.[13] In *opera buffa*, physical imitation is at times permissible to raise a laugh, as in Rossini's *Il barbiere di Siviglia*, in the orchestral accompaniment to Don Basilio's words "come un colpo di cannone."[14]

But I must classify as oddities those imitations that pertain to the graphic aspect of music [*musicografia*], such as that which Grétry boasts about: in *Silvain*, at the words "mais dans un doux esclavage," he uses notes whose pitches form a circular shape to represent the bond that joins husband and wife.[15] I would frankly be unable to praise Rossini if, in the second-act recitative from *Guillaume Tell*, his intention was to draw a mountain with the notes, at the words "L'avalanche roulant du haut de nos montagnes."[16]

---

11. The first-century Roman rhetorician Quintilian reports the anecdote by which a young Caesar told a practicing reader: "If you are singing, you are singing badly; if you are reading, you are singing" (*Institutio oratoria*, 1.8.2: "si cantas, male cantas: si legis, cantas"). See Quintilian, *The Orator's Education*, ed. and trans. Donald A. Russell, 5 vols. (Cambridge, MA: Harvard University Press, 2001), 1:200–201.

12. Joseph Haydn, *Die Schöpfung*, ed. Annette Oppermann, *HW* XXVIII/3 (2008), N. 1a, Einleitung: Die Vorstellung des Chaos (Introduction: The Representation of Chaos), mm. 85–86.

13. See Meyerbeer, *Les Huguenots*, N. 20, Choeur de la dispute ("Nous voilà! félons, arrière!").

14. N. 6 ("La calunnia è un venticello"), mm. 58–62, in which the orchestral sforzato associated with the cannon shot includes a very prominent bass drum.

15. See André-Ernest-Modeste Grétry, *Mémoires; ou, Essais sur la musique* (1789), 2nd ed., 3 vols. (Paris: Imprimerie de la République, Pluviôse, an V [1797]), 2:193. The passage is in Hélène's Air "Ne crois pas" from scene 3 of Grétry's *Silvain* (Paris: Comédie-Italienne, 1770).

16. *Guillaume Tell*, N. 12, Final 2ᵉ ("Des profondeurs du bois immense"), mm. 292–94. Basevi's two examples of "musicografia" are not, however, in the same category: Grétry's symbolism is purely visual ("eye music"), whereas Rossini's is also clearly audible ("tone painting").

To return to Jacopo's piece in *I due Foscari*, here the imitation of the breeze is certainly not to be condemned so long as we hear the orchestra only. But it may be viewed as at least unnecessary after the entry of the voice. It is always preferable for music and text to unite to express the inner sense of the psyche, rather than, as in this piece, to highlight the physical impression made on the external senses.[17]

The andantino "Dal più remoto esiglio" is in ⁶⁄₈ time, accompanied mostly by what I shall call "empty" triplets [*terzine vuote*]: these have a rest in place of the second note or chord of the group. Let me make some comments on this meter, tempo, and rhythm; the musical laity may skip these without much harm, but musicians may find them useful.

Time is the principal—indeed the prime—element of music. In the final analysis, the difference in pitch between two notes boils down to variations in the duration of the oscillations of vibrating bodies; thus it is time that produces these differences. And not only notes but, through rhythm, all melodies stem from time. Among the various sorts of meter that merit special study I shall limit myself to a consideration of ⁶⁄₈. This has a special character that makes it suited to expressing things appertaining to the pastoral and hunting. It is no less suited to barcaroles, ballads, etc. Note also that the effect and expression will differ depending on whether the speed is slow or quick, and on the accompaniment figure; in fact, when slow, the pattern of empty triplets lends itself wonderfully to the lullaby. One must therefore proceed with tremendous caution in the use of that meter and that accompaniment pattern.

The special character and expressive limitations of ⁶⁄₈ time have often deterred composers from using it. Verdi himself employed ⁶⁄₈ time not at all in *Nabucodonosor* and only once in *I Lombardi*, in the chorus "La bella straniera."[18] The same holds for *Ernani*, where ⁶⁄₈ was used in the opening chorus[19]—and note that both these choruses are in a quick, brisk tempo. In Jacopo Foscari's andantino, the empty triplets give the melody a languor that is most appropriate to his mood but that the audience is perhaps not obliged to share: art must seek truth, but not unpleasantly burdensome truth.[20] The cabaletta ["Odio solo, ed odio atroce"] is full of fire but contains nothing singular.

---

17. This terminological opposition of "senso interno" and "sensi esterni" was widely (and diversely) used by philosophers and physicians of Basevi's time.

18. N. 8, Coro nell'harem ("La bella straniera").

19. N. 1, Introduzione ("Evviva! beviam!").

20. Traditionally, the combination of ⁶⁄₈ meter, moderate tempo, and the rhythm | ♪ ♪ ♪ ♪ | (or | ♩♪ ♩♪ |) was often associated with boats and rowing (and in specific cases with Venice

The cavatina for Lucrezia (soprano)[21] is among Verdi's best. Here again we find a seven-measure introduction that expresses Lucrezia's character and is repeated with an identical or similar rhythm each time she appears. The chorus of women that precedes the andante maestoso is very poor, tossed off without care—a rare occurrence with Verdi. The melody of the andante maestoso, "Tu al cui sguardo," is very tender and poignant. Note that when the first period of a melody is beautiful, Verdi very shrewdly follows it with a little four-measure period, in order to return quickly to the first. Note too that these intermediate periods in Verdi's melodies generally vary greatly in both their harmonies and their rhythms. In the allegro of this cavatina we find one of those highly popular *di slancio* periods on the words "O patrizi, etc." A fine effect is produced here by the transition from D minor to a D-major seventh chord resolving immediately onto a chord of G. At the repetition of the cabaletta, the first melodic period, which preceded that beginning "O patrizi," is omitted.[22] Verdi did the same in the soprano aria in the second finale of *I Lombardi*, where the cabaletta is not repeated from the beginning.[23] The chorus of senators[24] is too raucous; the music would be more fitting for a crowd of savages.

The *romanza* of Francesco (baritone)[25] is a ⁶⁄₈ andantino with empty triplets in the first melodic period. This piece too is very afflicting.

In the duet "Tu pur lo sai, che giudice,"[26] the andante is highly varied [*variato*], following the form first used in *Nabucodonosor*. The allegro too is

---

and gondolier songs). Donizetti, for instance, had used the pattern to accompany a barcarole sung by a gondolier in act 2, scene 1, of *Marino Faliero* (Paris: Théâtre Italien, 1835)—another opera with a Venetian setting. It is remarkable that Basevi should not mention this topos when discussing the use of ⁶⁄₈ for the andantino: here, Jacopo's evocation of his nostalgia for Venice is occasioned by his looking at the city's waters from a balcony. The topos recurs later in the opera, in the third-act barcarole "Tace il vento, è queta l'onda." Verdi would soon return to the convention in *Alzira*, where a similar lilting rhythm is associated with the image of a boat (N. 5, Cavatina "Da Gusman, su fragil barca").

21. N. 4, Scena ("Nò . . . mi lasciate . . ."), Coro ("Resta, . . . quel pianto accrescere"), [ed] Aria Lucrezia ("Tu al cui sguardo onnipossente").

22. Basevi deduces this "omission" from his description of the cabaletta as starting with the first quatrain ("La clemenza? . . . s'aggiunge lo scherno!"). A different description is one by which, in Budden's words, "only the second [quatrain] ('O patrizi') forms the material of the cabaletta proper. The first ('La clemenza?') is set as a minor-key preparation for it in a [. . .] slightly slower tempo" (Budden, 1:185).

23. See pp. 34–35 above.

24. N. 5, Coro ("Tacque il reo!"; "Al mondo sia noto").

25. N. 6, Scena ("Eccomi solo alfine!") e Romanza Doge ("O vecchio cor, che batti").

26. N. 7, Scena ("L'illustre dama Foscari") e Duetto [Lucrezia e Doge] ("Tu pur lo sai, che giudice").

varied ["Se tu dunque potere non hai"]; while the soprano's phrase is banal, the entry of the bass in a slower tempo is very arresting ["O vecchio padre misero"]. The composer benefited here from a variation in poetic meter.[27]

The second act begins with a short prelude, played only by a solo viola and a solo cello, with a very doleful effect. Did Verdi aim at this effect deliberately? If he did—perhaps to signify the perpetual night that reigns in Jacopo's dungeon—it does not seem to have been a very good idea. The ensuing prayer for Jacopo is certainly not among our composer's best efforts.[28]

A duet for Lucrezia and Jacopo follows.[29] The $\frac{3}{8}$-time andantino is in varied form, and contains some pleasing phrases. In the first soprano phrase, the theme unfolds over a descending motion in the orchestral bass, but as this is not followed up later—to the contrary, this distinctive motion is completely forgotten—it seems to me that it would have been better not to use it in the first place. The melody of the allegro of this duet ["Speranza dolce ancora"] is very tender; in form and in character it belongs to the same family of melodies as "Verranno a te sull'aure" in Donizetti's *Lucia di Lammermoor*.[30] The third time the melody "Speranza dolce ancora" is repeated in this duet, the soprano and tenor sing it in unison, and the accompaniment consists of a harp arpeggio, with the violins and violas providing the harmonies, pianissimo, in a high register. From this pianissimo the piece shifts to fortissimo with a fine effect of contrast.

The *terzetto* for Lucrezia, Jacopo, and Francesco[31] is preceded by a *parlante melodico* that, contrary to Verdi's usual procedure, is perhaps too long. The andante is of a unique sweetness. The tenor begins with a three-period melody, whose final four-measure period ["Quest'innocente figlio"] is *di slancio*. The bass follows with a different melody for two periods, and then,

<hr>

27. The poetic meter moves from *decasillabi* ("Se tu dunque potere non hai") to *settenari* ("O vecchio padre misero"); Verdi shifts musical meter and tempo at this juncture.

28. N. 8, Introduzione, Scena ("Notte! . . . perpetua notte"), ed Aria Jacopo ("Non maledirmi, o prode").

29. N. 9, Scena ("Ah sposo mio! . . .") e Duetto Lucrezia e Jacopo ("No, non morrai; che i perfidi").

30. See Donizetti, *Lucia di Lammermoor*, N. 3, Scena ("Lucia, perdona") e Duetto Lucia ed Edgardo ("Ei mi abborre . . ."; "Sulla tomba che rinserra"), whose stretta "Verranno a te sull'aure" indeed presents several similarities in design to "Speranza dolce ancora."

31. N. 10, Terzetto [Lucrezia, Jacopo, e Doge] ("Ah padre! . . ."; "Nel tuo paterno amplesso").

singing in thirds with the tenor, repeats the latter's final *di slancio* period. The soprano enters with a broken, breathless rhythm of the kind for which Verdi has often shown a fondness. In the *mossa* of this melody for Lucrezia, which is only one period long, there is an example of musical accentuation out of its natural place. As the soprano sings, the other voices join in. All then take part in a somewhat disconnected period, after which they repeat the *di slancio* period together and fortissimo; this marvelous piece then ends immediately with a cadential phrase. It will be clear that Verdi has followed the varied form used in the final *terzetto* of *Ernani*,[32] here too employing a melodic period that, repeated at opportune moments, gives the piece a degree of unity.

The quartet that follows ["Ah sì il tempo che mai non s'arresta"][33] is virtually a waltz, and does not seem to me suitable for describing the anguish of the characters. You may note some effects of "counteraccentuation," one of which is in the twenty-eighth measure of the presto,[34] whose first note is slurred to the last one of the previous measure and carries no accent.

The chorus that precedes the second finale[35] is too monotonous and uniform. The sextet ["Queste innocenti lagrime"] is a most moving andante agitato begun by the tenor and continued by the soprano; then the chorus enters and continues the musical discourse along with the other characters. At the thirteenth measure after the entry of the chorus there is a ten-measure period containing some fine effects of counteraccentuation in the seventh, eighth, and ninth measures.[36] After a repetition of this last period an obbligato recitative follows immediately, and then a short, more song-like passage ["Ai figli tu dell'esule"], after which the final six measures of the aforementioned last melodic period are repeated with more vigorous orchestral accompaniment. The act ends with an ordinary cadential passage. The repetition, following the recitative, of the fine counteraccented phrase takes place after the audience's attention has been distracted; it thus produces no effect, especially since it does not conform to the requirements of the drama. In truth, Verdi never had

32. See p. 54 above.

33. This "quartet" is still part of N. 10, which began as a *terzetto* but now adds the part of Loredano.

34. N. 10, m. 206.

35. The chorus ("Che più si tarda? . . ."; "Non fia che di Venezia") in fact opens N. 11, Finale atto secondo, in which it is followed by Basevi's "sestetto."

36. The period begins at m. 226, and the "effetti di *controaccento*" are the prominent accents on the third or second beat (mm. 232–33 and 234, respectively).

much aptitude for the repetition of themes—something at which Meyerbeer excelled, perhaps above all others.

The chorus that opens the third act is slight, the melody of the following barcarole lovely and quite catchy.[37]

The tenor aria "All'infelice veglio" is notable for its form.[38] The third melodic period is sung by the soprano; then the tenor continues with another melodic period up to a sort of obbligato recitative. After this, the tenor has another eight-measure period, which is repeated fortissimo by the five voices together with the chorus, in harmony. The tenor then sings the first phrase of a new melodic period that is completed by everyone in harmony, and the piece ends with a short cadential passage.

In the soprano aria "Più non vive"[39] note one of the usual *di slancio* periods on the words "Sorga in Foscari."

Francesco's final aria[40] is the most beautiful piece in the opera; it must be added that this is also the drama's finest and most poignant scene. The grief and remorse of the doge, who has lost his son without having used his power and influence to save him; his anger at seeing himself stripped of the dignity he had hoped to maintain all his life; his humiliation at being forced to cede the dogal vestments: these are all highly momentous circumstances that move the audience to pity the fate of the unhappy old man. Verdi profited from this solemn situation, and he wrote one of those pieces that reveal his consummate genius in all its power.

This opera leaves one with a feeling of melancholy that accords well with the plot. The effect is bolstered by the frequent use of the minor mode, which is in much greater evidence here than in the other operas we have examined. Nor is the score enlivened by the slow ⅝ time with empty triplets that is used in two arias, or by the slow ⅜ with the same accompaniment pattern that is found in one duet. It is curious that no cantabile is in adagio tempo; this decreases the variety that is so necessary to bring music to life. Moreover, the text—with its continuous lamenting, its uniformity of content, and its virtuous but not very moving conjugal love—never enlivens the *colorito* of the drama or, therefore, of the music.

---

37. N. 12, Introduzione-Coro ("Alla gioia, alle corse") e Barcarola ("Tace il vento, è queta l'onda").

38. N. 13, Scena ("Donna infelice") ed Aria Jacopo ("All'infelice veglio").

39. N. 14, Recitativo ("Egli ora parte!") ed Aria Lucrezia ("Più non vive! . . .").

40. N. 15, Scena ("Signor, chiedon parlarti i Dieci . . .") ed Aria Doge ("Questa dunque è l'iniqua mercede") e Finale ultimo.

5

GIOVANNA D'ARCO

In February 1845 the first performance of another new opera by Verdi took place at the Teatro alla Scala in Milan: *Giovanna d'Arco*.[1]

Although Solera was strongly inclined toward sacred subjects and was able to instill a certain fervor into his characters, he was not as lucky with his operatic adaptation of this miraculous tale of the shepherdess of Domrémy as he had been with *Nabucodonosor* and *I Lombardi*.

It is known that in the first half of the fifteenth century Joan of Arc, believing herself divinely inspired, went to the King of France promising to free her country from the English occupation. After many examinations to ascertain whether it was God or the devil who counseled her, it was decided that nothing about Joan seemed contrary to sound religion. With a sturdy contingent of soldiers she then went to Orléans, and kindling universal enthusiasm in the French—who had been disheartened by misfortune—she liberated the city, which for seven months had been under siege by the English. She was victorious in subsequent battles, and fortune seemed to favor her until she finally

---

1. The critical edition of *Giovanna d'Arco*, by Alberto Rizzuti, was published as *WGV* I/7 (2008).

fell into the hands of the enemy, who, adjudging her possessed by the devil, burned her alive as a heretic.

The subject of *Giovanna d'Arco* gives me the opportunity to offer some thoughts on the fantastic and the supernatural that may provide some enlightenment and guidance to writers who wish to treat subjects of the kind we are discussing.

Most people tend to confuse the fantastic and the supernatural, but the difference is great indeed. The fantastic is what the human imagination produces when, drawing on elements stored in the memory, it puts together mental images that, not translating into actuality, meet with no obstacles in material reality. Able thus to go beyond what is possible, they may assume the *guise* of the supernatural. But the supernatural proper does not originate or remain in the sphere of the imagination; as a product of superhuman power, it is manifested in actual deeds that seem completely contrary to the laws of matter.

As a product of the imagination, the fantastic must satisfy the intellect; and in order to have a useful function it should have a "tempering" aim—that of impressing the principles of wisdom more firmly on the mind by embodying them in various fictional deeds, in such a way that the senses are agreeably affected, and will aid the memory through the workings of delight.

The supernatural, on the other hand, lies beyond the reach of our will, and derives its effectiveness from the surprise it causes. In no way is reason involved in the consideration of those deeds in which it is overpowered either by our faith or by our credulity.

The fantastic takes the form of fiction, such as allegories, fables, and so forth; the supernatural draws its subjects from the scriptures or from folk beliefs, provided that these still live in the heart of the audience. *Robert le diable*, which personifies and contrasts man's good and evil inclinations, is a good example of a fantastic drama, while *Mosè* may be counted among the finest subjects based on the supernatural.[2]

In the enterprises of Joan of Arc we discern neither the fantastic nor the supernatural; Joan therefore remains suspended, as it were, between heaven and earth. Indeed, seeing her as inspired by heaven does not make her any more venerable—as we are not dealing here with sacred history—and serves to minimize her heroism since we do not perceive it as stemming solely from

2. A miniature score of Meyerbeer's *Robert le diable* (Paris: Opéra, 1831) would later be printed by the Florentine publisher Guidi (*Roberto il diavolo*, 1863), with whom Basevi collaborated. On *Mosè*, see chapter 1, n. 6, above.

nobility of spirit. Hence, we must not be surprised if the French have never shown much fondness for their liberatrix. To the contrary, Voltaire wrote a poem[3] intended to insult and deride her—which would have caused no offense to the patriotism of the French: we read that toward the end of the last century, in the tumult of revolution, the furious populace tore down a modest stone monument to the girl in a street of Orléans.[4] It does no good to cite the poem to Joan's glory by Chapelain, a poet justly derided by Boileau, or the tragedy by Soumet, a truly slight thing, or the two *Mességniennes* of Delavigne:[5] while attractive, these lack the development the subject would have demanded had it been truly close to the nation's heart.

Foreigners have displayed greater devotion to this French heroine. Southey wrote a poem about her that is not without merit.[6] And it is a fact that, almost simultaneously with the aforementioned desecration of Joan's memory at Orléans, an author was booed at London's Covent Garden who, in a mimed performance, had hoped to please the audience by showing the French heroine carried off by devils in the final scene. On succeeding nights she was seen accompanied instead by angels—to universal applause.[7]

Schiller wrote a fine tragedy on the subject; yet it will be clear from even a moderately attentive reading that the splendor of its form, its poetic conceits, its abundance of incident, and its large number of characters all blind us to the intrinsic defectiveness of the principal character.[8]

3. Although there had been pirated editions of the poem since 1755, Voltaire first published *La pucelle d'Orléans* in 1762. See the critical edition by Jeroom Vercruysse, in *Les oeuvres complètes de/The Complete Works of Voltaire*, ed. Theodore Besterman et al. (Geneva: Institut et Musée Voltaire; Oxford: Voltaire Foundation, 1968–), vol. 7 (Geneva: Institut et Musée Voltaire, 1970).

4. Basevi is probably referring (albeit imprecisely) to an event documented to have taken place in Orléans in 1792, when a bronze monument to Joan of Arc was destroyed to make cannons for the city's Garde Nationale.

5. On its publication, Jean Chapelain's *La pucelle; ou, La France délivrée* (1656) was satirized by the poet-critic Nicholas Boileau. Alexandre Soumet's tragedy *Jeanne d'Arc* (1825), on the other hand, was well received. Casimir Delavigne published "La vie de Jeanne d'Arc" and "La mort de Jeanne d'Arc" as *Deux mésséniennes; ou, Élégies sur la vie et la mort de Jeanne d'Arc* (Paris: Ladvocat, 1819).

6. Robert Southey's epic poem *Joan of Arc* was first published in 1796.

7. This anecdote is reported by Southey in later editions of his poem, beginning from the third: Robert Southey, *Joan of Arc*, 3rd ed. corrected, 2 vols. (London: Longman, Hurst, Rees, & Orme, 1806), 1:9–19 ("Preface"), 18.

8. The "romantic tragedy" *Die Jungfrau von Orleans*, first staged in Leipzig in 1801, was one of Schiller's most performed plays in the nineteenth century. It had already served as the source for Giovanni Pacini's opera *Giovanna d'Arco* (Milan: Teatro alla Scala, 1830).

But what becomes of this subject when, as in Solera's libretto, everything is reduced to a heroine of questionable heroism, a spineless, nearly idiot king—with whom Giovanna is made to be in love—and a father (Giovanna's) who is unnatural, superstitious, and fanatical to the point of accusing his own daughter of witchcraft and not blanching at the thought of seeing her dragged off to the stake? Furthermore, the choruses of good and evil spirits added by Solera have something of the fantastic about them, but they do not mesh well with the rest of the drama and are out of place.

I must say in all frankness that Verdi simply could not find inspiration in this subject, rather putting into his craft and his care over the form all the substance that he was unable to feed into the ungrateful terrain of the libretto.

The *sinfonia*[9] draws attention with its ingenious andante pastorale, in which the flute, clarinet, and oboe stand out, beautifully intertwined and in exquisite taste.

In the chorus of townspeople[10] that opens the prologue [act 1],[11] we find a melody first sung by everyone in unison, then repeated in a harmonized version; this yields a variety of a new kind. Note the instrumentation of this piece, especially the movement of the bass.

As in *I due Foscari*, so in *Giovanna d'Arco* the tenor's cavatina[12] is a ⁶⁄₈-time andantino accompanied by empty triplets [*terzine vuote*]. Although punctuated by the chorus, the melody still comes off as monotonous and heavy. Then comes a chorus of townspeople, who describe a scene of witches and demons ["Nell'orribile foresta"]. In its first measures, this ⁶⁄₈ allegro vivace recalls—in its character, if not in its melody—the chorus of witches in Mercadante's *Ismalia*,[13] one of that composer's best pieces and one that is justly cited as a

9. N. 1, Sinfonia.

10. N. 2, Introduzione ("Qual v'ha speme?").

11. The four parts of *Giovanna d'Arco* are labeled as a prologue and three acts in various early sources (including the libretto of the premiere) but as four acts in Verdi's autograph score. Early printed vocal scores—and Basevi with them—follow the libretto but number all the finali, with the result that act 1 concludes with a Finale secondo, and so on. We will refer to Verdi's subdivision in square brackets.

12. N. 3, Scena ("Nel suo bel volto qual color!") e Cavatina Carlo ("Sotto una quercia parvemi").

13. Saverio Mercadante, *Ismalia, ossia Morte ed amore* (Milan: Teatro alla Scala, 1832). The chorus of witches "Quando solo al fischiar de' venti" is part of the opera's opening number, Introduzione-Coro [interno] ("Beltà pudica e tenera") e Sortita Azila ("Al suono de' liuti"). See the vocal score (Milan: Ricordi, [1832]). Basevi refers to the opera as "*Ismelia.*"

model of its kind. The cabaletta ["Pondo è letal, martiro"] bears the imprint of Verdian vehemence.

The andante of Giovanna's cavatina[14] is most graceful. In the *tempo di mezzo*[15] the choruses of evil and celestial spirits ["Tu sei bella"; "Sorgi! o diletta Vergine!"][16] are lacking in *colorito*, particularly the first. Granted, the infernal spirits have disguised themselves with a view to penetrating Giovanna's soul more effectively, concealing their true nature as best they can. Even so, their musical portrayal should not reach the point where hypocrisy is no longer distinguishable from true virtue. Music is so rich in expressive devices that it can simultaneously depict widely differing sentiments so that some cloak the others—which is what would be required here. See how the celebrated Meyerbeer dealt with the character of Bertram in *Robert le diable* and you will be convinced of what I say.

The cabaletta ["Son guerriera che a gloria t'invita"] is properly impetuous. Note as an extraordinary thing for Verdi that the first melodic period is composed of two seven-measure phrases.[17] This sort of irregularity is not unfitting where passion powerfully dominates, as it does at this point, where Giovanna takes up the helmet and the sword.

The *terzettino* for unaccompanied voices ["A te, pietosa Vergine"] is very slight indeed. After this, the three voices, nearly always in unison, repeat with great vigor the soprano's cabaletta beginning with its second melodic period.[18] And thus ends the prologue [act 1].

In act 1 [act 2], a chorus of little account[19] is followed by the baritone's aria,[20] which reminds us of Verdi's majestic manner in the andante "Franco son io"—but nothing else.

14. N. 5, Scena ("Oh ben s'addice") e Cavatina Giovanna ("Sempre all'alba ed alla sera").

15. In Verdi's autograph what Basevi calls "tempo di mezzo" is in fact already the beginning of N. 6, Finale primo ("Paventi, Carlo, tu forse?"; "Tu sei bella"), which of course covers the remainder of the act (Basevi's later "cabaletta" and "terzettino" reflect further subdivisions found in printed vocal scores of the time).

16. In Verdi's autograph the words that open the angelic chorus read "Sorgi! o diletta Vergine! Maria, Maria ti chiama"; most sources give a censored version, "Sorgi! I Celesti accolsero / La generosa brama!"

17. The period that starts with the anacrusis to m. 166 is in fact more regular than is suggested by Basevi.

18. Measures 282ff. are a reprise of 181ff. only melodically, as they set a different poetic text.

19. N. 7, Introduzione atto secondo ("Ai lari! . . . Alla patria!").

20. N. 8, Scena ("Questa rea che vi percuote") ed Aria Giacomo ("Franco son io, ma in core").

The *romanza* "O fatidica foresta"[21] is a ⁶⁄₈ andantino—this time without empty triplets—which is not very suited to the situation or to the words; the melody, however, is pleasant.

In the second-finale duet for soprano and tenor[22] we find first a *parlante* whose orchestral part recalls that of the introductory chorus in the second act of *Ernani*. In the cantabile "Dunque, o cruda," pitches outside the harmony are used as essential notes of the melody, in the manner often adopted by Bellini; this makes the cantabile more deeply affecting. Observe too the allegro "Vieni al tempio," which clearly draws on "Speranza dolce ancora" from *I due Foscari*.[23] A characterless chorus of evil spirits has been grafted onto it.

In act 2 [act 3] there is nothing else worthy of note aside from the andante of the final *terzetto*, "No! forme d'angelo."[24] Here again we find ⁶⁄₈ time but with a rich and varied accompaniment. The form may be called "Mercadantesque," as it is based on a long musical idea, sung first by the soprano alone and then in unison with the tenor with the addition of the other voices.[25] The stretta is very weak.

The closing scene is without doubt the finest in the opera.[26] Following Schiller, who paid no attention here to history, Solera has Giovanna perish of a wound received in battle. In a poignant tableau we see the moribund Giovanna, now understood by her father to be innocent, dying contented to have obeyed heaven and saved her country. Verdi painted it with the ability and talent one would expect of him. Still, this final scene is certainly inferior to that of *I due Foscari*.

It is now fifteen years since this music was written—surely not too soon for a cool-headed assessment. Both careful study of the score and the public's reception of the opera pronounce it inferior to the four that preceded it.

21. N. 9, Romanza Giovanna ("Qui! Qui! . . . dove più s'apre"; "O fatidica foresta").

22. N. 10, Duetto–Finale secondo ("Ho risolto!"; "Dunque, o cruda e gloria e trono"). See n. 11 above.

23. See *I due Foscari*, N. 9, Scena ("Ah sposo mio! . . .") e Duetto [Lucrezia e Jacopo] ("No, non morrai; che i perfidi"), mm. 169ff., and Basevi's discussion of the passage, p. 66 above.

24. N. 13, Finale terzo ("Te, Dio, Lodiam"; "No! forme d'angelo non dà l'Eterno"; "Fuggi, o donna maledetta").

25. See mm. 148ff. and 171ff.

26. N. 16, Finale ultimo ("Un suon funereo d'intorno spandesi"; "S'apre il Ciel . . . Discende Maria").

6

ALZIRA

Although written with skill and care, the music of *Giovanna d'Arco* added nothing at all to its author's reputation, and indeed the envious and malicious smiled inwardly. It was thus with great eagerness that the premiere of the next opera, *Alzira*, was awaited, so that Verdi's talents might be better judged.[1]

In August 1845, the opera was performed at the Teatro San Carlo in Naples, where it achieved a succès d'estime—which is to say that disapproval was inhibited by respect for the composer.

Cammarano,[2] a poet of some worth, modeled his libretto on Voltaire's noted tragedy *Alzire*.[3] But this subject was no better suited to the operatic stage than was that of *Giovanna d'Arco*.

It was Voltaire's principal aim to contrast the good fruits harvested from religion when properly understood with the evil ones that sprout from

---

1. The critical edition of *Alzira*, by Stefano Castelvecchi with the collaboration of Jonathan Cheskin, was published as *WGV* I/8 (1994).

2. *Alzira* marks the beginning of Verdi's collaboration with the prominent librettist Salvadore Cammarano, which would later give rise to *La battaglia di Legnano*, *Luisa Miller*, and *Il trovatore*.

3. *Alzire; ou, Les Américains* (Paris: Comédie-Française, 1736).

superstition and fanaticism. The main theme of this work is reflected in the following lines, which a dying Gusman addresses to his killer:

> Des Dieux que nous servons, connois la différence:
> Les tiens t'ont commandé le meurtre et la vengeance,
> Et le mien, quand ton bras vient de m'assassiner,
> M'ordonne de te plaindre, et de te pardonner.

> [Know the difference between the gods we serve:
> yours have required of you murder and vengeance,
> and mine, when your hand has just slain me,
> requires me to pity you, and pardon you.]

These were not badly imitated by Cammarano, as follows:

> I numi tuoi, vendetta atroce . . .
> Misfatto orribile . . . ti consigliar . . .
> Io del mio Nume odo la voce,
> Voce che impone di . . . perdonar!

> [Your gods counseled . . .
> atrocious vengeance . . . horrible sin . . .
> I hear the voice of my God,
> a voice that commands me . . . to forgive!]

This is all well and good, but it is taken in only by the philosophically minded portion of the audience—a small portion indeed. Besides, nowadays this topic lacks even the advantage of allusion, which always serves to arouse passion; it had this of course in Voltaire's time.

The philosopher of Ferney, preoccupied with the doctrine he was concealing "beneath the veil of mysterious lines,"[4] paid no attention to characterization or to the customs and times of the setting. All the merit of this tragedy, if indeed it has any, lies in the philosophical ideas, and in the maxims he puts into the mouths of his characters. Now, music holds nothing in greater horror than undiluted philosophy. Music is the indeterminate language of the

---

4. Basevi's "*sotto il velame delli versi strani*" is a quotation (marked by his italics) that would have escaped few educated Italians (Dante, *Inferno*, 9.63).

heart, not the precise language of the mind; if at times it expresses philosophical ideas, it does so only when these are cloaked in human passions. In this
respect, then, Cammarano could not have been more poorly advised in his
choice of subject. Besides, on today's musical stage the mores that win the
best reception are those closer to us—to the extent that this is possible—and
within the ken of the spectator: otherwise the drama will be unable to sustain
the music with due efficacy. A rapid look at the history of opera reveals that
fabulous and heroic subjects were chosen at first, as in the earliest operas of
Dafne, *Euridice*, and *Arianna*.[5] With the passage of time, material from ancient history came to be used. Now at last, music having extended its means
of expression, it is easier to take on contemporary subjects—or at least those
that foreground passions and feelings that are valid for all places and times.

The action of *Alzira* is set in Peru at a time when the inhabitants of that
land were still in a state of savagery. But who really are the Peruvians in Voltaire's tragedy? On close scrutiny they prove to be nothing more than Frenchmen disguised as savages. But Cammarano took these Peruvians seriously and
did not notice that in their speech and their actions they show signs of having
at least lived in Europe for a good long time. Verdi was more perceptive, and
to escape this predicament he treated them all in his music as sons of the Old
World.

Cammarano took up all Voltaire's contradictions and added some of his
own. The Peruvian Zamoro begins by giving proof of great moderation and
generosity in saving the life of the Spaniard Alvaro, and ends by treacher-
ously murdering his enemy and rival Gusmano. Gusmano, on the other hand,
is shown at first to be pitiless and driven by the greatest cruelty toward the
vanquished; in the end, he pardons Zamoro, who has mortally wounded him,
and cedes Alzira to him. Which of these characters are we to hate and which
to love? Then, in Voltaire's tragedy, Alzire is a savage in love with Zamore.
Believing him dead, and at her father's insistence, she marries Gusman; according to Cammarano's text, on the other hand, it is Gusmano himself who
forces Alzira to give him her hand in marriage by threatening to have Zamoro
killed if she refuses. This change transforms Gusmano's love into brutish lust.
Indeed, one could not otherwise explain why, to satisfy his love, he would

5. These are all subjects chosen by the early librettist Ottavio Rinuccini. *Dafne* was first set
by Jacopo Peri and Jacopo Corsi (Florence, 1598), *Euridice* by Jacopo Peri and Giulio Caccini (Florence: Palazzo Pitti, 1600), and *L'Arianna* by Claudio Monteverdi (Mantua: Palazzo
Ducale, 1608).

use the very arguments that should heighten his jealousy: those that testify to Alzira's love for his rival Zamoro.

Verdi nonetheless applied his notes to this ungrateful canvas, counting perhaps too heavily on the effectiveness of the music alone.

The prologue [act 1][6] is dominated by the tenor, who occupies nearly all of it with a long cavatina;[7] the andante ["Un Inca! . . . eccesso orribile!"] does not lack a certain expressiveness, but the allegro ["Dio della guerra"] is ordinary. Ternary meters predominate throughout the prologue; we find them in the introductory chorus[8] as well as in both the andante and the allegro of the cavatina. We do not encounter empty triplets [*terzine vuote*]; on the other hand, we find those chordal triplets for the abuse of which Verdi has often been chastised. It is true that, unless performed slowly, triplets take on a gay, easy, animated character that will keep the listener alert; because of this asset, it is not strange that Verdi tended to use them. In Verdi's first operas, reproof seems a bit unjust. His abuse of triplets is more noticeable in the later works, as you may see from the following survey.

Examining the main lyrical sections[9] in Verdi's operas, we find that barely one-fourth of *Nabucodonosor* has accompaniments of simple or compound triplets, *I Lombardi* one-third, *Ernani* a little less than one-third, *I due Foscari* about half, *Giovanna d'Arco* something more than two-fifths, and *Alzira* two-fifths exactly. Listing the operas of Verdi in ascending order of use of triplets, we have the following sequence: *Nabucodonosor*, *Ernani*, *I Lombardi*, *Alzira*, *Giovanna d'Arco*, and *I due Foscari*.[10]

Alzira's cavatina[11] is the piece that stands out in the first [second] act, but it seems to me that, because of a certain whimsical and graceful something, it would be more apt on the lips of some young woman of our hemisphere than on those of this untamed daughter of the Incas.

---

6. The three parts of *Alzira* are labeled as prologue and two acts in the libretto of the premiere and as three acts in Verdi's autograph score—a difference variously reflected in early sources. Verdi's titles will be indicated in square brackets.

7. N. 2, Scena Zamoro ("A costoro quel nume perdoni"; "Un Inca! . . . eccesso orribile!") e Finale primo ("Dio della guerra").

8. N. 1, Introduzione ("Muoia, muoia coverto d'insulti").

9. Basevi's phrase here is "pezzi cantabili." See chapter 2, n. 53, above.

10. Of course the survey covers only the operas already discussed at this point in Basevi's book.

11. N. 5, Cavatina Alzira ("Riposa. Tutte, in suo dolor vegliante"; "Da Gusman, su fragil barca").

The largo of the first finale[12] is well constructed, but there is no sign of that rich Verdian imagination: the whole piece can be reduced to a single main idea, stated first by the soprano ["Il contento fu per noi"] and then by the soprano and tenor in unison, with the other voices singing in harmony. The melody the bass and baritone sing at the beginning is little more than an obbligato recitative or a *parlante misto*.

In the second [third] act, the duet for baritone and soprano is worthy of note.[13] The andante agitato is very expressive, and here we also find the breathless rhythms so dear to Verdi. The cabaletta ["Non di codarde lagrime"] of the tenor's aria should also be mentioned.[14]

We must wait for the final scene of the opera ["I numi tuoi, vendetta atroce . . ."] to find something remarkable.[15] The dramatic situation is moving, and the music does not express it badly; this notwithstanding, the scene fails to match not only the final scene of *I due Foscari* but even that of *Giovanna d'Arco*.

This unfortunate opera made some effort to stand on its feet, but its congenital paralysis was incurable, such that it very soon fell "as a dead body falls."[16]

12. N. 7, Finale [secondo] ("Qual ardimento! Olà!"). The section in question is the adagio "Nella polve, genuflesso."

13. N. 9, Scena ("Guerrieri, al nuovo dì") e Duetto [Alzira e Gusmano] ("Il pianto . . . l'ambascia . . . di lena mi priva . . .").

14. N. 10, Scena ("Amici! . . . Ebben?") ed Aria Zamoro ("Irne lungi ancor dovrei").

15. N. 11, Finale ultimo ("Tergi del pianto America"), mm. 179ff.

16. As earlier in the chapter (see n. 4 above), Basevi quotes from Dante's *Inferno* ("*come corpo morto cade*," 5.142).

7

ATTILA

It is commonly said that in adversity it becomes easy to distinguish true friends from false; it is no less true that misfortune also enables us better to gauge the strength of our enemies. The latter was Verdi's case. After writing *Nabucodonosor*, *I Lombardi*, and *Ernani*, he had every reason to doubt that his adversaries could do him any harm, thanks to the prestige he had so suddenly and unexpectedly acquired and then maintained. When later—having withdrawn from the battlefield, so to speak, with *Giovanna d'Arco* and *Alzira*—he saw no one emerging to take his place, Verdi was able to take no small comfort in this, for he saw that he had on his side not only his own powers but also the weakness of his rivals.

If Verdi could find consolation in his enforced dictatorship, those who think to the future can only grieve at the obvious decadence of Italian musical talent. We must not delude ourselves as Verdi's blind allies do, crediting him with such dazzling light as to render the lesser stars invisible, even if these stars would arguably shine brightly in their own right in his absence. Nor, on the other hand, must we join his enemies in viewing him as a corrupter of good taste to the point of having completely blunted the audience's sense of beauty, so that if some brilliant genius now appears, he withers before he can germinate, like a seed deprived of water. Those two views are equally distant from the truth.

I regret to say that for the most part music is subordinate to fashion, at least for the moment. Composers must write to please theatergoers, and end up in the position, if you will pardon the comparison, of courtiers—not to say parasites.[1] "Courtier" music will never be worthy of the name of art—nor would painting, sculpture, poetry, etc. if they were forced into that position. But fortunately music is only a temporary courtier, for I am convinced that as it develops it will gain its proper independence and dignity.

We must thus consider, in Verdi's music, the courtier side as well as that of truth and progress that is proper to art. Courtier elements are frequent, and we will not hold that against him, for they are a temporary necessity. As for the great luster that Verdi's work lends to Italian music, whatever its significance it can be denied by no one who carefully observes the trend toward a stronger union between music and drama.

Operatic music is still in its infancy; a large dose of genius is needed to make it develop so that one day it may burst from its chrysalis to become a butterfly soaring freely in the air. On the other hand, not everybody is up to courting the audience, as some would suggest. Indeed, it is so difficult that we continuously see musical courtiers faring not unlike the donkey in the fable: envying the dog the master's caresses, he tried to imitate—with the grace we are all familiar with—that nimble animal's frolicking.[2]

Now sure of his strengths, Verdi was nevertheless being careful not to abuse them. When he began work on the new opera, his goal was that it should not turn out to be the sister of *Alzira*.

Solera based his new libretto on the celebrated deeds of Attila, *flagellum Dei*.[3] There is a touch of the miraculous in this subject, but this does not offend common sense or detract from the stature of the central character. None-

1. The overtones of the passage are not easily translated: Basevi uses both *cortigiano*—as a noun (meaning "courtier") and as an adjective (with connotations of "obsequious," "servile")—and *cortigianeria* (meaning "deference," "flattery"); moreover, the feminine *cortigiana* can denote either a female courtier or a courtesan.

2. The fable is Aesop's "The Donkey and the Pet Dog" (Ademar 17, Perry 91). For a readily accessible English translation, see *Aesop's Fables*, ed. and trans. Laura Gibbs (Oxford: Oxford University Press, 2002), p. 162.

3. Attila, the fifth-century ruler of the Huns, was also known as *flagellum Dei*, "the scourge of God." Solera's more immediate source was Zacharias Werner's "romantic tragedy" *Attila, König der Hunnen* (1808). The critical edition of Verdi's *Attila*, by Helen Greenwald, was published as *WGV* I/9 (2013).

theless, Solera's Attila is very different from the Attila of history, as he is from the Attila so dear to our fancy. He speaks, it is true, of massacres, of pillages, of victims in the dust, but he is also able to admire the courage of his enemies, to the point of presenting his sword to his prisoner Odabella without concern that in her hands it could be turned against him. Also, that fine moralist rebukes Ezio, the Roman ambassador who, thinking to betray his country, offers Attila the universe (understood not to include the sun or the planets) if Attila will leave Italy (not included in the universe) to him. Later on, just as her lover Foresto is about to kill Attila, Odabella reveals Foresto's treachery. And do you know why? Because she wants to kill Attila herself, and to achieve this she intends to marry him. Do you not admire her judgment and sagacity?

None of the characters of this libretto can inspire either real sympathy or unequivocal aversion. Still, as the librettist had imbued them with vigor, Verdi managed to make the most of them. For the rest, there are some situations that, though episodic and perhaps none too rational, gave scope to the composer's imagination.

Attila was first performed in March 1846 at Venice, with most gratifying success.[4]

A brief *preludio* introduces the opera.[5] It is dominated by sentiment, with the result that the audience is not suitably prepared for a story such as Attila's—atrocious and barbarous.

In the prologue, the music of the introductory chorus, "Urli, rapine,"[6] aptly expresses only the first of those two words.[7] The march accompanying Attila's arrival is very weak. The ensuing hymn, "Viva il re," sung by the Huns, is catchy and popular in taste, but—besides lacking the rhythmic variety found in other, similar compositions by Verdi—has no trace of the proud, barbarous character proper to Attila's soldiers. Here we cannot restrain ourselves from wondering, Where is the composer of the choruses from *Nabucodonosor* and *I Lombardi*?

The cavatina for Odabella (soprano) is certainly among the opera's finest pieces in terms of expression, variety, and form.[8] The andantino bears the clear stamp of Odabella's indomitable spirit. This piece, which exhibits the composer's special fire, contains one of those *di slancio* melodic periods so

4. The venue was the Teatro La Fenice.
5. N. 1, Preludio.
6. N. 2, Introduzione ("Urli, rapine").
7. "Urli" means "screams."
8. N. 3, Scena ("Di vergini straniere") e Cavatina Odabella ("Allor che i forti corrono").

favored by Verdi, here employed with great skill on the words "Ma noi donne italiche." After this *di slancio* period comes a *parlante* period of the kind we have seen elsewhere, although here Attila, on the words "Bella è quell'ira, etc.," sings in unison with the orchestra for a stretch, to good effect.[9] The allegro too ["Da te questo or m'è concesso"] is full of power and energy, and its vehemence shows it to have sprung from the same source as "Salgo già" from *Nabucodonosor*. In terms of form, however, this allegro displays nothing new. In the original score, which I have examined, the first version of this cabaletta was crossed out; it was very ugly and trite. It is interesting to see how by means of a number of seemingly trivial alterations it was transformed into one of the loveliest of Verdi's cabalettas to date.[10]

A duet for Attila and Ezio (bass and baritone) follows.[11] The andante is worthy of the name of Verdi. Ezio's melody is broad, grand, and expressive, and is suited both to his imposing personality and to the boldness of the plans that motivate him. The first phrase has but one change of harmony (to the dominant) without seeming either tedious or insignificant. Attila's response—in the minor mode, with different rhythm and accompaniment and a faster pace—and the arrival of A-flat major on the words "Là col flagello mio" produce the finest of effects. Then suddenly—a welcome surprise—Ezio repeats his striking phrase "Avrai tu l'universo." The final measures of the *a 2*, however, do not equal what preceded them and close the piece a little too coldly. The allegro ["Vanitosi! che abbietti e dormenti"] is banal in conception, and follows the old model for this type of piece.

Next we hear the prelude to a chorus of hermits, which seeks to convey an impression of a storm by means of repeated diminished sevenths.[12] The chorus itself is suitably grave and religious. The following section imitates the sunrise. But this cannot properly be called "imitative" music, as it makes its effect rather by analogy: it is in fact a gradual crescendo, a feature that can appertain equally well to sound, to light, or to many other things. Moreover, it aims to express the pleasure we feel in the transition from darkness to light

---

9. Basevi is here referring to the second appearance of the phrase "Bella è quell'ira," which occurs in the new, allegro section (mm. 67ff.).

10. This appears to be the only case in which Basevi examined the autograph full score of a Verdi opera for the preparation of his *Studio*.

11. N. 4, Duetto Attila ed Ezio ("Uldino, a me dinanzi"; "Tardo per gli anni e tremulo").

12. N. 5, Scena ("Qual notte! Ancor fremono l'onde") e Cavatina Foresto ("Ella in poter del barbaro!").

by making us experience a pleasure derived from the transition from piano to forte and from minor to major, and from the resolution of dissonant chords—which is at its greatest when the dissonances are prolonged in order to increase the urgent need for resolution. It seems to me that Verdi has not quite achieved his goal in this piece—not because of anything lacking in the crescendo, in the change from minor to major, etc., but because I cannot grasp the meaning of the rhythm he has used. Its scintillating quality would, I believe, have better imitated a fire than a sunrise. I prefer Félicien David's sunrise in *Le désert*—however inferior to the example in Haydn's *Creation*.[13]

Portions of the tenor's cavatina are praiseworthy. The andantino ["Ella in poter del barbaro!"], accompanied by the usual triplets, has the easy, frank quality that Verdi has used so well to win his listeners over. After fifteen measures, the chorus interrupts for four measures, following which the tenor gracefully resumes the *di slancio* passage "Io ti vedrei fra gl'angeli." The first phrase of the allegro ["Cara patria"] is weak, but the second eight-measure phrase is lovely and vigorous; it is repeated to advantage by the chorus in unison.

Odabella's *romanza*, which opens act 1, offers nothing of note except an accompaniment that imitates the sound of the river and the rustling in the air.[14] But the heartache of a woman awaiting her lover is in no sense expressed.

The duet for soprano and tenor merits some attention.[15] The andante is in varied form [*forma variata*], like that which we observed in *Nabucodonosor* and elsewhere. The allegro ["Oh t'innebria nell'amplesso"] then employs an uncommon rhythm that in its outlandishness recalls the style of Pacini, although with the benefit of chiaroscuro and without excessive choppiness. The voices are always in unison, and—when the singers are in tune—the effect is very beautiful.

---

13. David's *ode-symphonie* of 1844, whose third and final part opened with a "Lever du soleil," had a significant influence on composers of descriptive music. There is no evidence that Verdi went to hear the piece when it was performed in Milan in 1845 (which he may have done, as he was then in the city); it is certain that he saw its score. See *WGV* I/9, xviii. As for Haydn's sunrise, see the instrumental passage that opens N. 6b, Recitativo ("In vollem Glanze steiget jetzt"/"In splendor bright is rising now"), in *Die Schöpfung*, ed. Annette Oppermann, *HW* XXVIII/3 (2008).

14. N. 6, Scena ("Liberamente or piangi . . .") e Romanza Odabella ("Oh! nel fuggente nuvolo").

15. N. 7, Duetto [Odabella e Foresto] ("Qual suon di passi?"; "Sì, quello io son, ravvisami").

The bass aria is without doubt one of the composer's best.[16] The andante is a broad, austere melody onto which certain harmonic sequences are well grafted to accompany the words that Attila repeats as he heard them in his vision;[17] this section finishes, very pleasingly, in the major mode. The form has novelty, and variety is employed without offending the unity of the design. The cabaletta ["Oltre quel limite"] is sinewy, and is well matched to Attila's character.

In the finale of this act[18] Verdi displays his talents at their best. The situation too is very effective: Attila—who despises every material obstacle, who tramps over heaps of corpses, who fords lakes of blood—now, before the voice of God, halts, lays down his weapons, and prostrates himself. This scene is wonderfully enhanced by the music; Attila's reverence is well observed and well expressed, finely matched by the devout emotion of those present at this miraculous manifestation of divine power. The ensemble is among the finest, and closes the number and the act in a marvelous fashion.

In that piece, which is a largo in $\frac{6}{8}$ time, a sequence begins at the twenty-fifth measure[19] and is prolonged for six measures, then resolving in a cadence, the first time simply, the second time in a more complicated way. Note in this sequence that leads to the cadence an effect that—as it arouses in us a strong desire to arrive at the cadence—may be named the "anticipation effect" [*effetto di ansietà*]. And indeed, when he has the wish and the skill to do so, a composer may induce in the listener a feeling greatly akin to anticipation. Before melody came to master it, this effect lay altogether in the realm of harmony. Perhaps the first, and certainly the most stupendous, harmonic example of this effect is found at the end of the chorus "The heavens are telling" in Haydn's *Creation*, where the cadence the listener so eagerly desires finally arrives to tremendous satisfaction.[20] Perhaps the first instance of this

16. N. 8, Scena ("Uldino! Uldin!") ed Aria Attila ("Mentre gonfiarsi l'anima").

17. These are the words that, crucially, presage those uttered by Pope Leo in the ensuing first-act finale.

18. N. 9, Finale [primo] ("Parla! Imponi!"; "No! non è sogno . . . che or l'alma invade").

19. Given his description of the music, Basevi must mean twenty-five measures after the beginning of the tutti at m. 127 (m. 152 of the entire first-act finale).

20. Cited in Italian by Basevi as "Palesano i cieli," this is the chorus that concludes the first part of the oratorio; he is obviously referring to the passage that begins at the upbeat to m. 175 and eventually reaches the tonic at m. 190. See Joseph Haydn, *Die Schöpfung*, ed. Annette Oppermann, *HW* XXVIII/3 (2008), N. 6c, Chor ("Die Himmel erzählen die Ehre Gottes"/"The heavens are telling the glory of God").

effect as adorned by melody is in the magnificent second finale of Spontini's *La vestale*, beginning at the thirty-seventh measure following the chorus "De son front."[21] The devices that can be used to produce this anticipation effect are many and varied. Here are the principal ones: sequences; harmonic vacillation—that is, repeated alternation between one harmony and another; the reiteration of rhythms, or even of single notes, whether syncopated or not; a succession of several dissonances; certain rhythmic traits suitable for representing agitation, joy, etc.; imitation among the various parts; crescendo, either alone or followed by smorzando; stringendo, possibly followed by allargando; and other devices too numerous to list. The finest example from a modern opera is in the last finale of Bellini's *Norma* at "Padre tu piangi."[22] To tell the truth, the anticipation effect in the present piece in *Attila* is not among the most effective—nor, indeed, does the dramatic situation demand this.

The anticipation effect must not be abused. Above all, there must be a certain balance between the desire provoked and the satisfaction given. In the *introduzione* to Mercadante's *La vestale*, at measure 27 of the chorus "Una possa che i barbari," the sopranos sing a syncopated F for three measures, while the harmony vacillates three times between a chord and its dominant. But all this preparation ends in nothing but the simplest and most strangulated cadence.[23] Now consider, again in Mercadante's *La vestale*, the second-act bass aria: at the thirtieth measure of the melody beginning "Spargiam d'immonda cenere" there are two and a half measures of a syncopated F, but this leads to a much more ample, properly proportioned cadence.[24] Mercadante used a similar effect in the largo of the first septet in *Il bravo*: after five measures of uniform rhythm with a stressed high G on the first beat of every measure, you

21. See Gaspare Spontini, *La vestale* (Paris: Opéra, 1807), N. 13, Final ("Sa bouche a prononcé l'arrêt"), pp. 312ff. of the orchestral score printed by Erard (Paris, n.d. [between 1814 and 1820]), reproduced in *ERO* 42 (1979). The passage discussed by Basevi begins on the second half of p. 331. Spontini's *tragédie lyrique* was one of the most successful French operas of its time.

22. See the concertato "Deh! non volerli vittime," part of *Norma*'s N. 8, Finale dell'atto secondo. The passage in question follows the shift to the major mode.

23. See Saverio Mercadante, *La vestale*, Preludio e Preghiera mattutina ("Salve, o Dea protettrice di Roma"). The passage in question is on p. 11 of the vocal score (Milan: Ricordi, 1840) reproduced in *IOG* 22 (1986).

24. Ibid., Scena ("Ah! il foco . . ." "È spento!") ed Aria Metello ("Versate amare lagrime"). See the più animato at p. 145.

arrive with a fortissimo at the final cadence with a fine sonority effect [*effetto di sonorità*]—and with a feeling of great pleasure.[25]

These anticipation effects must not be confused with the effect of crescendos, for although the crescendo gives pleasure, it does not do so by fulfilling a need. As noted, however, the two effects may be combined, as they were by Spontini, Mercadante, Bellini, and Verdi in the pieces I have cited.

Act 2 begins with the baritone's aria, which neither in the andante nor in the allegro rises above the common stock of such pieces.[26]

I mention in passing the lively and lighthearted chorus of priestesses ["Chi dona luce al cor? . . ."].[27] But it is the *pezzo concertato* in the finale of the second act ["Lo spirto de' monti"] that demands attention. It begins in the minor with the lightest instrumentation; at one point, with a certain eccentricity, there is a sort of conversation between the flute, piccolo, oboe, and first violins, on the one hand, and the violas, clarinet, and second violins, on the other. A certain generalized confusion is not inappropriate to this scene, where a harsh wind extinguishes the torches, provoking universal terror. When the sky is again becalmed, the piece goes into the major and the melody becomes more agreeable. At the nineteenth measure of this major-mode section, note a diminished-seventh chord whose top note rises a semitone to resolve onto a six-four chord:[28] a fine harmonic effect. In the first finale of Halévy's *La juive*, there is a similarly fine diminished-seventh effect on the words "O ma fille chérie."[29] These examples show that even ordinary things can become singular. The act ends with an extremely commonplace stretta.

In the third and final act we must pause a moment at the tenor's *romanza*,[30] not because it has especial merit, but because its rhythm provides an oppor-

25. Mercadante, *Il bravo* (Milan: Teatro alla Scala, 1839). Basevi is referring to the concluding twelve measures of the largo ("Ei si mostra, e ognun tremante") from the opera's first finale ("Sì giustizia, vendetta tremenda").

26. N. 10, Scena ("Tregua è cogl'Unni") ed Aria Ezio ("Dagl'immortali culmini").

27. N. 11, Finale [secondo] ("Del ciel l'immensa volta"/"Chi dona luce al cor? . . ."/"Lo spirto de' monti"), mm. 80ff.

28. Basevi appears to be referring to the *thirteenth* measure of the major-mode section (m. 249), in which case the "diminished-seventh chord" of this passage is actually a German sixth.

29. Fromental Halévy, *La juive*, ed. Karl Leich-Galland (Saarbrücken: Lucie Galland, 1985), N. 7, Finale ("Noël, tout là-bas le cortège s'avance"), mm. 510ff. A facsimile of the full score printed by Schlesinger (Paris, [1835]) is presented in *ERO* 36 (1980), where the passage mentioned by Basevi is on p. 201. The opera was premiered at Paris's Opéra in 1835.

30. With this *romanza* for Foresto we have already entered the opera's final number, which forms the entire third act: N. 12, Scena ("Qui del convegno è il loco . . ."), Romanza ("Che non avrebbe il misero"), Terzetto ("Che più s'indugia? . . ."; "Te sol, te sol quest'anima"), e

tunity for comment. The rhythm of the short phrase "Che non avrebbe il misero" is one of those most often used in Italian melody. It is not always presented in exactly the same way, but we will not make much of those modifications that do not greatly alter its general appearance. Foreigners use it only exceptionally, and very rarely is it found in any but the most recent works. For anyone who is interested in examples, I can cite Cola's aria "Napoli bella e cara" in Paer's *Camilla*[31] and the duet "Alle più care immagini" from Rossini's *Semiramide*.[32] Examples are more frequent in Bellini's music. In *Norma* this rhythm, with little variation, is found in five pieces. Nor did Donizetti ignore it: it appears four times in *Anna Bolena*.[33] As for its use by Verdi, we find it three times in *Nabucodonosor*, six in *I Lombardi*, two in *Ernani*, three in *I due Foscari*, five in *Giovanna d'Arco*, four in *Alzira*, and six in *Attila*, in the following pieces: "Bella è quell'ira, o vergine," "Dove l'eroe più valido," "Sì, quello io son, ravvisami," "Vieni . . . Le menti visita," "Dagl'immortali culmini," and "Che non avrebbe il misero."[34]

In this final act, it is worth mentioning the affecting *terzettino* ["Te sol, te sol quest'anima"] for soprano, tenor, and baritone; this is organized so as to place the three voices in individual relief, each having a different melody at the beginning. The baritone's initial phrases ["Tempo non è di lagrime"] are beautiful; here Verdi employs a fine effect of vibrant, staccato notes.

Considered as a whole, the music of *Attila* seems to be of much greater value than that of *Alzira* and, in several places, even than that of *Giovanna d'Arco*. But it would be vain to hide the fact that it is greatly inferior to that of *Nabucodonosor*, *I Lombardi*, and *Ernani*. Nonetheless, *Attila* has been performed a number of times in various theaters, and has often had the happiest of receptions.

Quartetto–Finale ultimo ("Non involarti, seguimi!"; "Tu, rea donna, già schiava, or mia sposa").

31. The aria is N. 2 of Ferdinando Paer's *Camilla, ossia Il sotterraneo* (Vienna: Kärntnertor-theater, 1799): *PaWV*, 317.

32. N. 6, Duettino [Semiramide ed Arsace] ("Serbami ognor sì fido il cor"), mm. 71ff. (allegro giusto "Alle più care immagini"). Basevi writes "calde" rather than "care."

33. Milan: Teatro Carcano, 1830.

34. See *Attila*, N. 3, mm. 67ff.; N. 4, mm. 60ff.; N. 7, mm. 58ff.; N. 9, mm. 63ff.; N. 10, mm. 42ff.; and N. 12, mm. 44ff.

8

MACBETH

On the example of a number of celebrated transalpine composers, Verdi decided to set a "fantastic" subject (that is, supernatural of the secular kind).[1] Neither the success of Meyerbeer and Weber in this genre of music nor a certain aversion on the part of Italian composers to dealing with extraordinary events of this sort was enough to discourage Verdi from entering this dangerous arena. I say "dangerous" because the fantastic genre, of transalpine origin and nature, requires music appropriate to its character, and the Italian composer must abandon the beaten paths he knows so well to venture into a labyrinth where the Northern mind may freely wander without becoming lost.

Piave took no great trouble to seek the fantastic subject that would best suit the Italian genius, but ran his eye over Shakespeare's tragedies and chose *Macbeth*.[2] Here we do not find the kind of fantasy that is inoffensive to our

1. See Basevi's discussion on p. 70 above.

2. The critical edition of Verdi's *Macbeth*, by David Lawton, was published as *WGV* I/10 (2005). It presents the materials for both versions of the opera, of 1847 (Florence: Teatro alla Pergola) and 1865 (Paris: Théâtre-Lyrique). In his *Studio* of 1859 Basevi can of course refer only to the first. Following *WGV*, all numbers followed by an *a* (for example, N. 5a or m. 177a) will refer to the first version as edited there.

fastidious minds: the kind that beneath its extraordinary, supernatural exterior conceals some wise precept or embodies human vices or virtues. Today, we find *Macbeth*'s witches and magical deeds meaningless and utterly ridiculous. Still, if we give careful consideration to this creation of Shakespeare's great mind, we can see that—under a thick veil, it is true—the witches represent the power of destiny. But what is destiny if not the effect of a power that knows no obstacles? And in this instance what is that power if not Macbeth's ambition, fueled by his wife and not resisted strongly enough by his virtue? Did Piave understand this? It really seems not.

But Piave made another enormous mistake in choosing a drama in which love plays no part. Neither Meyerbeer nor Weber committed this error in *Robert le diable*, *Der Freischütz*, or *Oberon*. Love is the emotion best suited to music. Here Nature herself can instruct us: not only do many species of animals sing more often and more richly in mating season, but species otherwise mute acquire voices at that time.

We will not waste our time noting all the incongruities, ill graces, and blunders in this shameful libretto of Piave's.[3] I am sure that my readers will be grateful to me for this. I shall give only a brief résumé of the plot. Macbeth, general to the King of Scotland, encounters a group of witches, from whom he learns that he is destined for the Scottish throne, but that his successors will be descended from the line of Banquo. He reveals the witches' predictions to his wife, who, overweeningly cruel and ambitious, eggs him on to murder King Duncan, so as to hasten the desired events. Macbeth secretly kills the king, to whom he is giving hospitality under his very roof. Raised in this way to the throne, and not content with that alone, he lays an ambush for Banquo with the intention of killing him and his son; the assassins succeed only in murdering Banquo himself. The enormity of these sins weighs heavily on Macbeth and his lady. Meanwhile, from all quarters, the oppressed populace moves against the usurper, who loses his life in the fray.

Verdi's new opera appeared in Florence at the Teatro della Pergola in March 1847. It was given a good reception, but more out of regard for the presence of the composer than because of the music, which never more than half pleased. The opera had the same fortune in other principal theaters. This shows not only that the judgment of the Florentines was sound, but also that the performance of this opera—one of a genre that was less than common

---

3. The libretto for *Macbeth* also includes interventions by another poet, Verdi's friend Andrea Maffei (who would write the libretto for the composer's next opera, *I masnadieri*).

for Italians—had left nothing to be desired. Whatever difficulties there might anyway have been, the orchestra of the Pergola would have surmounted them as well as any other. Where a Pietro Romani is the musical director, and where the orchestra has an Alamanno Biagi for its leader, there need be no fear for the perfect execution of the music.[4] This is confirmed by the great success of *Robert le diable*, *Les Huguenots*, and *Le prophète* on the stage of the Pergola, where they were performed for the first time in Italy.

As soon as we hear the first part of the witches' chorus in the *introduzione* we have a fair idea of how Verdi conceived of these imaginary beings.[5] He saw them as nothing but ugly old women—bizarre, spiteful, and silly. Those are the lines along which Verdi wrote his music, and for that reason it lacks what is most important: an expression of supernatural and evil power that can arouse fright and horror. Verdi had nothing in mind if not Mercadante's famous chorus of sorceresses, which displays the same shortcomings.[6] The music of the witches' dance ["Le sorelle vagabonde"], in the major mode, is built on a melody that is graceful yet even less appropriate to the witches than the preceding piece in the minor. But it is not entirely the fault of the composer if the character of the witches is not well depicted; it is largely to be blamed on the librettist, who, truth to tell, presents them as more mad than evil. In fact, in the first scene, which most improbably turns Shakespeare's three witches into three *groups* of witches, the second group says, "Ho sgoz-zato un verro!" ["I have slaughtered a boar!"], which is utterly ridiculous and mad coming from a group. In the English tragedy, we find the opposite: that a single witch has killed several swine ("Killing swine"), which is more evil than mad.[7] Also, Piave has "whirling"[8] through the minds of his third group of witches a seaman's wife who had sent them to hell, don't ask me why; then, for vengeance, they want to make her husband, who is on the high seas, fall prey to the waves. Shakespeare, on the other hand, does not have

---

4. These are the very musicians who a couple of months later would be involved in the first (and only) production of Basevi's own opera *Enrico Howard*. Moreover, Pietro Romani had been a composition teacher of Basevi's, and Alamanno Biagi would later win a prize in the first Concorso Basevi (1861), for the composition of a string quartet.

5. N. 2, Introduzione ("Che faceste? dite su!"). N. 1 of the opera is the orchestral Preludio.

6. See chapter 5, n. 13, above.

7. *Macbeth*, act 1, scene 3. (First Witch: "Where hast thou been, sister?" Second Witch: "Killing swine.") The two quoted words are in English in Basevi's Italian text.

8. Basevi's "Piave fa *frullare* nel pensiero"—and later "Shakespeare, invece, non fa *frullar* nulla"—is a derisory reference to a line in Piave's opening scene, his italics marking the use of an idiom he clearly found unsuitably bizarre or silly.

anything "whirl" through anyone's mind, and puts the threat into the mouth of a single witch—not madly and without cause, but as revenge for the sailor's wife having denied her some chestnuts. Verdi then exaggerates this madness with his music—as in the second scene, when the witches say, "Macbetto e Banco vivano!" and vanish.

The ensuing duet between Macbeth and Banquo (baritone and bass) is finely contrived.[9] Macbeth's solo is grand and solemn where he is gripped by horror at the thought of shedding the blood of his king in order to fulfill the witches' prophesy by usurping the throne. That phrase is notable for being a lengthy musical idea in one sweep [*di getto*], continuing for twelve measures without growing stunted or abstruse, even though it has frequent harmonic changes, with harmonies distant from the home key. The transition from C to D-flat at the twenty-first measure is bold. Movement from one key to a second, unrelated key, using a single pitch [*unisono*] rather than a complete chord, must be employed carefully, and only when it yields a good effect. In act 2, scene 17, of *Don Giovanni*, Mozart goes from the key of D to the key of F by means of the single note of E.[10] In the duet for Arnold and Guillaume in Rossini's *Guillaume Tell*, the tenor begins his melody "Ah Mathilde" in G-flat after the instruments have moved from a chord of B-flat seventh to a unison B-natural and then a C, with the result that the tenor, taking up the succeeding D-flat, suddenly finds himself in the key of G-flat.[11]

The chorus the witches sing on their return to the stage ["S'allontanarono!"] is well written but has the defects I have already noted.

The cavatina of Lady Macbeth (soprano) is full of energy, with the old Verdian stamp.[12] The andantino is bold and majestic. There is considerable abuse of high notes—or screams, which were in fashion at the time. In the

---

9. Though early printed vocal scores treat this "duet" ("Due vaticini compiuti or sono . . .") as a separate number, in Verdi's autograph score it is still part of the *introduzione* (N. 2, at mm. 295ff.). Basevi's "twenty-first measure" later in this paragraph is thus m. 316.

10. See N. 24, Finale ("Già la mensa è preparata"), mm. 116–18—the nimble move to the F major in which the musicians accompanying Don Giovanni's dinner play an excerpt from Giuseppe Sarti's comic opera *Fra i due litiganti il terzo gode*. The critical edition of *Don Giovanni*, by Wolfgang Plath and Wolfgang Rehm, appeared as *NMA* II:v/17 (1968): the passage is actually in act 2, scene 13.

11. N. 2, Récitatif ("Contre les feux du jour que mon toit solitaire") [et] Duo [Arnold et Guillaume] ("Où vas-tu? quel transport t'agite?"), mm. 166–68. Rossini uses the same device at the parallel mm. 245–47, though the reprise is (unusually) a tone higher.

12. N. 3, Cavatina Lady Macbeth ("Nel dì della vittoria le incontrai"; "Vieni! t'affretta! accendere").

allegro ["Or tutti sorgete"] we find one of the usual *di slancio* phrases on the words "qual petto percota." Note the first melodic period of this cabaletta; while it is composed of the usual two phrases, the second is longer than the first, going against the customary symmetry. Donizetti supplies a similar example in the cabaletta from *Anna Bolena* "Nel veder la tua costanza."[13] Fine in its melody, though not in its character, is the rustic music announcing the arrival of the king; its disappearance into the distance is most effective.[14]

The duet for Macbeth and his wife is the opera's climactic number.[15] Macbeth's recitative ["Sappia la sposa mia"], which precedes it, is notable for its expressiveness and for certain instrumental combinations. The *tempo d'attacco* of this duet, which begins "Fatal mia donna!" is its finest part.[16] It is a true flash of Verdian genius, and must be numbered among the most beautiful creations of the "Swan of Busseto." Macbeth's terror at the crime he has committed, his remorse when he tells of his inability to repeat the word "amen," and, finally, the contrast with the evil indifference of his wife could perhaps not be better expressed in music. Splendidly daring, and impossibly so for anyone but a great talent, is the lively, almost *opera buffa*–like melody on Lady Macbeth's words "Follie! follie, etc." This does not destroy the horror of the scene, but actually increases it with a blood-red glow. The magical effect of the whole is enhanced not so much by the melody as by the simple but effective instrumentation. The second violins, muted, play a sort of murmur over which the first violins and the English horn[17] play the melody pianissimo. Other instruments join later, always with magical effect. In this work Verdi reaped much profit from his blending of woodwind instruments, a blending that has something of the fantastic about it—or rather one that is suited to the depiction of the fantastic, as shown by Weber, Meyerbeer, and others. The ⅜-time andantino that follows ["Allor questa voce"] is in a unique form, and

13. See [N. 10, Recitativo] ("Tu pur dannato a morte") [e] Aria Percy ("Vivi tu, te ne scongiuro"), mm. 113ff. I am indebted for this reference to Paolo Fabbri, whose critical edition of Donizetti's *Anna Bolena* is forthcoming in *EN*.

14. N. 4, Recitativo ("Oh donna mia! Caudore!") e Marcia.

15. N. 5/5a, Scena ("Sappia la sposa mia, che pronta appena") e Duetto [Lady Macbeth e Macbeth] ("Fatal mia donna! un mormore").

16. This is the first occurrence in the book of the phrase *tempo d'attacco*—an expression that has had much currency among more recent generations of musicologists. Here, as elsewhere, Basevi's use of italics signals a technical term, though in the broad sense suggested in the glossary.

17. It is in fact the clarinet (though see the critical commentary to *WGV* I/10, 88 n.1).

the bass's phrase "Com'angeli d'ira" is majestic.[18] The remainder of the duet is truly mediocre.

The first finale[19] displays a grandeur most suitable to the amazement and indignation everyone feels at the murder of King Duncan. Its design and *colorito* bring to mind the composer of *Nabucodonosor* and *I Lombardi*. Act 1 ends without a stretta; here we must commend Verdi for lending his authority to the destruction of one of those bonds by which Italian composers believed themselves to be shackled, one does not understand just why.[20] But I do not want to malign strettas: if they are like some by Rossini and Pacini, I will welcome them. In the act 2 soprano aria "Trionfai! securi alfine"[21] Verdi gave an example of exaggeration of his own method—exaggeration of the kind to which we have long been accustomed by the works of his imitators.

The chorus of assassins[22] has some nice chiaroscuro effects, but it is not very—indeed, not at all—expressive. Here I must praise the change in orchestration at the repetition of the theme, which is placed in higher relief over a quick motion in the violas. It is time we freed ourselves from literal reprises. In this piece the timpani are cleverly used not merely as underpinning but as essential instruments.

The entire banquet scene through the end of the act is very well constructed.[23] A brisk instrumental part with a broken, leaping rhythm reminiscent of German dance and band music is repeated several times through the entire scene; it serves also for a *parlante*. The *brindisi* ["Si colmi il calice"] is somewhat banal. Afterward, the oboe repeats the theme while the clarinet and the bassoon descend by semitones,[24] giving it a lugubrious color, most

---

18. Macbeth is a baritone; Basevi refers to him at times as a baritone and at times as a bass (probably because of the clef in which the part is notated).

19. N. 6, Finale primo ("Di destarlo per tempo il re m'impose"; "Schiudi inferno la bocca, ed inghiotti").

20. Dispensing with a possible *tempo di mezzo* and a concluding stretta, Verdi brings the finale to an end with the concertato (the final, thirty-one-measure allegro is rather a coda to the preceding adagio and sets words from it). Prominent Verdian examples of "internal" finali lacking a stretta are the first-act finale of *Luisa Miller* and the second-act finale of *La traviata*.

21. N. 7a, Scena ("Perché mi sfuggi, e fiso") ed Aria Lady [*Macbeth*] ("Trionfai! securi alfine"). Basevi gives the incipit as "Trionfai secura alfine."

22. N. 8, Coro di sicari ("Chi v'impose unirvi a noi?").

23. N. 9/9a, Convito ("Salve, o Re!" "Voi pur salvete"; "Si colmi il calice"), Visione ("Che ti scosta, o Re mio sposo"), e Finale secondo ("Va! . . . spirto d'abisso! . . . spalanca una fossa"; "Sangue a me quell'ombra chiede").

24. It is in fact oboe 1 and clarinet 1 that have the melody, while clarinet 2 and bassoon 1 have the descending line. (See also n. 17 above.)

apt for the moment in which it serves for a brief *parlante* dialogue between Macbeth and one of the assassins. Contrast between a theme and its accompaniment was first employed—and with great effect—by Gluck in *Iphigénie en Tauride*, where Oreste sings a theme suited to the words "Le calme rentre dans mon coeur" while the accompaniment is dark and agitated.[25] At the first rehearsal the players tried to sweeten this accompaniment, which they thought contradicted Oreste's words, but (as related by Mme de Staël in *De l'Allemagne*) Gluck, nearly losing his temper, exclaimed, "Pay no attention to Oreste; he is not at all calm; he is lying."[26] In the largo of the finale, "Sangue a me," there are eighteen changes of harmony in the space of eight measures, executed with such taste and judiciousness that the melody is easily followed throughout. In the ensuing sixteen measures the soprano alternates most expressively with the other voices. Then a lovely twenty-two-measure *pezzo concertato* begins, accompanied by a triplet figure; this contrasts well with the preceding material and ends the act. The crescendo in the theme "Biechi arcani, etc.," specifically beginning with Macbeth's entry on the words "Il velame del futuro," gives me occasion to alert scholars to a particular melodic procedure. Note here that the rhythm begun by the bass in the first half of the measure is taken up by the soprano in the second; this continues for three measures but with harmonies that change, in order to keep the listener in a state of anticipation and make him yearn for the resolution, which comes with a forte in the fourth measure.[27] This is followed by a fortissimo in the next measure, which contains the completion of the melodic thought. Here we have another example of the anticipation effect [*effetto di ansietà*] on which I digressed in the previous chapter.

The witches' chorus that opens the third act[28] is long and, with the exception of a few measures at the beginning, lacking in character. The end, in the major mode, by no means expresses, even to the least degree, the fierce joy of

25. See, in act 2, scene 3, of Gluck's *tragédie* (Paris: Opéra, 1779), Oreste's Air "Le calme rentre dans mon coeur." The critical edition of the opera, by Gerhard Croll, is *GGA* I/9 (1973).

26. Mme (Anne-Louise-Germaine) de Staël, "Des beaux-arts en Allemagne," in *De l'Allemagne*, 3 vols. (Paris: H. Nicolle, 1810; reprint, London: John Murray, 1813), 2:380–99, 395 ("N'écoutez pas Oreste: il dit qu'il est calme; il ment"). Basevi's description ("l'accompagnamento è tetro ed agitato") is lifted from Mme de Staël's text ("l'accompagnement de cet air est sombre et agité").

27. See mm. 431a–34a. The "bass" is, again, Macbeth.

28. N. 10a, Coro ("Tre volte miagola la gatta in fregola").

these evil beings. See how Meyerbeer succeeded in fitting music to demonic joy in the celebrated Infernal Waltz from *Robert le diable*.[29]

The apparition scene[30] is unworthy of the name of Verdi: it has no overall conception, no order, and no effect whatsoever. And as though to prove the composer's lack of concern in the quest for new harmonic, melodic, and rhythmic combinations, the scene ends, when Macbeth sings "Oh mio terror! dell'ultimo," with one of those very old rhythms already used six times in *Attila*—a rhythm that in the course of *Macbeth* appears also in "Oh qual'orrenda notte!" and "Come dal ciel precipita."[31]

The chorus "Ondine, e Silfidi" is graceful and most apt.[32] Some passages recall a dance movement in *Robert le diable*.[33]

The third finale, "Vada in fiamme," is extremely commonplace.[34]

The chorus "Patria oppressa!"[35] with which the fourth act begins is characterized by gravity, and it produces a certain effect—not, however, a fresh one. The rhythm itself is timeworn. Even more timeworn—and without effect—are the rhythms of both the adagio and the allegro of Macduff's aria.[36]

Verdi aimed to recoup with Lady Macbeth's sleepwalking scene,[37] and he wrote a piece that, while not offending the ear, certainly gratifies the mind. The meticulous accompaniment is dominated to great effect by a dark *tinta*; from time to time a sort of lament is heard in the English horn, which somehow captures the inner cry of the conscience.

---

29. N. 10, La valse infernale ("Noirs démons, fantômes"), in act 3 of the opera. *ERO* 19 (1980) is a facsimile of the full score published by Schlesinger (Paris, [1831]).

30. N. 11a, Recitativo ("Che fate or voi, misteriose donne?"), Apparizioni ("Dalle basse, e dall'alte regioni"; "Fuggi, regal fantasima"), Ballabile ("Ondine, e silfidi"), ed Aria Macbeth ("Ove son io? Fuggiro! . . . Oh sia ne' secoli"; "Vada in fiamme, e in polve cada").

31. Compare the vocal part in N. 11a, mm. 164a–65a, with those in N. 6, Finale primo, mm. 16–17, and N. 8½, Scena Banco ("Studia il passo, o mio figlio!"; "Come dal ciel precipita"), mm. 22–23.

32. N. 11a, mm. 205a ff.

33. Compare mm. 294a ff. here with the 2me Air de ballet ("Séduction par le jeu") in Meyerbeer, *Robert le diable*, ed. Wolfgang Kühnhold and Peter Kaiser, *MWA* I/10 (2010), N. 15, Final [of act 3].

34. N. 11a, mm. 438a ff.

35. N. 12a, Coro ("Patria oppressa! Il dolce nome").

36. N. 13a, Scena ("O figli! o figli miei! da quel tiranno") ed Aria con cori Macduff ("Ah, la paterna mano").

37. N. 14, Sonnambulismo di Lady Macbeth ("Vegliammo in van due notti"; "Una macchia . . . è qui tutt'ora!").

Macbeth's aria, which follows, offers nothing of note;[38] I observe only that here too a very old rhythm is used. In this connection I would mention that rhythm is so great a part of melody that a composer who forms new themes on old rhythms, altering only the pitches, does not deserve to be called original. The much-praised memorability of many Italian arias comes in great part from the familiarity of their rhythms.

Would you like a recipe for composing facile, catchy melodies? Take an old rhythm, one of the most clear-cut. It does not take much work to adapt new notes to it, for there are nearly fixed rules for choosing a pleasing sequence of pitches, such as those recommending leaps of a fourth when rising, and of a major sixth, a third, or a fifth when descending, and so on and so forth. As to the way the piece unfolds, or its form, feel free to follow, as from a pattern, whatever is in vogue at the moment, without taking the trouble to introduce the least modification. For the harmonies, you have those of the key of the piece, and there are additional useful rules for when you wish to make other pleasant modulations. It is in this way that many pieces of music usurping the title "new" are created. Then, the musical epicures go to the theater and cry, "Lovely, lovely! This is music you can immediately understand! You should never go to the theater to study!" These foolish judgments fly from mouth to mouth; if they were to be heeded by anyone truly touched by the sacred hand of genius, they would very soon drag the art of music to its final stages of decay.

Because the poetry of modern languages is content with a number of accents, and places no importance on the contrast between long and short syllables, music must take the best possible advantage of rhythmic richness.

One of the principal causes of rhythmic uniformity is the lack of metric variety in modern librettos. Good examples of this variety are to be found in the poetry of Chiabrera, Parini, Monti, and others.[39] The librettist must cultivate such variety, for otherwise musical rhythm will inevitably remain as impoverished as it is today.

---

38. N. 15a, Scena ("Perfidi! All'anglo contro me v'unite"/"Pietà, rispetto, onore"), Battaglia ("Ella è morta!" "Qual gemito!"; "Via le fronde, e mano all'armi"), [e] Morte di Macbeth ("Mal per me che m'affidai").

39. The experiments in metric variety of the poet Gabriello Chiabrera (1552–1638)—partly inspired by classical and French models—influenced the work of later, neoclassical poets such as Giuseppe Parini (1729–99) and Vincenzo Monti (1754–1828). All three poets also produced librettos.

9

I MASNADIERI

In but a few years Verdi had scaled such great heights that other nations, slow to acknowledge our glories, finally began to pay attention to this new composer, who was unrivaled in his popularity on the major stages of Italy. Verdi wrote the opera *I masnadieri* expressly for London, with a libretto by the celebrated poet Andrea Maffei, who took the subject from Schiller's well-known tragedy.[1]

A youthful work of Schiller's, this tragedy was truly the product of a spirit impatient of restraint and of a mind not yet moderated by experience. "Because of my ignorance of men and their destinies," Schiller later wrote with reference to this play, "my brush inevitably missed the midpoint between angel and demon. I therefore produced a monster that, luckily, has never existed in this world and that I would want to preserve only as an example of a creation derived from the strange union of subordination and genius. I am

1. Schiller's drama *Die Räuber* was first published in 1781 and staged in 1782. Andrea Maffei had already provided a number of additions to Piave's libretto for *Macbeth*. The Italian translator of all Schiller's dramas, Maffei was a friend and literary adviser of Verdi's, also supplying the words for several of his chamber songs. The critical edition of Verdi's *I masnadieri*, by Roberta Montemorra Marvin, was published as *WGV* I/11 (2000).

speaking here of *Die Räuber*."[2] And yet this play—however false its basic premise and its aim—was given such beauty by the power of genius that some naive youths, utterly dazzled and overwhelmed by their own blind enthusiasm, took to the woods like Carlo Moor to lead a life of brigandry.[3]

This Carlo, son of Massimiliano, Count Moor, has a brother, Francesco, who is perfidy personified. For in order to speedily gain sole possession of the entire family fortune, he puts Carlo into the bad graces of his father, widening the rift with lies and slander. Finally, he convinces his father that Carlo is dead. Impatient to enjoy the fruits of his iniquity, he then announces his own father's demise and succeeds to his title and wealth. Though believed dead, Massimiliano has been incarcerated in a horrible tower. One of Francesco's accomplices grows repentant, and confesses the atrocious sin to Amalia, Carlo's fiancée. Carlo returns and frees his father but, overcome with remorse for the infamous life he has been leading, flees from everyone, including his beloved Amalia. The libretto's denouement leaves Francesco in the throes of remorse, Massimiliano prostrated by grief, Amalia in a faint, Carlo fled, and the brigands angered at their abandonment by their captain.[4]

Such a subject is not well suited to music—though Maffei asserts otherwise[5]—because, as affirmed by Aristides (famous for his ancient treatise on music), the goal of music is the love of beauty.[6] In *I masnadieri* we are expected to love baseness. Not even the character of Amalia, which represents

2. The passage is in the "Ankündigung" (advertisement) Schiller prepared in 1784 for his forthcoming periodical *Rheinische Thalia*. See it in *Schillers Werke: Nationalausgabe*, vol. 22, *Vermischte Schriften*, ed. Herbert Meyer (Weimar: Böhlhaus, 1958), 93–98, 94.

3. We have kept to the Italianized names used by Basevi (Carlo, Massimiliano, and Francesco for Schiller's Karl, Maximilian, and Franz), given that his discussion moves seamlessly between drama and libretto.

4. In fact, Carlo stabs Amalia at the end of both Schiller's play and Verdi's opera. There is evidence, however, of at least one case in which the finale was indeed altered so that Amalia would simply faint. See the libretto printed for the production of *I masnadieri* at Rome's Teatro Apollo in the carnival season of 1848. My thanks to Roberta Montemorra Marvin for providing me with this piece of information.

5. In the preface to his libretto for *I masnadieri*, Maffei had written that—because of the emotional and dramatic intensity of *Die Räuber*—he could think of no literary work that would be as suited to operatic treatment.

6. Aristides Quintilianus, who left a substantial treatise on music (*Peri mousikes/De musica*), is thought to have been active in the third–fourth century (see Thomas J. Mathiesen, "Aristides Quintilianus," in *Grove*, vol. 1). In bk. 3, chap. 18, of the treatise, having associated the ratios of intervals with both bodily proportions and virtue, he concludes, "This is what the noble Plato means when he says that the objective of music is love of the beautiful." Andrew Barker, ed., *Greek Musical Writings*, 2 vols. (Cambridge: Cambridge University Press, 1984–89), 2:519.

virtue, helps this work retain the dignity, nobility, and purity of the human conscience.

Maffei's *melodramma* did not come up to the expectations that many had formed when this worthy poet undertook the task. Perhaps not a few recalled the view of some men of letters, including Quadrio, Crescimbeni, Gravina, Muratori, and even Apostolo Zeno, that opera is essentially a monstrous bastard, unworthy of inclusion among the family of fine arts.[7] Yet it so happens that men of no lesser stature in wisdom and erudition have believed the contrary—and, it seems to me, with greater justification.

Opera, a theatrical genre born about two and a half centuries ago, having been initially designed for pure pleasure, had to yield unquestioningly to many unavoidable whims that interfered with its natural development. But even without the aid of guiding precepts, it was still able to make progress, piloted by the talents of gifted composers who, through instinct more than learning, were able to guide it along the right route. We still have need of a poetics of opera—one that, starting out from a profound exploration of the nature of both music and poetry, might teach the way of union, conciliation, and mutual assistance for the two sister arts. Poetry and music must form a single composition where either separated from the other would lose the savor and effectiveness born of their intimate union.

I masnadieri was performed in London in July 1847.[8] Its reception was not up to expectations; brought to Italy it has survived with neither condemnation nor praise.[9]

Before beginning my examination of this work I want to clear up a doubt that may occur to the reader about my methods. It might well be objected that by examining an opera through analysis, as I do, one is bound to overlook many of its virtues and defects—indeed, the most essential ones, appertaining to the work *as a whole*.[10] But please consider that the synthetic method cannot

7. Francesco Saverio Quadrio, Giovan Mario Crescimbeni, Gian Vincenzo Gravina, and Ludovico Antonio Muratori are among the most distinguished Italian *letterati* active in the period from the late seventeenth century to the mid-eighteenth. The reason Zeno is singled out is that he was a prominent librettist himself.

8. The premiere took place at Her Majesty's Theatre.

9. Basevi's phrase here ("senza infamia e senza lode") is another of his Dantean references (though this one is graphically unmarked, as it had probably already become a current expression in Italian): *Inferno*, 3.36.

10. Basevi's claim that music analysis is *bound* to miss the most essential features of the work as a whole might seem surprising. Here as elsewhere, however, he uses terminology that has philosophical overtones: "analisi," in explicit opposition to the synthesis of the following

be used in music criticism on account of opera's still limited development: an opera cannot legitimately be compared to a statue or a painting, where the *whole* is considered in the first instance. In its music we search in vain for a well-defined central idea, around which all the individual numbers might cluster, as if to form a unified whole. The music may, however, find in the general concept behind the drama a support, a center toward which the various pieces that make up the opera converge—to a greater or lesser degree, depending on the composer's talent. This is how what we call a *colorito* or overall *tinta* is attained.[11] But the attainment of a *colorito* is not the musician's goal; rather it is the means by which the various pieces of the opera can be suitably brought together in relation to the drama. This *colorito* is of different kinds, depending on its degree of specificity. In the case of a wholly sacred subject, a matching musical *colorito*, however appropriate it may seem, will still be too vague to appertain to one oratorio rather than another. The same holds true for comic subjects and so forth. But creative composers have been able to find less vague *tinte* that are better suited to a specific libretto. Without leaving the operas of Verdi, I shall note that the sacred *colorito* in *Nabucodonosor* is in no way different from that of Rossini's *Mosè*; in *I Lombardi*, on the other hand, there is a more specific *colorito* whose freshness makes it wonderfully suited to a Christian sacred subject. This attainment alone would suffice to place Verdi among the greatest masters. *I due Foscari* too has its own *tinta*, which, though not so vivid as that of *I Lombardi*, is more so than in other operas by the same composer; others yet have no *colorito* whatsoever. Indubitably, the overall *colorito* of an opera reveals better than anything else a composer's genius, for it shows us his disposition to synthesis. When a composer has managed to conceive what is necessary to impart this much-desired *colorito* to the music, through the organization of the melodies, the use of harmony, the choice of instruments, etc., then he has created something like a type, a modus operandi, a ready point of reference for individual pieces, themes, accompaniments, and so forth; the result is a whole that surprises and irresistibly attracts the listener, who full of wonder is compelled to acknowledge the work of a great genius.

sentence ("metodo sintetico"), is the breaking down of a complex object into smaller, more elemental components.

11. The term *tinta* (hue, coloring)—and the idea that an opera can have an overall quality of its own—is one that has found considerable favor with opera scholars in recent decades (see also the glossary).

In *I masnadieri* we see no trace of such an overall *tinta*; indeed, it feels like a patchwork of assorted pieces stitched together, rather than a continuous canvas with various images.

The tenor's cavatina follows a short *preludio*.[12] A recitative and a brief off-stage chorus ["Col pugnale e col bicchier"] lead us to a ⅜-time andantino accompanied by empty triplets [*terzine vuote*], on the text "O mio castel paterno." It is monotonous and, on account of its rhythm, excessively flaccid. While this kind of singing might have been suitable for Jacopo Foscari, it is inappropriate to the proud Carlo Moor. Emotions do not express themselves in the same way in all people, for not everyone feels in the same way. The allegro "Nell'argilla maledetta" is better suited to this character's temperament. In its rhythm it recalls the phrase from *Attila* on the words "È gettata la mia sorte."[13] This rhythm brings great energy to the melody and produces a brusque effect by placing an accent on the second quarter of the measure, which is one of the so-called weak beats. Placing strength on a position where the ear is used to finding weakness is a means that other composers too have used to lend a sung melody this kind of energy, which represents very well a mind churned by vehement emotions. The form of this cabaletta is not new, and the composer has employed a hackneyed effect, repeating a phrase of the cabaletta in the unison chorus.

The baritone's aria follows.[14] In the andante "La sua lampada vitale," the music is associated with words expressing a thought that is among the most abominable—that of a son who, with complete calm, undertakes to hasten his own father's death. If Verdi had managed to imagine music suited to this thought, he would have discovered a world hitherto unknown to the art of music, for it is held by many illustrious philosophers that music cannot accurately express foul thoughts. This is a blessing of Providence, inasmuch as evil is thus deprived of the aid of a great enticement. Music, however, is able to paint evil passions—but because they are passions, not because they are evil. And all passions—even those that often completely evade the rule of reason—carry with them, if not their own justification, certainly a mitigation

12. N. 1, Preludio; N. 2, Scena ("Quando io leggo in Plutarco") ed Aria Carlo ("O mio castel paterno").

13. This is the stretta of Ezio's second-act aria "Dagl'immortali culmini" (N. 10), which indeed opens with an identical rhythm.

14. N. 3, Recitativo ("Vecchio! Spiccai da te quell'odiato") ed Aria Francesco ("La sua lampada vitale"). Basevi gives the incipit as "Quella lampada vitale."

of their sinfulness. Perhaps with a view to underlining music's inability to express absolute evil, Verdi linked the fearful words of Francesco Moor to a melody that could perfectly well be put into the mouth of the tenderest lover. Verdi could have availed himself here of abstruse harmonies, broken rhythms, and so on and so forth, but he did not; he would therefore have done better not to set these foul words at all. The allegro "Tremate, o miseri!" in which Francesco Moor's emotions grow violent, is adequately expressive. Here again we find novelty neither of rhythm nor of form, but only straightforward and energetic melody.

Organizing the musical numbers with scant wisdom, Maffei follows these two arias with the soprano's cavatina.[15] The rhythm of the andante mosso, "Lo sguardo avea degl'angeli," strays from the usual in its first measures, but the melody then continues with very ordinary, poorly connected rhythms and ungraceful harmonic shifts; it thus appears long, incoherent, flabby, and inflated. Besides, the theme seems to me too sparkling to suit Amalia as she thinks of her betrothed, who has been unjustly banished by his father.

There follows a *duettino* for bass and soprano that offers nothing of note.[16]

The well-fashioned final quartet of act 1 draws our attention with a reminiscence of the *terzetto* from *Attila*,[17] too obvious to attribute to chance, where Francesco repeats for the second time the words "Grazie, o Dimon! lo assalgono." For the rest, this piece is a fine example of the grand, composed, solemn side of Verdi's music.

In act 2, an unattractive chorus ["Godiam ché fugaci son l'ore"] is followed by the adagio of Amalia's aria,[18] which proceeds well enough without offering much that is new. The allegro ["Carlo vive?"] is full of *slancio* and begins with a rhythm that is not much used.

---

15. N. 4, Scena ("Venerabile, o padre, è il tuo sembiante") e Cavatina Amalia ("Lo sguardo avea degl'angeli"). Basevi gives the incipit as "Lo sguardo aveva degli angioli."

16. N. 5, Duettino ("Mio Carlo! . . ." "Ei sogna! . . ."; "Carlo! io muoio, ed, ahi! lontano") e Quartetto finale dell'atto primo ("Un messaggero di trista novella! . . ."; "Sul capo mio colpevole").

17. Compare mm. 161ff. of this N. 5 of *Masnadieri* with mm. 170ff. ("Tempo non è di lagrime") of *Attila*'s N. 12, Scena ("Qui del convegno è il loco . . ."), Romanza ("Che non avrebbe il misero"), Terzetto ("Che più s'indugia? . . ."; "Te sol, te sol quest'anima"), e Quartetto–Finale ultimo ("Non involarti, seguimi!"; "Tu, rea donna, già schiava, or mia sposa").

18. N. 6, Scena ("Dall'infame banchetto io m'involai") ed Aria Amalia ("Tu del mio Carlo in seno"). The chorus is already part of this number.

Then follows a duet for soprano and baritone containing no great original-ity.[19] The andantino is modeled on that of the first-act duet:[20] both end with a delicate, pianissimo *a 2* in thirds and sixths. But it must be noted that in the present duet the words strongly oppose the music. The allegro ["Ti scosta, o malnato"], besides lacking a novel theme, is modeled on the old form calling for three repetitions in the cabalettas of all duets.

The chorus of brigands is very trite.[21] The tenor's *romanza* ["Di ladroni attornïato"] is notable only in that it shows Verdi's ability to fashion new out of old.

The second finale ["Su, fratelli! corriamo alla pugna"] gives fresh proof of Verdi's limited aptitude for writing strettas.

The third act begins with a duet for tenor and soprano that is among the best things in the opera.[22] The andantino ["Qual mare, qual terra"], begin-ning as a dialogue and ending *a 2*, is not inexpressive; only toward the end does its form lapse into the old-fashioned. The allegro ["Lassù, lassù risplen-dere"] obeys the old rule of threefold repetition; its theme is sparkling and not without effect.

The chorus of brigands[23] has no distinctive character; but because of a cer-tain variety and some chiaroscuro effects, it may, with a good performance, succeed in pleasing a lay audience. The melody Verdi uses in this chorus of cannibals—who refer to "the last breaths of murdered fathers, the cries and screams of wives and mothers" as "music" and "diversion"—would be more appropriate to a band of carefree youths giving full rein to their innocent mirth. Verdi could, however, excuse himself by laying the blame on the poet, who put on stage things one would never encounter in real life.

The *racconto* of the bass (Massimiliano) ["Un ignoto, tre lune or saranno"] is not very original, though in some places is not without expression.[24] The oath ["Giuri ognun"] that follows makes use of the sonority effect [*effetto della sonorità*] more than anything else; the remainder offers nothing of note.

---

19. N. 7, Recitativo ("Perché fuggisti al canto") e Duetto [Amalia e Francesco] ("Io t'amo, Amalia! io t'amo").

20. This is of course the *duettino* that is part of N. 5.

21. The chorus opens N. 8, Finale secondo ("Tutto quest'oggi le mani in mano"), which also entails the two ensuing sections named by Basevi.

22. N. 9, Scena ("Dio ti ringrazio!") e Duetto [Amalia e Carlo] ("T'abbraccio, o Carlo"/ "Amalia, abbracciami").

23. N. 10, Coro di masnadieri ("Le rube, gli stupri, gl'incendi, le morti").

24. N. 11, Finale terzo ("Ben giunto, o capitano!"), mm. 172ff.

The dream with which the fourth act opens,[25] though having some praise-worthy passages—notably in its accompaniment—if viewed as a whole is seen to have a number of disparate parts that are poorly connected. The duet between Moser and Francesco, deficient in melody and in realization, is singular in its form, but not terribly attractive.[26]

The duet for Carlo and Massimiliano is a hackneyed thing in which Verdi lowers himself to the level of his most unremarkable imitators.[27]

The opera ends with a *terzetto* that bears the mark of Verdian genius; on its own terms it merits great praise, although other *terzetti* by Verdi are far superior.[28]

Our examination of its various pieces shows that *I masnadieri* did not add a single laurel leaf to Verdi's wreath. If we cast our gaze over the entire score, comparing its various parts, we soon realize what a feeble expenditure of inventiveness Verdi needed to complete this opera. The life that had so often gushed copiously from his imagination to imbue his creations had now failed him, so he on this occasion had recourse to an artificial semblance of life, with which he was able merely to "galvanize" a corpse.[29]

Triplets reign supreme in this score. If you go through the main pieces of the opera, you will find barely half to be without them. In general, the rhythms are not very varied or spontaneous. Four times in the principal themes Verdi used an accent on the second quarter of the measure; with such repetition this loses its effectiveness, which consists mainly in surprise. Moreover, common time is so sparingly used that, out of twenty-six principal melodies, it is found only fifteen times; thus, tempos appear even quicker owing to the shortness of the measures. Note that, when abused, quick tempos do not impart gaiety and brio to music but render it cloying and unpleasant—even more so when quick motion and short measures are compounded by notes of small value, as they are in *I masnadieri*. In *Nabucodonosor*, Verdi used many quick tempos,

25. N. 12, Sogno di Francesco ("Tradimento! Risorgono i defunti! . . ."; "Parea, che sorto da lauto convito").

26. N. 13, Scena ("M'hai chiamato in quest'ora") e Duetto [Francesco e Moser] ("Trema, iniquo! il lampo, il tuono").

27. N. 14, Scena ("Francesco! mio figlio!") e Duetto [Carlo e Massimiliano] ("Come il bacio d'un padre amoroso").

28. N. 15, Finale ultimo ("Qui son essi!" "Capitano!").

29. Basevi the physician here uses the verb *galvanizzare* in its root sense, for the sake of his simile: the dead body of an uninspired opera was only seemingly brought to life by an external force (presumably that of the devices described in the following paragraph) in the way the muscles of dead frogs contracted when electrically stimulated, as discovered by the eighteenth-century Italian physiologist Luigi Galvani.

but he very shrewdly balanced their effect through the use of common time (there are only two appearances of ¾ in the opera); moreover, he used larger note values—the so-called round notes [*note tonde*].

Observe, too, that while many pieces in *I masnadieri* will seem pleasant, or at least not tedious, if heard individually, when heard in succession as arranged in this opera they leave an impression, if not of unpleasantness, certainly not of satisfaction. This is a very useful example for study by composers who write one piece at a time, concerned only to bring that piece to its own good end—so that, when it seems pleasing on its own, they set the piece aside and begin another in the same way, paying no further attention to what has come before. This way, having written separately all the pieces making up their opera, they feel overjoyed and think that nothing else is required to make their work perfect. But what is lacking after the various parts are finished is the necessary interrelation; if the melodies, the contrapuntal devices, and so forth lack the cohesive links from which they mutually profit, the discerning listener can never be completely satisfied. It is not rare for a piece to seem more beautiful when preceded by others that prepare the listener suitably. And it also happens very frequently that a piece that is lovely in itself will appear unpleasant simply because the listener is badly disposed to it by the previous pieces. To these considerations we owe the abandonment of long and very tedious recitatives and the greater care taken with *parlanti*. We are now far indeed from the time when Traetta, seated at his harpsichord, had to call for the attention of an audience distracted by scene after scene of insipid recitatives by announcing, "Attention, ladies and gentlemen! The next piece is a lovely one!" And only then would they cease their chattering.[30]

30. One account of this alleged practice of Traetta's is that provided by Carpani—a likely source for Basevi. See Giuseppe Carpani, *Le haydine, ovvero Lettere su la vita e le opere del celebre maestro Giuseppe Haydn* (Milan: Buccinelli, 1812), 23.

10

JÉRUSALEM

The Paris Opéra also wished to host the music of Verdi, and in November 1847 it presented *Jérusalem*.[1] Messieurs Royer and Vaëz wrote the libretto in such a manner as to enable the composer to insert some pieces from *I Lombardi* as well as to add new ones.[2]

These reshuffles and patch-ups, though endorsed through use by celebrated composers including Rossini, Donizetti, and others, are to be deplored as contrary to the progress and dignity of music. Such works as the new version of Rossini's *Mosè*[3] do not contradict this: in these apparent exceptions, either the changes made in the reworked opera have not actually altered it in any essential way, or the composer's powers of invention have managed only to mask, not to remove, the inevitable contradictions between words and music. Our veneration for the great Rossini will not be diminished if we observe

1. References below are to the vocal score *Jérusalem: Grand opéra en quatre actes* (Paris: Bureau central de musique, pl. no. B.C. 1256, [1849?]), with only minor amendments to the verbal text.

2. Alphonse Royer and Gustave Vaëz had already collaborated in preparing French translations of librettos of operas by Rossini and Donizetti and in writing an original libretto for Donizetti (*L'ange de Nisida*, later reworked into *La favorite*). Verdi's reformulation of *I Lombardi* for the French stage entailed the composing or reworking of a large amount of music.

3. See chapter 1, n. 6, above.

that in the new *Mosè* there is a stylistic disparity between the new pieces and the old—which is certainly not the source of that masterpiece's appeal.

In order to develop suitable criteria to guide us on this important question, we need to consider three cases: first, when the music is altered but the words remain; second, when the same music is used for different words; and finally, when additions, deletions, and rearrangements change the original order of the pieces that constitute the work.

When associated with poetry, music takes up the main thought or situation, animates it with its most vivid colors, and holds back, so to speak, the flow of time while "painting" in a way that addresses the ear rather than the eye. Not all composers are equally gifted in creating such musical pictures, which can take an infinite number of forms. Hence, no harm will befall art if the same text is set by different composers, or by the same composer in different ways, for the mediocre and the bad do not have the strength to usurp the beautiful and the sublime. The fathers of opera, Peri and Caccini, both set Rinuccini's *Euridice*; they were motivated by no other, less noble thought than that of gentlemanly competition. But when music has been properly united with a given text, it is not a good idea to cudgel the brains in search of a different melody: the powers of the imagination (by their nature limited) must not be abused. It is said that Hasse, "The Saxon," wanting to set the aria "Se mai senti spirarti sul volto," which had already been beautifully set by Gluck,[4] had to start afresh a good eight times without success; he finally hit on a second melodic period, which led him back to the first [i.e., Gluck's]—so strongly had Gluck's theme impressed itself on his mind. On the other hand, since, unlike its sister arts, music loses its charms with time—as it were through an aging process—something that may not be feasible in one time may become so in another. Hence, nothing prevented Cimarosa or Paisiello from setting the text "Se cerca se dice," even though Pergolesi had used it in an aria

---

4. The aria text "Se mai senti spirarti sul volto" is found in act 2, scene 15, of Metastasio's libretto *La clemenza di Tito* (1734), which was set by about forty different composers. Among them was Johann Adolf Hasse (often referred to as "Il Sassone," as Basevi does here), who set the text in 1735 (Pesaro, as *Tito Vespasiano*) and then again in 1759 (Naples). Between Hasse's two settings came Gluck's (1752, Naples). Gluck's setting of "Se mai senti" made a great impression, so much so that almost three decades later the musicographer Saverio Mattei could still write, "How can one possibly set to music [. . .] 'Se mai senti spirarti sul volto' after Gluck?" Saverio Mattei, "La filosofia della musica, o sia La riforma del teatro," in *Opere del signor abate Pietro Metastasio*, 15 vols. (Nice: Società tipografica, 1783–85), 3 (1783):iii–xlviii, xxviii–xxix ("com'è possibile, che uno scriva [. . .] *Se mai senti spirarti sul volto*, dopo Cluk [*sic*]?").

deemed insuperable.[5] As melodies age, younger ones, their descendants, take their place, so that one could write—and with interesting results—a "musical genealogy."

In its ability to accommodate the same poetry in differing ways, music is akin to the other fine arts, which are likewise able to depict a single subject or story in diverse manners. But where music differs from its sister arts is in the reverse procedure, where a given melody is applied to different words. Within certain limits, music can indeed do this, for in essence it is not an imitative art. When the text is changed, one of two cases will apply: either the meaning will remain the same, or it will change along with the words. The first case is that of a translation, which requires great expertise in the poet if the music is not to be severely weakened and lose both its accentuation and the appeal that it often acquires from the words. In these cases I would not oppose freeing the poet from the obligation to rhyme, which is at times a great burden in such translations. Here I share the view that Tommaseo stated in his brief essay on the relationship of music to poetry: "If it were not for the fear of violating rhyme, opera librettos and epic poems would less often violate reason."[6] Certainly, when music is transferred from one language to another something of its original vigor and character will always be lost; nonetheless, good translations must be encouraged lest nations be deprived of masterworks created abroad. In cases where the meaning changes along with the words, it is possible to use the same music when there remains at least some analogy, even a distant one, so long as there is not absolute opposition. Here, the best guide is the composer's common sense and good taste. Composers have often made use of this flexibility of music; if some of their operas do not achieve the desired success, they attempt to salvage from the wreck the pieces whose only fault was the bad company they kept. Music has not infrequently profited from this. In Bellini's first opera, *Adelson e Salvini*, on the words "Ecco signor la sposa, io salva te la rendo," we find the beautiful melody that Bellini subsequently adapted so successfully to the text "Meco tu

5. Basevi had already mentioned Pergolesi's version of the aria (see chapter 1, p. 24 and n. 57, above). "Se cerca, se dice" is in *L'olimpiade* (1733), one of Metastasio's most successful librettos, having been set by about sixty composers. Cimarosa's version was premiered in 1784 (Vicenza), Paisiello's in 1786 (Naples).

6. See Niccolò Tommaseo, "Della musica nelle sue relazioni con la poesia," in *Della bellezza educatrice* (Venice: Gondoliere, 1838), 69–78, 72. Tommaseo (1802–74) is especially known as a leading lexicographer of the Italian language.

vieni o misera" in *La straniera*.[7] But the composer must avoid taking melodies from popular or very well-known operas—even if composed by himself. In an opera, reminiscences distract the listener's attention and instantly transport his mind to where he first heard the melody. Such distractions diminish the dramatic effect. What should we then say when entire very well-known pieces are given new words—particularly when, as often happens, they fit less well or, indeed, badly? When a composer has been truly inspired to set to music a fine dramatic situation expressed in suitable poetry, that music can never be as successful in a new situation. There are unfortunately composers who believe their music able to express the most disparate things equally well; this music usually has no more variety of expression than castanets or the bass drum have variety of sound.

When, having given an opera's words some new music and its music some new words, the composer then adds, removes, and reorders pieces, we run into new difficulties and drawbacks that are no less significant than those mentioned above. The overall *tinta*—if there was one in the first place—disappears, and pieces lose the appeal they had acquired, as if by reflection, from their position in relation to the others.

Having made these observations, we shall briefly examine Verdi's *Jérusalem*. We immediately see that in this libretto the Lombard crusaders have become Frenchmen and that Milan has ceded place to Toulouse in France. Viclinda and Giselda, the wife and daughter of Arvino, have been merged into the single character of Hélène, daughter of the Count of Toulouse (Arvino from *I Lombardi*). *I Lombardi*'s Oronte is replaced by Gaston, Viscount of Béarn (who, however, has never even dreamed of being a Muslim). The count gives him Hélène's hand in marriage to make up an old quarrel. Fueled by powerful jealousy, Roger, the count's brother, orders that Gaston be killed,

---

7. This may not be as straightforward a case of self-borrowing as it appeared to Basevi on the basis of the sources available to him. Bellini began reworking his three-act *opera semiseria Adelson e Salvini* (Naples: Collegio di San Sebastiano, 1825) into a two-act version that he never finished. The two-act version that circulated later was completed after Bellini's death (1835) by others, who adopted the melody for Salvini's "Ecco signor la sposa" (in the second, and now last, finale) either from Bellini's working materials for the second version or directly from *La straniera* (Milan: Teatro alla Scala, 1829). In *La straniera* it figures in [N. 7], Scena ("Udimmo. Il tuo racconto") e Aria di Valdeburgo ("Sì, li sciogliete, o Giudici"), as the melody of the cabaletta "Meco tu vieni, o misera" (mm. 174ff.). For information on *Adelson e Salvini* and *La straniera*, I am indebted, respectively, to Davide Daolmi and Marco Uvietta, who are preparing critical editions of the two operas (to appear as vols. 1 and 4 of *ECB*). Basevi owned a vocal score of *Adelson e Salvini* in the two-act version (Paris: Schonenberger, [1854]: *Catalogo Basevi*, 122).

but by mistake it is the count who is wounded. To save Roger, the assassin accuses Gaston, who is banished from France and journeys to Asia, where he is taken prisoner. Hélène accompanies her father, the leader of the crusaders, to Palestine, where she encounters a repentant Roger and also Gaston, whose innocence is finally vindicated. Because of this transformation, the plot of *I Lombardi* has lost its best scenes to make room for others that are very colorless indeed.

The prelude of *Jérusalem* is not that of *I Lombardi*.[8] It shows great craft, though to no purpose.

The new material in act 1 comprises a very poor *duettino* for soprano and tenor that serves as an *introduzione*,[9] a depiction of the sunrise that certainly does not eclipse that of *Attila*,[10] and the cabaletta of the bass's cavatina, which has been changed for the worse.[11] There are also new recitatives and *parlanti* as well as other mutations not worth mentioning. The Ave Maria, with new words, has been transferred to a position following the aforementioned new *duettino*. The music of the introductory chorus of *I Lombardi*, altered and abbreviated, was adapted to the chorus that follows the sunrise.[12] Also conserved, for the most part, was the music of the two *Lombardi* quintets, which was infused into the two sextets in this act.[13]

Transferred to *Jérusalem*, the music of many numbers from *I Lombardi* has lost its effectiveness, having been badly used—sometimes to the point of nonsense. The theme of the chorus of cutthroats is found here in a chorus of

---

8. The prelude is titled "Introduction" in the French score.

9. Récit ("Non, ce bruit, ce n'est rien") et Duo [Hélène [et] Gaston] ("Adieu, mon bien-aimé"). The brief duo is unnumbered, as if it formed a single unit with the preceding instrumental introduction.

10. The instrumental "Lever du soleil" is appended to N. 1, Ave Maria [Hélène] ("Ave Maria, ma voix te prie"), which is derived from the Ave Maria in N. 3 of *I Lombardi*.

11. Pagano's "Sciagurata! hai tu creduto" in N. 2 of *Lombardi* has been recast as Roger's "Oh! dans l'ombre, dans le mystère" in N. 4 of *Jérusalem*, Choeur de femmes ("Viens! ô pécheur rebelle") et Air [Roger]; but Pagano's original cabaletta "O speranza di vendetta" is substituted by Roger's entirely new "Ah! viens! démon! esprit du mal!"—part of the ensuing N. 5, Choeur de buveurs ("Fier soldat de la croisade").

12. Compare "Era Viclinda" (in *I Lombardi*, N. 1, mm. 120ff.) with "Non, plus de guerre!" (in *Jérusalem*'s N. 2, Choeur "Enfin voici le jour propice," mm. 82ff.).

13. One of Basevi's "quintets" is the concertato for five characters and chorus "T'assale un fremito!" within *I Lombardi*'s *introduzione* (N. 1, mm. 272ff.), which becomes the passage for sextet with chorus "Je tremble encor" in *Jérusalem*'s N. 3, Sextuor et Choeur ("Avant que nous partions pour la croisade sainte"). The other "quintet" is the concertato passage for five characters and chorus "Mostro d'averno orribile" in the first finale of *Lombardi* (see chapter 2, n. 17, above), reworked into that for six characters and chorus "Monstre, parjure, homicide!" in *Jérusalem*'s N. 7, Final du 1er acte ("Mais quel tumulte!").

drinkers.[14] In the largo of the second sextet, the music does not fare so well as it does in the second quintet of *I Lombardi*, for there the focus of the action was the bass (Pagano), while in the new number it is the tenor (Gaston). The stretta of this piece ["Sur ton front est lancé l'anathème"] is a mixture of the new and the old.[15]

The second act is now without the fine chorus of ambassadors, and opens with a *gran scena e romanza* for the bass, which is "Ma quando un suon terribile" from *I Lombardi*.[16] A *polacca* for soprano follows, to the music of "Non fu sogno! . . . ,"[17] and afterward the theme of "O Signore, dal tetto natio" is used in a chorus of pilgrims.[18] The grand march of the crusaders is new, but it has no virtues that will make us forget the vivacious march from *I Lombardi*.[19] Now comes a trio for three basses—also new, but trite in its rhythm and its unison effects.[20] I preferred the *duettino* "Sei tu l'uom della caverna?" which has been excised.[21] The tenor then has his cavatina to the same theme as "La mia letizia infondere," the cabaletta of which has been cut.[22] The duet for soprano and tenor from the third act of *I Lombardi* has furnished the music for the finale of this act.[23]

The third act begins with a chorus of slaves, the same as "La bella straniera."[24] There follow several dance movements, which do not stand out for

14. Compare the chorus "Niun periglio il nostro seno" (part of N. 2 of *I Lombardi*) with "Fier soldat de la croisade" in *Jérusalem*'s N. 5.

15. Compare the stretta of the first finale in *I Lombardi*, "Va! sul capo ti grava l'Eterno" (N. 4, mm. 134ff.).

16. In *I Lombardi*, the second act opens with the chorus "È dunque vero" (N. 5); in *Jérusalem*, it opens with Roger's Invocation "Grâce! mon Dieu!" (N. 8), in which the adagio "Ô jour fatal! ô crime!" is a reworking of Pagano's *romanza* "Ma quando un suon terribile" (in N. 7 of *I Lombardi*).

17. N. 9, Polonaise [Hélène] ("Quelle ivresse!"), is a transformation of Giselda's cabaletta "Non fu sogno! . . ." (in N. 14 of *Lombardi*).

18. The celebrated chorus from *I Lombardi* (see chapter 2, n. 50, above) turns into *Jérusalem*'s N. 10, Choeur des pèlerins ("Ô mon Dieu! ta parole est donc vaine!").

19. N. 11, Marche. In *I Lombardi*, the march of the crusaders had been heard in N. 7, Scena ("E ancor silenzio!"), Marcia de' crociati, ed Inno ("Stolto Allhà!").

20. N. 12, Choeur des croisés ("Le Seigneur nous promet la victoire"): the chorus is led by the count, Roger, and the papal legate, thence Basevi's definition of the number as "a trio for three basses" (the count is a baritone—as we have seen, not a relevant difference for many purposes).

21. The duet between Arvino and Pagano was part of N. 7 of *I Lombardi* (mm. 193ff.).

22. N. 13, Air [Gaston] ("Je veux encor entendre") is derived from the cantabile of Oronte's Cavatina (*Lombardi*, N. 6).

23. N. 14, Duo [Hélène et Gaston] ("Mon Hélène! . . ." "Gaston! . . ."); see *Lombardi*, N. 11, Recitativo ("Dove sola m'inoltro?") e Duetto ("Teco io fuggo!").

24. N. 15, Choeur dansé ("Ô belle captive"); cf. N. 8 in *Lombardi*.

having a particular *tinta*.[25] After these dances there is a *gran scena ed aria* for the soprano that employs the music of the *rondò* from the second finale of *I Lombardi*.[26] However, the situation has been weakened, in that Hélène no longer has Giselda's strong motivation to rail bitterly against her father and against the crusaders' enterprise. In *I Lombardi* Giselda is overwhelmed by desperation because she believes her lover to be dead—and by her father's hand. Hélène, on the other hand, sees her husband *threatened* with death. Therefore, her anger—in a situation that is not desperate and in which a supplicating tone might have been more effective—does not make a strong impression on the spectator. The finale of this act is new and very fine. The French librettists created a scene in which Gaston is dishonored at the hands of the executioner. It begins with a funeral march and closes with a *gran scena ed aria* for the tenor.[27] The march has character but without originality. The threefold declaration of Gaston's guilt is moving. Verdi set it in the simplest way—even too simply, for he did nothing but transpose the same music up a half tone each of three times. This may make a fine effect with a few measures of music, but in this piece eighteen measures are repeated. The situation is so powerful in itself, however, that it conceals this flaw. The stretta ["Frappez bourreaux!"] has energy and is suited to Gaston's distress. Taken as a whole, this number does not lack effect; nonetheless, it does not bear comparison with other beautiful pages by Verdi. The fact is that it has no merit other than that of not diminishing the effect of the dramatic situation.

The final act opens with the processional chorus, "Jérusalem."[28] Then comes a trio modeled after the famous one from *I Lombardi* but without making the same effect.[29] This is because—apart from the omission of the violin solo that predisposed the listener so well—the dramatic situation is different; it no longer deals with the solemn moment at which a Muslim receives

25. For the substantial ballet that was typical in a *grand opéra* Verdi wrote fifteen dance movements included in four "Airs de ballet" (separately numbered from the rest of the opera's pieces: N. 1, Pas de quatre; N. 2, Pas de deux; N. 3, Pas solo; N. 4, Pas d'ensemble).

26. N. 17, Air [Hélène] ("Mes plaintes sont vaines!"), after Giselda's "Se vano è il pregare" in the Finale secondo (N. 9) of *I Lombardi*. Basevi's comments on the differing dramatic contexts refer to the following passage, Hélène's rage scene ("Non . . . votre rage, indigne outrage"), based on Giselda's "No! . . . giusta causa."

27. N. 18, Marche funèbre, and N. 19, Grande scène ("Barons et chevaliers") et Air [Gaston] ("O mes amis, mes frères d'armes").

28. This is N. 20, Choeur de la procession ("Jérusalem la sainte")—a reworking of the chorus "Gerusalem! . . . Gerusalem! . . . la grande" that opens the third act of *I Lombardi* (N. 10).

29. N. 21, Trio ("Dieu nous sépare, Hélène!"), derived from "Qual voluttà trascorrere" in the N. 13 that concludes the third act of *I Lombardi*.

baptism as he nears death, but rather with a mere blessing from a hermit. After an instrumental movement meant to signify a battle, the opera ends with
a quintet and hymn into which, for the most part, is infused the music of the
terzettino and hymn that close *I Lombardi*.[30]

I Lombardi is barely recognizable through the disguise of *Jérusalem*, owing to the loss of its freshness and appeal. This was inevitable given that the
best ideas and scenes were altered in the transformation, that the action was
moved under a new sky, and that many good pieces disappeared or were muti-
lated and many more deprived of the life and energy found in the others. This
resulted in a swollen, disjointed work, without the *colorito* that is the greatest
virtue of *I Lombardi*.

Jérusalem has been translated into Italian; this third-generation reshuffle
peeped out from a few Italian stages and then hid itself away.

It was a truly unreasonable pretension to present anew on the stages of Italy
an opera that in another form had made such a deep impression on the Italian
spirit as *I Lombardi*. There are some impressions that are not easily effaced,
even when the virtue of greater beauty is put up against them. What hope
is there that they will be supplanted with new ones when these have a lesser
power—in the present case, that of the music and libretto of *Jérusalem*?

30. The instrumental Bataille and the Final du 4ᵉ acte (both unnumbered pieces) are reworked from the Finale ultimo of *I Lombardi* (N. 15). The *terzettino* "Un breve istante" and the
hymn "Te lodiamo" have now become "Un instant me reste encore" and "À toi gloire ô Dieu
de victoire."

11

IL CORSARO

Verdi wrote the new opera *Il corsaro* for Trieste, where it was performed in October 1848.[1] The work's reception did not live up to the hopes it had engendered; according to some, the composer himself acknowledged that the opera was lacking in inspiration. Lacking in inspiration! Is that not to say lacking in effect, in raison d'être, in everything? When his inspiration fails him, the true artist is no longer distinguishable from the false artist. Though lacking the creative gifts necessary to cultivate artistic soil, the false artist still works on fruitlessly, motivated by vanity. For in everyone's soul there are two mirrors, one of which, the mirror of vanity, conceals all our defects and reflects nothing but our virtues, real or imagined, infinitely magnifying them; the other, the mirror of the conscience, reflects only the naked truth. The self-respecting artist does not avert his gaze from the mirror of the conscience, whereas the false artist dares look at himself only in the deceitful mirror of vanity. If only the man of genius took no other counsel than that of his own conscience! Then we should not see him so often stooping to embolden false

---

1. The venue was the Teatro Grande. The critical edition of *Il corsaro*, by Elizabeth Hudson, was published as *WGV* I/13 (1998).

artists, who believe themselves raised to the heights when they see great men lowered to their level.

But what are the works of a false artist? The critical eye easily sees that they contain no living element that truly belongs to their author, but only imitations as cold as death. And what, indeed, can be imitated in the works of the great apart from external appearances? Is it at all possible to penetrate the soul of the true artist to taste of the pure beauty that gives life to works of genius? Certainly not. So what happens? The false artist simulates a feeling he does not have, and that he nevertheless persuades himself to have, deceived by his own vanity. He reminds us of an old man, his heart now closed to all joy, who tries nonetheless to put on a laughing face, and who forces himself to imitate the radiant smile of a girl of fifteen. But try as he might, the smile that hangs from the old man's lips cannot penetrate the souls of others because it does not come from *his* soul.

I do not want the reader to think that my harsh words about imitation extend to the study of classical and other fine authors, on the grounds that there is no point in studying if imitation is forbidden; nothing could be further from my intention. The true artist does not reject imitation at its proper time. But as he uses it to implement his ideas in a more effective way, it is a means, not an end in itself. The true artist must spend many years in detailed study of the works of others in order to be able to draw on the labors of his predecessors and to strengthen his own powers, which on their own would be too weak to defend and augment the riches of art. It is foolishly presumptuous to close one's eyes to the past and consider oneself an artistic pioneer, as though we could disdain the works of the many great minds who have gone before—as though there existed a man able to advance art without outside assistance, or even to maintain it at its present level.

False artists are so blind that at times they themselves do not know what they wish to imitate. Hence the greatest oddities, eccentricities, and lunacies in the world. There was a time when every poetaster, eager to imitate Petrarch, affected to have fallen in love on Good Friday.[2] And do we not see even greater follies in music? Music enjoys greater freedom than other arts, for it is not bound by those threatening models from nature that to some extent restrain the ill-considered steps of false artists in other fields. Composers of the

2. By Basevi's time, Petrarch had been a model for writers of lyrical poetry in Italian for five centuries; he had in various places mentioned Good Friday as the (symbolic) date of his first encounter with Laura, the woman idealized in his writings. See, for example, *Rerum vulgarium fragmenta* (*Canzoniere*), 3.62.

lowest sort, always intent on courting the latest fashion, receiving no stimuli from either their taste or their imagination, "create" new pieces with scant labor. As I have said, they use old rhythms festooned with different notes so that their melodies should appear new. Once they have found, one way or another, a musical idea, they develop it according to a template found in some successful composer, without considering that not all ideas can be developed in the same way. Thus conceived, the piece is orchestrated in the easiest possible way, using as a model the least-known pages of other composers, and taking care only to avoid confusing the ophicleide with the flute.[3] Then, to add a dash of pepper to their insipid music, they sprinkle some so-called effects [*punti d'effetto*] here and there—mainly shrieks from the singers and fortissimos from the orchestra. If our ears are still intact, it is certainly not thanks to these composers. We are too often made to exclaim with Salvator Rosa,

> Musica mia, non so se sì molesti,
> Come son ora i professori tuoi,
> Eran già quei martelli onde nascesti.[4]

> [O my Music, did those hammer blows
> from which you were born
> ever grate as much as our musicians do?]

While inspired music reaches and touches the heart, this other kind stops at the tympanic membrane, deploying all its power in stimulating the sense of hearing. We see hacks taking the utmost trouble to patch their operas together with tunes calculated to tickle the ear. And to this end they do not hesitate to ransack dance music and similar material, to draw out of it some idea or other, paying no heed to the philosopher, at whom they rudely laugh.

In *Il corsaro*, Verdi, while always a true artist, acted no differently from imitators. True, he imitated mostly himself—but did it to such an extent that

3. The ophicleide is a family of brass instruments whose use peaked in orchestras of the second quarter of the nineteenth century. In modern performances, its part can be realized by a bass trombone.

4. The quotation is from a poem dedicated to music by the seventeenth-century artist and poet Salvator Rosa ("Satira prima: La musica," lines 241–43). The allusion to the birth of music from hammers is a reference to Pythagoras (sixth–fifth century BCE), who was credited by Boethius with having discovered the numerical laws of consonance by observing the relationship between the weights of blacksmiths' hammers and the intervals between the pitches they produced. See *De institutione musica*, 1.10. Basevi mistakenly has "più molesti" in the first line.

he was no longer Verdi. On the other hand, it must not be denied that this libretto is totally incapable of stirring a dormant imagination, let alone firing it into life.

Piave took the plot of *Il corsaro* from a short poem by Byron of the same title.[5] This choice was certainly no better than Maffei's with *I masnadieri*. Corrado the corsair much resembles Carlo Moor. Though gentle by nature, both become cruel beyond measure after great suffering caused by the injustice and evil of men; and both become bandits, one on the sea and the other on the land, in order to vent the hatred they have conceived for all of human society.

Poetry, so capable of penetrating the deepest corners of the human heart, succeeds in making some characters less odious than they might seem at first, but music paints with broader brushstrokes and is incapable of the precision needed to follow the poetry. Being the great librettist that he was, Felice Romani had the skill in a similar case to avoid the rocks on which Maffei and Piave foundered. In *Il pirata* by the lauded Romani, note how Gualtiero's abominable profession is judiciously placed in shadow, so that it is barely discernible. The poet has rather brought to the foreground the unhappy lover, who, after dangerous trials, recovers his beloved Imogene, the wife of his enemy. The torments of that enamored spirit, his furies, his vengeance, and his sad end, move and arouse the sympathy of the spectator to the point that he completely discounts the fact that the unfortunate Gualtiero is a pirate.

As we have said, the music of *Il corsaro* was condemned by its own author; this will not prevent us from passing it briefly in review.

After a very poor *preludio* containing a theme from the final *terzetto*,[6] act 1 opens with an unaccompanied chorus in 6/8 time that tries unsuccessfully to attain a fine, pleasing quality through the use of chiaroscuro.[7] The andante of the tenor's aria, also in 6/8 , gives us an old rhythm with triplet accompaniment whose melody smacks somewhat of *I Lombardi*, but that seems rather out of place here. The instrumentation is rich where the first period of the andante is repeated in the orchestra while the voice proceeds as though in a *parlante*.[8] Although without the least scent of the new, the cabaletta has energy ["Sì: de' Corsari il fulmine"]; to give it greater power, Verdi presses into service the old ploy of having the chorus repeat in unison one of the phrases of the solo.

5. Byron's verse narrative *The Corsaire* was first published in 1814.
6. Compare N. 1, Preludio, mm. 34ff., with N. 13, Finale ultimo, mm. 181ff.
7. N. 2, Coro ("Come liberi volano i venti"), Scena ("Ah sì, ben dite . . ."), ed Aria Corrado ("Tutto parea sorridere").
8. Measures 124ff.

The *romanza* for the soprano, Medora, also in ⁶⁄₈, is very sad and lovely, and is one of the few pieces that truly appear to have been mined from the vein of the master.⁹ In the *mossa*, the unexpected transition from the chord of C minor, which dominates the first measure, to the A-flat major found in the second measure accords well with Medora's distress at how far away her lover is. A soprano-tenor duet follows.¹⁰ The soprano's part in the andante mosso contains rhythmic novelty, but its melody is overly labored and mannered; in the meno mosso, the tenor responds with a different melody, and then the two parts continue together even more slowly, alluding in the major mode to the theme earlier sung in the minor by the tenor. There is no allure in this section. In the ⁶⁄₈ allegro ["Tornerai, ma forse spenta"], Verdi makes use, to rather good effect, of *sotto voce* and, in the reprise of the melody, an accompaniment in the violins' upper register.

A chorus of odalisques opens the second act; it is a brillante assai in ⁶⁄₈ time.¹¹ The ⁶⁄₈ "empty" triplet [*terzine vuote*] andantino of the cavatina for the soprano (Gulnara) is heavy, and even a certain ornate passage in its accompaniment cannot rouse the listener.¹² While built on an extremely trite idea, the cabaletta ["Ah conforto è sol la speme"] is not unpleasant. After an inconclusive chorus, the bass sings a majestic hymn that calls to mind many of Verdi's less good pieces;¹³ here too the unison chorus repeats after the bass a phrase from his hymn. It is not worth detaining ourselves with the ensuing *duettino* for tenor and baritone,¹⁴ or with the vocal-instrumental hash that is meant to express the confusion caused by the pirate attack—and that does so all too well.¹⁵ The quartet of the second finale opens with a ¾-time andante in which the bass has a truly decrepit vocal line of rare uniformity ["Audace cotanto mostrarti pur sai?"]: the same figure appears in fourteen consecutive

---

9. N. 3, Romanza Medora ("Egli non riede ancora!"; "Non so le tetre immagini").

10. N. 4, Scena ("È pur tristo, o Medora, il canto tuo!") e Duetto Medora e Corrado ("No, tu non sai comprendere").

11. N. 5, Coro ("Oh qual perenne gaudio t'aspetta"). The tempo marking is simply "Allegro" in Verdi's autograph.

12. See N. 6, Cavatina Gulnara ("Né sulla terra creatura alcuna"; "Vola talor dal carcere"), mm. 33ff.

13. N. 7, Coro ("Sol grida di feste") ed Inno ("Salve, Allah! . . . tutta quanta la terra"). The "basso" is Seid, who is rather a baritone: as in other cases, Basevi's vocal designations are relatively flexible (Seid will be called "baritono" in the description of N. 8 and then again "basso" in the discussions of NN. 9, 10, and 11).

14. N. 8, Recitativo ("Giunge un Dervis fuggito alle catene") e Duettino [Corrado e Seid] ("Dì: que' ribaldi tremano").

15. The passage opens N. 9, Finale atto secondo ("Ma qual luce diffondesi intorno?").

measures. As though that were not enough, the tenor then regales us with twelve measures more of the same—though at least not twelve measures in succession. Rhythmic uniformity is sometimes required in the interests of expression, notably where the subject is profound terror; we see this in Rossini's *Semiramide* at "Qual mesto gemito." It is also suitable for rebuke and penitence, but only at solemn moments such as "Qual cor tradisti" in Bellini's *Norma*.[16] The ensemble section ["È demone o nume"] begins with a broad phrase of four measures' length, à la Verdi; when this has been repeated, the various voices share the first eight measures of the tenor's melody. Then, a sequence and a brief crescendo lead to a fortissimo followed by a diminuendo—and this happens twice in the same way; the section finally ends with a brief cadential passage. When used sensibly, such sequences, crescendos, and diminuendos will never fail to stir an audience strongly, on account of the effect I have elsewhere labeled "of anticipation" [*ansietà*].

The third act begins with the bass aria.[17] The 6/8 andantino, with empty triplets, employs a very heavy[18] rhythm—which becomes no lighter when it moves from the vocal to the instrumental part. The cabaletta ["S'avvicina il tuo momento"], with its weak-beat accents, recalls *Attila*—and we are none the happier for this. After a long *parlante* and obbligato recitative, the duet for soprano (Gulnara) and bass[19] contains an allegro in which the soprano responds with a pianissimo to the bass's fortissimo—but more than that would be required to enliven this piece! The soprano then sings a duet with the tenor;[20] its first andante mosso includes a sung dialogue of the kind that in general should be preferred to *parlanti*, particularly in serious operas. There is nothing of note in the next andante mosso ["Non sai tu che sulla testa"], which forms a sort of "middle cabaletta." Then this extremely long duet has

16. See the concertato ("Qual mesto gemito," mm. 414ff.) of *Semiramide*'s N. 7, Finale primo ("Ergi omai la fronte altera"), and the concertato "Qual cor tradisti, qual cor perdesti," part of *Norma*'s N. 8, Finale dell'atto secondo. In the two passages, the rhythmic obsessiveness is found both in the vocal parts and in instrumental ostinatos.

17. N. 10, Recitativo ("Alfin questo Corsaro è mio prigione!") ed Aria Seid ("Cento leggiadre vergini").

18. The 1859 print here reads "gradevole" (pleasant), probably the result of a typographer's misreading of "gravoso" (heavy): that Basevi intended the latter is suggested both by his original wording in the article on which this chapter is based ("uno dei soliti ritmi gravosissimi" [one of the usual very heavy rhythms]: Piovano, 221) and by his continuation here ("non acquista maggior leggerezza").

19. N. 11, Duetto Gulnara e Seid ("Eccola! fingasi!"; "Sia l'istante maledetto").

20. N. 12, Scena ("Eccomi prigioniero!") e Duetto [Gulnara e Corrado] ("Seid la vuole: inutili").

a bit of storm music, and finally an allegro ["La terra, il ciel m'abborrino"] that serves as the true cabaletta—not one of the worst in this score.[21] The final *terzetto*[22] is without doubt the most praiseworthy piece in the opera— particularly from its D-flat andante ["O mio Corrado, appressati"], for the ¾-time allegro that precedes it ["Per me infelice"] would be more apt as a waltz than as an expression of the piteous words with which it is associated.[23] In the remainder of this piece we find that majestic manner of Verdi's that, when coupled as in this case to an important situation, produces a strong im- pression. In the twenty-ninth and thirtieth measures of the andante is a lovely passage on the words "pietà, perdon da Dio, etc.," where the soprano melody contains very effective counteraccentuation. Verdi later availed himself of the same idea in the soprano-baritone duet in act 2 of *Rigoletto*.[24]

To compensate for this opera's lack of vitality, Verdi had recourse to the artificial brio that comes from quick tempos in short measures. No adagio is to be found in twenty-two of the most prominent pieces. Common time is found only eight times and ⁶⁄₈ seven times. I do not mean to reprove Verdi for using one meter or tempo rather than another, but I think it useful to note this fact because it seems to me not to accord with his grave yet impetuous talents. His virtue of conciseness resides not so much in brevity of the measure or of the phrase as in his banishment, for the most part, of the clichés that once stuffed scores without a reason in the world.

A great lesson we must learn from study of this score is that we need to be more cautious about basing our assessment of a composer's creative pow- ers on only some of his work. After *Il corsaro*, who would not have believed Verdi's vein to have been exhausted? And who would have thought that af- ter one more unfortunate essay he would acquire still greater vigor and write masterpieces surpassing everything he had done before? This is an important lesson for all who have the advancement of art at heart: they must not be too hasty in condemning the numerous composers who in their first few flights suffer as many falls. Woe to Verdi if this lapse of inspiration had occurred at the very beginning of his road—and woe too to Italy, which today would not be able to boast this great genius!

---

21. At 402 measures, N. 12 is indeed an "extremely long duet"—and one whose unusual, dramatically pliable shape understandably puzzled Basevi the formalist.

22. N. 13, Finale ultimo ("Voi tacete . . . io non oso").

23. The section is in fact an allegretto assai moderato.

24. Compare mm. 208–9 of this N. 13 with *Rigoletto*, N. 10, Scena ("Mio padre!") e Duetto [Gilda e Rigoletto] ("Tutte le feste al tempio"), mm. 153ff.

12

LA BATTAGLIA DI LEGNANO

Political passions were running high in Italy, and everything was colored by them, when Verdi turned his hand to the political opera *La battaglia di Legnano*.

Music and politics have always had the closest of relations, a fact that did not escape the acute gaze of the ancient Greek philosophers. Indeed, if we consider spontaneous national movements, we will see that they grow out of a nation's mode of feeling—nor could it be otherwise. Now, if music is the freest manifestation of modes of feeling—that is, of inclinations and dispositions toward some passion or emotion—it is clear that in this sense it can be viewed as symbolizing and representing the political vicissitudes of a people, or even of civilization, as is true of philosophy with respect to modes of thinking; for music is concerned with human emotions in the same way that philosophy is concerned with the mind. It is because of this that Plato, Aristotle, and other great philosophers rightly viewed music as an art of the greatest importance to the education of the heart.

The limits of this study do not allow us time for a proper treatment of this theme, so we will confine ourselves to sketching in a few lines the historical course of music, so that its connection with the development of the human spirit may be easily discerned.

For the sake of reasonable brevity we shall begin in the Middle Ages—when, with the decline of Latin, new forms of language arose, and when the construction of a new civilization slowly began on the ruins of the old pagan culture.

Though opposed in its first steps by tremendous persecution, Christianity survived through faith and constancy, and developed such vigor that it turned and assaulted paganism head on, wiping it out until only its memory remained. The first centuries of the new belief passed in darkness, and the rough, barbarous, ignorant populace knew no discipline save that of faith. Thus were the sciences, letters, and arts buried; something resembling light gleamed only in a few ecclesiastics. The need to ally music to prayer spurred Saint Ambrose in the fourth century, and Saint Gregory in the sixth, to regulate ecclesiastical chant, which remained unaltered until the eleventh century, a time of no little splendor for Italy owing to the musical method discovered by Guido.[1] Thus, music was at first a reflection of the daring faith of Christianity's first centuries.

Having sung the praises of God, music sought to sing those of heroes, and to express love in dulcet tones. But this required poetry, and hence a certain linguistic cultivation—indeed, a greater gentility of spirit. The Provençaux, the first to perfect language, fostered the rise of the numerous poet-singers, the troubadours, who traveled to the most distant lands to inspire love for poetry and for chivalrous deeds. This had no little effect on the refinement of manners. The role of the troubadours became redundant when their disciples surpassed their masters. This occurred especially in Italy with the appearance of the *Divine Comedy*. After such a poem, mankind had no further need for the troubadours, who gradually declined, fell out of favor, and were eventually ousted from all parts toward the end of the fourteenth century after two hundred years of splendor. Music, which by its association with the poetry of the troubadours had depicted the generous and tender emotions that were reawakening in mankind, took on another form when that poetry deteriorated, and did so in accordance with the new order of human society.

As customs grow more refined, a need is soon felt for certain comforts of life, of which people take little or no heed in a state of barbarism. Some

1. Though Ambrose, bishop of Milan, was active as a composer and musical innovator, his reputation as the originator of the tradition named after him (Ambrosian chant) is largely legendary. Even more conjectural is the role of Pope Gregory I (Gregory the Great) in the development of so-called Gregorian chant. The music theorist Guido of Arezzo (early eleventh century) was largely credited with the invention of the solmization syllables (*ut re mi fa sol la*).

of these must be procured from distant lands, while others must be manu-factured; hence, trade and industry developed to satisfy the new needs. The location of certain Italian cities, combined with the energies of their inhabit-ants, very soon resulted in the rise of a number of trading centers. The peoples of Venice, Genoa, and Pisa may be compared to the ancient Phoenicians and Carthaginians. After the Arabs the Italians held supremacy on the seas, and retained it until the discovery of a new route to the East Indies via the Cape of Good Hope. In the fourteenth century, trade so flourished and industry so prospered in many Italian cities that sumptuary laws were enacted to temper the unrestrained luxury born of immoderate wealth. Meanwhile, in northern Europe, the hardworking, thrifty, determined, and united Flemish people also flourished in trade and industry. Ghent and Bruges corresponded in the north to what Venice and Genoa were in the south of Europe.

Music partook of this spirit of industry and itself grew industrious through the craft of bringing several melodic parts together in accordance with the rules of harmony. The patience and perseverance of the Flemish gave them the palm of having been the first to perfect this skillful kind of music. Such music depicts a society whose members, while following different roads and inhabiting different places, work with the greatest accord toward the same ends. That was the picture more of the Flemish than of the Italians; this may be why the Italians achieved excellence in counterpoint not only after the Flemish but after the Germans and the French as well.

This "industrious" music began to be corrupted by its own excesses, for it gave utmost priority to a grand display of subtle and very studied contrapuntal artifice. Music penetrated the church with these defects, to the detriment of the devotions of the faithful. Thus many clerics, in the spirit of the Council of Trent, were of the opinion that music should be banned from churches, or—which amounted to the same thing—that it should be stripped of its en-tire backbone. Then, with the composition of his celebrated *Pope Marcellus Mass*, Palestrina made it obvious that, without jettisoning its latest develop-ments, music was fit for association with sacred rites, which would gain, not lose, in majesty. Thanks to Palestrina, Italy regained supremacy in the fine art of sound, and from then on was rich in excellent musicians. It was for Italy, which had gained such splendor from Catholicism, to find in music a forceful new argument for an embattled religion.[2]

2. The battle in question is that of Reformation and Counter-Reformation. The Mass mentioned by Basevi is Palestrina's *Missa Papae Marcelli* (published in 1567), which according

The age of religious battles was succeeded by that of philosophy, which, in conformity with the courses charted respectively by Locke and by Kant, split into two branches that were opposite from one another in many ways. At first, the sensualism of Locke found capable supporters in France, among whom must be mentioned Condillac, who drew the ultimate conclusions from that system. Kant, on the other hand, considered sensations as *matter* that lacked *form*,[3] which he assumed to be innate to the human mind. Fichte then took Kantian philosophy to the point of negating matter altogether and admitting nothing but the *I*. Condillac and Fichte are direct opposites—as France and Germany were around that time. Music too took its outlook from philosophy. Gluck, though German by birth and Italian by musical education, found fertile ground in France for his philosophical reform of theatrical music. This reform consisted of relating everything to poetry, just as, for Condillac, everything was related to the senses. In Germany, on the other hand, music followed idealism, that is, a path independent of "matter"—which, in opera, is poetry. This led to a perfection that was limited to instrumental music. Haydn began this reform, which Beethoven took so far as to create a musical form of *transcendentalism*.

While not yet having entered a new period, music in Italy, without so to speak leaving the wider orbit of philosophical music,[4] has nonetheless covered a more limited trajectory: a reflection of the historical progress of the general mode of feeling.

If we are to follow this trajectory as far as Verdi, the subject of our discussion, we must begin with Rossini.

That great genius began to shine at a time when, weary of the Napoleonic wars, Italy—and Europe—earnestly desired peace. The nature of Rossini's

---

to legend rescued the use of polyphony from a possible ban by the Catholic Church; the legend emerged in the early seventeenth century, and—as testified by Basevi's account—survived well into the nineteenth. It is in any case true that generations of musicians regarded Palestrina as a paragon of contrapuntal writing and his settings as models of balance between musical quality and intelligibility of the words (the latter being an important post-Tridentine concern). Verdi himself revered Palestrina as the "Eternal Father" of Italian music (see his letter of November 15, 1891, *Copialettere*, 373).

3. As elsewhere, Basevi italicizes some words in this paragraph in order to emphasize their specialized use, here as technical terms from philosophy: *materia*, *forma*, *l'io* (Fichte's *das Ich*), *trascendentalismo*.

4. In the few decades that led to the time of Basevi's *Studio*, Italians had come to use *musica filosofica* largely to designate music that is inflected, stretched even, so as to follow closely the

genius is at once one of war and one of peace: of war in the profound impressions that events left on the memory; of peace in the inclinations of the heart. Rossini's music is as unconstrained, frank, open, vehement, and enthusiastic as a soldier, while at the same time as carefree, pleasant, happy, and sensual as an epicurean. With good reason might Rossini be said to have represented his time.

But the calmer minds soon began to seek new emotions—naturally inclined to movement as they are. The majority inclined toward tender and melancholy affections, to which the music of Rossini was not well suited. Then Bellini arrived on the scene and quickly rose to dominance. But his reign was of no long duration, for untimely death cut off this brilliant enchanter. Donizetti remained, but, too eclectic, never truly held the scepter. Verdi was more fortunate.

Verdi may be viewed as the opposite pole to Rossini in the same way that the times of one are the reverse of those of the other. Rossini won admiration when a period of turmoil was yielding to one of peace and tranquility, whereas Verdi arrived when the peoples [of Europe], surfeited by the quiet life, were preparing to venture onto the turbulent seas of civil unrest. If compared with Rossini's, Verdi's genius is similarly seen to be as frank, unconstrained, and vehement as a soldier, but it differs in that it is also as brusque, disdainful, irritable, sad, and manic as a hypochondriac.

It would be a grave error to conclude from our discussion that the music of Rossini and Bellini is no longer of any value because it is no longer in vogue. Thank God, music is not so founded on fashion that it must follow all its fortunes. And if, owing merely to changes in general attitudes, it no longer has the same effect, it will still not be forgotten by artists or by anyone else who cares about the progress of art, as long as it contains passages that are to be valued for their expressive truth.

The title of representative of the musical taste of his time is well suited to Verdi, who has reigned alone in Italy since 1842. As such he was bound to write an opera corresponding to the new general mood in 1848. He did so, and had no reason to reprove himself as Grétry had done when—seeing his musical scepter seized by Méhul and Cherubini, who were better suited to the new mode of feeling during the French Revolution—he wrote in his *Essais*,

---

meanings of words and drama—usually by contrast with the more abstract quality of the "ideal music" associated with the Italian vocal tradition (increasingly referred to as "bel canto").

"I am in effect pale and feeble by comparison with the revolutionary music of our times."[5]

Italy's troubles were coming to a head when *La battaglia di Legnano* was staged at Rome in January 1849.[6]

Cammarano, who wrote the libretto, made clever use of the Italians' most splendid military feat.[7] Yet this subject did not engage him enough to stop him from abandoning it frequently in favor of an episode of love and jealousy that was remote from the central plot.

The opera was well received in Rome, but was less successful elsewhere.

The *sinfonia* is a fine piece; it might be compared with that of *Nabucodonosor*, though it does not surpass it technically.[8] After a martial theme elaborated in several ways, we come to an andante espressivo handled with equal ingenuity. This is followed by an allegro, which, after hinting at that first martial theme, develops into a sparkling melody that is then presented in different form and with different accompaniment; it finally reappears with the martial theme, to which it serves as a counterpoint.

The first chorus[9] is unaccompanied, and employs the martial theme from the *sinfonia*. It is perhaps too symmetrical and uniform, and therefore corresponds little with warlike impetuosity. The tenor's cavatina ["La pia materna mano"] is an andante similar to many others by Verdi. The *romanza* for the baritone ["Ah! m'abbraccia . . . d'esultanza"] has an allegro theme whose first phrase is made up of notes of equal value; such simplicity of rhythm would have required the compensation of a more appealing melody. The oath ["Tutti giuriam difenderla"], at its most important point, gives us a trite

5. See André-Ernest-Modeste Grétry, *Mémoires; ou, Essais sur la musique* (1789), 2nd ed., 3 vols. (Paris: Imprimerie de la République, Pluviôse, an V [1797]), 2:81 ("je suis pâle et foible, matériellement, auprès de la musique révolutionnaire de nos jours").

6. The venue of the premiere was the Teatro Argentina.

7. Cammarano grafted onto the narrative of a French drama (Joseph Méry's *La Bataille de Toulouse*, 1828) the historical event of the battle of Legnano of 1176, in which the imperial forces of Frederick I Barbarossa were defeated by the Lombard League, an alliance of cities from northern Italy that was backed by the pope. Basevi refers to the Lombard League plainly as "the Italians" (as does Cammarano's libretto, more or less explicitly), and indeed the battle of Legnano had long enjoyed iconic status in the national imagination. A couple of years before Verdi's opera Goffredo Mameli's text for *Il canto degli italiani* (1847)—later to become Italy's national anthem—mentioned Legnano as one of the crucial moments in Italy's centuries-old struggle against foreign domination.

8. N. 1, Sinfonia. The segmentation into pieces and their numbering are largely based on Martin Chusid, *A Catalog of Verdi's Operas* (Hackensack, NJ: J. Boonin, [1974]).

9. N. 2, Introduzione ("Viva Italia! Sacro un patto").

unison sequence with fifteen measures of uniform rhythm ["Domandan vendetta"], depending entirely on a *crescendo poco a poco* for any effect. This rep-
etitiousness is among the least desirable of things. Evidently, Verdi wanted
this sequence to imitate the effect of the magnificent one in the first finale of
Rossini's *Mosè*, at the words "Dio così stermina."[10] But he did not succeed,
because, though ascending, this sequence does not move with the quickness
and energy of the descending one from *Mosè*. After a very mediocre chorus
of maidens, the soprano's cavatina follows.[11] The andante's first melodic period is cast in a single sweep [*di un sol getto*]. For the rest, the form is among
the simplest and most common. A certain refinement is to be noted in the
accompaniment, where the musical accent falls on the second fourth of the
measure, that is, on a weak beat. The cabaletta ["A frenarti, o cor, nel petto"]
has a certain brio but nothing else. The duet for soprano and tenor that closes
act 1 is not without a certain dramatic sense.[12] Moreover, the form of the piece
is out of the ordinary. Note the tenor's phrase "T'amai, t'amai qual angelo,"
which is five measures long, that is, asymmetrical. The soprano's answer is
fashioned in the same way.[13]

The chorus that opens the second act does not stand out;[14] nor does the *duettino* for tenor and baritone. In the quartet that concludes the act, the stretta
["Il destino d'Italia son io!"] is finer than the adagio, being more appropriate
to the situation. Though its meter is ¾, its rhythm still reveals its membership
of that great family of strettas descended from the famous one by Rossini, in
the quartet from his *Bianca e Falliero*.[15]

10. See mm. 526ff. of N. 5, Finale [primo] ("All'etra, al ciel"), in *Mosè in Egitto*, ed. Charles
S. Brauner, *EC* I/24 (2004). Basevi, however, may have derived this reference from the score
of *Mosè* (the Italian translation of the French revision *Moïse et Pharaon*), in which this piece is
unchanged. See chapter 1, n. 6, above.

11. N. 3, Coro ("Plaude all'arrivo Milan dei forti"), Scena ("Voi lo diceste, amiche"), e
Cavatina Lida ("Quante volte come un dono").

12. N.4, Scena ("Sposa . . .") / "Oh momento!") e Duetto [Lida e Arrigo] ("È ver? Sei
d'altri? . . .").

13. Basevi might seem to imply here that the formal peculiarity of the duet consists in this
phraseological irregularity alone. But the piece is "out of the ordinary" in other respects, Basevi
himself explaining in the article from which this chapter is derived that it "adopts, in place of
the customary subdivision into adagio and allegro, a single movement" (*L'armonia*, January 15,
1858; see Piovano, 152 n. 243).

14. The second act is entirely occupied by a single number: N. 5, Coro ("Udiste? La
grande"; "Sì, tardi ed invano"), Scena ("Invia la baldanzosa"), Duetto [Arrigo e Rolando]
("Ben vi scorgo"), e Finale atto secondo ("A che smarriti e pallidi").

15. See mm. 238ff. of N. 10, Recitativo ("Donna chi sei?") e Quartetto ("Cielo, il mio labbro ispira"), in *Bianca e Falliero, o sia Il consiglio dei tre*, ed. Gabriele Dotto, *EC* I/30 (1996).

The introduction and oath scene in act 3 are not without merit.[16] The moment when the Knights of Death, descending into the crypt of the church of Saint Ambrose, join together to pronounce their agreed oath is well rendered. But the oath itself is inflated and mannered. In *Guillaume Tell*, Rossini treated a similar situation and created a masterwork. There you feel the fire that glowed in the breasts of the Parisians—and that, a few months after the Paris performance of *Guillaume Tell*, erupted terribly in those three days of July 1830.[17] The *duettino* for soprano and baritone[18] is exceptionally expressive, particularly in the baritone's part at the words "e dopo Dio la patria," a passage that imitates another very moving one—Julia's final aria in Spontini's *La vestale* at the words "Tout mon crime fut de t'aimer."[19] After fifty-one years this kind of expression is still effective! When truth is attained, neither the force of time nor the caprice of man can destroy the achievements of art. In the andante of the baritone's aria[20] we note an initial melodic period of nine measures, or "lame" [*zoppo*], which in no way damages the dramatic effect but in fact increases it. The cabaletta ["Ahi! scellerate alme d'inferno"] is ordinary at its beginning, and only in the last few cadential measures shows something of the adventurous.[21] In the final *terzetto* of this act[22] the allegro agitato is good, and suits Rolando's circumstances: he is furious at having surprised his wife Lida with Arrigo, whom he assumes to be her lover. This piece contains well-conceived six-measure phrases, which shows that it is not necessary to use two-, four-, or eight-measure phrases to construct a melodic discourse. The baritone's music continues to be apt in the andante mosso ["Vendetta d'un momento"]. But the final scene of the third act is not well painted by the music, even though it offered the composer a fine situation:

16. N. 6, [Introduzione] ("Fra queste dense tenebre"), Recitativo ("Campioni della Morte"), e Giuramento ("Giuriam d'Italia por fine ai danni").

17. See the oath "Jurons, jurons par nos dangers," mm. 337ff. of N. 12, Final 2ᵉ ("Des profondeurs du bois immense"), of *Guillaume Tell*. Basevi had already referred to the July Revolution of 1830 (see chapter 3 above), relating it—with a rather greater ring of truth—to Hugo's preface to *Hernani*.

18. N. 7, Scena ("Lida, Lida? . . . Ove corri?") e Duetto [Lida e Rolando] ("Digli ch'è sangue italico"). The "Duettino" found in Ricordi scores is the customary designation for one-movement duets such as this.

19. See mm. 7ff. of Air N. 20 ("Toi que je laisse sur la terre mortel") from *La vestale*, *ERO* 42 (1979), 415.

20. N. 8, Scena ("Tu m'appellasti . . .") ed Aria Rolando ("Se al nuovo dì pugnando").

21. This stretta may be "ordinary" in its melodic profile, but it is not in its overall shape, presenting the cabaletta period only once.

22. N. 9, Scena ("Regna la notte ancor") [e] Terzetto finale ("Ah! d'un consorte, o perfidi").

locked in the tower by a vengeful Rolando, Arrigo hears the summons of the Knights of Death, and to avoid the disgrace he would incur by not answering their call he hurls himself from the balcony, leaving Lida, who has been locked up with him, in the greatest desolation.

In the introduction to the fourth act, there is a well-thought-out combination of some offstage sacred singing, a soprano solo, and an onstage chorus.[23] The hymn of victory is too conventional.[24] The final *terzetto* ["Per la salvata Italia . . ."] is without doubt the best piece in the opera and may be counted among the finest fruits of Verdi's genius. Here Verdi shows that his music is better able to express the nobility of spirit of one who dies for his country, as in this piece, than the enthusiasm of those who dash en masse to free it.

23. N. 10, Preghiera ("Deus meus, pone illos"; "O tu che desti il fulmine"). The offstage chorus of basses in unison—representing a group of monks singing plainchant—intones a portion of a Latin version of Psalm 82 (Canticum Psalmi Asaph, "Deus quis similis erit tibi"), from verse 14 ("Deus meus pone illos ut rotam") to verse 17 ("[. . .] et quaerent nomen tuum Domine"), omitting only the opening words of verse 15 ("Sicut ignis qui comburit silvam").

24. The hymn "Dall'Alpi a Cariddi" is already part of N. 11, Finale ultimo ("Vittoria! vittoria!").

13

LUISA MILLER

The peoples that rose up in 1848—when, as if driven by a common ideal, they struggled to build new orders—appeared to be armed with that faith without which any edifice must crumble to dust. But alas, how quickly illusion dissolved when ideals were forged into deeds! Although dashed to pieces, the previous orders, strengthened by experience and practice, showed signs of greater life and sturdiness than the innovations that had everywhere been introduced with such momentum. But the people were not calmed by the restoration of the status quo ante. The unrest that persisted marked a substantial difference between the restoration of 1814 and that of 1849. Hence, it was not to be expected that there would be a notable change in the music in vogue, as there had been in the earlier case. A closer examination of this unrest reveals that it differed somewhat from that which had preceded the earlier upheaval. Earlier it had been accompanied by enthusiasm and the highest of hopes, whereas later it was nourished by disillusionment, fear, pessimism, resentment, and rancor. Skepticism waxed powerful, and materialism, its shadow, followed close behind. This was not a time when genteel methods could rouse spirits in this new mood; because of the preeminence of the senses over the mind and heart, physical pleasure had to take central place. Thus, the music bound to be most welcome was that which elicits strong emotions while at the same time pleasing the senses. Verdi's time, then, was not past; he had nothing to fear from a new Bellini, who would have been more in tune with the needs of tranquil spirits.

Verdi's talent nonetheless underwent certain changes that made it better suited to the new period. The exaggeration that had been so often condemned in his music came to be much tempered. Almost instinctively, Verdi realized that, if recent events had not calmed emotions, they had at least restrained them; people were not so vigorous in their feelings, and the violent methods so much used before were therefore no longer appropriate. This new, collective mode of feeling became ingrained in Verdi and gave his music a new quality, one so well defined and distinct that it constitutes a "second manner."

It would not be pointless to compare briefly the first and second manners; from this, the reader may derive some light by which better to study and understand Verdi's music.

In the first manner, the majestic predominated, attesting to the influence of the late works of Rossini. But alongside the majestic was the passionate, which dominated the music of this period to no less a degree. If considered in isolation, this passionate side seems flawed in its exaggeration, but looking at it together with the majestic music that surrounds it, we see that such exaggeration is used to maintain a certain balance, and as a counterweight to the majesty. It is important to note that by its very nature the majestic destroys, so to speak, anything individual or personal, making it collective; thus, though majestic music may be sung by a single character, it strikes the listener as though it were the expression of a nation, a caste, or an order of people. For this reason, to keep it in due proportion to the majestic, passion came to be greatly exaggerated, as though it were being expressed not by one person but by many. In Rossini's *Guillaume Tell* too, which contains passionate passages such as those in the trio and in Tell's third-act aria, passion is expressed with a certain exaggeration.[1] Without this exaggeration the majestic elements would, in a sense, suffocate the passionate ones. Verdi manifests this exaggeration mostly in those melodic periods I have labeled "di slancio." Another such sort of exaggeration is found in the sonority effects [*effetti di sonorità*], already in fashion at the time of Verdi's emergence. The trumpet had only recently become virtual mistress of the orchestra, having been enhanced first by keys and then by valves, and thus being able to play any note with ease. Composers

---

1. These are passages from *Guillaume Tell* that Basevi has already cited as examples of forceful, passionate singing: the Trio (see pp. 40 and 44 above).

vied with one another to pay it court by writing solos for it, by giving it frequent prominence in their works, and even by making it the companion of the voice, which it reinforced. Through their association with the trumpet, all the brass instruments grew in importance in the orchestra, so much so that the poor violin, the legitimate king, was all but completely banished. Indeed, Verdi himself made no little use of the ennobled trumpet. In his first manner, the melodies are often broad and grave and lend themselves to being sung by different voices, as though wanting to show that they belong to more than one character.

In the second manner, the majestic diminishes or disappears altogether, and each character represents no one other than himself. Passion, now individualized, no longer requires such exaggeration, and so the singing, though impassioned, proceeds with greater tranquility. The melodies are lighter and less broad; the rhythms are more varied and open; the themes are in general more catchy and trite. In the second manner, the greater need to caress the ear sees the revival of the *parlanti*, which Verdi had seemed to oust, so little are they used in his first manner. Sonority effects [*effetti di sonorità*] are employed much less frequently and, in the main, opportunely.

The difference between the two manners must not be thought so absolute that a characteristic of one may never be found in the other. Certainly not; in the operas of the first manner we see the germs of the second, just as in the second we find traces of the first; and other operas may be considered transitional. Then again all Verdi's operas have points of analogy, which together make up the Verdian style proper and are the expression of his genius.[2]

With his second manner, Verdi came closer to Donizetti. The difference between the two is found mostly in the fact that the more passionate Verdi more often strives to agitate and stir the listener, while Donizetti nearly always seeks simply to give pleasure.

Luisa Miller is the first opera that truly marks the beginning of Verdi's new manner.[3] It was first performed at Naples in December 1849, with the greatest success.[4]

2. The view by which *Luisa Miller* would open a new manner in Verdi is one that Basevi variously shares with commentators of his and later times—and one for which he has often been mentioned. But one should equally bear in mind the subtler shading of that distinction and the elements of continuity that Basevi himself points to in this paragraph.

3. The critical edition of *Luisa Miller*, by Jeffrey Kallberg, was published as *WGV* I/15 (1991).

4. The venue was the Teatro San Carlo, and the reception was rather less enthusiastic than asserted by Basevi (or even by more recent commentators). See Kallberg's introduction to *WGV* I/15, esp. xxiv–xxv.

The librettist, Cammarano, took his subject from Schiller's drama *Kabale und Liebe*.[5] This play is not counted among the author's best, for while it shows the great vigor of the poet, it also reveals the inexperience of the man; in this it stands together with that other youthful work, *Die Räuber*.[6] We nonetheless find in it violent passions that will stir even the most casual listener. And truly, who could be more monstrous than the blindly ambitious Walter, who threatens to kill Luisa's parents unless she swears not only to conceal her love for his son but also to feign love for another?[7] Verdi took advantage of the strong passions that are the pivot of this drama. And since audiences were no longer able to relish enthusiasm, characters who derived no obvious prestige from an ancient story, high station, or the consequences of their actions were not considered unseemly. For that reason this tragedy is referred to as "bourgeois"—what we would call "domestic."[8] Cammarano, however, did not tie himself strictly to his model. For example, Schiller had made Luisa's father a musician, but in the opera he is an old soldier. Perhaps this change, which gave the character greater energy, was more suited to Verdi's way of feeling.[9]

Turning to the music, note that the *sinfonia*[10] is based almost entirely on a single musical idea, which in a different meter will be used as accompaniment to the introductory chorus of act 3. This theme, first articulated in the minor mode by the violins, next becomes the object of imitations and sequences. It is then developed in the major mode by the clarinet and, after further imitations in various keys, is played twice, first by solo flute, oboe, and clarinet, then fortissimo with violin reinforcement until the cadence. Other musical ideas are present as episodes or interludes, but these are secondary. This overture

5. The play, labeled by Schiller "ein bürgerliches Trauerspiel" (a bourgeois tragedy), had first appeared, on stage and in print, in 1784.

6. As we have seen, *Die Räuber* was the source for Verdi's *I masnadieri*.

7. In the opera it is only Miller, Luisa's father, whose life is threatened.

8. Basevi uses "borghese" to translate the "bürgerlich" in Schiller's subtitle, and explains the genre with the widely used Italian expression "tragedia domestica." Schiller's play was influenced by eighteenth-century experiments in "bourgeois" tragedy—tragedy about the private lives of ordinary people in a contemporary setting. This would have been seen as unseemly by the classicist standards of tragedy in much of Europe—which, as Basevi hints, called for ancient settings and aristocratic characters whose deeds might inspire in the spectator an "entusiasmo" discordant with the mood of 1849. Whether *Luisa Miller* qualifies as a bourgeois tragedy in music depends on one's definition of the genre: its setting, at least two centuries old for the spectator of Verdi's time, could hardly be perceived as contemporary.

9. In a letter to Verdi, Cammarano indeed says that turning Miller into an ex-soldier would endow him with "some energetic impetus" ("qualche energico slancio"): Naples, June 4, 1849 (*Copialettere*, 472).

10. N. 1, Sinfonia.

model is rare in Italy, but examples are found in the works of musicians north of the Alps. The finest example of an overture on a single idea, in this case in the guise of a free fugue, is that of *Die Zauberflöte* by the great Mozart: a four-measure subject serves as theme from beginning to end of this miraculous piece. It is presented many times in the course of that overture: now in a similar form, now in imitation, now in stretto, now in question-and-answer, sometimes in one key, sometimes in another, and always employed so well that, rather than becoming dull, it returns ever more welcome. In the prelude to Meyerbeer's *Les Huguenots*, Luther's chorale ["Ein feste Burg"] appears in so many diverse guises, and is so skillfully handled, that you are filled with marvel.

The *introduzione* is a rustic chorus.[11] The instrumentation, simple at the outset, is enriched with fresh ornaments when the vocal melody is repeated. Verdi kept to that mode of expression, apparently true to life, that is used in music to allude to country folk, shepherds, and so forth. While music has undergone many transformations, it has remained static with respect to this mode of expression. Observe, for example, the old Swiss *ranz des vaches* and you will find the pastoral style as it is used today, and as the great Rossini took it for a model in his masterpiece *Guillaume Tell*. A review of works by a number of composers shows that all have expressed this kind of music in a similar fashion. Need I mention the chorus of peasants in Grétry's *Richard*, the pastoral aria in Paisiello's *Nina*, the chorus "Come, gentle spring" in *The Four Seasons* by Haydn, "Ricevete, o padroncina" from Mozart's *Le nozze di Figaro*, the chorus "Evviva il colle e il prato" in Mayr's *Adelasia*, the chorus of peasants in Weber's *Euryanthe*,[12] and, leaving others aside, the celebrated "Pastoral" symphony of Beethoven, particularly the part known as the Shepherds' Song? These examples lead us to conclude that the only music to suffer from the caprice of fashion is that whose worth derives from novelty and not

---

11. N. 2, Introduzione ("Ti desta o Luisa").

12. André-Ernest-Modeste Grétry, *Richard Coeur-de-lion* (Paris: Comédie-Italienne 1784), opening chorus "Chantons, chantons, célébrons ce bon menage." Giovanni Paisiello, *Nina* (Caserta: Belvedere, 1789): the shepherd's song "Già il sol si cela dietro alla montagna" was added for an early revival of the opera. Haydn, *Die Jahreszeiten*, ed. Armin Raab, *HW* XXVIII/4 (2007), N. 2, Chor des Landvolks ("Komm, holder Lenz!"). Mozart, *Le nozze di Figaro* (Vienna: Burgtheater, 1786), *NMA* II:v/16, N. 22, Coro ("Ricevete, o padroncina"). "Evviva il colle, il prato" opens Giovanni Simone Mayr, *Adelasia e Aleramo* (Milan: Teatro alla Scala, 1806); an early vocal score of the opera is reproduced in *IOG* 11 (1991). Carl Maria von Weber, *Euryanthe* (Vienna: Kärntnertortheater, 1823), chorus "Fröliche Klänge" within the first-act finale.

from truth. Truth is stable; it neither deteriorates with time nor wearies those who have savored it.

A *romanza* for soprano follows ["Lo vidi, e il primo palpito"]; it might better be called a cabaletta.[13] The first two measures of the *mossa* set the course of the whole number, for the remainder is the result of variations on them, if not with regard to the pitches, then surely with regard to the rhythm. Note in the phrase "Lo vidi, e il primo palpito," and consequently in the entire cabaletta, a staccato vocal line—one of Verdi's main characteristics. Indeed, if we stop to consider Verdi's vocal melodies, we find that the majority of them are composed of notes that are either *staccate* as a result of rests, or *puntate*—or indeed *legate*, though by artifice rather than by nature.[14] In this context it is worth observing that, in a number of circumstances, musical notes can exert mutual attraction or repulsion. Bellini—by instinct or by calculation—was able to organize his melodies in such a way that each note seems to gravitate toward the next. If you care to look into this secret, you will find it in his use of dissonances—whether appoggiaturas or passing notes—which eagerly seek consonance. And when the need was felt to give a consonant note a tendency to motion, the supporting harmony was judiciously changed so as to convert the note into a suspension, or to leave it consonant but as part of a new chord. But although it is easy to learn this secret, it is certainly difficult—perhaps impossible—to put it to work effectively without the aid of ingenuity and, even more, of an individual way of feeling. Verdi and Bellini, then, are opposites, inasmuch as the melodies of the former tend to the staccato and those of the latter to the legato. If we view the human larynx as an instrument (which it is), Bellini treated it as a wind instrument and Verdi, one would at times say, as a percussion instrument. I will not deny that Verdi has not infrequently written legato vocal melodies, but if you look at these carefully you will find that most of them contain staccato or vibrato passages.[15] In any case, legato is the

---

13. Luisa's *sortita* (mm. 198ff. of N. 2, Introduzione) is in fact neither a *romanza* (though it is called that in early vocal scores, to which Basevi must be referring) nor a cabaletta (the term Basevi would prefer, presumably because of its character). If anything, it is a "cavatina nell'introduzione": Cammarano calls it "cavatina" in a letter to Verdi (Naples, May 15, 1849: *Copialettere*, 78–80, 79).

14. In the ensuing "demonstration" that legato proper is marginal in Verdi—or at least in his vocal writing—we have retained Basevi's terminology: the notes in his first category are separated (*staccate*) by rests, as in the first measure of Luisa's cavatina; those in the second category are what *we* would call staccato (they are *puntate*, marked by *punti*—staccato dots).

15. "Passi *staccati*, o *vibrati*": "staccato" is to be understood, as often in Basevi, in a broader sense than the current one (see the glossary); "vibrato" must refer to his "note vibrate," notes

exception in Verdi's music, and where we encounter it we often find it to be artificial—that is, not the necessary result of attraction between notes.

In the *terzetto* that follows ["T'amo d'amor ch'esprimere"] we find again the staccato manner that I have discussed.[16] The melody of the allegro brillante is pleasing, and it is repeated to good effect at the end, for a fourth time, in unison by the tenor and the soprano.[17] This is then gradually lost in the distance, accompanied by a few detached chords sung pianissimo by the chorus, while the baritone's staccato line provides a sort of basso continuo. With regard to form: nothing special. The two-measure phrase "T'amo d'amor ch'esprimere" is the model for the whole piece. This method of building an entire piece on just a few measures would seem to make the path much easier for composers who are not overly inventive, yet it is amazing how few of them succeed even in such a simple compositional exercise. It shows that in such transformations too there is a need, if not for great genius, then certainly for exquisite taste if the initial kernel is to grow more attractive—or at least not lose its original appeal. Nevertheless, these predetermined forms smack too much of artifice, and are not appropriate in a passionate situation, for passion shuns all rules. The virtue of these pieces lies in their sonic beauty, and thus in the physical pleasure they induce via the acoustic nerve.

The andante of the baritone's aria, "Sacra la scelta è d'un consorte," provides an example of Verdi's majestic style;[18] then, at the words "mal dalla forza legge riceve," there is one of those vehement passages typical of our composer. This piece is a remnant of the first manner and is very clearly out of place in the second. As the piece develops it never loses sight of the rhythm of its *mossa*. Now, lest anyone confuse the majestic with the legato and find a contradiction in my considering majestic and staccato equally characteristic of Verdi's music, I want to point out that in majestic singing one has to "carry" [*portare*] the notes with the voice, which is an entirely artificial method and very different from legato, which arises from the mutual attraction between the notes. Indeed, the leaps between notes required by the majestic style bar

---

that are "vibrant," uttered with vehemence, animated—thus articulated individually rather than legato.

16. This *terzetto*, too, is still part of N. 1, Introduzione (mm. 288ff.), constituting its stretta. It is called "Terzetto e Stretta dell'Introd.^{ne}" in the first Ricordi edition of the vocal score (1850) and "Terzetto che chiude l'Introduzione" in Cammarano's letter mentioned in n. 13 above.

17. The melody is heard, rather conventionally, three times—sung by Luisa, then Rodolfo, then the two together; their fourth, telescoped statement of it comes as an afterthought (mm. 374ff.).

18. N. 3, Scena ("Ferma, ed ascolta!") ed Aria Miller ("Sacra la scelta è d'un consorte").

such attraction—so much so that Bellini, who may be unique in the legato kind of singing, is inferior to other composers in the majestic style. In the cabaletta of this aria ["Ah! fu giusto il mio sospetto! . . ."] we find yet another example of Verdian staccato. The form is routine and merits no special consideration.

The bass's aria follows, an andante that does not stand out.[19] In the major-mode passage on the words "Di dolcezze l'affetto paterno," note a grandiloquent phrase of the kind that Verdi used in his first operas, written according to the procedure I have called "economical." This piece is too long, and seems all the heavier for the relative insignificance of the dramatic action. Staccato and vibrato are not lacking here if you care to look for them.[20]

After a very graceful chorus on an overly uniform staccato theme comes the duet for contralto and tenor.[21] This scene, perhaps the finest in Schiller's tragedy, comes off coldly in Cammarano's libretto. This is because the librettist has made Federica virtuous, such that Rodolfo's rejection of her hand has no motivation other than his love for Luisa. In Schiller, on the other hand, Federica (Lady Milford) is the prince's favorite, which is the very reason Walter is seeking her as a bride for his son. She feels ashamed: she loves Walter's son and wishes to restore her good name; she tells him of all her good deeds and of all the evil ones she has prevented; and finally, repentant, she seeks in pure love the means to escape the mire in which she has lain. This is a magnificent scene—of which Cammarano did not take advantage. The ⁶⁄₈ andantino is distinctive and pleasant at first, but it continues with excessive uniformity. Note that this cantabile merges imperceptibly into a recitative, which in turn leads to the allegro or cabaletta ["Deh! la parola amara"]. We find this unusual form also in the larghetto of the duet for the two women in the third act of Donizetti's *Maria Padilla*.[22] I should be very pleased if this passage from one movement to another without the conventional distinctions that are the senseless custom were used more frequently. The entire allegro moderato, or cabaletta, is modeled on the first two measures of the *mossa*, where again you find staccato—which henceforth I leave readers to discover

19. N. 4, Scena ("Che mai narrasti! . . .") ed Aria Walter ("Il mio sangue, la vita darei").

20. See n. 15 above.

21. N. 5, Recitativo ("Padre . . ." "M'abbraccia . . .") e Coro ("Quale un sorriso d'amica sorte"), and N. 6, Recitativo ("Duchessa . . ." "Duchessa tu m'appelli!") e Duetto ("Dall'aule raggianti di vano splendor").

22. Although Basevi mentions the opera's third act, he is obviously describing the Scena ("Ines! . . . mia dolce suora! . . .") e Duetto ("A figlia incauta di reo trascorso") for Ines and Maria in the second act of Donizetti's *Maria Padilla* (Milan: Teatro alla Scala, 1841).

for themselves. The first measure has the same rhythm as that of the cabaletta "Viens! viens! je cède éperdu" in the final duet from Donizetti's *La favorite*—although Donizetti did not employ staccato.[23] Taken as a whole this duet has little value.

The unaccompanied chorus of hunters is most expressive.[24] In this genre, as in the pastoral one, Verdi has not pursued novelty but has most wisely imitated his predecessors. The added echo is extremely effective.[25]

The final quintet of act 1 is the finest piece in the opera and one of Verdi's outstanding creations. The dramatic situation is also extremely important. The *parlante* with which the finale begins, "Tu, Signor fra queste soglie! . . . ," has a very apt theme in the violins and cellos. The ⅜-time andantino ["Fra' mortali ancora oppressa"] is extremely beautiful; the baritone begins with a melodic period that is well suited to express Miller's barely repressed anger; a solo clarinet in its lower register accompanies him. The second period is magnificent for its solemnity at the words "A quel Dio ti prostra innante." The accompaniment is novel and consists of a figure in the violas and clarinet.[26] A little four-measure phrase ends the baritone's part. The tenor enters with a different melody, well suited to the passion that agitates him; he is interrupted twice by the bass, who completes the period. Following the entry of the soprano, the four parts are beautifully interwoven for fifteen measures. This serves as preparation for a lovely cantabile for the soprano ["Deh! mi salva . . ."], accompanied by a figure similar to that noted above in the violas and clarinet but performed this time by the tenor and baritone [bass], pianissimo, for another fifteen measures. After this, the first four measures of the soprano's entry are reprised fortissimo in harmony with the chorus, heard three times in an upward sequence. Nine measures of preparation follow; these include a general unison. After this, the last phrase of the soprano's cantabile is repeated fortissimo in harmony, though at first delaying[27] and only later reaching the final cadence of the piece. This is one of Verdi's finest pages. Beautiful, expressive vocal lines, good use of chiaroscuro, and richness of accompaniment make it a true gem. It is clear that, when it comes

23. See *La favorite* (Paris: Opéra, 1840), critical ed. by Rebecca Harris-Warrick in *EN* (1997), N. 15, [Final] ("Es-tu prêt?"; "Va-t-en d'ici!"), at mm. 284ff.

24. N. 7, Finale ("Sciogliete i levrieri . . .").

25. An offstage chorus in the left wing responds to another in the right, with a similar echo effect between horns also placed in opposite wings.

26. In both periods the clarinet is actually associated with a bassoon.

27. Basevi's "cadenza sospesa" would suggest a half cadence, which is not quite the case here.

to ensembles, one of Verdi's principal merits is that he has made them expressive. In the old days these pieces were mostly written in canon, which may be beautiful to the ear but not to the heart. When these canons came into some discredit, composers used meaningless phrases built into a crescendo to lead to fortissimos, smorzandos, and so forth, without any real purpose other than aural gratification. Many of Mercadante's and Pacini's concertati, and some of Donizetti's, have this defect: in them you can see four, five, six, or more singers come forward in a row to the stage apron, waving their arms as if in hand-to-hand combat with heaven, exchanging their function as actors for that of instruments. Rossini, as though wishing in *Guillaume Tell* to provide a model for everything that would be done later, wrote a most dramatic concertato in the quartet with chorus of the third act.[28] Among the truly dramatic ensembles we must not forget the *terzetto* in Donizetti's *Lucrezia Borgia*.[29] But Verdi nearly always made his concertati dramatic, and this is no small boast. The stretta of this finale is tantamount to an obbligato recitative, and does not much stand out.[30]

The chorus of country folk that opens the second act is expressive and full of character.[31] The unison *racconto* is well conceived. The andante agitato of Luisa's aria "Tu puniscimi, o Signore" is full of emotion, particularly where she says "non lasciarmi in abbandono." In this piece Verdi was so inspired that it did not occur to him to observe the usual "musical economy," and he spun a melody nearly all in one sweep [*di getto*] and independent of its opening measures—which, in fact, are not its finest. Note too the great variety with which the harmonies move. The allegro moderato that serves as a cabaletta ["A brani, a brani, o perfido"] is nothing more than ordinary at first, but later brings about a fine contrast at the movement to the major mode with a new rhythm at the words "Mi chiuda almeno i rai."

The *duettino* for baritone and bass is of little substance in every respect.[32]

28. N. 17-II, Quatuor ("C'est là cet archer redoutable").

29. See Donizetti, *Lucrezia Borgia*, N. 5, Recitativo ("Tutto eseguisti?") e Finale secondo ("Così turbata?"). The *terzetto* "Della Duchessa ai prieghi" is at mm. 361ff.

30. In fact, technically speaking this section is neither a stretta nor a passage of recitative. (Basevi may be calling it "stretta" in the general sense of "final section"—as indeed does the first Ricordi edition of the vocal score [Milan, 1850]—but then he appears disappointed at its not functioning like a "proper" stretta.) It rather resembles a *tempo di mezzo*—if it were not for the lack of a stretta to follow it.

31. N. 8, Coro ("Ah! Luisa, Luisa ove sei? . . ."), Scena ("Il padre tuo! . . ."), ed Aria Luisa ("Tu puniscimi, o Signore").

32. The piece is in fact for two basses: N. 9, Recitativo ("Egli delira"), Scena ("Ebben?" "Tutte apprestai"), e Duetto Walter e Wurm ("L'alto retaggio non ho bramato").

The unaccompanied quartet is very beautiful.[33] The soprano predominates, the other parts mainly providing accompaniment. Scudo compares it, not wrongly, to a madrigal.[34]

In the tenor's aria, the andante "Quando le sere, al placido" is rhythmically too uniform, but in the final measures it wakes up and enlivens the entire piece.[35] In *Maria di Rohan* Donizetti wrote a tenor *romanza*, "Alma soave e cara," that begins with the same rhythm and meter but that, lacking care in the final measures, ends coldly.[36] The allegro ["L'ara, o l'avello apprestami . . ."] is certainly not among Verdi's best, but it is impetuous and not unsuited to the dramatic situation.

The third act begins with a chorus of little moment.[37]

The following soprano-baritone duet is very fine.[38] The ⅜-time andantino, "La tomba è un letto," sung by the soprano, is most delicate, and though all its material is presented in the first four measures, it is spun out with taste. The baritone's più mosso ["Figlia! . . . Compreso d'orrore io sono!"] has a different character and is sufficiently well linked to the text. There is a well-calculated interruption when Luisa has said for the second time "È colpa amor?" Soon afterward the baritone begins another, very passionate melody at the words "Di rughe . . . il volto . . ." The orchestra accompanies with great truthfulness until Luisa tears up the letter, when the piece passes into a very appropriate, lively *parlante*. The parts alternate and then come together with great feeling until, without a break, they arrive at a recitative. The allegro "Andrem, raminghi e poveri" begins with a fine eight-measure melodic period. The soprano's repetition is similar but with a different ending. The baritone begins the second part in the same rhythm but then, together with the soprano, proceeds to another, different, part, which may be called cadential. At the repetition of the cabaletta, the baritone sings the first period while the soprano has some staccato notes in an identical pattern for four measures—an

33. N. 10, Scena ("Vien la Duchessa! . . .") e Quartetto ("Presentarti alla Duchessa").

34. The French critic Paul Scudo had written that this quartet could be called "a madrigal . . . rather than a page of theatrical music" ("un madrigal . . . plutôt qu'une page de musique dramatique"). *Revue des deux mondes*, October–December 1852, 1187–93, 1192.

35. N. 11, Scena ("Il foglio dunque?") ed Aria Rodolfo ("Quando le sere, al placido").

36. See *Maria di Rohan* (Vienna: Kärntnertortheater, 1843), critical ed. by Luca Zoppelli in *EN* (2011), N. 4, [Preludio, Scena] "Nel fragor della festa" [e Aria Chalais] "Alma soave e cara."

37. N. 12, Scena e Coro ("Come in un giorno solo").

38. N. 13, Scena ("Pallida! mesta sei! . . .") e Duetto [Luisa e Miller] ("La tomba è un letto").

apt expression of the persistence of beggars.[39] The clarinet attempts to imitate Luisa's voice, like a lament.[40] Then the two vocal parts interact differently from the first time, producing a fine effect where, on the weak beats of the measures, the soprano sings now an F-natural, now an F-flat, as major and minor appoggiaturas.

The soprano-tenor duet[41] is certainly not as beautiful as the preceding one, nor as adventurous. In the ⁶⁄₈ andante, nothing is notable aside from the phrase "S'è concesso al prego mio." The allegro "Maledetto il dì che nacqui . . ." was clearly inspired by the phrase in Donizetti's *Lucia*, "Maledetto sia l'istante."[42] The imitation is good, but I would find it difficult to justify the repetition in unison with the soprano—who certainly has no reason to yowl so on the words "Per l'istante in cui ti piacqui. . . ."

The final *terzetto* is a fine piece, in which Verdi succeeded in linking melody and expression as ably as one would expect of him. Luisa's part, which predominates, is most expressive. The broad, passionate melody that unfolds over an accompaniment of sextuplets and triplets ["Ah! vieni meco . . ."] recalls the similar manner found in the *terzetti* of *I Lombardi*, *Attila*, and other works.[43] The instrumentation of this piece is finely wrought.

If we consider the music of *Luisa Miller* in the most general terms, we find it to be Verdi's least noisy work thus far. Here the brusque ways noted in his other compositions are tempered. And yet that energy so characteristic of Verdi's music has not suffered in the least. In this opera, too, his music—owing to the use of staccato and the limited ornamentation (which used in moderation can have a softening effect)—has a somewhat rough and untamed character, striking you more often than it touches you.

---

39. A reference to the words in this passage: Luisa and her father resolve to escape and live together a life of vagrant poverty, begging for bread from door to door.

40. Basevi's wording here largely corresponds to Verdi's directions: the clarinet, which doubles Luisa for most of the passage (mm. 280ff.), is marked "imitating and following Luisa's voice in such a way that the clarinet is indistinguishable" and "like a lament" ("imitando e secondando la voce di Luisa in modo che non si distingua il Clarinetto"; "come un lamento").

41. N. 14, Scena ("Ah! l'ultima preghiera"), Duetto [Luisa e Rodolfo] ("Piangi, piangi . . . il tuo dolore"), e Terzetto finale [Luisa, Rodolfo, e Miller] ("Padre! ricevi l'estremo . . . addio!").

42. This is the curse, uttered by Edgardo, that gives rise to the stretta of N. 6, Finale atto secondo ("Per te d'immenso giubilo"), in *Lucia di Lammermoor*; it is the passage whose forceful execution had gained the tenor Gaetano Fraschini the epithet "il tenore della maledizione." For both incipits Basevi uses the spelling variant *maladetto*.

43. See *I Lombardi alla prima crociata*, N. 13, Scena ("Qui posa il fianco! . . .") e Terzetto-Finale terzo ("Tu la madre mi togliesti"), mm. 153ff.; and the Terzetto ("Te sol, te sol quest'anima") within *Attila*'s final number (N. 12), at mm. 154ff.

14

STIFFELIO

Piave took the plot for his libretto *Stiffelio* from the drama *Stifellius* by Émile Souvestre and Eugène Bourgeois.[1] The action regards the adulteress Lina, who, even though her guilt is caused by another's deception and betrayal, is at first repudiated by the priest Stiffelio; he then forgives her because, while preaching, he has chanced on the passage from the Gospels in which Christ pardons the adulteress. It is not entirely clear, however, how another's deception and betrayal might have caused Lina to err, as we do not know whether her case is the same as that of the wife of Filippello Fighinolfi [*sic*] in Boccaccio.[2] Indeed, judging by certain things she says, it would seem that she must once have felt at least some affection for her seducer. And the love that Lina declares she has always felt for her husband Stiffelio would need greater elaboration and proof to convince the spectator. But the strangest thing for a Catholic country like Italy is a married priest. How do you expect the majority of the audience, educated on entirely different principles, to be moved by

---

1. First printed and staged in 1849, the drama was actually entitled *Le pasteur; ou, L'évangile et le foyer*.
2. A reference to a tale by Boccaccio in which Filippello Sighinolfo's virtuous and faithful wife can be induced to betray him only through deception (*Decameron*, 3.6).

sentiments that Stiffelio's clerical garb turns into near sacrilege?[3] Lina's father, Stankar, plays a major role in the libretto, but one of no significance to the action; conversely, the character of the seducer Raffaele, whom we should like to know better, remains cloaked in shadow. Good situations and poignant scenes are not entirely lacking, but they do not add up to an altogether appealing work. Besides, Piave transformed to thickest darkness what little light the French authors had introduced into in their drama.

Verdi's opera was performed in November 1850 in Trieste, where it did not have the happiest of receptions.[4]

What strikes us first in this score is the distribution of voices. Stiffelio is a tenor, Raffaele the second baritone,[5] Stankar the first baritone, and Lina a soprano. There is nothing odd about the latter pair, but that cannot be said for the first two: a bass voice would seem more proper to the role of a priest, and a tenor voice to that of a lover. The distribution of voices certainly makes no little difference to the success of an opera. Each voice type is appropriate to a specific emotion: not all emotions are suitably expressed with sounds of the same pitch range, or of the same power, speed, or lightness; similarly, not all voice types—differing among themselves in pitch, power, lightness, and so forth—are equally suitable to characters that, because of the nature of their roles, must be dominated by one kind of affection or passion rather than another. For all that, the necessary distribution of voices has not always been given proper consideration, though this has often been due to special conditions among the singers rather than negligence on the part of the composer. If nothing else, we must recall the age of the castrati, who, with their little soprano and contralto voices, took on such roles as Pyrrhus. Yet the castrati were also the greatest singers in the world, and indeed after their time the art of singing fell into decline. Let a new Baldassare Ferri appear today—one able, like the first, to sing two trilled chromatic scales in one breath with perfect intonation at every step—and he will be welcome in the clothes of any character![6] Some will counter that no one today has the patience to study

3. Of course Stiffelio is a Protestant minister—a leader of the imaginary "Assasverian" sect.
4. The venue was the Teatro Grande. "Though not an unalloyed success, *Stiffelio* was given on the whole a warm reception at its premiere": Kathleen Kuzmick Hansell in the introduction to her critical edition of the opera, *WGV* I/16 (2003), xi–xxxix, xxiv.
5. Raffaele is in fact a second tenor (the first tenor being Stiffelio).
6. Ferri was an internationally acclaimed Italian soprano castrato of the seventeenth century. Basevi's "due scale semitonate" are elucidated by a number of sources; for example, Lichtenthal, 1:128 (s.v. *canto*), reports that Ferri "could in a single breath go up and down two full octaves, continuously trilling and marking all the steps of the chromatic scale with surprising

from a single sheet of paper for six years, as Farinelli did under Porpora.[7] This is quite true, for nowadays not six years but six months seems too long to spend on becoming an artist; and they are right if by *singers* they mean "shriekers"—for many of today's celebrated performers are nothing more than that. The bad habit of shrieking has caused the disappearance of contraltos and *bassi profondi*, with the result that the harmonies in concertati have become weak and incomplete.[8]

Returning now to our subject, it should be noted that the character of Stiffelio is so badly delineated that you truly do not know whether you are dealing with a priest or a jealous husband. Which is why a tenor or a bass would suit him equally well. Verdi seems to have paid little attention to Stiffelio's priestly aspects, realizing that he is a priest only for the sake of the effect one hopes to derive from it in the sermon of the final scene.

The *sinfonia*, which incorporates various themes from the opera, progresses well and produces a good effect.[9]

Act 1 begins with a recitative that is in no way original, and indeed follows the pattern of Verdi's other recitatives, most of which are the least carefully written things in his compositions.[10] Yet recitatives do not deserve such neglect, for they are where music's dramatic power can best be displayed. Hence it is perhaps easier to write a pleasing aria than an expressive recitative.

Recitative was the first thing the fathers of opera invented: the earliest operas of Peri and Caccini, *Dafne* and *Euridice*,[11] are nothing but extended recitative. At first, its dramatic expressiveness was certainly negligible, but a number of musicians gradually contributed both by precept and by example to its advancement. In the first half of the seventeenth century, Giovanni

---

exactitude" ("saliva e discendeva in un sol fiato due piene Ottave, continuamente trillando e segnando tutti i gradi della Scala cromatica, con una giustezza sorprendente").

7. Carlo Broschi (1705–82)—the *sopranista* better known as Farinelli, arguably the most famous castrato in history—was indeed a student of Nicola Porpora; the anecdote of the single sheet of singing exercises, however, is more often mentioned in relation to the formation of another celebrated pupil of Porpora, the mezzo-soprano castrato Caffarelli (1710–83).

8. This tirade shows Basevi to be at least partly in tune with a number of his contemporaries: toward the mid-nineteenth century, there emerges in Italy a retrospective, nostalgic celebration of the golden age of "bel canto"—an ideal form of singing that is supposedly being supplanted by the screaming of "canto declamato."

9. Some detail is provided in Budden, 1:454–55.

10. N. 1, Introduzione ("Oh santo libro, oh dell'eterno Vero"). Whether or not this passage deserves such adverse comment in terms of its quality, it was in fact original to open an opera with a setting of recitative verse rather than the usual chorus.

11. See chapter 6, n. 5, above.

Battista Doni wrote at length about theatrical music and proposed some wise rules about musical expression. He rightly censured those who tried to approximate everyday speech in their recitatives, as well as those who deployed all their skill in expressing individual words rather than the general meaning of a passage. That mode of expression remains alive, although we no longer encounter what Doni heard in a Roman church where, on the text "cuius regni non erit finis," everyone suddenly stopped singing to express the word "finis."[12] But we still have composers who, like the Prince of Venosa, would set the words "un'armonia mista" with notes containing all the musical accidentals,[13] or who, like Palestrina, would use sharp dissonances on the words "se amarissimo fiele."[14] And while such methods are the exception among great geniuses, they are sometimes to be found: even the great Mozart, in the quintet from *La clemenza di Tito*, used seven notes descending a twelfth from a high F to express "e nel tuo sen profondo."[15] Nor can I praise Spontini, who, in the third-act trio from *Fernand Cortez*, has an ascending chromatic scale on the words "que nos derniers accents montent vers l'éternel."[16] This is analogy, not expression. Bellini, on the other hand—who, after Gluck, must be numbered among the most careful composers in matters of expression—did not hesitate in *Norma* to set the words "Sì, sovr'essi alzai la punta . . ." with descending notes, for which, as I recall, he was censured by another musician.[17] Boieldieu too was unjustly criticized because in the ballad "D'ici vous

12. A phrase from the Credo ("whose kingdom shall have no end"). The episode is from "Trattato della musica scenica" (1630s), in Giovanni Battista Doni, *Lyra barberina*, 2 vols. (Florence: Stamperia imperiale, 1763), vol. 2, *De' trattati di musica*, 1–144, 74. (Basevi owned this eighteenth-century edition of Doni's writings: Piovano, 247 n. 284.)

13. The passage in question is in the madrigal "Tu che con vari accenti," from *Madrigali a sei voci* (Naples, 1626) by Carlo Gesualdo, Prince of Venosa.

14. This is the madrigal "S'amarissimo fele" ("If the bitterest gall") from Palestrina's *Delli madrigali spirituali a cinque voci* [. . .] *libro secondo* (Rome, 1594). The likely source for this example of expressive dissonance is Burney, whose words ("crude discords") are echoed by Basevi's ("crude dissonanze"). See Charles Burney, *A General History of Music from the Earliest Ages to the Present Period*, 4 vols. (London: printed for the author, 1776–89), 3 (1789): 194.

15. See *La clemenza di Tito*, ed. Franz Giegling, *NMA* II:v/20 (1970), N. 12, Quintetto con coro ("Deh conserve, oh dei"), mm. 96ff.

16. See Gaspare Spontini, *Fernand Cortez; ou, La conquête du Mexique*, 1st version (Paris: Opéra, 1809), N. 10, Hymne ("Amis voici l'instant d'un triomphe immortel"; "Créateur de ce nouveau monde"), mm. 4ff., in the vocal score *Fernand Cortez* (Paris: Imbault & M.elles Érard, [1809?]).

17. See the duet for Norma and Pollione ("In mia mano alfin tu sei") that is part of N. 8, Finale dell'atto secondo, from Bellini's *Norma*: the passage in question is toward the end of the opening cantabile.

voyez ce beau domaine" from *La dame blanche* he set the words "touchent le ciel" to a descending octave.[18] But let us return to recitative itself. To illustrate its longevity and perennial freshness when well written, I cite Agamemnon's magical recitative in the first scene of act 2 of Gluck's *Iphigénie en Aulide*, first performed in 1774.[19] Another beautiful example is the obbligato recitative in Spontini's *La vestale*, "Où vais-je? . . . ô ciel! . . . ," which contains a sequence that rises stepwise, gaining in intensity, to a fortissimo of matchless effectiveness on the words "la foudre est sur ta tête."[20] In today's recitatives, composers have in general adopted certain commonplaces that serve as indispensable fillers when their inventiveness fails. Verdi, who should know better, occasionally comes up with the trite chromatic motion that may be seen from the very first recitative of *Stiffelio*, and that will be noted again in the course of the opera.

Stiffelio's *racconto* ["Di qua varcando"], a sort of barcarole, is too simple in form.[21] Verdi could have taken better advantage of the astonishment of the chorus, the terror of Lina and Raffaele, and the suspicion of Stankar, all of whom are present for this narrative.

The ensuing septet ["Colla cenere disperso"] is well conceived; with great care and skill Verdi contrived to make different characters in turn predominate, according to their diverse feelings. In the stretta ["A te, Stiffelio, un canto"], only the chorus part is notable; we first encountered its theme in the *sinfonia*.

In the tenor's aria,[22] note that the first movement, usually reserved for the so-called adagio,[23] is the result of several melodies interrupted by short

---

18. Adrien Boieldieu, *La dame blanche* (Paris: Opéra-Comique, 1825), N. 3, Ballade. The descent in question is in the very first phrase ("D'ici voyez ce beau domaine dont les créneaux touchent le ciel!" which Basevi has as "les cieux").

19. Presumably Basevi is referring to the *last* scene of act 2 (scene 7), which includes an extended recitative for Agamemnon ("Tu décides son sort"), of which Gluck provided two versions. See *Iphigénie en Aulide* (Paris: Opéra, 1774), ed. Marius Flothuis, *GGA* I/5 (1987–89), vol. I/5a, pp. 309ff., and vol. I/5b, pp. 510ff.

20. See the recitative ("Sur cet autel sacré") that follows Julia's second-act Air N. 8 ("Toi que j'implore avec effroi"). In *ERO* 42 (1979), 230–38, 232–35.

21. The simplicity is in the modified strophic form; the "rowing" topos (⁶⁄₈ meter, moderate tempo, repetitious rhythms) is triggered by the boatman at the center of Stiffelio's *racconto*.

22. N. 2, Scena ("Non ha per me un accento! . . . non un guardo!") ed Aria Stiffelio ("Vidi dovunque gemere").

23. The terms *adagio*, *largo*, and *andante* are often used by Basevi with reference not (or not only) to a certain tempo or to a section in that tempo but to that lyrical section of a multipartite number to which we often refer as the cantabile. See the glossary, s.v. *cantabile*.

recitatives, both simple and obbligato, in one of which we again encounter that chromatic motion.[24] This first part of the aria transcends the ordinary in its variety—but that alone does not make it praiseworthy, as variety is beautiful only when combined with unity. And this section is lacking in unity; it is so disjointed that I cannot describe it better than by the expression "fallen apart" [*sfasciata*]. It is worth dwelling somewhat on this defect because it is found too often in the myriad obscenities that flow from the minds of the hundreds of composers who inundate Italy. It is useless for a vocal line, whether legato or staccato, to exhibit the unity that gives life to a musical phrase—and through the interrelation of phrases to an entire melodic period, and through the interrelation of periods to a larger musical discourse—if, instead of strengthening one another, these larger parts contradict each other and generate discord. The effectiveness of music springs from concord, and many composers, though perfectly able to compose a fine *mossa*, or even a musical period, are prevented by their limited talent from devising lengthier connections, producing disjointed pieces that leave no impression on the listener, even when they are not actually disagreeable. And this is something with which many unsuccessful, minor composers are unable to reconcile themselves: they see that their cavatinas, duets, and so forth contain beautiful melodies (or at least none any more disagreeable than those of other, fashionable composers) and even moments that are effective—and yet their operas do not please. This is because of the lack of cohesion within the various pieces, which end up resembling speeches written with the finest rhetoric, and with sterling words and phrases, but with no connection between ideas and no common sense. And just as common sense cannot be instilled in an orator who lacks it by nature, so the faculty of connecting the various parts of a musical edifice cannot be acquired by those who are inherently without it: hence the rarity of great geniuses. Verdi certainly has this connective faculty, and he must not be judged on the basis of a number of exceptions. In our times, however, the composer most generously endowed with this is Meyerbeer. Without it he could never have penned those grand, sublime pages of the fourth finale of *Le prophète* or those of the oath from *Les Huguenots*.[25]

In the cabaletta of this aria ["Ah v'appare in fronte scritto"] you find an even-note rhythm that seems to me better suited to expressing tranquil love

24. See mm. 115ff.

25. *Le prophète*, N. 24, Finale [4] N. 24a, Prière et imprécation ("Domine salvum fac regem nostrum"); *Les Huguenots*, N. 23, Conjuration et Bénédiction des poignards ("Des trouble renaissants").

or friendship than anger. As evidence I cite "Qui ribelle ognun ti chiama" from Donizetti's *Roberto Devereux* and "Sorgea la notte fosca" from Bellini's *I puritani*.[26] But those pieces contain greater variety; in this cabaletta, the uniformity is carried to such a pitch that nearly half the measures contain four equal notes, inducing tedium rather than delight.

The soprano's prayer is simple and contains nothing unusual.[27]

There are praiseworthy parts in the ensuing duet for baritone and soprano.[28] The allegro vivo, "Dite che il fallo a tergere," is well set; the first melodic period is of eight measures cast in a single sweep [*d'un getto*], which is appropriate where violent emotions are concerned, for these shun overly regular and symmetrical periodic repetition. The andante, sung by the baritone ["Ed io pure in faccia agl'uomini"], does not venture beyond the ordinary, and contains those passages of vibrant notes[29] of which Verdi made so much use. The soprano's answer has a rhythm conforming well to Lina's agitation—a repeated pattern of an eighth rest followed by two sixteenth notes, the first rushing into the second. The great effectiveness of this rhythm lies in the conflict between an artificial staccato and a natural legato—that is, where two notes that would by their nature tend to be joined are detached, such as when obeying the need for the resolution of a dissonance. The baritone, meanwhile, continues with a melody that is effectively set against that of the soprano. The cabaletta that closes the duet ["Or meco venite"] is trite. It imitates the rhythm of "Per me infelice" from *Il corsaro*; it is a waltz that returns three times.[30] The *a 2* cadential passage is prolonged excessively.

26. The first example is the cabaletta (mm. 133ff.) of N. 4, Scena ("Roberto . . . Che? . . . fra le tue braccia! . . .") e Cavatina Nottingham ("Forse in quel cor sensibile") from Donizetti's *Roberto Devereux, ossia Il conte di Essex* (Naples: Teatro San Carlo, 1837); Donizetti's autograph manuscript of the opera's full score was reproduced in *ERO* 26 (1982), where "Qui ribelle ognun ti chiama" begins on fol. 45r. For the second example, see Vincenzo Bellini, *I puritani*, ed. Fabrizio Della Seta, *ECB* 10 (forthcoming), [N. 3], Scena ("O amato zio") e Duetto Giorgio ed Elvira ("Sai com'arde in petto mio"); "Sorgea la notte fosca" (which Basevi has as "folta") is at mm. 169ff. Though Basevi's "ritmo a note uguali" implies notes of equal duration, his three examples (*Stiffelio, Roberto Devereux, Puritani*) also share other features (the likely reason for the association)—an anacrusis followed by four quarter notes of the same pitch (scale degree 3 of the passage's major key).

27. N. 3, Scena ("Tosto ei disse! . . . Ah son perduta!") e Preghiera Lina ("A te ascenda, oh Dio clemente").

28. N. 4, Scena ("Verrà! . . . dovrò risponder! . . . Che risponder?") e Duetto [Lina e Stankar] ("Dite che il fallo a tergere").

29. See chapter 13, n. 15, above.

30. See *Il corsaro*, N. 13, Finale ultimo, mm. 90ff.—a passage similarly censured by Basevi for being too waltz-like.

The completely staccato chorus that follows does not stand out.[31] During the repetitions of this chorus—first without and then with instruments—a recitative is heard.[32]

The first finale begins with Stiffelio's declamatory section "Non solo all'iniquo," which proceeds well but nothing more. The largo of the finale ["Oh qual m'invade ed agita"] begins with an eight-measure cantabile for the tenor that is repeated *sotto voce* by the three tenors in harmony, accompanied by a unison staccato figure for the baritone and the bass. After this, the same cantabile is recast in the seven principal voices, while the chorus basses, tenors, and sopranos alternate in a staccato accompaniment. Then the piece passes from G minor into the major, and with a slow crescendo that partly preserves the rhythm of the cantabile reaches a fortissimo followed by the cadential section, which drops to pianissimo. The structure of this piece is simple but well conceived, chiefly because of the effect of its sonorities [*effetto della sonorità*]. There is nothing unusual in the stretta ["Chi ti salva, sciagurato"], but its energy suits it well to the situation on stage.

In the recitative that opens act 2 we run once again into one of those chromatic motions.[33]

The andante of Lina's aria has the same rhythm and meter as "Quando le sere, al placido" from *Luisa Miller* and proceeds with the same uniformity;[34] at the end, however, there is a change that would provide another example of the disjointed manner [*stile sfasciato*] if unity were not maintained by the unusual accompaniment. The cabaletta ["Perder dunque voi volete"] is pleasant, but conflicts somewhat with the words.

Then comes a duet for tenor and baritone.[35] The orchestral part of the *parlante* "Scegli!" "Un duello?" with its martial *colorito* must be counted among the finest. For the rest, this duet does not contain the usual adagio and allegro

31. N. 5, Scena ("M'evitan! ma il colloquio"), Coro ("Plaudiam! di Stiffelio s'allegri il soggiorno"), e Finale primo ("Non solo all'iniquo ch'ha il Maestro venduto"; "Oh qual m'invade ed agita"). Basevi's "*coro* tutto *staccato*" starts at m. 100.

32. The superimposed dialogue is rather a *parlante*. Basevi at times designates as "recitativo" a dialogue passage within a number, even when it is not technically in recitative.

33. N. 6, Scena ("Oh cielo! dove son io?") ed Aria Lina ("Ah dalli scanni eterei"). The "progressione cromatica" is at mm. 43–49.

34. Compare N. 6, mm. 73ff., with *Luisa Miller*'s N. 11, mm. 67ff.

35. The duet of Raffaele and Stankar opens N. 7, Duetto ("Io resto." "Allor Rodolfo saprà tutto"; "Scegli!" "Un duello?"), Quartetto ("Era vero! . . . ah no . . . è impossibile! . . ."), [e] Finale secondo ("Dessa non è, comprendilo"; "Non punirmi, Signor, nel tuo furore").

sections, since the *a 2* with which it ends ["Nessun demone, niun Dio"] cannot be considered a cabaletta.[36] That section is completely at odds with the situation and with the text, because it is too symmetrical. Moreover, every two measures there is a general fermata, and this four times in a row. One wonders how it can be that two dueling enemies who are threatening one another by turns should at every step wait for each other under a fermata so as to begin the following phrase together. I do not say that we must be such slaves to truth and verisimilitude that we destroy art, which is based on a degree of convention, but neither should we deviate from them such that we affront the spectator's common sense.

In the recitative that precedes the quartet, on the words "Oh eccesso inaudito, etc.," we again find the usual chromatic motion, and this time with the greatest simplicity, in unison with the orchestra. The largo ["Era vero! . . . ah no . . . è impossibile! . . ."] begins with a very expressive passage for Stiffelio—a true model for declamatory song as conceived by Verdi. The setting of "Un accento proferite . . ." accords marvelously with the character's desperation. A fine contrast is then provided by a phrase of Lina's that contains a measure of common time within the ¾ meter of the largo. This change of meter in the midst of a piece, used often by the ancients, notably Lully, does not deserve condemnation, for it may greatly assist in true expression; it is a grave error to believe in the need always to maintain the same meter. At one time the same thing was believed of tonality, but today no one tries to remain in the same key throughout a piece—on the contrary, it is viewed as pleasing variety to depart from the key after a while. Among the moderns, Verdi is not alone in adopting such metric variety; Nicolai wrote a measure of ¾ time in the midst of a ⁹⁄₈ andante in the second-act duet from *Il templario*.[37] The largo from which our discussion has briefly strayed then continues in ¾ time. There is a very well conceived diminuendo, dominated by the soprano, in which a

36. Of course the passage is not a formal, detached duet (an independent number) but rather part of the larger N. 7.

37. See Otto Nicolai, *Il templario* (Turin: Teatro Regio, 1840), Scena e Duetto ("Ebben, piangente e supplice"), m. 18 of the andante: p. 147 in the vocal score (Milan: Lucca, 1841) reproduced in *IOG* 26 (1991). *Il templario* has an unfortunate connection with Verdi's career: the fiasco of his second opera, the comic work *Un giorno di regno* (1840), was partly due to miscasting, as the Teatro alla Scala employed for it the heroic-style singers who had just performed *Il templario* there.

downward motion of the voices through various harmonies leads very naturally to the reprise of the tenor's "Un accento proferite." In this largo, note too that, to represent a voice broken by sobs (on Lina's words "non negarmi tua pietà!"), the articulation of the syllables is displaced onto the second note of the triplets.[38] In sum, this largo is the best piece in the opera.

The offstage sacred chorus ["Non punirmi, Signor"] is very trite. The allegro sung by a nearly delirious Stiffelio ["Me disperato abbruciano"] is well coupled to the words. The interruption by the offstage chorus is very effective, as it influences the action of the characters on stage and gives scope for a good actor to show his worth.

In the baritone aria that opens the third act,[39] the rhythm of the andante is too uniform and hackneyed; the closing, however, has more life. The cabaletta ["Oh gioia inesprimibile"] expresses Stankar's convulsive joy very effectively.

There follows a duet for soprano and tenor.[40] The allegro sostenuto contains nothing of note. After an obbligato recitative the soprano sings an andante sostenuto ["Non allo sposo volgomi"]. This is followed by a short recitative that proceeds by the usual semitones and closes in an andantino ["Egli un patto proponea"], where the soprano has a sort of *parlante*. After another recitative comes the cabaletta ["Ah sì, voliamo al tempio"], which has no notable features aside from its triplet accompaniment, similar to that in Rossini's *Otello* at the words "L'ira d'avverso fato";[41] this gives the piece a sense of agitation that is fully communicated to the listener.

The unaccompanied prayer, sung by the chorus, Stankar, and Lina, is no more than commonplace.[42] I am still unable to find an explanation for the filler provided by the soprano when for many measures she sings a figure made up of three eighth notes leaping to a half note.

---

38. At mm. 225, 227.

39. N. 8, Scena ("Ei fugge! . . . e in questo foglio") ed Aria Stankar ("Lina, pensai che un angelo").

40. N. 9, Scena ("Dite ai fratei che al tempio") e Duetto [Lina e Stiffelio] ("Opposto è il calle che in avvenire").

41. "L'ira d'avverso fato" is the stretta of N. 7, [Scena] ("Che feci! . . . ove mi trasse") [e Duetto Otello e Iago] ("Non m'inganno; al mio rivale"). See Gioachino Rossini, *Otello, ossia Il moro di Venezia*, ed. Michael Collins, *EC* I/19 (1994).

42. N. 10, Preghiera ("Non punirmi, Signor, nel tuo furore") e Finale ultimo ("Stiffelio?" "Eccomi!"). Two more characters join in this prayer, but Basevi does not mention them as they simply follow chorus parts (Dorotea with the sopranos and Federico with the tenors).

The final scene is of no importance; here the fault is not so much with the composer as with the librettist and, if you like, with the plot.

Having made the circuit of several theaters under a different name[43] but with the same fate, *Stiffelio* was finally revised by its composer and, in the new guise of *Aroldo*, placed before the public once again.[44]

43. For reasons of censorship, the libretto of *Stiffelio* was heavily rewritten, and between 1851 and 1855 the opera was staged in various Italian cities under the title *Guglielmo Wellingrode*—a version of which Verdi always disapproved.

44. For *Aroldo*, see chapter 20 below.

15

RIGOLETTO

The laws of freedom are laws of trust: the more those for whom they were created prove worthy of them, the more effective they are. Checks that, though designed to oppose evil, may also get in the way of good are eliminated by wise legislators only when improved public behavior renders them superfluous. But that was not how Victor Hugo saw it when in 1832 he produced his play *Le roi s'amuse*, which was banned from the stage by government order immediately after the first performance.[1]

The drama—which while using historical names is actually the product of Hugo's imagination—hinges on three principal characters: François I, King of France, who, ruled by lechery, dishonors families of all stations; Triboulet, his jester, who incites him, eggs him on, and assists him in his infamous undertakings; and Blanche, the daughter of Triboulet, guarded by her father like a rare jewel and raised in virtue. She is in love with the king, whom she has often seen, but not recognized, in church. Abducted by courtiers who believe her to be the jester's mistress rather than his daughter, Blanche is taken

---

1. Hugo's *drame* was first staged at the Comédie-Française. Immediately prohibited, it returned to that stage only on its fiftieth anniversary, in 1882—by which time Hugo was an octogenarian and France a republic.

to the king, who defiles that blushing flower. When Triboulet learns of this, he resolves to take his revenge by having the king murdered by an assassin. But Blanche, driven by insane love, gives her own life to save his. The hired cutthroat places her in a sack and delivers her in place of the king to Triboulet, who on recognizing her is seized by immeasurable grief. This fulfills the curse that [Monsieur de] Saint-Vallier had once placed on the jester, who had lampooned and mocked the grief and anger of that venerable old man, whose daughter's honor had been sullied by the king.

This play is immoral in that it debases virtue and exalts vice. Virtue is debased when we find in the soul of Triboulet, that minister of obscenity, a sacred care for the honor of Blanche alone, as though virtue lacked the power to make itself loved wherever it appeared. And vice is exalted when Blanche, seduced and defiled by François I, in a sense takes her own life in order to save that of her seducer, rather than abominating her error and fleeing its cause. In short, Victor Hugo wished to make the audience pity the fate of a vile jester and of a girl martyred (as he would have it) to an immodest and sinful love.

Hugo defended himself against this charge of immorality, saying that the true substance of the drama was Saint-Vallier's curse.[2] But this defense does not hold up, for even the silliest women hardly believe in the effectiveness of such curses. And indeed, even if the defense were valid, it would not make virtue seem attractive, as the moralist would wish, but would rather make punishment seem fearsome. The dénouement of *Don Giovanni* is preferable for the latter purpose.

Piave took his *Rigoletto* from this drama of Hugo's. The most noticeable change is the mutation of François I into the Duke of Mantua.[3] For the rest, there are altered names: Triboulet becomes Rigoletto and Blanche Gilda. Piave nevertheless prided himself on having made the characters less immoral; to tell the truth, I find them only more insipid. This notwithstanding, the libretto contains several scenes that give the composer scope to display his talents.

We are now supposed to marvel at the choice of a deformed man as the central character of an opera, particularly as anything that diverges in the slightest from the beautiful and the sublime is purportedly unsuited to music. But if we consider the present depravity of taste—when audiences seek recre-

2. "The whole play develops from it: the true subject of the drama is *M. de Saint-Vallier's curse*." Preface to *Le roi s'amuse* (Paris: Eugène Renduel, 1832), i–xxiii, ix ("De ceci découle toute la pièce. Le sujet véritable du drame, c'est *la malédiction de M. de Saint-Vallier*").
3. This change was not immediate: Verdi had started sketching the opera using names modeled after Hugo's originals, later changing them at the request of the censors.

ation in the stimulus of the revolting, just as paralyzed limbs quiver at strong electric shocks—our wonderment is easily quelled.

Rigoletto was first performed in Venice, in March 1851, and was greatly celebrated from its first appearance.[4]

Verdi was truly inspired in setting this drama, which completely accorded with his vigorous way of feeling, always in search of contrasts.

After a short *preludio* we hear some brisk dance music, in the second part of which there begins one of Verdi's beloved staccato melodies, models for which may be found in the most recent dance music from Germany.[5] A recitative ["Della mia bella"] is sung during the dancing and playing.

A tenor aria ["Questa o quella"] follows; it is labeled a *ballata* because of its rhythm, particularly that of the accompaniment.[6] The melody has a defect of symmetry worthy of note: the first phrase is made up of a three-measure *mossa* followed by one measure of transition, and then three measures that reproduce the rhythm of the *mossa*. The phrase thus turns out to be of seven measures, or "lame" [*zoppo*]. Yet if we were to convert the ⁶⁄₈ meter into ¹²⁄₈, the result would be a four-measure phrase in which the irregularity, while no less noticeable to the ear, would be hidden from the eye.[7] It must be said, however, that such irregularities can, as in this case, add considerable easiness and grace to a melody by virtue of a certain *sprezzatura*. Nonetheless, few composers (and those rarely) are able to free themselves from the current mannerism that requires rigorous rhythmic symmetry and periodicity, and this precisely because they base the effectiveness of their music on the effectiveness of its rhythm, caring more about the impression on the senses than anything else. Whenever there has been a desire to increase the sensuous element in music, people have turned to rhythm, which, as dance music demonstrates, can pleasingly rouse our bodily fibers. Hence, theatrical music has

4. The venue was the Teatro La Fenice. The critical edition of Verdi's *Rigoletto*, by Martin Chusid, was published as *WGV* I/17 (1983).

5. N. 1, Preludio; N. 2, Introduzione ("Della mia bella incognita borghese"). Basevi's "melodia *staccata*" is from m. 25.

6. Whatever its meaning here, the label "ballata" is not present in Verdi's autograph, and was first introduced in the earliest printed vocal score (Milan: Ricordi, 1852).

7. The melody's first phrase in fact consists of not seven but eight measures, balanced by the eight of the following one. (In other words, "Questa o quella," "del mio core," and "La costoro" begin at regular intervals of eight measures—as implied by Basevi's ¹²⁄₈ experiment.) What is irregular is that *within* the first phrase Verdi brings forward the setting of the second line "a quant'altre" (soon restoring the balance by repeating "d'intorno"). Basevi is thus right to the extent that the first phrase presents a glaring metric irregularity ("a defect of symmetry").

gradually moved closer and closer to dance music and marches: in the absence of spiritual arousal, the muscles must be acted on. The influence of sonic impressions on our muscular system is well known; I hardly need to recall the convulsive starts induced in some people by unexpected loud noises, or the way in which hard work may be eased by means of music, as happens with laborers, soldiers, and others. We may all have noted that when we hear music with very uniform melodic periods and rhythms, a certain force disposes our muscles to a motion corresponding to it; if the rhythm is suddenly altered or broken off, the listener feels a shock rather like the discomfort caused by the abrupt halt of a carriage in which we are relaxing and that has transmitted its uniform motion to us. If we are in motion, rhythm influences our step. Grétry tells us that when he wished to make a companion of his walk more slowly without saying anything to him, he began to hum a march that he gradually made slower and slower; as a result, his companion unconsciously slowed his pace.[8] Writing of dance music in his *Istituzioni armoniche*, Zarlino too notes that it often induces us "to follow it with certain bodily movements."[9] And the invasion of the cabalettas, which depend principally on rhythm for their effect, was lamented by Simone Mayr in his time.[10] But it was Rossini who broke new ground with his lovely, rhythmically compelling melodies. Since Rossini's time, ever greater care has been taken with rhythm, and Verdi has followed the common practice, infusing his melodies with rhythmic regularity and uniformity so well that they accommodate themselves beautifully to band music and marches. Before Rossini these rhythmically regular melodies were not given such importance, and we often observe in operas the neglect of melodic ideas that, for the beauty of their rhythm, would today provide material for an entire piece. An exception is provided by almost the whole of

8. See André-Ernest-Modeste Grétry, *Mémoires; ou, Essais sur la musique* (1789), 2nd ed., 3 vols. (Paris: Imprimerie de la République, Pluviôse, an V [1797]), 1:264–65.

9. Gioseffo Zarlino, *Le istitutioni harmoniche* (Venice, 1558), part 2, chap. 7, p. 71 ("i balli, i quali spesso ne inducono ad accompagnar seco alcuni movimenti estrinsechi col corpo").

10. Basevi's "l'invasione delle *cabalette*" is a pun on *l'invasione delle cavallette*, "a plague of locusts." In a passage published posthumously in 1848, Mayr had complained that cabalettas "have ruined the study of music, for any youngster who may have hit upon eight measures of a rather pretty melody—invariably accompanied by those repeated notes or pizzicatos—believes himself a good enough composer, noting that today's imitators of Rossini do nothing but reiterate both such ditties [*cantilenette*] and such accompaniments and drum-beatings in every piece." See Girolamo Calvi, *Di Giovanni Simone Mayr*, ed. Pierangelo Pelucchi (Bergamo: Fondazione Donizetti, 2000), 216.

a cabaletta in Gluck's *Paride* on the words "Le belle imagini, etc."[11] The ancients did indeed have some rhythmically regular melodies, as can be seen in
some of their songs, but these were rarely used in operas. They are, however,
to be found—suffice it to note "Nel cor più non mi sento" from Paisiello's
La molinara.[12] Mozart too, in *Don Giovanni*, made good use of rhythm in the
aria "Finch'han dal vino"—an aria that Oulibicheff, the author of Mozart's
biography, regards almost as the mother of all rhythmic-effect arias in modern
opera.[13]

Another consequence of the importance given to rhythm is found in accompaniments, which used for the most part to be very irregular and to some
extent at odds with the melodies they supported, as you may see in the continuo parts of cantatas by Porpora and Scarlatti, in duets by Steffani and Clari,
etc.[14] These accompaniments later acquired a certain regularity, taking the
form of uniform groups of notes or arpeggios, in various patterns and guises,
with simple notes or with chords, and performed by a single instrument or
by a variety of instruments, either together or in alternation. But this kind
of accompaniment was not used in the music of eighteenth-century composers either so often or at such length as it was from Rossini on. And actually,
the practice of using ornamental notes in instruments playing with the voice
disturbed the regular rhythmic progression of the accompaniment, as well as
showing little concern for the melody by drowning it. Simple, periodic, uniform accompaniments do not distract the attention, which ought to be focused
on the melody; indeed, without your realizing it they communicate a pleasing
motion, like that of a moving carriage. Through their differing rhythms, such
accompaniments can give a melody a different gait and contribute much to
its appeal.[15] Verdi often makes use of the gentle movement of triplets, which
carries us forward at an easy canter without the least jostling. A lively and

11. Gluck, *Paride ed Elena* (Vienna: Burgtheater, 1770), ed. Rudolf Gerber, *GGA* I/4 (1954).
Paride's aria "Le belle immagini," which concludes act 2, is indeed characterized by rhythmic
insistence (though of course it is no "cabaletta").

12. Giovanni Paisiello, *La molinara* (Naples: Teatro dei Fiorentini, 1788). The second-act
duet "Nel cor più non mi sento" is this comic opera's most successful piece: it provided the
theme for sets of variations by a number of composers, including Beethoven and Paganini.

13. N. 11, Aria "Fin ch'han dal vino." See Aleksandr Ulïbïshev [Oulibicheff], *Nouvelle biographie de Mozart, suivie d'un aperçu sur l'histoire générale de la musique et de l'analyse des principales oeuvres de Mozart*, 3 vols. (Moscow, 1843), 3:132–33.

14. Nicola Porpora, Alessandro Scarlatti, Agostino Steffani, and Giovanni Carlo Maria Clari
were Italian vocal composers of the late seventeenth and eighteenth centuries.

15. Basevi will offer an example of this phenomenon later in the chapter, in reference to the
cabaletta "Sì, vendetta, tremenda vendetta."

pleasing impression can be caused when this gait changes, either through an increase or decrease in the number of notes making up the accompaniment, or through the speeding up or slowing down of the piece—so long as this is done gradually. Symmetry, regularity, and uniformity of rhythm produce their effect only after they have continued for a certain time: at first appearance they cannot transmit to us the propensity to motion that is their aim. But it must be mentioned that while on the one hand uniformity offers these advantages, on the other hand it can cause boredom if excessive. Hence, moderation is called for. In the accompaniment of this *ballata* in *Rigoletto* there is excessive uniformity, which Verdi could have avoided. And while I am on this point, I must add that it is a grave error to believe that regularity, rhythmic uniformity, and symmetry are the essential characteristics of Italian music. It is sufficient to glance at the music of Pergolesi or Jommelli or any of their predecessors to see that they took no account of uniformity or symmetry.[16] Moreover, the Italians were always celebrated for melody, while they were once held to be inferior to the French in rhythm, as we can read in the *Discorso sulla perfezione delle melodie* by G. B. Doni.[17]

After the *ballata* comes a minuet of the kind found in Mozart's *Don Giovanni*.[18] This serves as the instrumental part of another recitative ["Partite! Crudele!"]. A *perigordino* follows,[19] and then we hear again the dance music with which the *introduzione* began. Verdi then added a sort of cadential section, where we find a very odd abuse of the pedal point and of passing notes. This pedal is more implied than real, with the low E[-flat] heard on every quarter of the measure.[20] Looking at the clashes in the instrumental parts, we find that the E-flat of the *banda* melody jars with the E-natural of the melody of the first violins, oboes, and clarinets, and the F-natural of the

16. Giovanni Battista Pergolesi and Niccolò Jommelli were two leading composers of Italian opera in the eighteenth century.

17. Giovanni Battista Doni, "Discorso sopra la perfettione delle melodie," in *Compendio del trattato de' generi e de' modi della musica* (Rome: Andrea Fei, 1635), 95–125, 109–10: "the French perhaps surpassing us in rhythm, as the Italians certainly outdo all other nations in melody" ("superandoci [i Francesi] forse nel ritmo, come gl'Italiani senza fallo sopravanzano tutte l'altre nazioni nella parte melica").

18. N. 1, mm. 193ff. Compare *Don Giovanni*, N. 13, Finale [primo] ("Presto presto pria ch'ei venga"), mm. 220ff.

19. See mm. 255ff. The *perigordino* ("Perigordino" is Verdi's explicit label in the autograph score, as is the immediately preceding "Tempo di Minuetto") is a dance of French origin that emerges in the eighteenth century.

20. The passage discussed here and in the following sentences is at mm. 376ff. (The *low* E-flat is actually heard on alternate quarters.)

banda with the F-sharp of the violins. A measure later some rough parallel fourths rend the ear.[21] And this is nothing: the first violins, oboe, and clarinet play in unison with the chorus basses, while the latter clash with the bassoon and cello. In short, this is a devil of a passage, which it would take too long even to describe! The dissonances are so jarring that I can attribute it only to caprice on the composer's part. Verdi should not have been encouraged by the example of the great Beethoven, who in his third-period compositions occasionally allowed himself some harmonic license—or rather wrong notes. Anyone inclined to imitate these blemishes in the work of the great Beethoven should note that when that chosen spirit wrote those things he no longer possessed his sense of hearing. Meyerbeer too used crude dissonances in an off-stage women's chorus in the last act of *Les Huguenots*, but at what point in the drama? When the horrendous Saint Bartholomew's Day massacre is taking place.[22]

After a recitative containing the usual chromatic movement,[23] the stretta of the *introduzione* ["O tu che la festa"] has a unison passage that is not at odds with the universal anger at the insolence of Monterone (Hugo's Saint-Vallier) when he curses Rigoletto and the duke.

A duet follows between Rigoletto and the hired assassin Sparafucile;[24] the horror of this scene, during which Sparafucile offers his services as a cut-throat, is depicted with a fine combination of instruments. It is a sort of *parlante armonico*, one that is very expressive. The melody is played by a cello and a double bass, both muted. This instrumentation so effectively communicates the innermost psychological state of the characters that it may be used as evidence by those who hold that it is unnecessary for the main melody to be always on the lips of the singer. This piece also shows that there is no loss of effect in departing from the usual form for duets, which requires a *tempo d'attacco*, an adagio, a *tempo di mezzo*, and a cabaletta.[25]

Preceding a duet for Rigoletto and his daughter Gilda there is a recitative that, contrary to Verdi's usual practice, is very carefully written and

21. Presumably a reference to the (barely concealed) parallel fifths created by the *banda* melody against the general ascending chromatic line, between the two main accents of m. 377.

22. See Meyerbeer, *Les Huguenots*, N. 27 b, Choeur des meurtriers ("Abjurez, huguenots").

23. At "Slanciare il cane" (mm. 507ff.).

24. N. 3, Duetto [Rigoletto e Sparafucile] ("Quel vecchio maledivami!!").

25. "La solita forma de' duetti" is of course Basevi's best-known (and most-often-quoted) phrase. See p. xxiii above; and the glossary, s.v. *tempo d'attacco*.

expressive.[26] The allegro vivo entry of the orchestra after the words "Ah no! è follia!" depicts marvelously the sudden change from terror to joy in Rigoletto's soul. The andante of the duet, "Deh non parlare al misero," conforms well to the words and displays a fine variety of dramatic color, if no rhythmic novelty. The soprano has four measures in the minor mode with a rhythm that aptly expresses Gilda's agitation. The meter changes suddenly from ¾ to ²⁄₄ and the vocal parts continue together, but in a way that forces the soprano to articulate syllables on excessively high notes, which yields unattractive shrieking sounds. In the *tempo di mezzo* ["Il nome vostro ditemi"], which prepares for the cabaletta, there is a short obbligato recitative and then a solemn baritone melody that makes a fine contrast with the gay melody of the soprano that follows. The way in which Verdi here gave musical form to the ideas expressed in the poetry should be studied by those composers who churn out their melodies without paying any heed to the words, which can often help, as they do here, to guide the composer's imagination. The cabaletta ["Veglia, o donna, questo fiore"], which Rigoletto begins, is a moderato assai with a very uniform rhythm, which is by no means unsuited to the situation, as these words express not any strong passion but rather a mere warning. But I cannot approve of Gilda's repetition of the same musical idea, for she is moved by different emotions. Before the cabaletta is repeated *a 2*, Verdi sagaciously interrupts the duet to insert a recitative that follows it in the libretto but that would have been anticlimactic in that position. After this interruption, the baritone repeats his melody; during each long note in the baritone's part, the soprano sings staccato eighth notes that serve no purpose other than to decorate the melody. While this may please someone who cares little for subtleties, it does not suit me one bit, for it is antidramatic.

In the duet the soprano then sings with the tenor[27] the ³⁄₈-time andantino is lacking as much in invention as in expression. The cabaletta ["Addio . . . speranza ed anima"] is lively and full of fire. The number of times the lovers repeat the word "addio" is very natural in those who, because of their mutual love, can barely bring themselves to part. In addition, the cabaletta is out of the ordinary in that it is almost entirely cast in a single melodic sweep [*di getto*]: it is not repeated but rather progresses through apt imitation, which accords well with the identical emotions shared by the two lovers.

26. N. 4, Scena ("Pari siamo! . . .") e Duetto [Gilda e Rigoletto] ("Deh non parlare al misero").

27. N. 5, Scena ("Giovanna? . . . ho dei rimorsi . . .") e Duetto [Gilda e Duca] ("È il sol dell'anima").

I think the allegro moderato of the following soprano aria most delicate and tender;[28] Verdi here managed to turn a common cadential phrase into a pleasing melody. This melody is most tastefully wedded to very gentle instrumentation, acquiring a quality that, in the modern phraseology of certain critics, would be called "vaporous" or "ethereal." At intervals, two muted solo violins are heard as a distant echo, with a pleasing effect. The theme does not proceed as usual, but is transformed by means of variations, and is finally lost in the distance with a magical effect. Although I am among the adversaries of those passages of bravura and agility that have no purpose other than to show off the singer's skills, I cannot object to these particular variations or vocal flourishes, as Gilda might well sing to herself as she returns to her rooms to rest.[29] But now that music has been liberated from the tyranny of coloratura, we must not subject it to that yoke again except in extraordinary cases such as this one—even in order to hear a singer like Farinelli, who, for example, sang 146 notes, with incredible agility and precision, on the second syllable of the word "speranza" in an aria from Hasse's *Siroe*.[30]

As Gilda exits singing, we hear a chorus of courtiers who are preparing to abduct her.

After a very apt *parlante* ["Chi va là?"], the first act ends with a chorus ["Zitti, zitti, moviamo a vendetta"] that again displays the vibrato and staccato manner that is one of the characteristics of Verdi's music.[31] Without exhibiting great novelty, this piece proceeds well and is rich in fine chiaroscuro effects.

The tenor aria that opens the second act is mediocre.[32] The andante is affecting but spiritless, and the rest is of very little value.

The baritone aria is extremely well conceived.[33] The inner anguish that oppresses Rigoletto when he approaches the courtiers to find out where his abducted daughter has been taken is well hidden in his intermittent singing to

---

28. N. 6, Aria [Gilda] ("Gualtier Maldè! . . ."; "Caro nome").

29. Interestingly, the "agilità" defended here by Basevi is precisely what Verdi insisted was not a feature of Gilda's aria—provided it is performed, as it should be, at a moderate pace and *sotto voce* throughout. See his letter of September 8, 1852, to Carlo Antonio Borsi, in *Copialettere*, 497–98, 497.

30. See Charles Burney, *A General History of Music from the Earliest Ages to the Present Period*, 4 vols. (London: printed for the author, 1776–89), 4 (1789): 400, 438.

31. Both *parlante* and chorus are part of N. 7, Finale primo ("Riedo! perché?"). On Basevi's use of *staccato* and *vibrato*, see chapter 13, n. 15, above.

32. N. 8, Scena ("Ella mi fu rapita!") ed Aria Duca ("Parmi veder le lagrime").

33. N. 9, Scena ("Povero Rigoletto!") ed Aria [Rigoletto] ("Cortigiani, vil razza dannata").

himself. Rigoletto's anger at the courtiers who mock him is aptly expressed in the music. The point at which the jester, overpowered by paternal love, weeps and pleads is very moving indeed. Where the melody moves to D-flat, a solo cello provides an agitated accompaniment depicting Rigoletto's internal agitation. This aria will always stand as one of the finest pages of Verdi's music.

In the duet for baritone and soprano, the soprano's $\frac{2}{4}$-time andantino is very expressive.[34] The baritone's vocal line is majestic and passionate, its accompaniment expressing throughout the agitation of the miserable Rigoletto. Where it moves to D-flat, the melody is most affecting, and, when the parts join together, the soprano's sixteenth-note triplets, depicting a sort of caressing, contrast well with the baritone's grave melody, "Piangi, piangi, etc." The cabaletta ["Sì, vendetta, tremenda vendetta"] has great energy, and though modeled somewhat on the *mossa* of the duet "L'ira d'avverso fato" in *Otello* is handled differently, though with no less drive.[35] The reprise of the theme in the subdominant, though nothing new, is nonetheless stirring at this point. Uniformity of rhythm, while useful to depict calm, can also represent, as it does here, the kind of extreme anger that is manifested in the appearance of its opposite—just as we sometimes see laughter turn into tears, and vice versa. Using these extreme opposites without falling into absurdity clearly requires no middling talent. This cabaletta allows us to observe the effect and importance of the accompaniment. If you tried an accompaniment that marked the time only every half measure, you would deprive the melody of its impetuous character.

The beginning of the third act gives us the very popular *canzone* "La donna è mobile."[36] Close examination shows that this melody too begins with a common lilt, which one could easily continue by making the third motif of the first phrase repeat the second one a step lower, just as the second one repeats the *mossa* of the phrase. For the rest, this *canzone* is no different from the most ordinary material, and has no virtue other than that of expedient simplicity. Apropos of this most popular melody, I shall mention something that often happens in music, namely, that a theme that initially strikes us as something

34. N. 10, Scena ("Mio padre!") e Duetto [Gilda e Rigoletto] ("Tutte le feste al tempio"). Basevi mistakenly writes $\frac{3}{4}$.

35. "L'ira d'avverso fato" is in fact the stretta of N. 7, [Scena] ("Che feci! . . . ove mi trasse") [e Duetto Otello e Iago] ("Non m'inganno; al mio rivale") in Rossini's *Otello*.

36. N. 11, Scena ("E l'ami?" "Sempre") e Canzone [Duca] ("La donna è mobile"). The label "canzone" relates to the strophic nature of the piece and to its function within the drama (it portrays something heard as a song by the characters on stage).

we have heard before comes after repeated hearings to seem original—provided it is not merely a copy. This occurs with melody as with certain faces: some are so similar that at first it is nearly impossible to tell them apart; seeing them often, however, we not only learn to distinguish them but end up seeing no similarity at all between them. I remember that when "La donna è mobile" was first heard, everyone said, "Oh, that old tune again!" And now, through habituation, it is seen by many almost as a highly original and distinctive melodic type.

The ensuing quartet is one of those pieces that reveal the power of a great genius.[37] It is also one of those musical pictures [*quadri musicali*] worthy of being hung in the gallery that the history of art should establish to preserve for posterity the greatest monuments of each era. The stage is divided in two. On one side the duke flirts with Maddalena; on the other is Rigoletto, who, through a hole in the wall, shows Gilda the infidelity of the man she thought to be a devoted lover. Joy and grief, treachery and vengeance, love and jealousy: all had to be represented in this picture—and with the figures not, as in painting, next to and distinct from one another, but all together in the same space of time and without confusion. Verdi succeeded in this difficult task, and his glory appears all the greater given the simple means he used. The instrumental part of the *parlante* with which the piece begins is very pleasing. The andante "Bella figlia dell'amore" has a clear-cut theme, and a certain triteness that is appropriate to the foppish duke. In a little staccato sixteenth-note phrase, Maddalena laughs at the duke's declarations, as she knows that "tai baie costan poco" [such chatter is cheap]. Gilda has heard everything and, in a little phrase with a halting rhythm, recalls that the duke had used the same amorous expressions with her. Maddalena then repeats her phrase with different words, as does Gilda. Rigoletto tells his daughter that this is no time for tears, while the four parts proceed through various harmonies that prepare for the tenor's reprise of the first seven measures of "Bella figlia dell'amore." But this time, every two measures, where the duke's melody rests, Maddalena imitates her first coquettish phrase, and Rigoletto and Gilda proceed together with a broad melody constructed so as not to interfere with the other two parts. Gilda then continues with a broken vocal line similar to the one we noted in the soprano-baritone duet in the first act of *Stiffelio*,[38]

37. N. 12, Quartetto ("Un dì, se ben rammentomi").

38. See mm. 100ff. of the duet "Dite che il fallo a tergere" (*Stiffelio*, N. 4) and Basevi's discussion of it at p. 155 above.

which is most apt for depicting the agitation produced by intense grief. But here, besides being more fitting, it produces a stronger effect because of its better accentuation, and because the breaks are almost always between notes that would tend to be linked by their mutual attraction. From time to time, in gaps left by the soprano, we hear Maddalena's laughter. Meanwhile, the duke continues his sweet lovemaking, and Rigoletto promises his daughter that he will avenge her. The broken melody of the soprano, which had begun pianissimo together with the other parts, now grows louder and, keeping the same rhythm while introducing the kind of sequence that generates anticipation [*ansietà*] in the listener, climaxes in an emotion-venting fortissimo. But the pianissimo quickly returns, and having grown a second time to fortissimo, the piece ends with a cadential passage in keeping with Gilda's broken line.

A recitative follows, during which we hear the beginnings of the storm.[39] Verdi used human voices to imitate the chromatic sliding of the wind as it strikes various objects or passes through various openings at varying speeds: an offstage chorus aptly imitates these effects of the wind. The storm continues throughout the act and provides the background to its most gloomy scene. The mind's perception of events varies according to the impressions it receives from surrounding nature. This storm induces in one's soul such sadness and horror that it makes the bloody scene unfolding seem even more terrible. This makes it clear that it is not always necessary to use contrast to give greater life to the action, for sometimes surroundings increase the power of that action precisely through their similarity to it. Verdi depicted this storm with the greatest skill. After the storms of Haydn, Beethoven, and Rossini, little of novelty remained for Verdi to create in the technical particulars, but he cleverly managed to broaden the field, adding to it several pieces of music that, while losing none of their own effect, drew from the horrors of the storm an additional efficacy they would otherwise have lacked. Some may now ask when one should use analogy and when contrast. As a general principle it would seem advisable to use contrast in respect to things of the same nature and analogy in respect to things of different kinds. In the quartet discussed above you find fine contrast effects [*effetto di contrapposti*], but these all pertain to the psyche, which—although distinct in the various characters and driven by diverse emotions—still remains of the same nature, whereas the analogies in the aforementioned storm scenes pertain to things of differing natures,

39. N. 13, Scena ("Venti scudi hai tu detto?"), Terzetto, e Tempesta [Gilda, Maddalena, e Sparafucile] ("È amabile invero cotal giovinotto").

such as grief-stricken hearts on the one hand and an atmosphere heavy with mists and fearfully stormy on the other. Improperly used, contrast and analogy will destroy the very effect they were intended to enhance. For example, if you were to use analogy to place the wickedness of a tyrant in greater relief, by putting by his side other characters who are equally wicked, you would not achieve your intent; indeed, your tyrant would seem less odious. In the same way, it would be a mistake to locate the swearing of a conspiratorial oath atop a pleasant hill on a fine spring day, for here the contrast would destroy the effect you were contemplating.

The *terzetto* that is incorporated into the storm contains some fine phrases, but, owing to the unclear situation, there is insufficient musical development. This situation would have worked better as an obbligato recitative than as a *terzetto*—which in any event turned out to be little more than such a recitative. The lightning, thunder, rain, and wind are accessories that increase the impact of the scene. When Gilda enters Sparafucile's house, where she is killed, the storm is at its most powerful, but the musical expression contains nothing unusual at this point. The storm then calms, and a recitative of little musical importance takes place.

The final duet is of negligible effect.[40] One must not, however, forget that music has nothing to offer such a repugnant situation.

Taking advantage of some fine dramatic situations, Verdi created a series of superb musical pictures. He did what was possible, but *Rigoletto* also called for the impossible. It was impossible to render deformity appealing or to find music suited to material that we find utterly revolting. When the human spirit is inclined to find greater appeal in deformity and can be moved only by disturbing scenes like the finale of *Rigoletto*, it is a sign that music can have little power over that spirit—except perhaps for the dissonant, deafening music of the Chinese, which we have to no small degree approached.[41]

For these reasons, *Rigoletto*, though abounding in good qualities, and though moving and rousing in many places, has never left audiences with as strong a sense of satisfaction as other operas by the same composer. On the other hand, the vocal lines are more exposed, and certain bad sonority effects [*effettacci di sonorità*] are absent, as are *di slancio* phrases, abuses of unison

---

40. N. 14, Scena ("Della vendetta! alfin giunge l'istante!") e Duetto finale [Gilda e Rigoletto] ("V'ho ingannato! colpevole fui!").

41. A likely reference to *Rigoletto* itself. See, for instance, Basevi's earlier description of a passage from the opera as cacophonic (pp. 166–67).

reprises and repeats, and so forth. So *Rigoletto* continues on the road of musical improvement begun by *Luisa Miller*.

I have not yet spent a great deal of time on the instrumental side of Verdi's operas, because it seemed advisable to wait until the composer had produced a substantial number of works.

I shall briefly say something about the instrumentation of *Rigoletto*, which can also be extended to our composer's other operas.

The most cursory examination of the score reveals a similarity to Donizetti's practices. This should not be considered a flaw; we can, however, deduce from it that Verdi thought it wise to keep the orchestra somewhat in a position of servility, so that melody—a single melody—could be the absolute, even despotic sovereign.

I would certainly not advocate a republic of instruments and singers, of melody and harmony, in which all these components would enjoy complete equality, such as can be found in the scores of certain transalpine masters. But neither can I endorse the opposite extreme—an Oriental despotism carried to the point of stifling every virtue except that of a *single* melody, which is allowed to govern capriciously and without check.

Certainly, Italians of earlier times, while not possessing such a wealth of instruments, allowed greater justice to reign in the orchestra. The scores of Jommelli are ample proof of this—not to mention our great Cherubini.

Verdi has at times given the orchestra a more important role than that of handmaid to the melody. It would be desirable for him to do this more often. He does not lack great sureness in his handling of the instruments, such that he rarely fails to achieve the intended effect.

The neglect of orchestration stems principally from a jealous protection of rhythmic effects: one is afraid—and rightly so—to interfere with rhythm, from which we expect the music's principal effect to come.

Must we wait for these rhythmic effects to pass out of fashion before we see an improvement in the interplay of instrumental parts?

16

IL TROVATORE

The choice of an operatic subject is a matter of no little importance if one wishes to satisfy the prevailing taste and at the same time provide the composer with material that will be congenial to his creative nature. Verdi requires subjects that burst forcefully on the audience's senses, so subjects in the manner of Victor Hugo are very well suited to him. Cammarano's choice of the play *El trovador* by García Gutiérrez, a Spaniard of that school, was therefore a good one.[1] The plot is dominated by love, jealousy, and vengeance—emotions that are eagerly sought by the operatic composer, and that Cammarano drew skillfully into his libretto, for which he retained the title of *Il trovatore*. Here in brief is the story. Azucena is a gypsy whose mother was burned at the stake as a witch by order of the old Count of Luna. The dying woman's last words were "Avenge me!" and her daughter has fallen heiress to this fearful legacy of vengeance. To achieve that vengeance, Azucena kidnaps one of the count's sons with the intent of burning him alive, but her own son is consumed by the flames by mistake. In his place she has raised the kidnapped

---

1. Antonio García Gutiérrez's *El trovador* had appeared on stage and in print in 1836. Basevi refers to the play as "il *Trovatore* di Grazia Guttierez." The critical edition of Verdi's *Il trovatore*, by David Lawton, was published as *WGV* I/18A (1993).

child, naming him Manrico. Nearing death, the elderly count commands
another son steadfastly to seek his lost brother. But the young count, though
diligent in his quest, has never been able to find a single trace of him. He does
not realize that his brother is his rival in love and the beloved of Leonora. In
jealousy, they take up arms against one another, and only a cry from deep
within Manrico's soul restrains his blade and prevents him from unwittingly
killing his brother. But mendacious rumor asserts Manrico's death, and the
grieving Leonora decides to enter a convent. The young count tries to abduct
her, but Manrico arrives in time to free her and take her off to Castellor. In the
meantime, Azucena is captured by the count's men, charged with kidnapping
and burning the count's brother, and condemned to the stake. From a balcony,
Manrico sees his supposed mother in chains and rushes to save her, but he too
is taken prisoner. Motivated by love, Leonora pretends to love the count in
order to save Manrico, but at the same time secretly drinks poison. When
the count discovers this, he orders Manrico's death, but as the troubadour's
head falls the count learns from Azucena that he has committed fratricide. It
will be clear that this plot is not lacking in the implausible and even the absurd,
but as compensation there is plenty to stir the spectator's innermost fibers.

    This opera was successfully performed in Rome in January 1853.[2] In the
first instance, it is to be praised for its opportune use of the contralto voice,
which will disappear into undeserved oblivion if composers make no move
to rescue it. Yet that voice—which the castrati were able to employ so skillfully, and which after the Crescentinis and the Vellutis was maintained in high
esteem by a distinguished array of female singers—should not be overlooked
by those composers who seek to profit from all that nature offers in order to
increase the splendor of art. But today, the habit of pummeling the ears with
high-pitched shrieks is so entrenched that, if we continue on the same course,
the baritone voice too will gradually vanish and only two kinds of voice will
remain: the soprano and the tenor. Besides, if we foster in our singers no
other gift than that of sheer lung power, all grace, agility, and flexibility of
voice will disappear, and the art of music will be quickly ruined.

    Was the contralto voice well chosen for the character of Azucena? I think
so, for it suits a woman completely possessed by her thirst for revenge. Verdi
might perhaps have done better to make Lady Macbeth a contralto too, as in
my opinion this voice is far more appropriate to the expression of a woman
who has something of the masculine in her haughtiness and in the force of

---

2. The venue was the Teatro Apollo.

her passions than it is to that of a man moved by excessively tender and pite-ous emotions.

After a very brief prelude and recitative, a *racconto* by the bass, Ferrando, begins ["Di due figli vivea padre beato"].[3] This is composed of two parts. One of these is a common-time andante mosso of fourteen measures' length, and the other is a longer allegretto in ¾ time, where the principal theme is actually found. This theme has a very regular, symmetrical rhythm without interrup-tions, and bears the mark of dance music. It should be noted that, both in the first melodic period in E minor and in the second in G major, Verdi has followed the system I have referred to elsewhere as musical economy. And while the whole of this piece is almost slavishly modeled on the rhythm of the first phrase, the composer avoids the tedium that often results from uni-formity by occasionally breaking up that uniformity with great taste, as in the nineteenth, twenty-third, and thirtieth measures;[4] finally, the high Es in the last melodic period are very fittingly used to prevent the effect from growing feeble. Here we clearly see Verdi's paramount intention to make a pleasing impression on the senses. And as the briskness of ternary meters is of assis-tance in this respect, these are lavishly used in this opera. Half the main lyri-cal sections[5] are fashioned in those meters, including as many as seven of the first eleven, which make up act 1 and half of act 2.[6] In past centuries ternary meters exhibited that same quality; you may read in the *Institution harmonique* (1615) of Salomon de Caus that duple meters used to be employed in grave music and ternary ones in gay music.[7] The *introduzione* ends with a unison chorus ["Sull'orlo dei tetti"], also in ternary meter, with a bizarre and singu-lar rhythm, whose theme is continued by Ferrando until he is interrupted by the sound of a bell. It is the midnight bell, which provokes dolorous memories in all, who therefore erupt with great force in a curse on the witch, of whose

3. What Basevi calls a "brevissimo *Preludio*" is not a free-standing prelude or *sinfonia* (which Verdi did away with entirely for the first time here) but rather the orchestral measures that open N. 1, Introduzione ("All'erta!"). Basevi italicizes his word for Ferrando's narrative, "un *rac-conto*," as if to signal the technical designation of a musical genre—and indeed the term is from Verdi's score, where it is used as a title for the section in question.

4. Measures 97, 101, 108.

5. Basevi's term here is "*cantabili*." See chapter 2, n. 53, above.

6. Whereas the libretto of *Il trovatore* is divided into four *parti*, in his score Verdi called them "atti," the practice followed by Basevi here.

7. See Salomon de Caus, *Institution harmonique divisée en deux parties* (Frankfurt: Jan Nor-ton, 1615), "Partie deuxième," 5–6.

evil deeds they have just been told. A final cry in A major, suddenly springing from the key of A minor, is most effective.

The cavatina for Leonora (soprano) follows.[8] The ⅜-time andante is preceded by a little five-measure prelude that inclines the mind to the tranquil melody so aptly fitting the words "Tacea la notte." To obtain the needed variety, tempo and rhythm are changed in the little four-measure phrase at "dolci s'udiro e flebili." This kind of variety was known and used successfully long ago; one example is in Paer's cantata *Eloisa ed Abelardo*, where, at the fifteenth measure of the soprano cantabile "Funesti pensieri," there is a phrase ("Perché mi togliete la pace del core") in a new tempo and rhythm, which is even framed according to the "economical" system.[9] Verdi, who always aims at effect, ends this andante with a short melodic period shaped as a crescendo. Not satisfied with that, he repeats it a second time and reinforces it with a tremolo in the strings. It seems to me that this repetition is too obviously tacked on and does not grow as it should from the material that precedes it. See how Rossini handled the *romance* "Sombre forêt" in *Guillaume Tell*: the second time, rather than repeating anything, he created a new melodic period that provides a marvelous ending to the musical discourse.[10] The cabaletta of this cavatina ["Di tale amor che dirsi"] is very graceful and lovely, with a leaping—almost frolicking—rhythm that communicates great brio to the listener. Although the piece is constructed without variety, the rhythm of its *mossa* is so pleasant that we willingly hear it repeated. This may be counted among the loveliest of Verdi's cabalettas.

The *romanza* for Manrico (tenor) does not at all have the right character for a piece meant to take us back to the time of the troubadours, and greater harmonic simplicity would have been desirable.[11] Here are seventeen measures that would make precious little impression on the listener were the singer not forced to make a show of his voice at the end. Note too that this *romanza* is a

---

8. N. 2, Cavatina Leonora ("Ché più t'arresti?"; "Tacea la notte placida").

9. A reference to the fact that Verdi's four-measure *frasetta* just mentioned is also treated according to Basevi's "sistema *economico-musicale*" (see N. 2, mm. 57–64). A vocal score of Paer's cantata *Eloisa ed Abeilardo* [*sic*] *agli Elisi* was published by Artaria of Vienna around 1798.

10. N. 9, [Récitatif] ("Ils s'éloignent enfin . . . j'ai cru le reconnaître") [et Romance Mathilde] ("Sombre forêt, désert triste et sauvage"). Basevi refers to the piece in Italian ("[la] Romanza 'Selva opaca'"). His praise for the absence of musical repetition "the second time" refers not to the piece's second stanza (this is a *romance*, thus set strophically) but to the inner melodic construction of each stanza (the opening 8 + 8 measures could easily have been set as a conventional A A').

11. N. 3, Scena ("Tace la notte!"), Romanza ("Deserto sulla terra"), e Terzetto ("Qual voce! . . . Ah! dalle tenebre").

⅜ andante in which the minor mode dominates. Now, when we consider that the narrative and chorus of the *introduzione* are in the minor, along with the andante of the soprano's cavatina and, as we shall see, Azucena's act 2 *canzone* and *racconto*, we are prompted to ask ourselves whether all these minor-mode ternary rhythms do the opera any good. I think they do, for, when in the major, ternary meters inherently have something too sweet and cloying about them that can easily satiate—so that the minor mode, having some sadness to it, has a useful tempering effect.

Soon afterward comes a *terzetto* for Leonora, Manrico, and the Count of Luna (baritone).[12] A *parlante* precedes it; conforming to the custom in Verdi's second manner, this is fairly well developed. The instrumental part is brisk and has the staccato rhythm for which Verdi has always shown such fondness. The agitatissimo of this *terzetto* ["Di geloso amor sprezzato"][13] begins with a vibrant, energetic, and impetuous melody for the baritone; the phrase "Un accento profferisti" has no appeal other than its high notes. The soprano and tenor follow quickly in unison with an impetuosity that recalls Verdi's first manner as found in the first *terzetto* of *Ernani* and in the second-act quartet from *I due Foscari*.[14] The unison passage having ended, the baritone repeats a few measures of his melody and continues with a sort of connecting passage [*attacco*], or coda, that could be characterized as more typical of instrumental than of vocal music; it is very like the short coda in the overture to Rossini's *L'Italiana in Algeri* leading to the second theme of the allegro.[15] Verdi was so fond of this type of coda that he used it also before the *pezzo concertato* that closes the second act of this opera.[16] In Rossini's *Eduardo e Cristina* we find a similar effect in Giacomo's part during the ²⁄₄-time andante of the first finale, from the twenty-fourth to the twenty-eighth measure.[17] The aforementioned

12. This is the *terzetto* within N. 3. It opens with the *parlante* (mm. 93ff., "Qual voce! . . .") to which Basevi refers in the following sentence (he has the *terzetto* begin with the ensuing stretta).

13. Verdi's tempo is allegro assai mosso; Basevi derives the term "agitatissimo" from Verdi's performance direction for the count's opening phrase.

14. Compare this N. 3 at mm. 205ff. ("Un istante almen dia loco"/"Del superbo è vana l'ira") with *Ernani*, N. 4, mm. 153ff. ("Me conosci . . ."/"No, crudeli"), and *I due Foscari*, N. 10, mm. 179ff. ("Ah sì il tempo che mai non s'arresta").

15. *L'Italiana in Algeri*, ed. Azio Corghi, *EC* I/11 (1981), Sinfonia, mm. 68ff.

16. See N. 8, mm. 99–100.

17. Basevi is referring to the section "Oh dio! . . . Fia ver! . . . Ei"/"Tu stesso!" in Rossini, *Eduardo e Cristina*, N. 7, Finale primo ("A che, spietata sorte"). *Eduardo e Cristina* (Venice: Teatro San Benedetto, 1819) is a *pasticcio* that Rossini created largely by reusing earlier music of his own. The passage discussed here by Basevi originated in Rossini's *Ermione* (Naples: Teatro

bridge phrase in the baritone's part leads to a reprise of the soprano-tenor unison, during which the baritone proceeds in quarter-note motion in the manner of a basso continuo. A più mosso, serving as a cadential passage, brings the first act to an end.

Act 2 opens with a chorus of gypsies suitably prepared for by the orchestra.[18] The final part of the chorus, where the anvil strokes are introduced, is well conceived. A good contrast occurs when the chorus ends a cappella, apart from two cadential claps[19] in the orchestra.

The *canzone* "Stride la vampa!" is a ⅜-time allegretto in the minor mode, very symmetrical and simple, whose form offers nothing unusual.[20] Note that it ends not with a cadenza but rather, like the gypsy chorus, with two orchestral claps,[21] something one also finds in the work of others—for example, in the "Piff paff" song from Meyerbeer's *Les Huguenots*.[22]

If we now consider the first eight measures of this *canzone* and their possible harmonic relationships with the accompaniment, we will see that they could equally unfold in either G major or E minor without distressing the ear. This prompts me to expand somewhat on the relationship of melody to harmony in general. The influence of keys on melody is immediately seen in the different scale degrees that notes assume within the different keys. Taking the present case as an example, B, the note with which the *canzone* begins, is the third of the key of G and the fifth of the key of E; now, a third does not have the same relative sound as a fifth, and with a simple change in the accompanying harmony the same note will lose its initial relative sound.[23] It still has its absolute sound, but it is not from this that melodies are generated.

San Carlo, 1819). See the critical edition by Patricia B. Brauner and Philip Gossett, *EC* I/27 (1995), N. 7, Finale primo ("Amarti? Ah sì, mio ben!"), at mm. 178ff. (the cantabile "Sperar . . . "/ "Temer . . . poss'io?").

18. N. 4, Coro di zingari ("Vedi, le fosche notturne spoglie") e Canzone ("Stride la vampa!").

19. Basevi's word is "strappate," figuratively extending to the entire orchestra a term that applies to the strings (it refers to the use of the bow during multiple-stop chords).

20. As in the case of *Rigoletto*'s "La donna è mobile," the label "canzone" (used by both Verdi and Basevi) refers to the fact that here Azucena's singing represents something heard as a song by the characters on stage and to the associated strophic form (which explains Basevi's description).

21. We translate as "cadenza" Basevi's "comune" (one of the ways to refer to a fermata in nineteenth-century Italian). The "claps" are, again, Basevi's "strappate" (see n. 19 above).

22. Indeed two similar "strappate" conclude both stanzas of Marcel's song in the first act of *Les Huguenots*: N. 4, Scène et Chanson huguenote ("Piff, paff, piff, paff").

23. The concept of "relative sound" dates back at least to Rousseau's *Dissertation sur la musique moderne* (Paris: Quillau, 1743), 18–19.

Rameau saw very clearly that a melody changes its character and its melodic sense with the alteration of its fundamental bass, and is thus transmuted into a new melody.[24] From this he thought he could infer that melody is generated by harmony. But Rousseau disagreed, noting that harmony acts on melody only to the extent of determining the scale degree of each note in relation to the key, and that a melodic line exists as melody and not as harmony. In point of fact, were we to accept Rameau's claim strictly, we would have to discount entirely the element of succession, which is the veritable substance of melody. But it cannot be denied that a melody suggests its own harmony, which our ears long for without our realizing it. And truly, notes do not always derive their sound from their degree within the key, as Rousseau would have it, for in that case each note would be entitled to its own harmony as suggested by the key: at times they are rather appoggiaturas and passing notes, which have no meaning without reference to the harmony of the note onto which they resolve or pass. A melody would lose its character if these notes were harmonized as essential tones of the key. How does a melody suggest the most appropriate harmony? In various ways, but mainly by the natural tendency toward the easy and simple that is inherent in everything. In the *canzone* "Stride la vampa! la folla indomita" the last syllable, -*ta*, is on an F-sharp, which can belong to the chord of B if the piece is to be in E minor, or just as well to the chord of D major if we take the melody to be in G. In the latter case, the leap of a fourth from this F-sharp to the B at the beginning of the second phrase proves very awkward—so much so that, in order to make it smoother, we tend to imagine the B itself in the preceding chord together with the F-sharp; we therefore establish E minor as the key that is of most use in pitching the intervals of this *canzone*. Verdi was thus well served by his musical instinct in framing it in that key.

Melody may be considered from two principal angles in its relation to harmony: first, when the melody is either unaccompanied or accompanied by the harmony or one of the harmonies it suggests, and second, when it is set against a harmony with which it would not naturally be connected. There are two kinds of melody in the first category and two in the second. A first kind consists of those melodies that leave no doubt about the suitability of the harmonies with which they are associated. These are the most effective

24. The notion of the *basse fondamentale*, introduced by Rameau in his *Traité de l'harmonie reduite à ses principes naturels* (1722), refers not to the bass line notated in a score, which includes chords in inverted positions, but to the "real" bass line that can be derived from reducing all chords to root position.

and the most appealing, for they cause no uncertainty or labor in our minds, which accept them with the greatest pleasure. Could there be any doubt about the chords that harmonize the prayer "Dal tuo stellato soglio" from Rossini's *Mosè?*[25] Sometimes the composer will use harmonies that are not specifically implied but serve as ornaments and facilitate the natural chord progression; here the science of music comes to the aid of instinct. Another kind of melody is created out of those lines that can be fitted to a variety of harmonizations, and these are certainly not the most beautiful. Nonetheless, because of the surprise that certain harmonies can arouse, these can sometimes lend the melody a character that is well suited to expressing the dramatic situation. Thus, in the famous andantino from the trio in *Guillaume Tell*, at the words "Mon père, tu m'as dû maudire!" Rossini used distantly related chords that greatly add to the effect of the melody.[26] But it must be noted that in this case the melody is somewhat secondary; at that solemn moment no one would seek prettiness or tenderness in the vocal line. A third kind of melody comprises those created by composers, often as a display of learnedness, through torturing lines into forced association with harmonies they in no sense call for. As an example of this it is worth mentioning Wolfram's aria in act 3, scene 2, of Wagner's *Tannhäuser*, "O! du mein holder Abendstern." But what good is it, may I ask, to create melodies only to disturb them through harmonization? It would be better to counsel these composers to save learning for its proper place, pointing out that erudition is all the more to be prized when less obvious. Still, torturing melodies can at times prove useful, as may be seen in the final scene of Meyerbeer's *Le prophète*, when Jean de Leyde intones the drinking song for the third time; in this case the "inappropriate" accompaniment accords well with the horror of the scene.[27] There is finally a fourth kind of melody, those that have no significance by themselves without the support of harmony. Fétis, in his admirable treatise on harmony, states that nowadays melody is losing its purity because of the appetite for harmonic change that holds sway over composers; because of this, melodies are created that are meaningless without their harmony. And to prove his assertion he cites a passage from Rossini's *Soirées musicales*, more precisely from the *serenata* "Mira,

---

25. See *Mosè in Egitto*, N. 12, [Preghiera] "Dal tuo stellato soglio" [e Finale] "Ma qual fragor!"

26. See *Guillaume Tell*, N. 11, Trio "Quand l'Helvétie est un champ de supplices," mm. 100–101, 112ff. (Basevi quotes the phrase in the Italian translation by Calisto Bassi: "Il padre ahimé mi malediva.")

27. See Meyerbeer, *Le prophète*, ed. Matthias Brzoska et al., *MWA* I/14 (2011), N. 29, Final: 29 b, Couplets bachiques.

la bianca luna," namely, the phrase "Vieni alla selva bruna."[28] It seems to me, however, that while that melody modulates, this does not make it meaningless, for it still suggests the appropriate harmonies so clearly that it could survive admirably well without them. Melody is not incompatible with harmonic change, fine examples being found in the melodies "Assisa appiè d'un salice" from Rossini's *Otello* and "Ah! vorrei trovar parola" from Bellini's *La sonnambula*.[29] And if the time predicted by Fétis should come, when music becomes "omnitonic,"[30] melody will still not be destroyed, for the ear, accustomed to the new tonality, will be just as able then as it is today to suggest the proper harmonies for the new melodies. Now if anyone wants examples of melodies that are of little significance without their harmonies, he need only open those old books of cantatas, duets, and so forth built on the basso continuo. But for those who do not wish to go that far back, I shall mention the cabaletta "Oh! barbaro mio fato" in Mercadante's *Il giuramento*, where at several points the melody, rather than suggesting the harmony, depends on it for forward motion.[31] It will be clear from the above that one should opt for those melodies that best suggest their own harmonies; it must also be said that one must take great care not to generate boredom with too much harmonic monotony—or fatigue with an excess of harmonic change.

Azucena's *racconto* must unquestionably be counted among the finest pieces in this opera, and will be appreciated all the more for the difficulty involved in setting it.[32] Music and poetry both need emotions, but the first requires these to be more energetic and vehement. Narration is by nature more tranquil than action; in consequence the narrator is not as inflamed by passion as is the protagonist of the story. Still, the poet may succeed in being powerfully moving through the themes his art lends him and in which his ingenuity may kindle new life. But as an art that cannot use determinate language to bare

28. See François-Joseph Fétis, *Traité complet de la théorie et de la pratique de l'harmonie*, 2nd ed. (Paris: Schlesinger, 1844), 196–99; English translation in François-Joseph Fétis, *Complete Treatise on the Theory and Practice of Harmony*, ed. Peter M. Landey (Hillsdale, NY: Pendragon, 2008), 192–93. "Mira, la bianca luna" is N. 11 of Rossini's *Soirées musicales*.

29. "Assisa appiè d'un salice" is Desdemona's "Willow Song," part of the N. 10 that forms the entirety of the third and final act of Rossini's *Otello*. "Ah! vorrei trovar parola" is uttered by Amina at mm. 142ff. of Elvino's "Prendi: l'anel ti dono" in act 1 of Bellini's *Sonnambula* (Milan: Teatro Carcano, 1831). See Vincenzo Bellini, *La sonnambula*, ed. Alessandro Roccatagliati and Luca Zoppelli, *ECB* 7 (2009), [N. 3], [Recitativo e] Cavatina d'Elvino.

30. The "ordre omnitonique" was the ultimate phase in the history of Western harmony as Fétis viewed it. See chapter 1, n. 11, above.

31. This is the cabaletta of Viscardo's second-act aria "Fu celeste quel contento."

32. N. 5, Racconto d'Azucena ("Soli or siam!"; "Condotta ella era in ceppi").

the intimate feelings of the soul, music must make use of the accents of declamation. Now, declamation is not so vividly effective in a narrator as in the one who takes action; hence, music is none too appropriate to narration. But these considerations do not apply to scenes where most of the spectator's attention is naturally focused on the character who is listening to the narration, since he or she, receiving news that causes either joy or sadness, is moved directly, not vicariously. A good example of this is in *Norma*, where Adalgisa tells Norma of how she fell in love. The listener pays little heed to what Adalgisa is saying, but focuses on Norma, and is therefore shaken when, almost rapt in ecstasy, she sings, "O, cari accenti! etc.," one of Bellini's most beautiful inspirations.[33] This does not hold for Azucena's *racconto*. The spectator's attention is naturally focused on Azucena; because of this, the librettist was well advised to have her step out of her reminiscence,[34] and to enflame her as though she were once more in the midst of the events she is relating. This *racconto* begins with a ⁶⁄₈ andante mosso in the minor mode. Note that from time to time there is a groan in the accompaniment, as though that of Azucena's mother. Initially the theme, proceeding in the manner of a song, does not seem terribly well adapted to the words, and the composer's intention to caress the ear is obvious; but from the point at which Manrico responds, "La vendicasti?" the singing becomes expressive and declamatory, and the instrumentation suits the scene perfectly. Of fine effect is the orchestral repetition, in the violins' high register, of the theme of Azucena's *canzone* against a *parlante*;[35] and the crescendo that leads to the allegro agitato at "Mi vendica!" is most effective. From here, the *racconto* goes into common time and becomes completely declamatory, supported splendidly by the orchestra. Those high F-naturals on "il figlio mio avea bruciato!" which are a minor ninth above the bass, are searing.[36] After this supreme burst of passion, the composer depicts with great verisimilitude the draining of Azucena's spirit, which he communicates with marvelous effect by means of notes descending to the depths.

33. See, in the first act of Bellini's *Norma*, the *scena* and duet for Norma and Adalgisa that opens N. 5, Scena e Terzetto finale; the passage in question is at the twentieth measure from the beginning of the duet proper ("Sola, furtiva al tempio").

34. A reference to the fact that, when her *racconto* reaches its horrific climax, Azucena's words switch from the past tense of a narration to the present tense of a relived experience.

35. Compare mm. 71ff. with the preceding N. 4 at mm. 91ff.

36. Basevi's adjective is the same as Verdi's performance direction for the singer at this very point ("straziante").

The duet between Azucena and Manrico[37] has a cantabile for Manrico, allegro, that is little suited to the words but openhearted and clear. Azucena's meno mosso employs a rhythmic effect similar to that of Maddalena's entry in the *Rigoletto* quartet, although here it is more developed, and suits the character's fierce temperament.[38] The cabaletta ["Perigliarti ancor languente"] is an extremely quick ⅜ in the minor mode, in which Azucena sings first, expressing her maternal love for Manrico. This union of the harsh and the tender in the gypsy's soul is rather apt. When she says, "il tuo sangue è sangue mio!" [your blood is my blood], a pedal and an ascending figure of four semitones suggest the falsity of her claim. Manrico's major-mode answer has a too openly dancelike character, and no expressiveness is added by the accent that Verdi places on the penultimate sixteenth note of each measure. The melodic period that Azucena and Manrico sing in unison, and that concludes the theme begun by Manrico, is at odds with the words.

The aria for the Count of Luna follows.[39] The largo is majestic and proceeds with a certain gravity. The second melodic period, which is fashioned according to the economical system, is rich in changes of harmony, which progress without affectation and to good effect.[40] Note here that when the phrase is repeated for a second time it is no longer accompanied by the same harmonies. This is a sort of variety that, used with reserve, produces a fine effect. In the final melodic period, the tessitura of the vocal line is so high that one would think the baritone had turned into a tenor. In the *tempo di mezzo* there is a staccato chorus with rapid answers among the voices, representing the lively interchange of many people talking among themselves. A similar procedure is found in the first finale of Rossini's *Eduardo e Cristina*, in the 2/4-time andante, where it provides a sort of vocal accompaniment to the principal melody.[41] Something along the same lines may be heard in the chorus "Pan! pan!" in *Les diamants de la couronne* by Auber.[42] The cabaletta of the count's aria ["Per me ora fatale"] is energetic but offers nothing unusual; at

37. N. 6, Scena ("Non son tuo figlio? . . .") e Duetto [Azucena e Manrico] ("Mal reggendo all'aspro assalto").

38. Compare mm. 92ff. ("Ma nell'alma dell'ingrato") with *Rigoletto*'s N. 12 at mm. 64ff. ("Ah! ah! rido ben di core").

39. N. 7, Aria Conte ("Tutto è deserto!"; "Il balen del suo sorriso").

40. Measures 42ff.

41. See the reference in n. 17 above.

42. Daniel-François-Esprit Auber, *Les diamans* [*sic*] *de la couronne* (Paris: Troupenas, [1841]), N. 3, Choeur ["Amis, dans ce manoir"] et Ballade ["Le beau Pédrille"]. The opera was premiered at Paris's Opéra-Comique in 1841.

times it recalls the piece "Ite entrambi" from Bellini's *Beatrice*.[43] On the other hand, there is a certain novelty at the end of this piece, where the chorus joins in and—retaining the staccato rhythm and the answering texture noted in the *tempo di mezzo*—concludes by dying away to excellent effect. This shows how erroneous is the opinion of those who, for the sake of effect, would have all pieces end in a riot.

The second finale begins with an offstage sacred chorus;[44] there follows an imitative alternation of several short, staccato phrases between the onstage chorus and the baritone; toward the end of the piece these phrases accompany the offstage chorus's final melodic period to fine effect. The *pezzo concertato* follows ["E deggio e posso crederlo?"], an andante mosso in common time, begun by the solo soprano with a cantabile melody whose first period has a staccato rhythm based on three sixteenth notes followed by a sixteenth rest. The rhythm changes in the second, very brief period, and again in the final one, to which Verdi attached some importance, as we will see. The baritone follows with a phrase that is completed by another phrase for the tenor; this occurs twice. These phrases call to mind the final *terzetto* of *Attila*.[45] Then the baritone initiates a melodic period that the tenor, joining him, continues and that the soprano finishes, singing in ensemble with the other voices. After this, the tenor and the baritone in unison sing a phrase of instrumental character that functions as a bridge or coda, and leads to a very fine ensemble in which the theme is taken by the soprano, with the others providing what amounts to an accompaniment. This theme has the staccato rhythm we pointed out in the first melodic period of the andante mosso, although here it continues for as many as eighteen measures. This insistence produces an effect that could not have been achieved with fewer repetitions. The perceptive composer must give serious consideration to this asset of rhythmic insistence: Verdi had already benefited from it in the *Rigoletto* quartet. A fine example is found in Bellini's *La straniera*, in the chorus "Qui non visti."[46] Verdi's intention in using the rhythm in question was no doubt to express joy. Mozart had already used it to that end, as may be seen in *Die Entführung aus dem Serail*,

43. See the second-act quintet with chorus "Al tuo fallo ammenda festi" from *Beatrice di Tenda* (Venice: Teatro La Fenice, 1833): the passage mentioned by Basevi is on pp. 94ff. of vol. 2 of the score (Rome: Pittarelli, n.d.) reproduced in *ERO* 5 (1980).

44. N. 8, Finale atto secondo ("Ah! se l'error t'ingombra").

45. See, in the Terzetto ("Te sol, te sol quest'anima") within *Attila*'s N. 12, the exchanges that begin at m. 170.

46. "Qui non visti" is part of the first-act huntsmen's chorus "Campo ai veltri."

where Belmonte says, "Klopft mein liebevolles Herz."[47] But although many composers have employed this rhythm, they have prolonged it very little in vocal parts, as you may see also in the third act of Rossini's *Otello*, where, after repeating for the final time the first eight measures of her *romanza*, Desdemona sings, "Ma stanca alfin di piangere, etc."[48] A similar rhythm has been repeated at greater length in instrumental parts, and Mercadante made good use of it in *Leonora*, where Strelitz narrates the death of Guglielmo.[49] After an allegro vivo ["Urgel viva!"] that takes the place of a *tempo di mezzo*, the act ends with a repetition of the final melodic period of the soprano's cantabile, noted above at the beginning of the ensemble ["Sei tu dal ciel disceso"]. This reprise of a forgotten phrase is somewhat odd. Verdi did something similar in *I due Foscari*, at the end of the second act—but to what effect?[50] Very little indeed. To make a good impression with reprised phrases, one has to create an expectation for them, or present them with adornments that will arouse marvel in the audience. Meyerbeer is unique in his ability to render his themes more agreeable each time, presenting them newly clothed with ever greater luxury and sheathed in the loveliest embellishments.

The third act begins with a chorus, in which the theme at the words "Squilli, echeggi la tromba guerriera" seizes our attention both through its rhythm and through its harmonies.[51] With regard to rhythm, it is because that of the first measure in no way presages that of the following ones—a two-and-a-half-measure succession of dotted-eighth-note-plus-sixteenth-note figures. This prolonged uniformity produces the effect of rhythmic insistence discussed above. With regard to the harmonies, one notes a certain *sprezzatura* where the order of the chords of the first two measures is changed in the third measure with the aim of reaching a dominant chord in the fourth. There is lovely variety in the accompaniment to this piece.

The *terzetto* for Azucena, the count, and Ferrando is none too charming.[52] Here again Azucena begins with a minor-mode section in ⅜ time, which shifts to the major in its final melodic period. When Azucena's cantabile has ended,

47. N. 4, Recitativo ed Aria ("Konstanze! dich wieder zu sehen!—O wie ängstlich, o wie feurig klopft mein liebevolles Herz!"), mm. 9–13. *NMA* II:v/12 (1982), ed. Gerhard Croll. Basevi refers to the opera as *Il rapimento* and quotes in Italian ("come batte questo core").

48. See Rossini, *Otello*, N. 10, mm. 230–33.

49. In the Finale terzo of the opera (Naples: Teatro Nuovo, 1844). The passage is at pp. 210ff. of the vocal score printed by Lucca in Milan in 1845 (pl. nos. 5181–5201).

50. For Basevi's discussion of the passage, see pp. 67–68 above.

51. N. 9, Coro ("Or co' dadi").

52. N. 10, Scena ("In braccio al mio rival!") e Terzetto ("Giorni poveri vivea").

the piece continues as a *parlante* interspersed with lyrical passages until the cabaletta—where Azucena's theme is trite. The count's is a little better, and the chorus is well matched to it. At the reprise of Azucena's theme, the count, Ferrando, and the chorus, in mutual imitation, join in the singing.

Now comes the tenor's aria, which contains a fine adagio.[53] In writing this tender melody, Verdi had in mind "Fra poco a me ricovero" from *Lucia*, as we can see also in the rhythm at the move to D-flat.[54] In the *tempo di mezzo* ["L'onda de' suoni mistici"] there is an uninteresting *a 2* for tenor and soprano, which I will point to as an instance of dawdling that is quite exceptional in Verdi's music. The ¾-time cabaletta in the major mode is dance music pure and simple ["Di quella pira"]. The rhythm of the entire piece is to be found in the first two measures. There are some *di forza* passages that please today's audiences, and this has therefore become a very popular melody. Note that while the first four measures suggest the chord of C major, Verdi used that of F minor in the third measure as a harmonic decoration; rather than upsetting the harmony suggested by the first phrase, this gives it renewed force in the fourth measure, because its arrival is more keenly craved. This is a useful example of an enhancing subsidiary harmony.

Act 4 begins with the beautiful "Miserere" scene.[55] The little ten-measure prelude has a dark and mysterious character that disposes the soul to sadness. Leonora's adagio "D'amor sull'ali rosee" is of great sweetness and unfolds with much variety. Some of the harmonic changes in the final melodic period follow hard on one another, but they do not cause confusion, for the melody itself demands them. The offstage chorus that follows ["Miserere d'un'alma già vicina"] is solemn, and the occasional distant tolling of the bell arouses a terror that is well expressed in the ensuing melody for Leonora, "Quel suon, quelle preci." This contains a rhythm that is repeated several times at short intervals until everything appears to become confused at the words "che tutta m'investe, al labbro il respiro, i palpiti al cor!"[56] For two measures after this, the melody successfully imitates Leonora's agitation by means of triplets with rests [*terzine vuote*] in place of the first eighth note. We then hear the offstage voice of Manrico, who, singing in the major mode, makes an effective con-

53. N. 11, Aria Manrico ("Quale d'armi fragor"; "Ah! sì, ben mio, coll'essere").

54. This is the cantabile in Edgardo's final aria from Donizetti's *Lucia di Lammermoor*: N. 9, Ultima scena ("Tombe degli avi miei"; "Fra poco a me ricovero").

55. The "Miserere" is part of the fourth act's opening number, N. 12, Scena ("Siam giunti") ed Aria Leonora ("D'amor sull'ali rosee").

56. Basevi mistakenly has "ai palpiti il cor."

trast with the doleful minor used until now. The tenor sings an eight-measure phrase in which the portion on the words "a chi desia, a chi desia morir! . . ." is extremely moving; a great part of its effect is the result of the harmony, which at this point follows a most natural progression and serves as good preparation for the cadential "addio" that follows. The offstage chorus is heard again and then Leonora's sad melody, now intermixed with the chorus periodically singing "miserere." The tenor soon repeats his tender melody; the effect of the progression of which I spoke is improved with the alteration of the words to "Non ti scordar di me! . . ." When this is completed, Leonora responds, in a very impassioned one-measure phrase, "Di te scordarmi?" which is repeated. During these two measures the tenor has begun his melody for the third time; it has been compressed and now occupies only four measures. The soprano, who had had her impassioned little phrase in the first two measures, in the other two continues by filling in. In the meantime, the offstage chorus at intervals sings "miserere," which combines well with the melodies of Manrico and Leonora. And thus are formed four measures of ensemble that are truly masterly and of magical effect. These last four measures are repeated, and then a simple prolongation of the harmony concludes this marvelous piece, which has had the power to deeply move spectators everywhere. Composers in particular must take note above all of the simplicity and clarity of this scene. The soprano's allegro ["Tu vedrai che amore in terra"] that follows this beautiful scene has little effect. But it is true that, after so fine a piece, it would be difficult to please or move an audience.

At the beginning of the duet for the count and Leonora[57] there is a very vivacious and natural *parlante*, in typical Verdian style, that leads to an andante mosso, in which Leonora has a very clear, symmetrical, and pleasant cantabile. The count responds with a different rhythm, energetic and vibrant, and infused with a full measure of Verdian impetuosity. Then the parts intertwine, employing the rhythms already used. For several measures there are some very effective little broken phrases in the soprano part, on the words "Mi svena! . . . calpesta . . . il mio, etc."; they contrast with the baritone's angry line. After the *tempo di mezzo* ["Conte!" "Né cessi!"] there is a very quick-paced cabaletta ["Vivrà! . . . Contende il giubilo"], each of whose melodic periods is composed of a single eight-measure phrase, except for the last, which is extended to twelve measures. The first part is sung by the soprano

57. N. 13, Scena ("Udiste? Come albeggi") e Duetto [Leonora e Conte] ("Qual voce! . . . come! . . . tu donna? . . .").

and the second by the baritone; the soprano then repeats her first phrase, after which, in a più mosso, the two parts interact until, having reprised the first phrase almost entirely in unison, they bring the piece to a close with a short cadential passage.

A *duettino* for Azucena and Manrico follows.[58] The ⅜-time andantino with which Azucena's cantabile begins is in the minor mode ["Sì . . . la stanchezza"], and Manrico continues in the major. After this, Azucena sings the lovely melody "Ai nostri monti . . . ritorneremo! . . ." The tenor repeats his phrase, and Azucena continues with broken phrases well suited to someone who is dropping off to sleep.

The *terzettino* for Azucena, Manrico, and Leonora has few charms. The andante ["Parlar non vuoi! . . ."], begun by the tenor, includes a fine phrase on the words "Ha quest'infame l'amore venduto!" that recalls a phrase from the first quintet of *I Lombardi*;[59] this phrase dominates the *terzettino* while it still has the appearance of a duet for tenor and soprano. When Azucena repeats the cantabile "Ai nostri monti," the other two parts, in a sense, provide the accompaniment; this weakens and cools off the action, focusing the spectator's attention on the sleeping character and distracting it from the other two, who are the most important at this point.

In the final scene we find nothing of note except the few measures of andante that Leonora begins with the words "Prima . . . che d'altri . . . vivere. . . ." The soprano's line, with its breathless rhythms, joins with those of the tenor and baritone to great effect.

Although it belongs to Verdi's second manner, *Il trovatore* has a certain exaggerated quality in common with the first. We nevertheless find in it more than a few praiseworthy pieces, which have rightly made this opera one of the most popular on the stages of Italy and the world.

There is a French translation entitled *Le trouvère*, which Verdi enriched with four pieces of ballet music, inserted into act 3 after the chorus of soldiers.[60]

---

58. We have in fact reached the opening of the opera's last number—N. 14, Finale ultimo ("Madre . . . non dormi?"). The first printed vocal score (Milan: Ricordi, 1853) marks this as "Finale quarto" but typically goes on to subdivide it into smaller numbers, and the titles found there ("Duettino," "Terzettino," "Scena finale") are reflected in Basevi's discussion.

59. Compare mm. 226ff. of this finale with the concertato "T'assale un fremito!" in *I Lombardi*'s N. 1, Introduzione, at mm. 278ff. ("Di gioia immensa") (a section to which Basevi has already variously referred as "quartet" and "quintet").

60. *Le trouvère* (Paris: Opéra, 1857) also presents a modified, extended version of the opera's ending. The critical edition, in preparation, will appear as *WGV* I/18B.

17

LA TRAVIATA

The subject of this opera prompts me to make a number of observations about the immorality of today's literature.[1]

In the present century, during which industry and the natural and physical sciences have advanced so splendidly, we have also seen advancing at an equal pace—and almost side by side—certain false doctrines that aim to corrupt the soul of man and to undermine his conscience. France—the source, it is said, of the light of truth—has sent us instead the shadow of error. Epicureanism has set down deep and wide-spreading roots in that country, and the various branches of that evil plant have penetrated into every sphere: civil, moral, and religious. "Man is born for pleasure; hence, let us enjoy as much as we can": here in a single article the entire code of these neo-Epicureans. Pleasure was elevated to the level of a religion with Saint-Simonism and took the form of a science with Fourierism.[2] While these absurd and baleful doctrines remained within the confines of a laughable religion or an insane form of knowledge the damage was not too great, but soon (and it is now scarcely

1. The critical edition of Verdi's *La traviata*, by Fabrizio Della Seta, was published as *WGV* I/19 (1997).
2. A reference to the doctrines of two early socialist French theorists from the first half of the nineteenth century, Henri de Saint-Simon and Charles Fourier.

thirty years later) these same doctrines used the seductive power of novels
and the theater to extend their influence, and to poison the hearts of the
simple and the ignorant. The theme that novelists and playwrights chose for
development in a thousand guises was this: that "passion, when spontaneous
and sincere, can justify any human error and rehabilitate the sinner." Fourier
had already said that passions are a kind of divine revelation, and that a man
disobeys God when he fights his passions rather than obeying them. Limiting
myself to speak only, and as briefly as possible, about matters concerning love,
I shall demonstrate how we have gradually come to the glorification of fallen
women [*traviate*]. It began with attacks on the bonds of wedlock. Beyle, in his
book *De l'amour*, writes that "a woman belongs by right to the man she loves
and who loves her";[3] Balzac followed in Beyle's footsteps in *La physiologie du
mariage* and other books, Sand in the novels *Valentine, Lélia, Indiana, Jacques*,
and others, and Sue in *Le juif errant* and elsewhere.[4] Of others we will not
speak for the sake of brevity. Once marriage came to be viewed as an often
tyrannical law, a justification was found for adultery, which was seen as "nature's rebellion against civilisation." Such loathsome precepts will be found in
Dumas's *Antony*, in Balzac's *Père Goriot*, and in many books by Sand and others.[5] The ultimate consequence of these doctrines is free love; indeed, Sand
states in *Jacques* that "a bond more human and less holy will replace marriage; it will ensure the existence of children, who will be born of a man and
a woman without severely limiting forever the freedom of either."[6] Concubi-
nage will thus be the crowning of social progress. In *Horace* and *La comtesse de
Rudolstadt*[7] these doctrines are even more clearly set out and preached, to the
effect that the only law of marriage is love. But this free love is portrayed not

3. Marie-Henri Beyle is the writer best known under the pen name Stendhal. In the essay on
love cited by Basevi (2 vols., Paris: Librairie universelle, 1822) he had in fact written: "A woman
belongs by right to the man who loves her and whom she loves *more than life*" ("Une femme
appartient de droit à l'homme qui l'aime et qu'elle aime *plus que la vie*": 2:254 [Stendhal's
italics]).

4. Basevi refers to books that variously defend the rights of nature and the passions against
social conventions (such as marriage) or religious intolerance. Balzac published his satirical
essay in 1829; George Sand's novels mentioned here are from the years 1831–34; Eugène Sue's
novel was published in 1844–45.

5. Both Dumas's drama (premiered in 1831) and Balzac's novel of 1834–35 deal will the
theme of extramarital relationships.

6. Basevi's translation contains one interesting misreading—perhaps the subconscious
result of his dislike for this passage: Sand's text reads "a bond more human and *no* less holy"
("un lien plus humain et *non* moins sacré" [emphasis added]). George Sand, *Jacques*, 2 vols.
(Paris: F. Bonnaire, [1834]–37), 1:73–74.

7. Novels by George Sand, published in 1842 and 1843, respectively.

merely as permissible but as meritorious. And therein lies the greatest ill of modern literature. In *Lucrezia Floriani*, Sand says, "He who loves is greater, though he err, than he who walks straight, along a path that is solitary and cold."[8] In *Marion Delorme* and *Angelo*, Victor Hugo had already depicted the courtesan purified and ennobled by love.[9] Balzac, Dumas, Gautier, and many others have professed these disreputable opinions in their writings. But the writer who more than any other treated the theme of rehabilitation through love—in the most splendid form and with the greatest craft—was Alexandre Dumas fils, in the novel and the play of *La dame aux camélias*, from which the plot of *La traviata* is taken.[10]

It is my duty to note that, while the poison came to us from France, it is also in France that an antidote has been sought. In 1856, the Academy of Moral and Political Sciences of Paris launched a competition [for an essay] on the following topic: "Describe and evaluate the influence of contemporary literature on French mores, considering particularly the theater and the novel." The entry of Eugène Poitou was rightly chosen. Poitou's prize essay, entitled *Du roman, et du théâtre contemporains, et de leur influence sur les moeurs*, is warmly recommended to all who value public morality, which must be protected with equal energy against those who, wishing to eradicate certain social misconceptions, exceed the limits without respect for the most sacred of principles, and against those others who, although it is their intention to defend morality, actually disfigure it by associating it and identifying it with a profusion of errors.

Piave had the task of reducing the play of Dumas fils to a libretto, and he succeeded quite well. I shall draw no comparisons between the play and the libretto, but shall merely sketch briefly the plot of the latter.

Violetta Valery is a courtesan who passes her time in accordance with the maxim that

8. See George Sand, *Lucrezia Floriani* (Paris: Proux, 1846), 3 ("celui qui aime est plus grand, lors même qu'il s'égare, que celui qui va droit, par un chemin solitaire et froid"). *Lucrezia Floriani* is generally understood to be a roman à clef about Sand's relationship with Chopin.

9. Both works are dramas. *Marion Delorme* (Paris: Théâtre de la Porte-Saint-Martin, 1831) would become the source for Ponchielli's opera of the same title (Milan: Teatro alla Scala, 1885); *Angelo, tyran de Padoue* (Paris: Comédie-Française, 1835) had already provided the basis for Mercadante's *Giuramento*, and would again for two operas premiered within a couple of months of each other in 1876—Cui's *Andzhelo* (St. Petersburg: Mariinsky Theater) and Ponchielli's *Gioconda* (Milan: Teatro alla Scala).

10. Dumas had published the novel in 1848 and then adapted it into a successful play (Paris: Théâtre du Vaudeville, 1852). Although Verdi knew both works, it is the latter that constitutes the main source for his opera.

Tutto è follia nel mondo
Ciò che non è piacer.[11]

[All is madness in the world
that is not pleasure.]

Alfredo Germont is introduced to Violetta, whom he has secretly loved for a year. He confesses his love, but Violetta, who has not yet experienced this emotion, does not believe him. Alfredo's words nonetheless leave a vivid impression on her soul. Thus Violetta, who had wished

Di voluttà ne' vortici finire

[To perish in a vortex of pleasure][12]

is then struck with a violent love for Alfredo, so much so that she goes to live with him in the country near Paris.

For Alfredo's father, this illicit union constitutes an obstacle to the marriage of his daughter, who is engaged to a man who loves her deeply but is at the same time very jealous of his family's honor. He decides to go directly to Violetta. She agrees to sacrifice her love for Alfredo and, in order to sever all intimacy with him, pretends to love another. In revenge for his abandonment by Violetta and inflamed with jealousy and rage, Alfredo publicly insults her, hurling money down at her feet and saying to the others,

Qui testimon vi chiamo
Ch'ora pagata io l'ho.[13]

[I call you all to witness
that I have now repaid my debt.]

Germont père, who knows Violetta's true feelings, castigates his son for this base act, which has angered the bystanders. Violetta, who has for some time been afflicted with latent tuberculosis, sickens seriously, rapidly ap-

11. Act 1, scene 2.
12. Act 1, scene 5.
13. Act 2, scene 14.

proaching the grave. Alfredo now learns of the sacrifice made by the woman he had judged unfaithful and a traitress and arrives in time to beg her forgiveness. And, as the elder Germont accepts Violetta as a daughter, she dies.

Piave adds his endorsement to the passport to heaven that had been issued to the fallen woman by Dumas fils, saying to her,

> Vola a' beati spiriti;
> Iddio ti chiama a sé.[14]

> [Fly to the blessed souls;
> God calls you to his side.]

Dumas fils had pardoned her with the phrase "a little love restores a woman's lost chastity."[15] This seems an opportune moment to mention the comparison that, in his *Cours de littérature dramatique*, Saint-Marc Girardin makes between ancient tragedy and modern dramas: "Ancient tragedy taught that a single evil passion was enough to condemn a soul, whereas the morality of our modern dramas has it that a single good quality is sufficient to pardon a multitude of sins."[16]

Verdi could not resist the temptation to clothe in music—and in consequence to render more attractive and acceptable—a foul and immoral subject that is universally enjoyed at present only because the very vice it depicts is itself universal today.

The opera was first performed in Venice in March 1853.[17] The reception at the first performance was not very gratifying, but Verdi did not lose heart; number 11 (March 13, 1853) of the *Gazzetta musicale* of Milan contained an extract from a letter by the composer that said, "Last night *La traviata* was a fiasco. By whose fault? . . . Mine or that of the singers? . . . I do not know. Time

---

14. Act 3, scene the last.

15. The reciprocal love of Armand and Marguerite is explicitly associated with her moral regeneration in a number of passages in both drama and play (see n. 10 above)—perhaps most prominently in the play's final line: "Sleep in peace, Marguerite! Much shall be forgiven you, for you have greatly loved!" The sentence echoes Christ's words about Mary Magdalene ("Her sins, which are many, are forgiven; for she loved much" [Luke 7:47]), to which Dumas had already made reference in the novel's third chapter.

16. Basevi's quotation is abridged from Saint-Marc Girardin, *Cours de littérature dramatique; ou, De l'usage des passions dans le drame*, 5 vols. (Paris: Charpentier, 1843–68), 1 (1843): 401. Basevi cites the title in Italian (*Corso di letteratura drammatica*).

17. The venue was the Teatro La Fenice.

will decide." And time *has* decided—that it would become one of the most popular operas there has ever been in Italy.

La traviata is a work of a kind that, in the nature of its characters, in its domestic sentiments, and in its lack of spectacle, approaches comedy. Here Verdi began a third manner that in many ways approaches the French genre of *opéra comique*. Music of that kind, while not yet tried in the Italian theater, is not unknown in the drawing room. In recent years the principal exponents of this music, called *da camera*, have been Luigi Gordigiani and Fabio Campana.[18] With *La traviata* Verdi very successfully transferred to the stage this *musica da camera*, to which the chosen subject lends itself admirably. In this score we find greater simplicity than in the composer's other works, especially in the orchestra, where the strings almost always dominate. *Parlanti* occupy a great part of the score, and there are a good number of arias that are repeated in the manner of *couplets*.[19] Finally, the principal melodies are by and large set in "small" binary and ternary meters,[20] and generally do not have the expansiveness characteristic of the Italian spirit. Moreover, Verdi has infused great emotion into this music, but without the exaggeration sometimes to be found even in his second manner; for this reason, he has never succeeded in expressing love with less affectation than in this opera. But the love he depicts here is voluptuous and sensual—completely devoid of the angelic purity found in the music of Bellini. Bellini's music always retains an innocence and candor that fill one's heart with tenderness, even when it is associated with a less than virtuous character. The difference between the kinds of love that inform Bellini's and Verdi's music testifies to the dissimilar ways of feeling in the times of the two composers. But since the character of the *lorette*[21] is still not

18. The "chamber music" in question is accompanied vocal music (for one or more voices); Gordigiani (1806–60) and Campana (1819–82) had attained European success especially through their *romanze da camera*. (Campana was from Livorno, like Basevi; also like Basevi, Gordigiani was an adoptive Florentine.)

19. A reference—as is the use of the term "romanza" several times later in the chapter—to the presence of strophic forms in arias in *La traviata*, an unlikely trait in the Italian operatic tradition and one with strong French connotations (especially because of the presence of these forms in *opéra comique*).

20. Probably a reference to the tendency to use shorter metric units, such as the $\frac{3}{8}$ of, for example, "Libiamo ne' lieti calici," "Un dì felice eterea," "Ah forse lui," and "Parigi, o cara"— surely all among Basevi's "cantilene principali."

21. *Lorette* is a "polite" term that emerges around 1840 to designate the young women who were kept as mistresses by many upper-class Parisians. (It derives from Notre-Dame de Lorette, the church of the district where many such women resided.)

deeply rooted in Italy (and we must hope that it never shall be), Verdi erred in leaving the nature of Violetta unaltered, rather than Italianizing it a little, thereby making it less loathsome. If it is true that Bellini depicted a guilty woman in *Norma*, he at the same time presented her as so blinded by passion that she could not see the enormity of her sin. Moreover, Norma's sin is less offensive to us, since, owing to the remoteness of the times and the differences in social mores, it is difficult for our conscience to identify with that of the character. This is not true of *La traviata*, where we find characters near to us not only in time and mores but also in social condition. In this opera, everything exudes lasciviousness and sensual pleasure: even old Germont himself, in his piteous scene with Violetta and in the other where he gently reproves his son, though motivated solely by paternal love, reveals an understanding of the appeal of those corruptions that his age barely gives him the strength to timidly condemn.

The *preludio* is composed of several melodies from the opera, notably the phrase "Amami, Alfredo," which on second hearing is richly embroidered by the first violins.[22]

The *introduzione* unfolds in the form of a *parlante*.[23] The principal instrumental theme is reminiscent of that of the introduction to the first act of *Alzira*, but here it is more capricious, and accords well with the festive scene it represents.[24] Because this *parlante* is very long, several other, secondary themes alternate with the main one in order to provide variety. Meanwhile, there is dialogue among various characters, and the chorus too takes part.

The *brindisi* ["Libiamo ne' lieti calici"] begins. It is in an unusual rhythm: the first phrase is of ten measures' length, which, reduced to $\frac{6}{8}$ time, would yield five measures, resulting in a so-called lame [*zoppo*] phrase. The rhythm of the *mossa* is modeled on that of the barcarole "Voyez du haut de ces rivages" from *La muette de Portici* by Auber.[25] In his chansons, ballads, and

---

22. Compare N. 1, Preludio, mm. 18ff., with N. 6, Scena Violetta ed Aria Germont, mm. 81ff.

23. N. 2, Introduzione ("Dell'invito trascorsa è già l'ora").

24. Compare N. 2, mm. 6ff. and passim, with *Alzira*'s N. 3, Coro ("Giunse or or, da lido ispano"), mm. 3ff. and passim. On Basevi's reference to "the first act" here, see chapter 6, n. 6, above.

25. The piece opens act 5 of the opera (Paris: Opéra, 1828) and is N. 17 in the score (Paris: Troupenas, [1828?]) reproduced in *ERO* 30 (1980). This is not an unlikely association: there is a melodic resemblance between Auber's and Verdi's incipits that goes beyond the rhythmic parallelism highlighted by Basevi; moreover, the first phrase of Auber's song is of ten measures.

barcaroles, that composer almost always avoided the rhythmic regularity he employed elsewhere. Indeed, this license is not inappropriate in pieces where the composer wishes above all to avoid an effect of unnaturalness. There is a nice chiaroscuro effect in the seventh measure of this *brindisi*;[26] otherwise, nothing in the form is so different from other, similar compositions, except that when Alfredo (tenor) and Violetta (soprano) repeat the *brindisi* together, the chorus and the other characters imitate the string accompaniment, with a certain novelty. Next comes a waltz—somewhat in the German style and reminiscent of the chorus with dance from act 3 of Weber's *Oberon*[27]—during which a dialogue between Violetta and Alfredo takes place.

When the waltz music ends, the *duettino* for Alfredo and Violetta commences ["Un dì felice eterea"]. Alfredo's part contains nothing of note except the melody at "Di quell'amor che è palpito," which is distinctive, and is repeated several times in this act. Its first period, which is fashioned "economically" and is the most expressive part of the melody, descends through an octave; in a way it thus embodies the image of baseness. Place this theme next to that from *I puritani*, "A te, o cara, amor talora," and see the difference between sensual love and the angelic love that Bellini's music expressed so well.[28] The melody with which Violetta replies is jocular, and suits her personality. Alfredo repeats part of his characteristic melody, the two voices intermingle, and, with a cadenza in the same vein, the piece ends. Immediately afterward the waltz is heard again, during which there is more dialogue; as the melody of the waltz fades away, Alfredo and Violetta say farewell. A chorus ["Si ridesta in ciel l'aurora"] follows, constituting the stretta of the *introduzione*.

Now comes Violetta's aria.[29] The andantino is straightforward, but perhaps too melancholy at this point. It is treated as a *romanza*, being twice repeated. In this andantino Alfredo's characteristic melody, "Di quell'amor," is repeated; here, however, it is accompanied more richly by the clarinet, arpeggiating in triplet motion. The cabaletta ["Sempre libera"] smacks a little of *opera buffa*; it is, however, pleasant in rhythm and has a very attractive spar-

26. There is often a sudden drop in sonority in the seventh measure of the *brindisi*'s main melodic phrase. See, for example, mm. 190, 200, 311, 321.

27. This is "For thee hath beauty," N. 21 of Weber's "romantic and fairy opera" (London: Covent Garden, 1826).

28. Vincenzo Bellini, *I puritani*, ed. Fabrizio Della Seta, *ECB* 10 (forthcoming), [N. 4], Coro ("Ad Arturo, onore!") [e Cavatina d'Arturo] ("A te, o cara, amor talora"), mm. 243ff.

29. N. 3, Aria Violetta ("È strano! è strano!!"; "Ah forse lui quest'anima").

kling character.[30] The tenor's theme follows, which he sings from off stage; here this makes for an effective contrast.

The second act opens with the tenor's aria.[31] The andante is notable because the melody is cast almost entirely in a single sweep [*di getto*], though the rhythm is repeated. The cabaletta ["Oh mio rimorso! . . ."] has an unusual rhythm, but it is not a particularly beautiful moment.

A duet follows for Violetta and Germont (baritone).[32] The form of this duet is absolutely new in the variety of its melodies. The first cantabile, for Germont, in common time, allegro moderato, employs a conventional rhythm that unfolds with great simplicity, and is not lacking in affecting tone. With great cleverness, Verdi next uses a *parlante* in place of the simple recitative called for by the text.[33] Then Violetta has a quick theme in ⁶⁄₈ time; the rhythm of the *mossa* is repeated too much, and those three measures of the note E at the move to C major seem to me antimelodic. After a brief "a piacere," another *parlante* follows, an andante in ²⁄₄ time; this leads to an extended melody on the words "Un dì, quando le veneri," which is flawed by too much rhythmic uniformity. The music is beautifully expressive where Germont says, "Violetta, deh pensateci"; Violetta's answer, in a broader form, yields nothing of note. Her cantabile ["Dite alla giovine"], which opens the andantino in ⁶⁄₈ time, is very poignant—sixteen measures in a single sweep [*di un solo getto*] and full of passion. There is no less feeling in Germont's passage "Piangi, piangi," where well-employed appoggiaturas and harmonies bestow on the vocal melody an almost Bellinian melancholy. Then Violetta repeats her earlier sixteen measures, while Germont joins her with an independent part. The following measures of *a 2* are very lyrical and piteous and close the andantino. A short recitative ["Imponete"] and a *parlante* ["Tra breve ei vi fia reso"] lead to the cabaletta of the duet ["Morrò! . . . la mia memoria"], which does not have a very unusual form; nor is it of great effect. The ending has a certain novelty; in a sort of farewell recitative, the composer brings back a phrase of the cabaletta to evoke the way in which, in taking leave of someone, we often remind them of the things that mean most to us.

---

30. As in other cases, Basevi's choice of word ("brillante") is prompted by Verdi's score (the cabaletta is marked "Allegro brillante").

31. N. 4, Scena ("Lunge da lei per me non v'ha diletto! . . .") ed Aria Alfredo ("Dei miei bollenti spiriti").

32. N. 5, Scena ("Alfredo? Per Parigi or or partiva") [e] Duetto [Violetta e Germont] ("Pura siccome un angelo").

33. The verse passage starting at "Ah! comprendo . . ." is recitative-like in poetic meter (*versi sciolti*).

The following *duettino* for Violetta and Alfredo is entirely cast in the form of a *parlante*.[34] Up to the point where the piece enters the key of F, note the magical effect that can be drawn from music when, rather than being governed by rhythmic symmetry, it proceeds with the same freedom as the emotions. The orchestra depicts the state of Violetta's emotions wonderfully. Of great effect are the trilled appoggiaturas that the violins play first alone, then with flute, then piccolo, creating a very effective crescendo.[35] The rhythm becomes regular when the piece goes into the key of F at the words "Amami, Alfredo." Here Verdi surely had in mind the famous phrase in Isabelle's aria from *Robert le diable*, on the words "Grâce, grâce pour toi même, etc.," which, on its third repetition, has a fortissimo that makes you shiver.[36] But note in this orchestration that, at the loudest point, Verdi has the trumpet playing in unison with the soprano, but does not employ either the trombones or the cimbasso.[37] Other composers of the day would have added a cannon.

The andante of the baritone's aria is affecting, recalling somewhat Weber's last thought.[38] It unfolds in the manner of a *romanza* that repeats, and its rhythm is perhaps too uniform. The cabaletta ["No, non udrai rimproveri"] is of little interest.

A chorus of gypsies ["Noi siamo zingarelle"] has nothing in it worthy of mention; another of matadors ["È Piquillo un bel gagliardo"] is in a gracious ⅜.[39]

---

34. The passage is already part of the recitative that opens N. 6, Scena Violetta ("Dammi tu forza, o cielo . . .") ed Aria Germont ("Di Provenza il mar, il suol").

35. See N. 6, mm. 63ff.

36. See mm. 85ff. of Isabelle's N. 18c, Cavatine ("Robert, toi que j'aime"; "Grace!"), part of the fourth-act finale of Meyerbeer's *Robert le diable*, ed. Wolfgang Kühnhold and Peter Kaiser, *MWA* I/10 (2010). As is often the case, Basevi draws a parallel between passages that present richer analogies than he mentions: in both cases the downbeat is marked by a switch to F major, *ff*, tremolo in the strings, and a sustained f″ in the soprano, and is prepared by an ascending line toward the f″ (in the first violins in *Traviata*, in the voice in *Robert le diable*).

37. In Verdi's time, the term *cimbasso* was used in Italy to refer generally to the lowest brass instrument in the orchestra (and could designate any of a number of morphologically diverse instruments).

38. By "l'ultimo pensiero di Weber" Basevi alludes to a piece that enjoyed a certain popularity in the nineteenth century, the fifth of Carl Reissiger's *Danses brillantes pour le pianoforte*, op. 26 (1822); this waltz became widely known under later titles such as *Webers letzter Gedanke* or *Dernière pensée de Weber*, and its incipit indeed bears a motivic resemblance to that of "Di Provenza il mar, il suol."

39. The two choruses are already part of N. 7, Finale secondo ("Avrem lieta di maschere la festa").

The gambling scene is set as a *parlante* ["Qui desïata giungi . . ."]; in the orchestra, Verdi sought to express the oppression that weighs on the gambler. The result seems to me too gloomy—and also somewhat unnatural, as the company is composed of young scamps and reckless old men; besides, let us not forget that the time and setting are those of a party. The phrase that Violetta repeatedly interjects ("Ah perché venni! etc.") is striking. Alfredo's anger is well delineated in the passage "Ogni suo aver tal femmina, etc.": twenty-one measures, all in one sweep [*tutte d'un getto*], of the greatest effect. The reply of the others suitably depicts their indignation.

The finale begins with a largo ["Di sprezzo degno"], in which Germont reproves his son with a melody that is severe and noble, and well coupled to the words.[40] The passage then sung by Alfredo, expressing his remorse, is too uniform. The brief ensemble that follows is of majestic cast, but I do not much like the modulation to B-flat, even though it is composed in accordance with all the rules, because it seems to me that we continue to desire to remain for a time in the key of E-flat major. Violetta's vocal line is also very uniform here; it is only toward the end that it acquires the variety and breadth it needs to prepare sufficiently for the grand melody of the tutti that closes the act. This melody is accompanied to fine effect, with short chords for the chorus on each beat, and with three bass voices imitating the orchestral bass line in a rhythmic figure that puts the melody into clear relief. We find this figure also in *Mosè*, in the viola and cello parts that accompany the cantabile "Non è ver che stringa il cielo."[41] This section recalls Verdi's first manner, and for that very reason I consider it out of place in the present context.

The third act opens with an orchestral introduction whose first seven measures were also heard in the *preludio* to the opera.[42] The harmonies, composed of the sounds of high violins, are of magical effect. The melody that follows is extremely touching: a sad and gentle melodic line of thirty-three measures, almost all in one sweep [*di un getto*], that induces profound melancholy. This introduction is a valuable model not to be disregarded by composers.

---

40. Of course, this point is in fact well into the Finale secondo as delimited in Verdi's autograph score. It is perhaps remarkable that, given his usual focus on formal practices, Basevi omits to mention that Verdi concludes the act with this *largo concertato*, dispensing with the customary stretta.

41. Compare the figure at mm. 724ff. of this Finale with the almost identical one in Rossini, *Mosè in Egitto*, N. 3, Duetto [Elcia e Osiride] ("Ah se puoi così lasciarmi"), mm. 73ff.

42. N. 8, Scena Violetta ("Annina?" "Comandate?"; "Addio del passato bei sogni ridenti").

The aria "Addio del passato" must be numbered among the most expressive. Here is the bitter sadness so appropriate in a woman who sees all her beautiful dreams disappear.[43] The rhythm too is most fitting, as it imitates poor Violetta's agitation. And certain interruptions in the vocal line, where the oboe dominates, could not be more effective. This aria too repeats in the manner of a *romanza*.[44]

After an offstage bacchanal chorus,[45] useful for suspending the scene of pain and agony for a time, comes a *duettino* for Violetta and Alfredo.[46] The melody "Parigi, o cara," which belongs to the same family as "Ai nostri monti . . . ritorneremo! . . ." from *Il trovatore*, is very gentle.[47] The chromatic passages for Violetta are very apt, as with these Verdi wished perhaps to imitate the instability of her voice, caused by the illness that afflicts her; it strikes me, however, that they are too heavily reinforced by the orchestra. The allegro "Gran Dio! . . . morir si giovine" suitably expresses Violetta's desperation; for that reason I do not approve of Alfredo's repetition of the same melody with different words expressing different emotions.

There are several poignant melodic phrases in the final scene, but they do not seem to be well linked.[48] Also, by this point the dénouement has become all too predictable, and the spectator has been prematurely moved.

A great part of this opera's vogue is clearly due to the passion that it places in relief and that is so well expressed by Verdi's music. I am certain that with the mores observed in Italy ten or fifteen years ago *La traviata* would not have been such a success; perhaps Verdi, a true representative of the taste of the public, would not then have set such a subject, or would not have set it so successfully as now. Elevated by the lofty sentiments displayed in *Nabucodonosor* and *I Lombardi*, he would have been unable to descend to ennobling a harlot. And if music is a mirror of the soul of a people, it is earnestly to be desired that the musical Italy of *La traviata* should revert to that of *I Lombardi*.

43. In the earlier version of this chapter (the 1858 article in *L'armonia*), Basevi went on to pay Verdi a remarkable tribute: "There is nothing more delicate or affecting: here we could almost say, Bellini *redivivus*" ("Nulla di più delicato, di più penetrante nell'anima: in tal punto si potrebbe dire Bellini risorto"; see Piovano, 296).

44. What repeats is of course the music, while the words are new—a second stanza that is cut in many modern performances. (See the glossary, s.v. *romanza*.)

45. N. 9, Baccanale ("Largo al quadrupede").

46. N. 10, Duetto [Violetta e Alfredo] ("Signora . . ." "Che t'accadde?"; "Parigi, o cara, noi lascieremo").

47. Compare *Il trovatore*, N. 14, mm. 125ff.

48. N. 11, Finale ultimo ("Ah Violetta!" "Voi . . . signor?").

Today *La traviata* is obviously a favorite opera among a great portion of the fair sex. I would wish because of this, not to accuse them of nurturing less than modest sentiments, but rather to warn them of the peril of such entertainments. They introduce poison into our souls—poison we do not notice until it has taken possession of us.

The artist has an obligation similar in a sense to that of a priest: he must not only conserve but also improve and propagate public morality. The influence of artists on mores is such that it is no surprise that the ephors condemned the celebrated musician Terpander for adding a few strings to the lyre: they deemed so small a change capable of corrupting the mores of the Greeks.[49]

To give greater weight to my words, I append those of Planelli, who, in his valuable *Trattato dell'opera in musica*, having recommended that [dramatic] poetry should not offend morality, says:

> Music, dance, painting, and the decorative arts must all pass a diligent and severe test: that none of them should exude debauchery and license, but that all should contribute to making this form of spectacle [i.e., opera] worthy of a civilized nation. But to be certain that opera does not offend public propriety, it is not enough that all the arts that combine to form it should have been scrutinized. That is indeed the least part. The greater part lies in the integrity of the actors and dancers. You may castigate the above-mentioned arts as much as you like, but all is for naught if the singers and dancers—and particularly the women in both these categories—do not count decency among the virtues most necessary to their profession.[50]

49. According to classical sources, the lyric poet Terpander of Lesbos (seventh century BCE) was condemned by the ephors—high-ranking Spartan magistrates—for the addition of strings to the lyre. Whatever its historical basis, the story is one of many to testify to the classical-age belief in the powers of music.

50. Antonio Planelli, *Dell'opera in musica* (Naples: Donato Campo, 1772), 256.

18

GIOVANNA DE GUZMAN
(LES VÊPRES SICILIENNES)

Who does not know about the Sicilian Vespers? Everyone does, of course, except for Messieurs Scribe and Duveyrier, who composed this libretto— if they really sought to deny the facts of the massacre known by that name. But it seems that those authors wished to deny nothing but the conspiracy and the premeditated plan to murder all the French in Sicily simultaneously. And in this they would agree with our most erudite Michele Amari and other distinguished historians.[1]

1. "Sicilian Vespers" is the standard way of referring to the uprising of 1282 in which the Sicilians killed thousands of their French occupiers. The Sicilian historian Michele Amari had published an important book on the subject, *La guerra del vespro siciliano*, for the first edition of which he had been obliged by the censors to adopt the more anodyne title *Un periodo delle istorie siciliane del secolo XIII* (Palermo: Empedocle, 1842); the book presented the historical episode as the result not of a conspiracy but of a spontaneous popular uprising of oppressed Sicilians. In a prefatory note to their libretto for Verdi's *Les vêpres siciliennes* (Paris: Opéra, 1855), Eugène Scribe and Charles Duveyrier wrote that "there was never any such thing as the general massacre known as 'the Sicilian Vespers.'" In reviewing the opera, the noted critic Paul Scudo quoted this passage and criticized the librettists for ignoring Amari's study. Basevi's more balanced comment implicitly countered Scudo's review (which he knew, as he refers to it later in this chapter), the librettists having simply claimed that the so-called Sicilian Vespers had not been a "massacre général," planned to take place simultaneously throughout Sicily, but was rather a spontaneous uprising of the people of Palermo, not immediately related to a series of later

Since in Italy this score circulates with the words of the libretto *Giovanna de Guzman*, I think it will be more useful to the majority of my readers to examine it in that new guise, which was given to *Les vêpres* in order to mollify suspicious censors.[2]

I shall not judge the Italian adaptation severely, for I know very well what tortures are in store for a poet who must perform the harrowing operation of transforming French verse into Italian with the least possible alteration to the music. The music has suffered a little, but the poetry so much more: in both language and content it has become a monstrosity; moreover, the musical and verbal accents do not always correspond.

In the libretto of *Giovanna de Guzman* the action takes place at Lisbon in 1640, when the Portuguese were suffering under the Spanish yoke.[3] Act 1 opens in the plaza at Lisbon, where we discover Spaniards and Portuguese, who look askance at each other. Giovanna de Guzman, whose brother had been killed by the Spaniards, is extremely angry and contemplates vengeance. The Spaniards and the Portuguese are about to fall on one another when the governor of Portugal, Vasconcello, approaches and prevents the fight.——Enrico, a Portuguese officer and Giovanna's lover, arrives and, in a scene with Va-

---

events on the island. See Scribe and Duveyrier's "Note" in *Les vêpres siciliennes, opéra en cinq actes* (Paris: Michel Lévy Frères, 1855); and Paul Scudo, "Revue musicale: *Jaguarita—Jenny Bell—Les vêpres siciliennes*," *Revue des deux mondes*, July 1, 1855, 213–27, 218–19.

2. In *Giovanna de Guzman* (Parma: Teatro Ducale, 1855), with Italian words by Eugenio Caimi, the action is transposed to seventeenth-century Portugal. For this version of the opera, we refer to the vocal score by Luigi Truzzi, Alessandro Truzzi, and Henri-Hippolyte Potier (Milan: Tito di Gio. Ricordi, [1856]). (Basevi always refers to it using the Italianized title *Giovanna di Guzman*.) Caimi's translation largely survives in later Italian versions of the opera, which are usually titled *I vespri siciliani* (restoring the medieval Sicilian setting) and are performed much more often than the original French version.

3. Since readers are much likelier to encounter librettos, scores, productions, and recordings based on *Les vêpres siciliennes* (or on *I vespri siciliani*), we provide here—for the main characters mentioned by Basevi in his summary of the plot—the original names accompanied (after the slash) by those of their reincarnations in *Giovanna de Guzman*: La Duchesse Hélène (la Duchessa Elena), sister of Duke Frederick of Austria/Giovanna de Guzman, sister-in-law of the Duke of Braganza; Guy de Montfort (Guido di Monforte), governor of Sicily on behalf of Charles of Anjou, King of Naples/Michele de Vasconcillos, governor of Portugal on behalf of Philip IV of Spain (this name form is used in the dramatis personae; in the body of the libretto he is referred to as "Vasconcello"); Henri (Arrigo), a young Sicilian/Enrico, a young Portuguese; Jean Procida (Giovanni da Procida), a Sicilian doctor/Don Giovanni Ribeiro Pinto, Portuguese gentleman. Vasconcillos is based on the real historical figure of Miguel de Vasconcelos, who governed Portugal until he was killed in the revolt of 1640. In our references below, for the sake of brevity, the names from *Giovanna de Guzman* are paired with the respective ones in *Vêpres*—but not *Vespri*; and in order not to encumber the main text with double poetic incipits (French/Italian), we more often provide them in the footnotes.

sconcello, expresses his hatred of the Spanish domination of his land. Vasconcello does not lose his temper at this, but contents himself merely with
forbidding Enrico to visit Giovanna. Enrico does not submit and goes off in
the direction of Giovanna's residence.——In the second act we are in a valley
near Lisbon. Pinto, a Portuguese captain, has returned after having visited
many lands seeking help against the Spaniards. France has been the most
generous, responding that it will send help if all of Portugal rises.——But
the Portuguese seem to be disinclined to rise; there is a need to rouse them,
to cause a tumult. For this, a strong hand is needed, and Enrico volunteers.
Giovanna promises to marry Enrico if he will avenge her brother. A Spanish
officer now arrives and, on behalf of the viceroy, invites Enrico to a ball; he
refuses and is forcibly dragged away by soldiers. A nice invitation!——The
stage gradually fills with people; all is festivity, for several weddings are to take
place. At the height of the excitement, there is a new edition of the Rape of
the Sabines: the Spaniards abduct the Portuguese women. The Portuguese,
who had stood by to witness this scene without lifting a finger, now gather
and discuss avenging the affront. Meanwhile, some Spanish officers pass by
on a boat, singing a barcarole.——In the third act, Vasconcello is in his study
reading a letter written by his wife on her deathbed. In it she begs him to save
the life of their son Enrico if it should ever be threatened. That woman had
been abducted by Vasconcello, and she had later abandoned him and hidden
their child from him for fifteen years. Enrico, invited with the ill grace that we
have seen, comes before Vasconcello, and learns that he is his father. At this
he rushes out in horror.——We are in a ballroom. Giovanna and Pinto enter,
masked, and give Enrico a blue ribbon, a sign of recognition for the Portuguese. Enrico, knowing the danger his father is in, warns him. Vasconcello
ignores him, and when Giovanna goes to kill him, Enrico shields him with
his body. Vasconcello has all the conspirators arrested save Enrico—who is
deemed a traitor by his own people.——In the fourth act we see the courtyard
of a fortress. Enrico comes to see the prisoners in order to exculpate himself. Giovanna enters, and Enrico reveals that Vasconcello is his father, but
at the same time assures her that he does not hate the oppressors of his land
any the less for that. The order comes to take the conspirators to their death.
Enrico begs Vasconcello to spare their lives; he agrees, on the condition that
Enrico call him father. Giovanna tells Enrico not to utter that word, but he
does not have the heart to see her sent to her death and cries, "Father." Vasconcello now pardons everyone, and even consents to the union of Enrico
and Giovanna. Universal jubilation. And thus the drama would seem to have

ended. But it has not. There is a fifth act, which takes place in the gardens of Vasconcello's palace. Universal happiness reigns at the approaching marriage of Giovanna and Enrico, who are content and no longer have so much as a thought for the oppressed Portuguese. Pinto comes to remind Giovanna of her quickly forgotten patriotism, and of her oath of vengeance for her slain brother; he tells her that the bell that will ring to mark her wedding will be the signal for the uprising. To prevent the slaughter, Giovanna refuses to marry Enrico, who, ignorant of all this, waxes wroth—and Pinto even more so than he. Vasconcello arrives and, against Giovanna's will, intends to unite the couple; meanwhile, the wedding bells peal out. The Portuguese hurl themselves at the Spaniards, and here the drama truly ends. The reader may imagine himself to have read the original French libretto if he replaces Vasconcello with Guido di Monforte, Pinto with Giovanni da Procida, Giovanna with the Duchess Elena, Lisbon with Palermo, the Spaniards with the French, the Portuguese with the Italians, and the year 1640 with the year 1282.

There would be no lack of fine scenes in this libretto, but as they are not well connected to the whole or placed in their best light they do not seem very alive. They form a too obvious mosaic whose seams are far too coarsely made.

Verdi accepted the subject of the Sicilian Vespers without hesitation, though, as Scudo rightly observed, it was hardly an appropriate choice for an opera written by an Italian composer for the French stage.[4]

The opera was first performed in the theater of the Académie Impériale de Musique[5] in Paris on June 13, 1855.

With this score, Verdi had to combat very powerful competitors who ruled the French operatic stage, foremost among them Meyerbeer.

Many wrongly think that when setting a French libretto a composer is obliged to bow to French taste, but if that were true the French would never translate Italian operas. And if Verdi was asked to compose an opera to French words, that was not so that he would bow to French taste, but rather because the French had relished his Italian music and wished to hear more of it. The real difficulty for an Italian who sets a French libretto lies in the need to compose pieces that require new forms, as the poetry intended for the lyrical movements in French opera is sometimes too short, sometimes too long,

---

4. See Scudo, "Revue musicale," 218.

5. This is the theater generally known as the Opéra. (Basevi refers to it simply as "Accademia di Musica.")

sometimes repeated many times, and sometimes interrupted by recitatives. These and many other things impede the use of the musical forms now accepted in Italy. Because a change in form inevitably entails a change in the way pieces are handled, where the composer wishes to retain the Italian style he is obliged to pass quickly over the verse lines that exceed the length required by Italian forms, or to draw things out where the lines are scant. Setting a French libretto in the Italian style, then, amounts to filling out the music and overburdening it with redundancies. Verdi found himself precisely in that position. The most concise of composers, he has become verbose and grandiloquent in *Les vêpres siciliennes* for those very reasons. The result is that this is the least dramatic of Verdi's operas. Here he found too much material to shape according to his impatient nature. We will all have observed that, when someone who is driven by intense passion has to explain himself at length, that agitation becomes less perceptible to others, as though with every word a particle of the passion were dissipated. So as not to allow his natural impetuosity thus to be lost ineffectively, Verdi concentrated it all in a few pieces, and the others were left completely without it. But the heat of one number could not overcome the chill of the others.

It is untrue that all the music of this opera is written in accordance with French taste, just as it is untrue that it is perfectly molded to the taste of the Italians. The most applauded pieces have invariably been those that, written in the Italian style, were least encumbered by their French poetry. I am convinced that if Verdi had chosen a French libretto that had the form of Italian librettos, the result would have been music more homogeneous and therefore more pleasing both to the French and to the Italians. This assertion can be substantiated by the great success of the French translation of *Il trovatore*.

Given these difficulties that Verdi had to surmount, and judging the score impartially, we find in it no signs that the composer's creative vein was becoming exhausted, but only a manifest lack of ease.

As we cast a rapid glance over the various pieces of the score, we shall stop to examine on the way whatever seems most worthy of note.

The *sinfonia* is composed of several themes from the opera, principal among them that of the tenor-baritone duet.[6] That theme is repeated several times, accompanied and embellished in diverse ways; the final time it

---

6. The theme first heard in the cellos during the overture (marking the allegro agitato's second key area of G major) is that heard various times in the third-act duet between Henri/Enrico and Montfort/Vasconcello (see below).

produces a fine effect—not a new effect, however, and one of which the Franco-German school was especially fond. The cellos, which dominate, give the theme a well-crafted vividness.

In the introductory chorus ["Beau pays de France!"/"Al cielo natio"], the difference and discord between the Portuguese and the Spanish (or French and Italians) are not expressed well; several times, particularly in cadential passages, the two groups sing in unison. Before the repetition of this chorus, there is a *parlante* with a very uniform instrumental part; this could almost be defined a *parlante di ripieno*, and does not even prepare for the reprise of the chorus, which arrives unexpected and unwanted.[7] In the introduction to Meyerbeer's *Robert le diable* we see how a chorus may be repeated several times without becoming tiresome—indeed, even delighting the listeners greatly.[8] In this *introduzione*, Verdi did not opt for a purely Italian form, nor did he venture to embrace the form that Meyerbeer had used with such success in his French operas.

The *parlante* on the words "Qual s'offre al mio sguardo" is really another *parlante di ripieno*.[9] Euphony is not enough to make a *parlante* pleasing.

Giovanna's cavatina begins with a series of resolving diminished-seventh chords; accompanied by motion in the basses, these are meant to signify an impending shipwreck, as expressed in the text.[10] Then the largo theme "Deh! tu calma" begins in the melodic form Verdi uses so often: the "economical" form.[11] For the rest, this short largo has nothing to arrest our attention. It is accompanied by a tremolo in the very high violins: what the composer intended here escapes me. After a sort of obbligato recitative we arrive at the cabaletta "Coraggio, etc."[12] This is in Verdi's style; besides recalling *Macbeth* and *Attila*, it brings to mind the operas of other composers. That notwithstanding, it produces a fine effect for listeners fond of the impetuous, frenzied

7. For this section ("Vive Guy de Montfort"/"Evviva, evviva il grande capitano") Basevi introduces the term "parlante di ripieno," which is not part of his earlier classification of *parlanti* (see pp. 36–37 above). Although he gives it the dignity of a technical term (italicizing it, and indexing it at the end of the *Studio*), he is unlikely to mean anything other than that a given *parlante* is a filler, used as a connecting or preparatory section (he uses "ripieno" in similar ways elsewhere in the book).

8. This is the chorus passage "Au seul plaisir" in N. 1b, Introduction—Choeur des buveurs ("Versez à tasses pleines"), mm. 31ff., of *Robert le diable*, ed. Wolfgang Künhold and Peter Kaiser, *MWA* I/10 (2010).

9. This is the French score's recitative "Quelle est cette beauté."

10. "In alto mare e battuto dai venti" (Hélène's "Au sein des mers et battu par l'orage").

11. "Deh! tu calma, o Dio possente" (Hélène's "Viens à nous, Dieux tutélaire!").

12. "Coraggio, su coraggio" (Hélène's "Courage! . . . du courage!").

style propagated by Verdi in his first manner. Since there are too many verse lines, the composer, after a few inconclusive measures, had to begin a new theme, "Ardir, etc.,"[13] which is poorly linked to the rest and is what we call lame [*zoppo*] as it contains five-measure phrases. After a chorus in one of the usual rhythms favored by Verdi, the first phrase of the cabaletta is reprised in unison with the entire chorus, producing one of the many timeworn effects that continue to survive even in the face of common sense: in this case the Portuguese and the Spaniards ought to sing different music from each other. This very energetic cabaletta is appropriate to a woman of a proud, indomitable, irascible personality; the rest of the opera does not confirm the opinion we form of this character on the basis of this piece, which is therefore at odds with her nature. Few composers take care to proportion the expressive quality of a melody to the temperament of the character for whom it is destined. Yet such proportionment is required not only by wisdom but also by the goal of achieving the greatest effectiveness for dramatic music. What would we say of a playwright who did not make the personalities of his characters consistent? The same must hold for composers. See how Rossini depicted the personality of Othello: in love, in jealousy, in friendship, in vengeance, you always recognize the same Othello. He cannot love like Romeo—who, on the other hand, cannot burst into a fury like Othello. Music has its proportions, just as poetry does, and they must be used appositely. It is from these proportions, well or ill used, that the spectator sometimes derives a satisfaction or dissatisfaction that he himself cannot define.

The quartet that follows, for the most part unaccompanied, is an academic exercise that is out of place in this opera.[14] Perhaps Verdi wished in this score to include every kind of music for the sake of variety, but what good is this if all does not join in a single unified conception?

The duet for tenor and baritone[15] begins with a *parlante* that, because of its instrumental part, must be counted among the *parlanti di ripieno*. The *cantabile grandioso* is very beautiful, but is not suited to the words "Di giovin audace,"[16] which demand impetuous music and a more animated rhythm. In its breadth, this theme is completely at odds with the French style. While the tenor sings the cantabile, the baritone sings a part that would suit the words quite well if it did not have such long stretches of silence. When the tenor

13. "Ardir, ardir! Al mugghiare dell'onda" (Hélène's "Debout! Debout!!!").
14. "D'ira fremo all'aspetto tremendo" (originally "Quelle horreur m'environne").
15. Enrico and Vasconcello's "Qual è il tuo nome?" (Henri and Montfort's "Quel est ton nom?").
16. "Punis mon audace!" "Cantabile grandioso" is Verdi's direction for the section.

repeats the cantabile, the baritone changes his first theme, and takes up another that seems to me to interfere with the tenor's line. The baritone begins the allegro with an energetic melodic period formed in economical fashion.[17] The ensuing theme for the tenor is commonplace; its syncopated accompaniment is among those least used by the Italians.

After a brief prelude, the second act opens with the aria of the *basso profondo*, Pinto.[18] The largo is very tender, and the words and music are properly united. Here we find lovely variety, well employed. There is richness and variety in the accompaniment as well. The cabaletta,[19] however, is no real match for the largo; besides, it lacks the virtue of novelty: in its form it is a slavish imitation of the second-act aria from *Il trovatore*.[20]

The duet for Giovanna and Enrico is perhaps the best piece in the opera.[21] The tenor's *cantabile con passione* is very tender and is without exaggeration.[22] The ⁶⁄₈-time andantino is the culmination of the duet. A sad accompaniment, with a low flute part, is given to the words "Presso alla tomba, etc."[23] The first period has an elusive melody that nonetheless leads gracefully to the second period, "Tu, dall'eccelse sfere," which is most pleasing.[24] The tenor sings another melodic period with an accompaniment similar to that of the earlier sad one, and the parts intertwine in an *a 2* including a very gentle[25] passage that gains much from being sung pianissimo, especially in the case of the tenor. A declamatory passage—or rather a nine-measure recitative—follows, and with an ample cadenza this jewel of a duet closes. Its form is unusual. And yet by reason of its small proportions the piece does not figure well in a colossal opera like this one. Composers must ensure that the individual pieces, especially those in the most important scenes, display a sense of proportion

17. "Temerario! Qual ardire!" ("Téméraire! téméraire!").

18. "O sacra terra" (Procida's "Et toi, Palerme"/"O tu, Palermo").

19. "Nell'ombra e nel silenzio" (originally "Dans l'ombre et le silence").

20. The reference is to the cabaletta "Per me ora fatale" from *Il trovatore*'s N. 7 (the count's aria "Il balen del suo sorriso"). The similarity (which does not quite extend to Basevi's "slavish imitation") lies in that both pieces frame the soloist's statements of the cabaletta theme with pianissimo, staccato passages in which the chorus takes part.

21. "Quale, o prode, al tuo coraggio" (originally Hélène and Henri's "Comment, dans ma reconnaissance").

22. "Ma le tue luci angeliche" ("Vous détournez les yeux et mon audace est grande!"). The section is an allegro giusto: "cantabile con passione" is Verdi's direction for the tenor.

23. Giovanna's "Presso alla tomba ch'apresi" (Hélène's "Près du tombeau").

24. Hélène's "Et du haut, du haut des cieux."

25. Basevi's term, "dolcissimo," is lifted from the performance direction in Verdi's score at this point.

to the whole. That is precisely what is lacking in the present score. This kind of proportion is no less important than the kind mentioned above with reference to the expression of emotions in accordance with the personality and temperament of the character.

The tarantella has character but becomes absurd when the abduction of the women takes place.[26]

In the second finale, the chorus "Il rossor mi coprì!" has one of the usual jerky Verdian rhythms.[27] As the distance between jerks is too great, it is obvious that it was devised to be sung together with the following barcarole ["Del piacer s'avanza l'ora!"]. When this chorus is later repeated, its rhythm is imitated between the jerks by three of the characters present; it is in this form that it then combines with the barcarole. The latter begins with a familiar theme, not entirely Verdi's own.[28] The two united choruses feel too studied and do not produce much of an effect. When not spontaneous, such combinations produce the opposite effect from what is sought. The uniting of themes first heard separately is not a new technique, but it is not, I think, generally useful for dramatic effect. At the very beginning of Guglielmi's *Paolo e Virginia*, Paolo asks Virginia to sing the song "La femmina innocente," after which Paolo sings another, "Se guardo il tuo volto."[29] They then beg each other to repeat their respective songs, and, neither wishing to precede the other, they sing them at the same time. Something similar is found in Cherubini's *Lodoïska*: Varbel sings a polonaise, and Floreski follows with another theme that is repeated over the polonaise.[30] The great Rossini too did something similar in the first finale of *La donna del lago*, where a chorus of bards is heard and later grafted onto a warriors' march.[31] It seems to me

26. By this point we have entered the final number of act 2.

27. This is the original "Interdits, accablés." Basevi writes "uno dei soliti ritmi verdiani *a scatto*"—his italics signaling, as often, what he considers a specialized term: the reference is clearly to the kind of writing that he elsewhere calls "ritmo staccato."

28. From the very beginning, a number of critics had connected this barcarole with a variety of southern Italian tunes. The composer-critic Ernest Reyer had given his solution to the problem as early as 1855: "It is, they say, a Neapolitan air; what does it matter?" See "Les vêpres siciliennes," *Revue française* 1, no. 2 (1855): 186–92, 188 ("c'est, dit-on, un air napolitain; qu'importe?").

29. Pietro Carlo Guglielmi, *Paolo e Virginia* (Naples: Teatro dei Fiorentini, 1817). Virginia's text is actually "La fiamma innocente."

30. See the Couplets de Floreski et Varbel in act 1 of Cherubini, *Lodoïska* (Paris: Théâtre Feydeau, 1791); they can be read on pp. 120ff. of the printed full score (Paris: Naderman, [1792]) reproduced in *ERO* 33 (1978).

31. See *La donna del lago*, ed. H. Colin Slim, *EC* I/29 (1990), N. 7, Coro ("Vieni, o stella") e Finale primo ("Quanto a quest'alma amante"), mm. 448ff., 566ff.

that Meyerbeer used this sort of combination with much greater dramatic effect in the third act of *Les Huguenots*, when the litany is combined with the "rataplan."[32]

A prelude of a few measures opens the third act.

The *mossa* of Vasconcello's aria recalls a passage in the oath from Meyerbeer's *Les Huguenots*.[33] Beyond that, the aria is well handled, and is the only one that can be said to conform to some extent to the French taste, as its melodic periods are not constructed in the Italian style. But it lacks the rhythmic variety needed to make these rather long pieces acceptable; hence, it is rather monotonous.

The duet for Vasconcello and Enrico is built on the theme that dominates in the *sinfonia*.[34] First, it is sung twice by the baritone, and then there is a rather inconclusive imitative passage *a 2*;[35] after the baritone has sung an adagio aided by the tenor,[36] we arrive at an obbligato recitative, which leads, in a faster tempo, to the reprise of the theme from the *sinfonia*. That theme is now sung by the tenor accompanied by the baritone.[37] The form of this duet, without being splendid or rich, is uncommon: rarely has the cabaletta used the same theme as the adagio or the andante, as happens here.

The music for the ballet of the Four Seasons does not stand out.[38]

The chorus "O splendide feste!" is another of the numerous versions Verdi has made of certain of his choruses.[39] It is divided up by a *parlante* with an orchestral figure similar to that found in the scene that opens the second-act finale of *La traviata*.[40] This figure, of which Verdi seems very fond, is also heard after the chorus, giving little pleasure to the listeners as it is without any expression whatsoever.

32. See chapter 2, n. 52, above.

33. Compare "In braccio alle dovizie" (originally Montfort's "Au sein de la puissance") with "Pour cette cause sainte," heard at various points in N. 23 of *Les Huguenots*, Conjuration et Bénédiction des poignards.

34. "Quando al mio sen per te parlava" (originally Montfort and Henri's duet "Quand ma bonté toujours nouvelle"); the theme is that which first appears at the words "Mentre contemplo quel volto amato" ("Pour moi, pour moi, quelle ivresse inconnue").

35. "Parola fatale!" ("Comble de misère!").

36. "Invano, o figlio, crudel mi chiami" ("Quoi, ma tendresse").

37. "Ombra diletta, che in ciel riposi" ("Ombre sainte que je revère").

38. This is the substantial score Verdi wrote for the danced *divertissement* that was expected by the audience at the Opéra.

39. The chorus (originally "O fête brillante") opens the third-act finale.

40. Compare the figure here at the words "Enrico! su te veglia l'amistade!" ("Henri! sur toi l'amitié veille!") with that in *Traviata*, N. 7, mm. 348ff. ("Qui desïata giungi . . .").

The third finale is worked out from a fine, broad, Mercadantean phrase, which is repeated in unison to great effect.[41] The movement to the dominant where Vasconcello and Don Diego take over the theme is well conceived.[42] The instrumental part of this piece too is very beautiful and is richly varied each time the theme is repeated. Verdi has displayed his great talent on this occasion. The third time the theme is repeated, in a full unison, a very fine effect is produced, but it is a sonority effect [*effetto di sonorità*] only; the dramatic aspect becomes secondary. Now, I believe that while one must not despise this sort of effect, it must not be viewed as the goal of music. I also believe that this fine piece does not accord much with the rest of the work, thus detracting from that unity of style and musical conception that constitutes the true beauty of an opera. The orchestration of this piece is very sophisticated; it results from various sorts of arpeggios, chromatic passages, etc. played mostly by the strings in sixteenth-note figures that contrast at many points with other rhythmic patterns. From this the accompaniment gains a certain agitation and nimbleness, nicely set against the tranquil, grave, slow motion of the melody.

The fourth act too begins with a prelude, followed by Enrico's aria, whose andante, "Giorno di pianto," is too uniform.[43] The harmonies of the first phrase are too studied and unnatural; the first three measures have three root-position triads in a row and on neighboring steps,[44] which does not produce a very nice sound. It is true that Palestrina did very much the same in the opening measures of his *Stabat mater*, but he may have wished to represent a sense of grief. In Verdi's piece, too, the words refer to tears and grief, but this is a grief that is in no way extraordinary. This first phrase is also an example of the class of melody that is meaningless, or almost so, without its harmonies.

The duet for Enrico and Giovanna follows; it is certainly one of this opera's praiseworthy pieces.[45] First there is a *parlante* that may be numbered among the *parlanti melodici*, and that recalls the theme from the overture to *Oberon*, noted once before.[46] Giovanna's andante, "Enrico! ah parli a un core," is very

41. "Terra adorata" (originally "Noble patrie").

42. Don Pedro and Don Diego are the Spanish officers who take the place of the original French officers Béthune and Vaudemont.

43. Henri's "O jour de peine."

44. This is the probable meaning of Basevi's "tre accordi perfetti di seguito, e vicini," especially given the reference to the opening of Palestrina's *Stabat mater* in the following sentence.

45. "O sdegni miei tacete . . . " (Henri and Hélène's "De courroux et d'effroi").

46. Compare the passage at "Non son reo! tremendo fato" ("Malheureux et non coupable") with those from Verdi's *Ernani* and Weber's *Oberon* specified in chapter 3, n. 39, above.

tender.[47] The movement from G minor to G major, falling immediately onto the chord of the subdominant, is rather singular. The allegro "È dolce raggio" is based on a delicate idea, and belongs in its effect to the family of duets *a mezza voce* that we began to note in *I due Foscari* and that we also found in *Rigoletto* in the first duet for soprano and baritone.[48] It is also similar to this latter piece in that at the third repetition of the theme the soprano sings certain decorations that I frankly find no more opportune in this duet than in the other.

The quartet that comes next has its good parts, but as a whole is disjointed and cannot please.[49] A measure of $\frac{5}{4}$ meter is bizarre and seems to indicate nothing but a caprice on the composer's part. I am not against $\frac{5}{4}$ time, but I would suggest that, for its use to make any sense, it should be prolonged so that the alternation of ternary and binary meters is clearly discernible. According to La Borde, Adolfati wrote the aria "Se la sorte mi condanna" from his opera *Arianna* in two unequal meters, that is, in quintuple time. Benedetto Marcello had done the same before him.[50]

The "De profundis" is a pallid imitation of the "Miserere" from *Il trovatore*.

The theme of the stretta of the quartet is very ordinary and is in the style of Donizetti. The only novelty consists in having the theme sung first by many voices in unison and then repeated only by Enrico and Giovanna, accompanied by Vasconcello and Pinto.[51] This procedure is contrary to common practice: the grand unison is usually saved for last.

47. "Ami! . . . le coeur d'Hélène."

48. The allegro is the original "Pour moi rayonne." The first reference is to "Speranza dolce ancora" (the stretta of Lucrezia and Jacopo's duet "No, non morrai," N. 9 of *Foscari*), which Basevi had likened to "Verranno a te sull'aure" from Donizetti's *Lucia di Lammermoor*; the second is to "Veglia, o donna, questo fiore" (the stretta of Gilda and Rigoletto's duet "Deh non parlare al misero," N. 4 of *Rigoletto*).

49. "Addio, mia terra" ("Adieu, mon pays"). This "quartetto" is also the finale of act 4, and includes the two sections next discussed by Basevi.

50. Both examples (Andrea Adolfati and Benedetto Marcello) are found in Jean-Benjamin de La Borde, *Essai sur la musique ancienne et moderne*, 4 vols. (Paris: Onfroy, 1780), 3:161; La Borde himself refers to Rousseau's *Dictionnaire de musique* as his source.

51. Though the stretta begins at "O mia sorpresa! o giubilo" ("O surprise! ô mystère"), the main theme to which Basevi refers—which Giovanna (Hélène) and Enrico (Henri) sing first in unison with the chorus's first sopranos and tenors, and then on their own with counterpoint from Vasconcello (Montfort) and Pinto (Procida)—is that at "Omai rapito in estasi" ("Je cède avec ivresse" / "O ma belle maitresse!").

The fifth act opens with a chorus partly off and partly on stage; it makes little effect, and is composed on a dance tune of no great novelty.[52]

The bolero is based on a very graceful musical idea, although its *mossa* is composed of notes forming a ninth chord and is therefore none too catchy.[53] The rhythm recalls somewhat the instrumental codetta to the bolero in Halévy's *La juive*.[54]

The tenor's *melodia* is very sweet but is studied at times.[55] Its nature is that of a parlor song. Thus, this piece, like others noted above, runs counter to the unity of style that should be maintained in an opera so that it may make a lasting impression on the listener.

In the ensuing *terzetto*, the largo is notable for its fine workmanship.[56] The stretta, although nothing new melodically, serves the poet's thought well, but it is too long;[57] like all the longueurs found in this opera, this is because of the French libretto.

The final scene contains nothing that demands our attention.[58]

We have reached the end of our journey through the opera *Giovanna de Guzman*. What have we learned? First, that Verdi has not written music appropriate in form to the French libretto; second, that it is this that has given rise to the longueurs in the opera; third, that the best pieces are those in which the old forms are retained; fourth, that the work does not abound in novelty; fifth, that, writing under constraint, it was impossible to compose homogeneous, consistent music with its own color; sixth, that it is not lacking in musical learning; and seventh, that Verdi does not show in this opera any drying up of invention, so that we still have much to hope for from him.

52. "Si celebri alfine" ("Célébrons ensemble").

53. Perhaps in an attempt at Sicilian local color, Hélène's "Merci, jeunes amies" (Elena's "Mercé, dilette amiche") is defined, puzzlingly, as a siciliana in scores of *Vêpres siciliennes* and *Vespri siciliani*. The definition of the piece as a bolero in the score of *Giovanna de Guzman* (Giovanna's "Il don m'è grato e pregio") and in the libretto of *Vêpres* makes more musical sense.

54. There are similarities between the opening phrase of the vocal part of Verdi's piece and the upper orchestral parts at mm. 58–59 in *La juive*'s N. 15, Boléro ("Mon doux seigneur et maître") (Eudoxie). (The piece is not included in the score reproduced in *ERO* 36 [1980].)

55. Enrico's "Scendono i zeffiretti" (Henri's "La brise souffle au loin," Arrigo's "La brezza aleggia intorno"). The French libretto calls this a "romance" (it is made of two *couplets*, like the preceding bolero), whereas Escudier's vocal score uses "mélodie"; though the two terms have a partly overlapping history, by Basevi's time the latter connoted greater dignity, both poetic and musical. Basevi borrows the Ricordi score's label "melodia"—clearly a simple adaptation from the French *mélodie*—but is quick to specify that this piece is rather a simple "canzonetta per camera."

56. "Sorte fatal!" ("Sort fatal!").

57. "M'ingannasti, o traditrice" ("Trahison! imposture!").

58. "Ah! vieni; il mio mortal dolore" ("Ah! venez compatir").

It is therefore impossible to establish to which manner this opera is most closely allied, for not only are there pieces belonging to all three of the manners noted thus far, but others—and not a few—approach the styles of other composers. Nor in the course of the opera does one particular quality emerge from all that variety to dominate the others and enable us to establish a new manner: indeed, the whole destroys or suffocates the variety of its parts. The orchestration, however, proceeds with a certain evenness and calm, with the strings dominating and the woodwinds used often as linkage.

This opera has also the very great defect of its length. Today's Italians cannot focus their attention on a performance for so many hours, whereas the French have this ability. Once it was different: in his *History of Music*, Bourdelot tells us that the operas of the French were at one time very short, while those of the Italians lasted five or six hours.[59]

But I am of the opinion that, like any other composition that cannot be interrupted, an opera must not be too long. If this type of spectacle is to serve as a refreshment from the toils of the day, it must not require further toil by the listener. In Italy there is the habit of conversation in the boxes, which would die out if operas were more continuously compelling than they generally are; it would be as it is with performances of tragedies and comedies, which are heeded with much greater attention. Most operas used to be divided into two acts of unbounded length; it was, I believe, very sensible to increase the number of acts to three, and nowadays to four, so as not to tire the audience's attention, which has become all the more necessary as our theatrical music has progressed.

59. The *Histoire de la musique et de ses effets depuis son origine jusqu'à présent* (1715) is the result of the efforts of various members of the Bourdelot family. The passage in question—which Basevi probably read in the 1725 edition of the *Histoire* he owned (Piovano, 313 n. 464)—originates in an earlier and better-known text, where we read that Italian operas "always last five or six hours, and . . . seem to last eight or nine." Jean-Laurent Le Cerf de La Viéville, *Comparaison de la musique italienne et de la musique françoise* (Brussels: Foppens, 1704), 43 ("durent toujours cinq ou six heures, & . . . vous paroitroient bien en durer huit ou neuf").

19

SIMON BOCCANEGRA

I had to read this libretto of Piave's no fewer than SIX TIMES, attentively, before I understood—or thought I understood—any of it.[1] I will endeavor to reduce to a scene-by-scene synopsis this monstrous operatic hodgepodge on which Verdi pinned such high hopes.

The libretto is divided into a prologue and three acts. Many years pass between the prologue and act 1. The action is set in and around Genoa in the first half of the fourteenth century.

Prologue

Scene 1. *A piazza in Genoa.* Pietro, a plebeian, and Paolo, a Genoese gold refiner, are in conversation.[2] Paolo promises Pietro gold and power if he will second the nomination of Simone, a corsair in the service of the Republic, to the rank of *primo abate.*

Scene 2. Paolo, alone, rails against the patricians.

---

1. Basevi consistently refers to the opera as *Simone Boccanegra*: we substitute throughout its generally accepted title.

2. We assign the two characters' activities following the libretto (Basevi had mistakenly reversed them).

Scene 3. Simone approaches hurriedly. Paolo tells him that all is ready for his nomination as doge.[3] Simone is reluctant, but agrees in the hope of being able to marry Maria, who is being held prisoner in the palace of the Fieschi. The reader of the libretto needs to know that Simone's love had been requited by Jacopo Fiesco's daughter Maria, who bore him a daughter, and that Fiesco would not permit their union.

Scene 4. Pietro, Paolo, artisans, and plebeians are on stage. They agree to elect Simone Boccanegra. (*Exeunt omnes.*)

Scene 5. Fiesco emerges from the palace, forgetting the key in the lock (!!!). He is lamenting the death of his daughter Maria. Women in mourning and servants come out of the house, cross the stage, and disappear.

Scene 6. Simone encounters Fiesco and begs his pardon, but this is denied. Simone insists, and Fiesco agrees on one condition: that Simone give him "the unfortunate innocent born of an impure love." This Simone cannot do, for he has lost her, and has long sought her in vain. Fiesco departs without granting his pardon. Simone enters the Fieschi palace, only to find the dead body of his Maria. He returns to the stage in horror.

Scene 7. The people proclaim Simone doge.

Act 1

Scene 1. *Palace of the Grimaldi outside Genoa*. A dejected Maria Boccanegra, Simone's daughter, living under the name of Amelia, awaits her lover.

Scene 2. Gabriele Adorno, a Genoese gentleman, arrives. He and Amelia express their mutual love.

Scene 3. It is announced that the doge [Simone], having returned from the hunt, wishes to visit the palace.

Scene 4. Amelia tells Gabriele that the doge is coming to request her hand for one of his favorites, and begs Gabriele to expedite their marriage.

Scene 5. On his way out, Gabriele encounters Jacopo Fiesco, who has taken the name of Andrea, and asks him for Amelia's hand. Andrea responds that Amelia is an adopted foundling to whom he had given the false name of Grimaldi in order to prevent the new doge from confiscating the wealth

3. In fact, Paolo initially mentions the office of *abate*, as he had already done in scene 1 (*abate del popolo* was a high-ranking magistrate in Genoa); it is only at Simone's refusal that he invokes the title of doge, which the Genoese will bestow on Boccanegra by the end of this prologue. Synopses of the opera tend to use "doge" from the very opening (and Basevi's slightly too early terminological switch suggests that he did not distinguish between the two roles).

of the exiles.[4] Gabriele is in love, and insists on his demands; Andrea agrees. (*Exeunt.*)

Scene 6. The doge enters with his train, etc.

Scene 7. The doge remains with Amelia. He discovers that she is his long-lost daughter.

Scene 8. Simone tells Paolo, now a favorite of his and in love with Amelia, that he must renounce her.

Scene 9. An irritated Paolo says to Pietro, another favorite of the doge's, that he wishes to abduct Amelia.

Scene 10. *A vast piazza in Genoa; upstage is the port, with dressed ships.* The anniversary of Simone's coronation is being celebrated.

Scene 11. Cries of treachery are suddenly heard. Gabriele enters with dagger drawn and makes for Simone, whom he believes to be Amelia's abductor.

Scene 12. Amelia arrives, having escaped, and declares that the doge is innocent. All cry anathema on the head of the traitor.

Act 2

Scene 1. *The dogal palace in Genoa.* Paolo tells Pietro to admit the two prisoners.

Scene 2. Paolo laments the doge's ingratitude.

Scene 3. The prisoners Andrea and Gabriele come forward. Paolo accuses Andrea, now known to be Fiesco, of having betrayed the doge—and then proposes that he murder the doge as he sleeps. Fiesco refuses.

Scene 4. Paolo makes the same proposal to Gabriele and, in order to rouse him to jealousy, adds that Amelia is with the doge and *the object of his villainous pleasures.*[5] Gabriele too refuses.

Scene 5. Gabriele remains alone, a prey to jealousy.

Scene 6. Amelia arrives, and Gabriele accuses her of infidelity, but she does not wish to reveal that the doge is her father.——The doge arrives, and Gabriele hides on the balcony.

Scene 7. Amelia asks her father if she may be Gabriele's bride. Although his enemy, the doge agrees. Amelia leaves, sorry at being unable to help the hidden Gabriele.

4. The Grimaldi brothers had been banished from Genoa; the infant orphan Maria had been secretly put in the place of their sister, the real Amelia Grimaldi, when the latter died.

5. Basevi marks in italics the words he has borrowed from the libretto, "*segno alle infami dilettanze.*"

Scene 8. The doge is alone and falls asleep. Gabriele takes advantage of the
situation and raises a dagger to kill him.

Scene 9. Amelia arrives and prevents the murder. The doge awakens and
rails against Gabriele, who, learning that Amelia is the doge's daughter,
begs forgiveness and receives it.——A tumult against the doge is heard
offstage. Gabriele offers Simone his sword in defense.

Act 3

Scene 1. *The scene as in act 2, with the hangings of the upstage balconies drawn.*
People and senators extol the doge on his victory. The doge invites
Gabriele into the church. Pietro tells Paolo that all is ready for vengeance
on Simone.

Scene 2. We hear a chorus announcing the marriage of Amelia and Gabriele.
Paolo is furious. He opens a door and brings in Fiesco, whom he tells that
Simone has been poisoned.

Scene 3. Fiesco is horrified at such a crime, and says that he will be able to
escape suspicion of such infamy through death. He withdraws.

Scene 4. The doge enters with Pietro and begins to feel the effects of the
poison.

Scene 5. The doge is left alone; Fiesco approaches and reveals himself. The
doge recalls that Fiesco had once offered to pardon him if he conceded
the orphan girl Fiesco mourned as lost; now he tells him that the orphan
lives—under the name of Amelia Grimaldi. Fiesco is amazed; he weeps
and reveals that a traitor has poisoned Simone.

Final scene. Enter Maria,[6] Gabriele, etc. The doge presents Fiesco to Maria
as her grandfather, blesses Maria and Gabriele, and dies. Gabriele Adorno
is proclaimed doge.

I do not know how much the reader may have understood from this detailed summary, but I can assure him that he would have understood less from
reading Piave's libretto.

I shall say nothing of history—even though it is not so much altered as
murdered—for, to my mind, one does not learn history from librettos. I would
allow Piave his historical license, but only on condition that he create for me
a story—or, if you like, a fable—in which I can find something worthy of my
attention.

---

6. For this final scene Basevi restores Amelia's birth name, Maria (as do a number of
primary sources).

The personalities of the characters are tentative, cold, often unnatural, and of no dramatic effect. The situations are all old hat, heaped up, without clarity, often unrealistic, and succeed one another without logical order. Lacking a focal point, the audience does not know where chiefly to direct its attention. The events, barely sketched, are too precipitate, dictated by chance, and without common sense, so that in the end they leave no imprint on the spectator's mind. Shall I speak of the verse? Piave's ability with verse is already well known. With regard to the distribution of the musical pieces—whether good or not—the composer is responsible, when that composer is a Verdi.

Verdi's new score was eagerly awaited by the public, the most varied opinions circulating as to the manner the celebrated composer would adopt. Some thought that, after the extremely happy success of *La traviata*, he would follow that same path; others thought he would continue in the direction of *Giovanna de Guzman*.

The great moment arrived. On the evening of March 12, 1857, the Teatro La Fenice in Venice resounded to the melodies of *Simon Boccanegra*.[7] The opera's reception was not good. Tested in other theaters, it found the public invariably severe, except in Naples. The fact is that—by seeking new forms suited to dramatic expression, by giving greater importance to recitative, and by being less concerned with melody—Verdi attempted in this opera a fourth manner somewhat approaching German music. At least judging by the prologue, I should say he was almost following—from afar it is true, but following nonetheless—in the footsteps of the famous Wagner, the subverter of present-day music. It is well known that Wagner would like, as far as possible, to render music a determinate language, almost a shadow of poetry.[8]

Wagner's system had, and still has, many opponents in Germany, even though that country does not appear as averse to harmonic abstruseness or as concerned about melodic simplicity as Italy. Wagner's *Tannhäuser* is performed in Germany, but it does not attract great crowds except through the novelty of the experiment; nor does it escape yawns, except when there is some melody or lyrical passage [*cantabile*] or ensemble [*pezzo concertato*]—things that, though contrary to the system, are still heard, if in small doses. Thus, if Germany itself does not desire these reforms, Italy should all the more hold them in horror. I will concede it as *possible* that Wagnerian reform

7. Basevi mistakenly gives the year as 1856.

8. As elsewhere, Basevi opposes music to verbal language because of the latter's greater semantic determinacy.

represents the *music of the future*, but I deny absolutely that it is the *music of the present*.[9] And if there is an art that should be keener to make itself immediately pleasing, it is unquestionably music, particularly theater music.

In the music of *Simon Boccanegra* there is certainly no abundance of bel canto, and the little we do run into feels like a very old acquaintance—one who, because of the listeners' deprivation, is often not unwelcome. In spite of this, the vocal style of this opera generally has the virtue of not being exaggerated by the impetuosity that characterizes Verdi's genius; hence, it approaches his third manner, which signaled notable progress in this respect.[10] The instrumental writing manifests less industriousness than sophistication—in the harmonies, in the use of pedal points, and in certain kinds of ornamentation, such that the vocal line often becomes subsidiary. The recitatives that are so abundant in this score do not stand out, and the themes of the *parlanti* are often unrelated to the words.

The *preludio* begins by outlining in staccato chords the hymn to the doge from act 1, a very old theme recalling a trite and timeworn cadence found in much church music.[11] Still, Verdi gave it great weight, for he made it one of the dominant musical ideas of the opera, and one that follows the doge like a shadow. We next hear some diminished-seventh chords resolving to six-five chords, which will later be used in the offstage chorus in scene 5 of the prologue for its cry of "È morta! . . . è morta! . . ." Soon comes the theme of the allegro from the duet between the doge and his daughter in act 1, scene 7.[12] This theme is given a certain importance, for the orchestra repeats it again during the doge's dream in act 2, scene 8. This melody too is far from new, and its rhythm not merely old but hackneyed: it is the rhythm on which Bellini wrote "Suoni la tromba, e intrepido."[13] Now comes the theme of the offstage chorus, "All'armi," from the second-act finale; this too is a commonplace—indeed trite—musical idea. Then, after a four-measure phrase from the duet

9. The ironic italicization of the terms (here and later in the chapter) is Basevi's; "music of the future" is a reference to Wagner's *Das Kunstwerk der Zukunft* (The artwork of the future, 1849); Wagner's *Zukunftsmusik* (Music of the future) had not yet appeared.

10. This is the stylistic turn that, according to Basevi, took place with *La traviata* (see p. 196 above).

11. The hymn "Viva Simon! . . . di Genova" is in the finale of act 1. The cadential formula is probably that outlined in the melody of mm. 9–15 of the *preludio*.

12. This is the stretta ("Figlia! . . . a tal nome palpito") from the Doge-Amelia duet "Dinne, perché in quest'eremo."

13. Vincenzo Bellini, *I puritani*, ed. Fabrizio Della Seta, *ECB* 10 (forthcoming), [N. 8], Duetto [Riccardo e Giorgio] ("Il rival salvar tu devi"), mm. 277ff. ("Suoni la tromba, e intrepido" is the cabaletta of the duet.)

for the doge and Fiesco in the fifth scene of the third act,[14] the *preludio* ends with a brief cadential passage.

The three scenes of recitative with which the opera opens are not as remarkable as they ought to be if they are to invite the audience's attention.[15] In general, Verdi has greatly neglected the recitatives of his operas. Yet it is in recitative that the composer can more easily display his genius with regard to musical expression, as he is not bound to certain kinds of symmetry and other regularities. Recitative is the true wellspring of opera. It was first created at Florence toward the end of the sixteenth century. Vincenzo Galilei, the father of the celebrated Galileo, was the first to write in an expressive mode for a solo voice, setting Dante's lines on Count Ugolino.[16] Giulio Caccini imitated his example, as did Jacopo Peri and others. The success of these monodies inspired a learned and illustrious society that met in the house of Jacopo Corsi to set an entire drama to music in *stile recitativo*. Ottavio Rinuccini was the poet, Peri and Caccini the musicians. Thus *Dafne* was the first opera—or rather the first attempt at opera.[17]

Recitative gradually improved. Vinci advanced it greatly, notably in a good part of the final act of his *Didone*[18]—so much so that, in Algarotti's words, "It must be believed that Virgil himself would have been pleased, so alive and terrible it is."[19] The celebrated Tartini tells us that in 1714 he heard in the theater at Ancona "a line of recitative accompanied by no instrument other than the bass, which caused, as much in us musicians as in the listeners, such emotion that each man looked from face to face to see a clear change in color wrought

14. See, in the duet "Delle faci festanti al barlume," the doge's part from the eighteenth measure of the largo "Piango, perché mi parla." (The musical phrase, of Basevi's "economical" type, actually takes only two measures in the duet version.)

15. Basevi calls these "scene" in the sense in which the term is used in librettos (Prologo, scenes 1–3).

16. Galilei's setting of Count Ugolino's lament (Dante, *Inferno*, 33), which was performed in Florence in 1582, does not survive. The same canto was set to music by Donizetti in 1828.

17. The *Dafne* of 1598 (of which only a few pieces survive) is widely regarded as the first opera, and had music by Peri and the nobleman Jacopo Corsi (rather than Caccini, who later made claims on it); it is the first *Euridice* (1600) that would have music by both Peri and Caccini—each of them soon publishing his own, independent setting of the entire opera. Basevi had published a series of articles about *Dafne* in the *Gazzetta musicale* in 1853–54, and in 1863 Guidi would print a modern edition of Peri's *Euridice*.

18. Leonardo Vinci, *Didone abbandonata* (Rome: Teatro delle Dame, 1726). Vinci was one of the most influential operatic composers active in the 1720s.

19. The quotation is from Francesco Algarotti's famous *Saggio sopra l'opera in musica*, though it does not appear in the work's very first editions (1755); it does appear in, for example, the edition printed in Livorno by Coltellini in 1763, p. 29.

in all present [. . .] . The drama was repeated thirteen times, and each time the same universal effect occurred."[20] In Burney's *History of Music* we read of the extraordinary case of the nightly encore of a recitative in Jommelli's *Attilio* sung by Serafini.[21] Benedetto Marcello, Porpora, Pergolesi, and others excelled in recitative, but it was the celebrated Gluck who brought it near to perfection.

We can distinguish two kinds of recitative: simple recitative, where all the expression is in the vocal part, and obbligato recitative, in which the orchestra is given greater importance. In simple recitative the music sometimes seeks to express the emotions contained in the poetry, and sometimes confines itself to setting the words to notes without troubling about anything else. In *opera buffa* particularly one finds this latter case; I myself would prefer simple spoken dialogue as in French comic operas. Obbligato recitative is sometimes so melodically adorned by the orchestra that it nearly approaches *parlante*. It is thus possible to construct a chain of the various classes of vocal music: in order, simple recitative, obbligato recitative, *parlante armonico*, *parlante melodico*, and finally aria.

Returning to Verdi's aforementioned recitatives, we will note a passage of a kind of which our composer is most fond, and that I consider to be often used inappropriately. I speak of the kind of recitative that is formed by using a monotone in the vocal part as though it were a pedal, while the harmony changes or the bass moves. This can depict nothing but immobility, gravity, and similar things—certainly no lively feeling. Paolo's words "Il prode, che da' nostri mari cacciava l'african pirata, e al ligure vessillo, etc." are set to twenty-three Cs in a row. Gluck used that sort of sung pedal very astutely in *Alceste*, in the chorus of infernal gods, where they say, "E vuoi morire, etc.," with thirty-eight Ds in a row across thirteen measures.[22] Rousseau judged that piece to be of sublime simplicity.[23] The same procedure was used by Mozart in *Don Giovanni*, when the statue of the commendatore speaks, and by Ros-

20. Basevi quotes from Giuseppe Tartini, *Trattato di musica secondo la vera scienza dell'armonia* (Padua: Stamperia del Seminario/Giovanni Manfré, 1754), 135.

21. Charles Burney, *A General History of Music from the Earliest Ages to the Present Period*, 4 vols. (London: printed for the author, 1776–89), 4 (1789): 463n. Jommelli's *Attilio Regolo* was first given at Rome's Teatro delle Dame in 1753.

22. See Gluck, *Alceste* (Vienna: Burgtheater, 1767), ed. Gerhard Croll, *GGA* I/3a (1988), act 2, scene 2, mm. 123–35.

23. See Jean-Jacques Rousseau, "Fragment d'observations sur l'*Alceste* italien de M. le chevalier Gluck," ed. Alain Cernuschi, in *Oeuvres complètes*, Raymond Trousson and Frédéric Eigeldinger general eds., 24 vols. (Geneva: Slatkine; Paris: Champion, 2012), vol. 12, *Écrits sur la musique*, 606–34, 623.

sini in act 1 of the new version of *Mosè*, when the mysterious voice is heard from afar.[24] I consider it incorrect to use this technique when the recitative expresses ordinary emotions. That recitative may still be effective nowadays is well demonstrated by the sixth scene of act 2 of *La traviata*, which is largely an obbligato recitative.[25] The Italians bear the responsibility of maintaining the good name of recitative, if for no other reason than that they have the most musical language in the world. The following piece for Paolo and the chorus is without effect, and almost without form. The allegro "L'atra magion vedete?" is a series of barely connected phrases; the vocal part often lies on a single note, a sort of pedal in which Verdi has taken great pleasure throughout this opera. A certain variety of orchestration is found in this piece, which attests to compositional care, but is no great help to expression.

Fiesco's *romanza* "Il lacerato spirito" begins in the minor mode with a much-used rhythm; after eight measures, the cantabile is interrupted by the offstage cry of "È morta! . . . è morta! . . ."; it then goes into the major with a different musical idea, which, proceeding together with the lamentations of the offstage chorus, ends with a certain effect on account of its simplicity. The lugubrious march that follows is poor.

The duet for the doge and Fiesco ["Simon? . . ." "Tu!"] has an unusual form. After a few bars of recitative, it shifts into a sort of *parlante melodico* with the words "Qual cieco fato"; then, at the words "Sublimarmi a lei," Simone has a true cantabile, which lasts no more than eight measures before giving way to a *parlante*, whose instrumental part has a rather studied sequence as well as some very hackneyed passages, all in the space of twenty-nine measures. After this, Fiesco has a six-measure cantabile ["Se concedermi vorrai"] that dissolves into an obbligato recitative of twelve measures. Simone then sings another cantabile on the words "Del mar sul lido," a ⅜ andantino of a pastoral nature that lasts no more than sixteen measures. Then the key of A-flat passes to E major, and the voice continues for eight measures, always on the same note, over a very simple accompaniment, until nine measures more of little-varied notes bring us back to A-flat; with a thirty-six-measure mixture of recitative, *parlante*, and a few scraps of melody, the piece comes to an end. It cannot be denied that the form of this duet is new, but not all

24. See *Don Giovanni*, recitative of act 2, scene 11, mm. 51ff., 59ff. The offstage "Voix mystérieuse" ("Moïse, approche-toi") is heard in N. 1, Introduction ("Dieu puissant, du joug de l'impie") of *Moïse et Pharaon*.

25. The scene corresponds to mm. 1–104 of *La traviata*'s N. 6, Scena Violetta ("Dammi tu forza, o cielo . . .") ed Aria Germont ("Di Provenza il mar, il suol").

novelty is beautiful; and we will not be so fond of novelty that we will not prefer the old things when they are more beautiful. Wagner would have happily
underwritten this piece; indeed, it is one of the most perfect models of a duet
as understood by the followers of the *music of the future*. It is so much *of the
future* that even Wagner himself would hardly dare to venture so far. In fact,
in the second scene of the first act of *Tannhäuser* there is a duet for Venus and
Tannhäuser in which the two characters not only sing together several times
but repeat the same lengthy and well-developed theme three times.[26]

If music were to aim at the goal to which Wagner and other innovators
would like to lead it—and to which Verdi in this duet seems for a moment
to have wished to direct it—its future would be a return to recitative, which
would fly hard in the face of history.

But music has been given this false direction because its true, vital relationships with poetry have not been given careful consideration.

These relationships exist on two levels: one is recitative and the other
aria.

I use the term *recitative* here not merely in a broad sense, but so extended
as to mean the kind of musical expression that timidly and slavishly, step for
step, follows the words and sentences of the poetry—not excluding those
brief melodies that interrupt the declamation and then vanish without linking with others, as found in the above-mentioned duet between Simone and
Fiesco. Recitative is the first step in the musico-dramatic art.

I also use *aria* in a broader sense, extending as far as the most colossal
ensembles.[27] Through the aria, music has attained a certain independence
and greater dignity, creating, as it were, musical pictures [*quadri musicali*]
that have their own substance even without the poetry. These are vague de-
pictions, but they are not without an effect on our feelings. The poetry with
which they are associated provides, in a sense, their interpretation, by which
their general meaning becomes particular and determinate. Thus, poetry is
here to music what arithmetic is to algebra: music supplies a formula that

---

26. See Richard Wagner, *Tannhäuser und der Sängerkrieg auf Wartburg* (1845 version), ed.
Reinhard Strohm, *SW* 5 (1980–95), act 1, scene 2, mm. 92ff., 181ff., 376ff.; it is Tannhäuser who
has the long melody three times (each time a semitone higher), though Basevi does not mention
that at this point the character is actually singing (and accompanying himself) within the
narrative.

27. In other words, in this passage the term *aria* is extended so as to embrace what we would
call set pieces or numbers, or at least their static sections.

poetry then applies to the particular case. Let us say that the fourth finale of Meyerbeer's *Le prophète* were to be performed without words beginning from the march.[28] This piece, a clear example of musical painting, could not fail to move the listener, although in an indeterminate way. Add the poetry, and the listener will understand the emotion he has felt. Now, the poetry increases the piece's effect not as poetry—that is, by virtue of its own art—but rather as an interpretation of the music.

This explains why the composer demands that the librettist produce not a work perfect in itself, but rather a skeleton that, when covered by concealing flesh, will not lose its own nature but impart it to its outer covering.

I am certain that the future of music lies in the improvement and expansion of these "musical pictures." The past is my guarantee for the future. This kind of progress is even more obvious in instrumental music than in vocal music: just compare a symphony by Lully with one by Beethoven. In vocal music, we may also observe that, having gradually developed arias, duets, and trios, composers wished to unite several scenes into a larger musical picture, which led to the creation of the finale, attributed to Logroscino, toward the middle of the last century.[29] When those early arias, duets, and so forth are compared with similar pieces from among the best modern ones, the latter display greater coherence, unity, and expression. Among the ancients, the musical discourse generally unfolded through many digressions or contained too many repetitions, whereas among the best of the moderns, if the musical discourse digresses somewhat, it is with a view to creating episodes that render the discourse itself more pleasant and strengthen and revitalize it. Just as recitative does not lose its character when it includes some stretches of melody, so an aria does not forfeit its identity when it contains some recitative passages.

In opera, recitative is no less necessary than aria, and it is for the composer's ingenuity to determine when and where it is needed. But he must never forget that aria has greater dignity than recitative.

These things elucidated, we will continue on our way.

---

28. The Marche du sacre (N. 23 in the score of *Le prophète* reproduced in *ERO* 21) introduces the fourth-act finale (N. 24) already praised by Basevi in chapters 1 and 14 above.

29. The opera composer Nicola Logroscino, who was especially successful in Naples in the 1740s and 1750s, began to be credited with the "invention" of the multisectional act finale in the 1790s—an attribution that has now been largely disproved.

After a lengthy recitative ["Oh de' Fieschi implacata, orrida razza! . . ."],
the finale of the prologue has an allegro assai vivo ["Doge il popol t'acclama!"]
that does duty for the choral acclamations and that we hear with pleasure after
the monotony and flabbiness of the preceding music. The theme of this allegro is similar to that wedded to the words of the chorus "Alle giostre, ai tornei
che prepara, etc." in Donizetti's *Parisina*.[30] And the effect it makes at this
point is proof of the influence pieces have on those that follow.[31]

The first act opens with Amelia's cavatina.[32] It is a ⅜-time adagio with
a not very expressive vocal melody, and offers nothing notable aside from a
very nimble string accompaniment, with chords spread out such that they
extend beyond the range of the vocal part. After twelve measures, we hear
eleven measures of ⅜ time that are not well linked with the preceding cantabile and do not prepare well for the rhythm that cantabile will take on when
it is repeated with a different accompaniment. The little offstage *canzone* for
Gabriele ["Cielo di stelle orbato"] in the *tempo di mezzo* is of little moment.
The cabaletta to this cavatina ["Il palpito deh frena"] is full of brio and recalls
the Verdi of the earlier operas; it stands out all the more for being almost
a melodic flower in the desert. Here Verdi forgot about Wagner and all the
musicians of the future and gave his allegro the form that, though old, is more
secure in its effect, if a bit trite. The *mossa* of this cabaletta is a common cadential passage.

In the duet for Gabriele and Amelia, Verdi has adopted the most frequently
used of forms. The attention the composer lavished on the accompaniment
to the ⅜-time andantino "Vieni a mirar la cerula" made him forget the vocal
melody, and for eight measures Amelia sings on the same note. In *I vespri siciliani*, where the same rhythm and vocal line were used on the words "Presso
alla tomba ch'apresi" (although in a different meter), at least they occupied
only a single verse line, not two, as they do here.[33] I noted above that these
sung pedals must be used sparingly and in what special cases they are useful.
After a few very badly connected phrases we reach the melodic period "Ri-
para i tuoi pensieri," which is repeated three times in the course of the piece;

30. See, in Donizetti's *Parisina* (Florence: Teatro alla Pergola, 1833), Parisina's first-act cavatina with chorus "Forse un destin che intendere": the choral passage is in the *tempo di mezzo*.
31. See p. 109 above.
32. Scena e Cavatina Amelia ("Come in quest'ora bruna").
33. See the opening of the andantino "Près du tombeau" from Hélène and Henri's second-
act duet "Comment, dans ma reconnaissance" ("Quale, o prode, al tuo coraggio"), discussed
on p. 212 above.

the melody of this period is fine, but its last four measures recall Adina's cavatina from *L'elisir d'amore*.[34] The allegro "Sì, sì dell'ara il giubilo" proceeds by brief, imitative answers—a very old technique, indeed one of the first adopted in the composition of duets. The duets of Steffani, Durante, Scarlatti, Pergolesi, etc. may be seen as examples.[35] I would certainly not ban this method, but it must be used judiciously, for not always—indeed rarely—does it give pleasure, as the brevity of the phrases and their frequent interruption obstruct the transfusion of dramatic power into the music.

Verdi returned to seeking novelty of form in the duet between Fiesco and Gabriele.[36] A long recitative prepares an andante mosso in which a four-measure theme peeps out on the words "Paventa, o perfido"—a most unappealing theme that is first sung by Gabriele over a timpani pedal and then repeated by Fiesco a fourth lower, also over a pedal in the timpani. After this, the parts proceed together for twenty-four measures in which I was unable to discern a musical idea. Furthermore, the dramatic situation is of little consequence; nor does the music help with its many repetitions of "paventa" addressed to someone who is not there to hear them. Once (at most) would have been enough. This is the poorest piece in the opera.

The form of the duet for the doge and Amelia is only half new.[37] The novelty lasts until the cabaletta ["Figlia! . . . a tal nome palpito"], which follows the old—indeed very old—custom for cabalettas, which in the case of duets were heard, as if by obligation, three times. On the other hand, in the first part of the duet, a recitative ["Il nuovo dì festivo"] is followed by a long *parlante* ["Dinne, perché in quest'eremo"] leading to the *racconto* "Orfanella il tetto umìle," pastoral in character but too long and badly connected. The doge then sings a rather characterless phrase of eight measures' length, after which the two parts continue together in a sort of cadential passage of nine measures that concludes with a gigantic cadenza—and an inopportune one at that. Could we not once and for all be freed of cadenzas? Are they not nonsensical? Are they

34. Compare this duet at the words "al porto dell'amor" with "Della crudele Isotta," Adina's cavatina within the *introduzione* to Donizetti's *L'elisir d'amore* (Milan: Teatro alla Canobbiana, 1832), at "Elisir di sì perfetta, di sì rara qualità." The example may also have occurred to Basevi because the two melodies show another similarity, in what he would call the *mossa*.

35. Agostino Steffani, Francesco Durante, Alessandro Scarlatti, and Giovanni Battista Pergolesi are important vocal composers active between the second half of the seventeenth century and the first half of the eighteenth.

36. Scena ("Propizio giunge Andrea!") e Duetto ("Paventa, o perfido"). Fiesco is here under the name of Andrea.

37. Duetto Amelia e Doge ("Dinne, perché in quest'eremo").

at all necessary? Do singers have no other way of demonstrating their ability? May composers ponder this and get rid of these antiartistic cadenzas. In the *tempo di mezzo* ["Dinne . . . alcun là non vedesti?"], a *parlante* leads us to the cabaletta "Figlia! . . . a tal nome palpito," which is the aforementioned theme in the *preludio*.

We shall pass over in silence a *duettino* all in *parlante* between Paolo and Pietro,[38] to arrive at the festive chorus;[39] this has some brio, which is perhaps heightened by contrast with the music that precedes it. The barcarole that follows the chorus is the least attractive Verdi has written up to this point ["Sull'arpe, sulle cetere"], yet he reuses its theme in the *ballabile* that comes immediately afterward.[40] The hymn "Viva Simon! . . ." is the one we have already noted in the *preludio*.

One would not think that the sextet ["Ella è salva!"] had been written by Verdi; in its first measures—an unheard-of thing!—it made the Florentine audience and the singers themselves laugh, particularly when they heard the many repetitions of the words "Ella è salva" at short intervals in the various vocal parts. Amelia's *racconto*, which follows, is not overly melodic ["Nell'ora soave"]; its accompaniment tries to imitate—or rather to translate—the words: a method that is remote from the dignity and the true purposes of musical art. And the stretta ["Giustizia, giustizia tremenda"] is an intertwining of parts that adds up not to order but to true chaos. I find very bizarre the sudden sound of the harps, which continues for sixteen measures, to accompany the word "giustizia."

In the second act we will proceed at once to Gabriele's aria.[41] Here we find a novelty: the allegro precedes the adagio. The allegro "Sento avvampar nell'anima" has a sixteenth-note accompaniment that rises and falls by semitones; this is of no great benefit to the vocal melody, which, after eighteen measures, almost dissolves and gives way to a brief obbligato recitative. The final part of the aria, the largo ["Cielo pietoso, rendila"], offers nothing worthy of comment except that it begins with the same rhythm as the bass's *romanza* from the prologue;[42] for the rest, it proceeds with excessive uniformity.

---

38. Scena ("Che rispose?") e Duettino [Pietro e Paolo] ("Che disse?" "A me negolla").
39. The chorus opens the Finale primo ("A festa, a festa, o Liguri").
40. This is the danced *divertissement* with chorus "Prode guerrier."
41. Scena ("Udisti?") e Aria Gabriele ("Sento avvampar nell'anima").
42. Fiesco's "Il lacerato spirito."

The ensuing duet between Amelia and Gabriele also departs in some ways from the usual forms.[43] The andante is of little beauty. The setting of the tenor's words "Dammi la vita o il feretro" with a descending chromatic line is wanting in the spontaneity without which any expression lacks true value.[44] There is no lack of passion in the più mosso ["All'ora istessa"], and the passage where Gabriele sings, descending chromatically, "Si compia il fato! . . . egli morrà!" is well conceived, nicely counterpointed by Amelia's part.

In the doge's dream the instrumental effect is negligible, although there is logic in the repetition of the theme of the allegro from the doge and Amelia's first-act duet under a very high-register accompaniment.[45]

The *terzetto* that closes the act contains some lovely musical phrases, especially Gabriele's "Dammi la morte; il ciglio." This piece ends with the offstage chorus "All'armi, etc.," during which Verdi gives a recitative to the three characters on stage—this, too, a novelty, but how effective?

We will hold our peace about the choruses that open the third act ["Vittoria, vittoria!"; "Dal sommo delle sfere"], and skip instead to the fifth scene, where the doge seeks the cool of the sea breeze ["Oh refrigerio! . . . la marina brezza! . . ."]. In this piece Verdi again misused imitative music, with regard both to the breeze and to the sea, whose undulations he was trying to imitate. Again, these imitations, accompanying words that already express the same thing, and do it better, resemble translations—and music's job is certainly not translation, for music is not a determinate or specific language.

The largo of the doge's duet with Fiesco presents a thin, unspontaneous, and inexpressive melody at the words "Delle faci festanti al barlume." An allegro that is neither pleasant nor moving follows on the words "Come fantasima, etc." Toward the end, we encounter a series of minor ninths that continue for many measures without real preparation or resolution, and that are intended to imitate tears and grief. Here Verdi makes shrewd use of the differences in strength and musical accent between the dissonant parts. Finally comes the largo "Piango, perche mi parla," in which we find passion rather than a cold combination of notes—and about time too!

---

43. Scena ("Tu qui? . . . ") e Duetto ("Parla, in tuo cor virgineo").

44. A reference to the setting of this phrase at its third appearance, a dozen measures into the major-mode section.

45. While the doge utters his daughter's name in his sleep, the orchestra recalls the stretta ("Figlia! . . . a tal nome palpito") from their recognition duet. We are already in the Scena ("Figlia?" "Sì afflitto, o padre mio?") e Terzetto ("Vecchio inerme il tuo braccio colpisce?"; "Perdon, perdon, Amelia") that concludes the second act.

The final quartet ["Gran Dio li benedici"] is the finest piece in the opera. Verdi produced an excellent musical setting of this dramatic situation, which is itself the best in the libretto and the only one that does not grate on common sense. He successfully devised a different melody for each of the four parts, every one of them most apt. A fine effect is also created by the ensemble passage in which, at the words "Ah! non morrai," Amelia has a syncopated, descending chromatic scale that is well suited to the desperation of one who weeps. A brusque interruption toward the end of this *pezzo concertato*, to make way for a lengthy recitative ["Senatori, sancite il voto estremo"], chills its effect. This piece provides an example of those musical pictures referred to above. Though not vast, it is a lively, beautiful musical depiction that, if divorced from the words, does not fade but remains effective and expressive, in the way in which this is possible for music.

This opera must be considered as Verdi's experiment in approaching German music, where the harmonic element dominates the melodic. But our composer lacked the principal thing: a suitable libretto. It has been said that "music sharpens the darts that the poet aims at the heart":[46] if these darts are fragile or have no power, what use is it to sharpen them? The fact is that when a libretto does not provide the stuff of dramatic, passionate music, all the composer can do is at least to make the music pleasing to the ear. Verdi did not even do this; rather, he seems to have made a conscious effort to create utterly unattractive, badly developed melodies, disconnected in their periods, without any vigor, lacking any relationships among themselves, and conflicting with rather than benefiting one another.

I do not wish to condemn German music, which I would in fact very gladly see more cultivated in Italy;[47] but this does not mean that I am glad to see certain harmonic refinements being given preference over expressive and passionate melody.

Let musical learning be brought onto the stage; this may—indeed must— be done; our Mercadante is particularly praiseworthy in this respect. But it must be introduced as it is by Meyerbeer, as it was by Mozart and others, who used it as a motive force, so to speak, to drive the art of music swiftly toward its rightful goal.

---

46. The sentence is found in Lichtenthal, 1:260 (s.v. *espressione*).

47. Indeed, Basevi would soon proceed to organize concerts and lectures that promoted German music from Haydn to Brahms (see the editor's introduction).

It is in this sense that I value classicism in music, and laud the few in Italy who honor it and cultivate it with love. Among these I should like to recall Teodulo Mabellini, Carlo Andrea Gambini, Giovacchino Maglioni, Ferdinando Giorgetti (celebrated founder of a school of violin playing), Salvatore Pappalardo, and Ruggero Manna. And if I omit to mention others it is not because I mean to detract from their merit.[48] If the study of the classics were more encouraged and valued in Italy, we should not see composers running to one of two extremes—either writing music that lacks robustness and is almost consumptive, or losing themselves in abstruseries, the musical equivalents of riddles and word games.

---

48. The musicians named here were all active in Florence. The only exception is Pappalardo, a Sicilian who established himself in Naples: a composer of chamber music among other things (the probable reason for his inclusion here), he would become a corresponding member of Florence's Istituto Musicale. From 1863, Mabellini would conduct the orchestra in the Concerti Popolari organized by Basevi. (On both the Istituto Musicale and the Concerti Popolari, see the editor's introduction.)

20

AROLDO

This opera is nothing more than a reshuffled *Stiffelio*.

The difficulties created by censorship and by the bad public reception of *Stiffelio* were what induced the composer both to transform the plot and to make notable changes in the music.

The main alteration in the plot was that the priest Stiffelio became the warrior Aroldo.[1] This change has removed some of the incongruities of the first libretto, but it has created new ones. The librettist has changed only the clothes of the protagonist, who has otherwise remained the same. Clearly, many situations that are appropriate for a priest are wrong—or at least seem strange—for a warrior. That is the case in the second-act finale where Aroldo faints, strongly moved by an offstage sacred chorus, and in the finale of the opera where—just like that—he pardons his wife on hearing the words of the Gospel about the repentant adulteress spoken by a hermit companion of his.[2] It is easy to see

---

1. In the reworked libretto—by Francesco Maria Piave, like that of *Stiffelio*—the setting is moved from nineteenth-century Austria to Britain ca. 1200, and the protagonist is "defrocked" into a Saxon knight.

2. In the finale of *Aroldo*, the "pious Hermit" Briano persuades the protagonist to forgive his repudiated wife by quoting the passage from St. John's Gospel, 8:7 ("Let him who is without sin cast the first stone").

how something that was natural in a preaching minister who has devoted all his life to study of the Holy Book becomes far-fetched in a warrior, even in one who has become a hermit—an act that if anything proves the depth of his grief at his wife's offense, and makes pardon the more improbable.

With regard to the music, some things from *Stiffelio* were preserved in *Aroldo* and others were changed or added.

Stiffelio's *racconto*, the first septet of act 1,[3] the prayer,[4] and the finale of the third act[5] were removed.

The first movement and the cabaletta of the tenor's aria were changed,[6] as were the last measures of the largo and the whole of the cabaletta of the soprano's aria.[7]

The entire fourth act is new.

Of these modifications, I cannot endorse the excision of the first septet from act 1 of *Stiffelio*, nor do I consider the altered cabalettas of the tenor and soprano arias to be improvements.

The newly made fourth act jars completely and too obviously with the general style of the score. In this act, Verdi continued to experiment with a fourth manner. In the introductory chorus ["Cade il giorno . . ."] we first hear, alternately from different directions, the voices of women at harvest, huntsmen, and shepherds, but without any clear and audible musical connection.[8] Afterward, the three choruses sing successively, but lacking suitable musical differentiation; they all end by singing the harvesters' theme in unison. Rossini produced a masterpiece in the scene with three choruses in the second act

---

3. The *racconto* "Di qua varcando" and the septet "Colla cenere disperso" are both parts of *Stiffelio*'s N. 1, Introduzione ("Oh santo libro, oh dell'eterno Vero").

4. This is *Stiffelio*'s N. 3, Scena ("Tosto ei disse! . . . Ah son perduta!") e Preghiera Lina ("A te ascenda, oh Dio clemente"). Mina (Lina's equivalent in *Aroldo*) is given a briefer first-act prayer ("Salvami tu, gran Dio! . . .")—a setting of what in the libretto appears as a mere three lines of recitative.

5. *Stiffelio*'s final number—N. 10, Preghiera ("Non punirmi, Signor, nel tuo furore") e Finale ultimo ("Stiffelio?" "Eccomi!")—was replaced by the added, entirely new fourth act of *Aroldo*.

6. Stiffelio's aria "Vidi dovunque gemere" (N. 2) becomes Aroldo's "Sotto il sol di Siria ardente," whose cabaletta, "Non sai che la sua perdita," replaces Stiffelio's original "Ah v'appare in fronte scritto."

7. N. 6, Scena ("Oh cielo! . . . dove son io! . . .") ed Aria Lina ("Ah! dagli scanni eterei"). A cut toward the end of the largo is likely to have already been at least an option in productions of *Stiffelio* (see Kathleen Hansell's critical commentary for mm. 96–97 in *WGV* I/16 [2003]). Lina's original cabaletta, "Perder dunque voi volete," is replaced by Mina's "Ah dal sen di quella tomba."

8. These choral groups, placed in three different positions, are initially not visible.

of *Guillaume Tell*.[9]——The general prayer ["Angiol di Dio"] is too studied, particularly in making the various parts repeat one by one the *mossa* of each melodic period. The storm with chorus ["Al lago"] is one of the usual imitative pieces.——The final *terzetto*-quartet ["Ah, da me fuggi, involati"] has some fine passages. Verdi has modeled the beginning of the largo ["Allora che gl'anni"] on his greatest dramatic *pezzi concertati*, although it does not make a great effect as the situation is none too well developed in the libretto.

Aroldo was sung for the first time in August 1857 at Rimini.[10] The composer's presence may have contributed to the applause that it received there and nowhere else.

A new Verdi opera will shortly be sung at Rome.[11] It is to be hoped either that the composer has perfected his fourth manner or that he has renounced it completely.

In artistic terms, it is my view that if in his fourth manner Verdi would endeavor to avoid sacrificing melody, but rather make it more pleasant and expressive by connecting it better with the harmony, adapting it more carefully to the human voice, and giving greater prominence to the various instruments, and if in addition he would put every effort into the development of musical pictures [*quadri musicali*], while not neglecting recitative but lovingly cultivating it, then he would have crowned his work worthily.

Composers who find themselves in popular favor for a time must not bow so deeply to the caprices of current taste as to enslave themselves entirely. It is in this respect that Verdi is to be warmly lauded when he strikes out on a path that, though divergent from the one the public treads today, may lead him to the only place where he might earn immortal laurels.

With the powers he has acquired thus far, Verdi can today be of immense service to art; I am convinced that this is—for it must be—his principal concern.

There was a time when Rossini was in a position to pursue the noble purpose of educating the public to a higher beauty than that usually prized. *Guillaume Tell* was the first opera he created with this intent; if only it had not been the last!

9. N. 12, Final 2ᶜ ("Des profondeurs du bois immense"). Basevi mistakenly refers to the opera's fourth (rather than second) act.

10. The premiere of *Aroldo* took place on the inauguration of Rimini's Teatro Nuovo.

11. *Un ballo in maschera* would have its premiere in February 1859.

CONCLUSION

1

Reason, in guiding our will, shows us the *end* of our actions, whereas our instincts and appetites conceal that end from us, governing us solely through the pleasure or pain that accompanies whatever *means* they adopt. Our propensity for glory is associated equally with reason and with appetite. Those who desire only to savor imaginatively the admiration of others are confusing the *end* with the *means*, counting glory among the appetites. That is how our Leopardi viewed glory, comparing it, in his "Parini," "to shadow, which, when it's in your hands, you can neither feel nor prevent from fleeing."[1] But glory is not limited to the vain pleasure of the ego. Reason views it as an *end* for works that are to be enduring in their truth, goodness, or beauty, the sole qualities in which we should take pleasure.

Those who cultivate the fine arts are particularly stimulated by glory, for they know that true beauty will never perish. Glory, then, must have as its counterpart a work's immortality. But is such immortality possible in music? Or will a musician's glory be a vain shadow? And if the art of music were unable to sustain glory, could we consider it to be a fine art worthy of the name?

---

1. Giacomo Leopardi, "Il Parini, o vero della gloria," in *Operette morali* (Milan: Stella, 1827), 117–61, 159.

Many say that music resembles a woman whose beauty diminishes with the passing of time, and that for this reason a composer has accomplished his task when his music succeeds in keeping the favor of audiences for a certain period, without any thought to the future. But let me make it clear that the comparison between the beauty of music and that of a woman is altogether false. In the case of a woman, it is not beauty itself that loses its powers over the beholder with the passage of time; it is rather her face, owing to the changes wrought on its features by the years. If you save the picture of a young beauty, this will always maintain its appeal, even though wrinkles have rendered the original unattractive. That is not true of music, for time does not modify or alter it in any way; thus, if its effectiveness diminishes, we must blame this on a change in the taste of the listeners. It is therefore inaccurate to say that music ages; better to say this of musical taste.

Now if the taste that judges musical beauty changes with time, it would seem that true beauty in music can never be determined, not so much because it is impossible to create it, as because it is impossible to assess it. The position of the art of music would then be strange and singular indeed. But it is not.

Perceptible beauty in a work of art is nothing but the expression of a higher beauty, an ideal beauty; the fine arts may be viewed as languages, each using different signs to express the same idea. Music being the vaguest, most indeterminate, and least obvious of these languages, its beauty is inevitably also more difficult to recognize. But we must not confuse true beauty with mere pleasantness, which is associated also with the nonaesthetic senses such as taste, smell, and touch. The ear is often—too often—used to savor the merely pleasant; this is the root of the flightiness of the public's taste.

To proceed with method in our judgment of Verdi's worth as an artist, we must consider music both in terms of pleasure and in terms of genuine beauty.

Viewed as something that simply gives pleasure, melody is certainly the least vital part of music, although it appears to be the most important. Individual melodies may die, so to speak, with the greatest of ease, but fortunately the nature of creativity is such that it compensates with extraordinary fertility. The way melodies change in this struggle between the inexhaustible imagination of composers and the ruthless sickle of Time is not a defect in the art of music, but rather one of its greatest virtues. In fact, since musical expression is vague by nature, a thousand melodies may express the same thing—hence our legitimate desire for variety. What perishes in a melody is not its meager expressive content, but only the portion that caresses the senses. The change-ability of taste is matched, as if by miracle, by the richness of the art of music and by the fertility of the imagination. In that sense, music is a language whose words or signs are continuously renewed. It is an astonishing thought that music, whose very matter is time, is also the art that produces the least durable works. One of the reasons for the variability of musical taste is precisely this essential aspect of music—that a certain length of time is required for its expression. Since length of time is one of the causes of boredom and satiety, musical taste is more easily tormented by boredom and satiety; and as novelty makes time seem to pass more quickly, it is desired in music more than elsewhere.

Hence melodies, by virtue of their ephemeral existence, cannot represent the beautiful, which is by nature unchanging, but only the fleetingly pleasant, and in this sense may be compared to the pleasing features of a woman who is not beautiful. The pleasantness of a face comes from certain expressions and characteristics that are agreeable to us because they conform somewhat to our way of feeling, or because they recall another face that is dear to us. These expressions and characteristics (or, if you like, features) are, in a sense, sem-blances of expression, and therefore without real cause (though the latter may be suggested to us by the power of analogy). Indeed, we often see faces with a smiling, angry, contemptuous, etc. expression, without there being any rea-son for them to be moved to laughter, anger, and so forth. Melody is similarly capable of assuming such features and expressive characters, without which it has no beauty. These expressive characters take a thousand forms, and are variously favored or rejected by changing tastes at different times. Some ap-pertain to a particular time, and all composers conform to them; others be-long to a single composer. If you look at serious music between Cimarosa and Rossini, you will find a solemn, grandiloquent, even inflated manner, as in, for example, "Se alla patria ognor donai" from *Gli Orazi* by Cimarosa.[2] That manner was then much in vogue, and accorded with the temperament of our fathers. Then consider the music of Rossini, and you will find that its special character is joviality; that of Bellini is melancholy; and in Verdi's music it is an impetuous, rustic mode. A composer's popularity depends principally on

2. See, in Domenico Cimarosa's *Gli Orazi e i Curiazi* (Venice: Teatro La Fenice, 1796), Marcus Horatius's first-act aria with chorus "Se alla patria ognor donai," N. 4 in the full score published in Paris by Imbault in 1802 (facsimile, ed. Giovanni Morelli and Elvidio Surian, Milan: Suvini Zerboni, 1985).

the way the expressive character of his music corresponds to the demands of the dominant taste. Note that the succession of these various kinds of expressive character does not proceed by leaps: their germs are found in earlier music. For example, who would not consider the third finale of Rossini's new *Mosè* to be Verdian in character?[3] It must be pointed out that, just as a composer gains favor when he satisfies the dominant taste, so, once he has risen to fame and preeminence, he influences that same taste, strengthening it and giving it form where before it was only a tendency or a desire. That is why the music of a composer's predecessors loses favor in proportion to his increasing predominance.

Verdi has certainly hit on new melodies, which, informed by his own temperament, have for some time given pleasure to those who hear them. This novelty must not, however, be considered absolute, for were we able to observe it from a certain distance of time (as we now observe old music, which all seems very similar to us) it would appear to be of little moment.

In melody, novelty can, after all, be easily introduced through the simplest of changes; if that were not so, the spring would dry up very quickly. The combination of notes, their various values, the meter, the tempo, the dynamics, the accents, the many kinds of chords, the arrangement of motifs, of phrases, of periods, and of rests, etc., etc.—all contribute to melodic variety. Moreover, older melodies may return after a time and seem new through only minor alterations. Similarity and dissimilarity may at times function in melody as they do in facial physiognomy. It may be observed that a portrait that is very like its model may not be recognizable, whereas one greatly altered—as in a caricature—may be instantly recognized by all. How does this come to be? By means of the *expressive character* that determines certain physiognomies, which is retained in the caricature but not in the portrait. That is true also of melodies, which may be rendered unrecognizable by the simplest changes, whereas other, more serious changes may not obscure their similarities if the expressive character is in some way preserved.

Rhythm, harmony, and form are the three principal components of melody. Let us see what novelty Verdi may have introduced in each of them. With regard to rhythm, he has followed the modern, "sensualist" school,[4] taking the greatest possible advantage of it; and since a melody takes on a new ap-

3. Rossini, *Moïse et Pharaon*, N. 12, Final ("Je réclame la foi promise"; "Grand Roi, délivre-nous").
4. See pp. 163ff. above.

pearance when new notes are placed on the same rhythmic frame, Verdi has employed many old rhythms, clothing them with fresh notes. Particularly after his first manner, he has preferred staccato rhythms. His harmonies are the customary ones, although at times he has displayed a richness that brings him closer to Mercadante. But the greatest novelty a master of great genius can introduce into music is in the realm of form. At first glance, it would seem that, precisely because it does not have external models to imitate, music would be so free as to give the artist full rein to introduce the newest and most unusual forms. But even conceding that the musician's imagination and fantasy might not be, like those of other artists, impeded by obstacles intrinsic to his art, they would find a potent one in the listeners. Precisely because music does not address the intellect with signs of specific meaning, it must proceed in conformity with the laws that govern memory. Now, memory would tire exceedingly, and would be unable to retain a melody at first hearing, were it not aided by similarities, analogies, symmetry, and other elements of regularity, which are all the more necessary the less clear and obvious the expressive mode, as is also true of architecture.

Hearing, aided by memory, cannot comprehend prolonged melody unless this has a form that in certain ways resembles a musical discourse: not an intelligible discourse, but one directed to the sense that must perceive it. This discourse is the product of phrases and melodic periods, either symmetrical, or analogical, or composed in a single sweep [*di getto*], etc. When we consider melody in its relationship to perception, we cannot look for unity proper, which lies in expression,[5] but only for what stands in for this unity: the predominance of one element over the whole. It is therefore necessary for there to be a specific expressive character, phrase, or period—or even, in the case of a long piece of music, a whole discourse—that, as if it were a main idea, dominates the composition. This musical idea may dominate in various ways: it can be surrounded by phrases, periods, and other elements whose rhythmic or melodic similarities to it make them its virtual shadows; it can be repeated after other melodies that cause the listener to desire it, so that it returns as welcome as an old friend; or it can be brought back several times, each time more richly adorned. The first way is the least consequential and is suitable for the smallest-scale pieces, such as arias and cabalettas. The second way requires larger proportions; Rossini was able to use it better than anyone. The third way is suitable for very large canvases [*quadri*], and Meyerbeer, who so

5. By "expression" Basevi here means the expression of determinate meaning.

broadened the field of musical representation, used it admirably. Verdi did not bring in great novelty of form and kept generally to the known methods, although he had the discernment to banish the many melodies that merit the term *pleonastic*—melodies that are used by composers with the intention of placing a musical idea in greater relief but that often generate tedium instead, which cannot be remedied by the reappearance of the idea they were supposed to serve. Verdi has, in a sense, proclaimed the equality of melodies: he did not want some to have greater or lesser importance than others. Thus, while he may have obtained equality, he has to some extent renounced unity. In this respect his conciseness is a somewhat negative attribute. In the grand duet for soprano and baritone in act 2 of *La traviata* that system is exaggerated.[6] In the final *terzetto* of *Ernani*[7] various musical periods succeed one another as though they were so many principal ideas—although there is among them a little phrase that is reiterated, providing a shadow of unity. I say "a shadow" because it is not always enough to repeat a musical idea to make it significant—something Verdi may have experienced in the second finale of both *I due Foscari* and *Il trovatore*.[8] The composer must use repetition only when a musical idea is worthy of dominating.

With regard to the form of arias, cabalettas, and similar pieces, Verdi has generally followed Donizetti and Bellini. The forms of his duets are modeled on the most varied examples by those composers, though not without returning a number of times to the old system of three repetitions. In ensemble pieces for three, four, and more voices, he has introduced greater variety than his predecessors usually displayed. It should be noted that where a number of characters come together motivated by differing emotions, given that [musical] unity is virtually impossible, it is better to use Verdi's system. And indeed Verdi has written ensemble numbers that are very fine in terms of dramatic truth. On the other hand, forms cannot always be changed as the composer pleases: he is at times obliged to accept and conserve at length those of others, if only because they still satisfy the general taste. Thus, we must not blame Verdi if he did not effect radical transformations. To everything its season.

6. For Basevi's discussion of the Violetta-Germont duet (N. 5 of *La traviata*), see p. 199 above.

7. See its discussion on p. 54 above.

8. Basevi had already discussed repetitions or reprises of thematic material in these two finali, in both cases finding the outcome ineffective and mentioning Meyerbeer as a composer who excelled in such an art. See pp. 67–68 and 187 above.

Every so many years musical forms change in a perceptible way; to prove
this it is necessary only to compare the early and late operas of Rossini, such
as *Tancredi* and *Guillaume Tell*. Radical change in musical forms is the reason
why old melodies—even independently of the changeability of taste—prove
less pleasing because less comprehensible. Because of such changes in form,
many pieces of music that were much in favor some time ago seem poor today.
It would be useful for the art of music to include a branch occupied specifically with form.

A "musical morphology" would reveal similarities that otherwise remain hidden. A "comparative morphology" of Verdi's music would prove
that in the forms of his pieces there has been little progress and no radical
transformation between *Nabucodonosor* and *Aroldo*. I do not wish to make any
absolute claim that Verdi has always copied the forms of others, for he has
now and then—and which composer has not?—employed unusual forms. It
is not my intention here to talk of these "accidental" forms, but rather of
forms that have received their final sentence, so to speak,[9] and of forms that
have obliterated the older ones and been firmly established in their place. Yet
Verdi did not grope blindly when he adopted other composers' forms, and
his work has often shown that he understands that not all forms are equally
suited to all melodies; whereas many other composers—lacking good taste or
judgment, and being all intent on blind imitation—because they do not know
how to choose (let alone create) forms suited to their melodies, use the very
forms that often emphasize elements that were better hidden while placing in
shadow elements that deserve all the light.

2

There are melodies that, though not among the most appealing or pleasing
to the ear, still seem to enjoy immortality because in their regard the general
taste does not appear to change at all. This miracle is worked through expression. Take the andantino of the trio from Rossini's *Guillaume Tell*[10] and see
what the melody of this piece basically amounts to; and yet, once it is joined
to the words, what could be more moving? Where music aptly expresses both

9. Basevi writes "forme *accidentali*," his italics generally signaling a technical use of a
term—here probably the philosophical one (meaning "nonessential"). The definition immediately following, "passate [. . .] *in giudicato*," is rather from juridical language, referring to cases
for which there has been a final judgment, leaving no room for appeal.
10. See Basevi's discussion of this passage, p. 182 above.

the words and the dramatic situation, we are so attracted by the beauty of the expression itself that we do not perceive the limited delight given to the ear: we consider the melody very pleasing, while in fact our pleasure comes principally from our being moved. It may also be asserted that the less music courts the ear, the greater chance it has to live a long life, as long as its expressive effectiveness makes it agreeable to us: in that case it does not owe its life to fickle taste and therefore cannot die by its hand.

Other melodies enjoy a long life and retain their effectiveness not by virtue of their expressiveness but by a "mnemonic" effect, as found in national anthems and so forth. Like artificial languages, these have no power except by virtue of the things they recall to memory.[11] Such mnemonic melodies thus have an uncertain life and cannot produce the same effect in all places or among all people. But the dignity of music lies in expression, and while it may sometimes suit a composer to use mnemonic effects in his works, he has to take as certain that the musically beautiful cannot entirely reside in them.[12]

It must be noted that not every kind of expression is sufficient to keep a melody perpetually alive. The features and expressive characters of individual melodies, discussed above,[13] are a first plane of expression, where there is but little life force. Some early music was considered very expressive in its time and yet today would be unbearable, such as that of Peri, Caccini, Galilei, Barbara Strozzi, and others.[14] Note, however, that those pieces were first steps in the expressive genre. The closer we come to our own time, the more examples we find of music of great expressive beauty—if not always throughout an entire piece, then certainly in some of its parts, as may be observed in the duet "Ne' giorni tuoi felici" from Paisiello's *L'olimpiade*.[15] And if the old comic

11. Basevi's "linguaggi *artificiali*" probably refers—as it does in other Italian writers of his time—to conventional languages (including verbal languages such as Italian or French), and he seems here to come close to the concept of arbitrariness found in modern linguistics and semiotics.

12. While Basevi's "il *bello musicale*" (which could also be translated as "musical beauty" or "the beautiful in music") might evoke the well-known book by the German aesthetician Eduard Hanslick, *Vom Musikalisch-Schönen* (1854), it should be noted that the phrase had long been in currency among Italian writers of the eighteenth and nineteenth centuries.

13. See pp. 243ff. above.

14. All the composers mentioned here are from a relatively narrow historical context, and were presumably chosen by Basevi because of their association with a style held to be especially expressive—the new manner of vocal writing that emerged in Italy between the late sixteenth century and the early seventeenth.

15. See the duet for Aristea and Megacle "Ne' giorni tuoi felici" in Giovanni Paisiello's *L'olimpiade* (Naples: Teatro San Carlo, 1786). Basevi owned an eighteenth-century manuscript

music of the same composer, and of Cimarosa, Guglielmi, and others, has survived better than their serious music, this is because of the greater importance it accorded to those words that give rise to laughter, which the music alone would be unable to elicit. Hence, it is to expression that comic operas owe their longer life.

In expression, truth must be distinguished from beauty. While beauty cannot be divorced from truth, truth may be found without beauty. To some extent, expressive music is governed by declamation. Now, just as one scene may be declaimed in several ways in accordance with truth, though only one of them is beautiful and effective, so music may express the same emotion in different ways, but only one of them will be the ideal type toward which the greatest artists will incline. It sometimes happens that, because of a certain fleeting disposition in the audience, a mode of expression that is very distant from the ideal type will make its effect simply because it conforms to the truth of the scene. But such effectiveness disappears with a change in that disposition. If the audience is agitated, for example, an exaggerated form of expression will be needed to rouse it, and so forth.

But who may judge true beauty in music? It is those mighty few who, as in all the fine arts, gain an irrefutable authority in the republic of letters through their exquisite taste and their fine and discriminating way of thinking. To tell the truth, those few do not seem at first glance to wield much power, and composers, eager for quick success, rather devote themselves to flattering the groundlings—the largest, most responsive, and least thoughtful part of their audience. They care nothing for the select few, whom they often even ridicule, without realizing that by doing this for the sake of a day's vainglory they are condemning themselves to eternal obscurity. But the thousand obstacles that composers face in seeking performances for their operas shamefully oblige the beginner to sacrifice art to the caprices of the crowd, as they make it imperative to gain an immediate, splendid success, which is measured by the impresario in terms of the number of tickets sold. Verdi paid his tribute to error in his first manner, with its frequent unisons, certain abuses of sonority [*sonorità*], and so forth; in his second manner, however, similar bad effects were far scarcer. The scepter won, his rivals beaten, he then sought new paths with *Simon Boccanegra*, where he seems to have set little store by the approbation of common audiences—and for that he must be praised.

---

copy of the full score of the opera's first act (in which this piece is found). See *Catalogo Basevi*, 74, 348.

The expressive character [of individual melodies] that we discussed earlier is sometimes a major obstacle to the proper expression of the words: some composers try to force music to express diverse, even opposite, emotions while still retaining that same character, on which they make all its beauty depend. This is like assigning the role of Medea to an actress whose figure is beautiful but whose features naturally express a smile—or like our prima donnas, who, relying entirely on the amplitude of their crinolines for their physical appeal, use them to portray even characters on whom they look absurd. Also damaging to expression are commonplaces such as certain kinds of cadential passages and harmonic progressions, some of the ready-made forms, and so forth, which may add flavor to music while they are in fashion but deprive it of it at every other time. We see this in many early arias, in which the very elements that once seemed to be adornments, providing all the piece's grace and beauty, are now viewed as blemishes. Verdi sometimes employed that impetuous character typical of his music even where it was inappropriate; but this defect must be attributed to his inability to tame his own temperament, which is naturally so inclined, rather than to cold calculation—as would be the case with the imitators and with the flatterers of the crowd, who do not copy but merely caricature.

Verdi did not force his music to express very diverse things, and he shone principally in strong, sudden, grand emotions. The rustic spirit found in his music manifests itself naturally in scenes of great surprise, admiration, worship, and unbridled liveliness—qualities that Verdi was always able to express aptly through music.

Does this Verdian mode of expression represent progress? With respect to quality, I cannot see that it does, for Rossini, Bellini, Donizetti, and Meyerbeer have provided examples of expression that Verdi has certainly not surpassed. Verdi never added to the pathos of Bellini, but he was more varied in his emotions; he equaled Donizetti in expressing the emotions of characters neither too elevated nor too humble; he surpassed Donizetti in accuracy and diligence but was not as fecund in unusual, euphonious melodies. He was a fine emulator of Rossini's majestic manner, particularly as found in the new version of *Mosè*[16] and in *Guillaume Tell*—except that Rossini's majesty conceals a smile and Verdi's a certain harshness that at times is not at all detrimental to effectiveness, and even increases it. Verdi has not, however, shown the inexhaustible creative vein attested by the diversity of Rossini's works.

16. See chapter 1, n. 6, above.

Verdi sometimes successfully imitated certain of Meyerbeer's effects in orchestration and theatrical music, but avoided imitating his forms; he did not try to fashion the vast musical pictures [*quadri musicali*] in which Meyerbeer is peerless and indeed alone on the path of true progress in music. Verdi was unique in Italy, however, in the serious expression of the emotions of characters belonging to our modern, prosaic society, such as in *La traviata*. The subject matter of *La sonnambula, Linda*, etc. is similar but not prosaic.

Although Verdi has shown no great desire to go in search of new forms—because he did not make such radical changes in music as to require them—neither was he such a slave to the old forms that he would not sacrifice them when necessary, as Donizetti too had done, often judiciously. In ensembles Verdi truly reigns, for he has been able to give them the dramatic expression of which they are susceptible, unlike many other composers who used them only as opportunities to make good counterpoint and nothing more. The quartet from *Rigoletto* will always be an example of Verdi's genius. In these pieces we also find the above-mentioned musical tableaux, although not of vast proportions.

Assuming that a composer has achieved expressiveness in his music, this will be of no use without performers to put it into effect. In painting and in sculpture the same artist conceives and executes; in architecture the executor need be little more than a machine or automaton; music, on the other hand, requires an intelligent performer, one so much so that he can almost identify with the composer. This unique condition of the musical art has given rise to, and constantly maintains, a competition, indeed a battle, between those who conceive and those who execute—a battle that has proved to be of grave damage to that art.

Singers have always sought primacy at the expense of the composer, and composers have always stealthily undermined the art of singing in order to subjugate the singer. Since the earliest times, composers have aspired to keep performers too far below them in status; even Guido of Arezzo, outraged by the effrontery of singers, writes in his *Micrologus* that, as composers understand what they do and singers do what they do not understand, the latter should be compared to beasts—"nam, qui facit quod non sapit deffinitur Bestia."[17] Tigrini compares singers to the donkey that carries the

---

17. "For he who does what he does not understand is termed a beast." The passage is in fact in Guido's verse treatise *Regule rithmice* (*Regulae rhythmicae*). See Dolores Pesce, *Guido d'Arezzo's "Regule rithmice," "Prologus in antiphonarium," and "Epistola ad Michahelem": A Critical Text and Translation* (Ottawa: Institute of Mediaeval Music, 1999), 332–33.

relics.[18] But these are exaggerations. Singers are not machines or beasts of burden, for they must have no little intelligence and feeling. Still, they must not exalt themselves to great heights and treat composers, as they too often do, as subalterns or people of no account. They want not only composers to be below them, but if possible also field marshals and ambassadors, as reflected in Gabrielli's riposte to Catherine II, Empress of Russia, and Caffarelli's to Louis XV, King of France.[19] The witty Benedetto Marcello, in his *Teatro alla moda*, commented ironically on the singers of his age: "When the modern virtuoso is walking with some great man of letters, he must not yield the right-hand side, for to the greater part of mankind the *musico* is esteemed a virtuoso and the man of letters a common man; indeed, he should persuade the man of letters—be he a philosopher, a poet, a mathematician, a physician, an orator, etc.—to become a *musico*, making him consider seriously that *musici* never want for money—not to mention their high status—while men of letters mostly starve."[20]

The age of the castrati was the most splendid for the art of singing, but it was also the time when singers had the greatest boldness and made composers suffer the greatest tyrannies. The eccentricities of many of these self-styled virtuosos are notorious; they wanted themselves and no one else to shine in an opera, trampling under foot all the laws of common sense. Algarotti tells us that in his time the singers had popularized silly contests between the voice and instruments such as the oboe, the trumpet, and so forth.[21]

The fall of the castrati must be attributed not to the war waged on them by composers but to sound principles of humanity—although composers were

18. A reference to the composer and music theorist Orazio Tigrini, who—after quoting the same sentence from Guido—had applied to singers an allegory (found in Andrea Alciato's *Emblematum liber*, 1531) in which a donkey swelled with pride to see people kneeling as he passed, not realizing that they were worshiping the sacred effigies he was carrying on his back. See Orazio Tigrini, *Il compendio della musica nel quale brevemente si tratta dell'arte del contrapunto* (Venice: Ricciardo Amadino, 1588), 52–53.

19. Caterina Gabrielli, a prominent soprano of the second half of the eighteenth century, sang in St. Petersburg in the 1770s; Caffarelli (Gaetano Majorano), one of the greatest castrati of the eighteenth century, sang in Paris in the 1750s. According to widely reported anecdotes, they insisted on better treatment than field marshals (Gabrielli to Catherine the Great) or ambassadors (Caffarelli to an emissary of Louis XV).

20. Benedetto Marcello's famous satirical pamphlet *Il teatro alla moda* was first published anonymously in Venice in 1720. The passage quoted here is from the section "A' musici" (To the *musici*): although the term *musico* was more frequently used to refer to a castrato, in this section Marcello alternates between "musico" and "virtuoso," and the content clearly addresses not just castrati but any male singers active in *opera seria* or as *parti serie*.

21. See Francesco Algarotti, *Saggio sopra l'opera in musica* (Livorno: Coltellini, 1763), 32.

encouraged by that fall to assume the superiority that is due them. Rossini removed from the singer's discretion the warblings and *fioriture* that, if sometimes used with wisdom, were more often abused so as to render the composer's music barely recognizable.[22] Rossini's talent and good taste enriched his music with ornaments that only the inventiveness of the greatest singers could have equaled—though certainly not surpassed. But he simultaneously took from these singers one of their most potent means of allowing their natural gifts to shine, an end for the sake of which they had willingly yoked themselves to long and tedious exercises, which they no longer considered necessary. Thus, the study of singing began to deteriorate. Bellini and Donizetti virtually banished *fioriture* and thereby further simplified the study of singing. They nonetheless gave singers a way of showing a certain grace in addition to their natural feelings. Meanwhile sonority effects [*effetti di sonorità*] came into fashion, thanks mostly to Mercadante and Pacini, and singing was replaced by shouting; thus, grace too was almost banished and gave way to emotions affected through such a display of energy that music came to be more widely called "dramatic"—though I would sooner call it frenzied. Singing received the coup de grâce. With his staccato and vibrato melodies,[23] his thrusts, and his frequent use of high notes—notably in his first two manners—Verdi has certainly not contributed to the betterment of the miserable state of singing. We have reached the point of paying a tenor forty thousand francs a month for a high C-sharp in full chest voice!

To this fall of bel canto, as well as to changed taste, must be imputed the fact that some pieces that once had great success seem today very cold indeed. Even if today's greatest singer were to perform the aria "Ombra adorata aspetta" from Zingarelli's *Giulietta e Romeo* it would make little or no effect. But who knows whether you would not be moved to tears, as was Napoleon I, if it were to be sung by a new Crescentini?[24]

22. This narrative—according to which from a certain point onward Rossini insisted on writing out all the ornamentation in his music so as to leave singers little or no freedom to alter it—was widespread in Basevi's time, undergoing serious revision only in the second half of the twentieth century.

23. On Basevi's use of *staccato* and *vibrato*, see chapter 13, n. 15, above.

24. Zingarelli's *Giulietta e Romeo* was premiered at Milan's Teatro alla Scala in 1796. The composer's original setting of the third-act aria "Ombra adorata" was soon replaced by a more successful one written by the great castrato Girolamo Crescentini (who had created the role of Romeo). Stendhal described Crescentini's performance of "Ombra adorata" as "the perfection of singing," making specific reference to the singer's art in extemporizing ornaments. *Vie de Rossini*, 2 vols. (Paris: Boulland, 1824), 2:446–52 (chap. 32), 451 ("la perfection du chant"). The episode concerning Napoleon took place in 1808, according to François-Joseph Fétis,

A resurgence of bel canto is not to be expected of singers, for they seek immediate applause above all else, being unable to leave any trace of their skills behind them or to place any hope in posterity. It does not matter to them that the audience's taste is depraved, their only concern being to flatter it. Composers foolishly abet the singers in their pursuit of frenzied acclaim, falsely believing that it is they who generate a great part of the applause; they do not consider the damage that art suffers at their hands.

Since composers have increasingly narrowed the scope of the study required by singers, the ability of those singers has declined accordingly; we must not marvel at the fact that today, with a few exceptions, they cannot show themselves off except by sheer lung power.

Verdi has, in fact, been no great adulator of the crowd; but with his impetuous way of feeling he has from the first reduced singing to a manner so emphatic that it has given neophyte singers a way of standing out without long study. And the graces that are certainly found in Verdi's music are not given the salutary preeminence one would wish for. Though it matters little, or not at all, to the singer that his trade is rushing to its ruin, such a decline cannot be a matter of indifference to the composer, for good music cannot shine without worthy performers. Besides, the mediocrity of singers clips the wings of the composer's creativity, for he can write only according to the insignificant ability of those singers. That is, he can write only music of little consequence, or music contrary to the sound principles of art and true beauty. We certainly cannot applaud Jommelli, who once, unable to find competent singers, consoled himself by saying, "Oh well, I shall make the violins sing."[25] But violins do not sing—they play. If composers will make good singers necessary, they will certainly not be lacking.

The art of singing, which was once one of the few incontrovertible glories of Italy, has today sunk so low that I would almost say it cannot descend any further. Who will bring about its resurgence? Young composers have too much to do in struggling against the tide, and cannot attempt such a difficult task. Verdi alone could, by capitalizing on his fame, if not accomplish this resurgence—for the bad habits are too deeply rooted—then at least begin it.

Biographie universelle des musiciens et bibliographie générale de la musique, 8 vols. (Brussels: Meline, Cans et Compagnie, 1835–44), 3 (1837): 216–17.

25. Basevi probably derives the episode from Giuseppe Carpani, *Le rossiniane, ossia Lettere musico-teatrali* (Padua: Minerva, 1824), 18 ("farò cantare i violini").

3

The composer of genius, when contemplating an ideal beauty found within himself, employs in his work the means that art provides to manifest his innermost feelings externally. Thus, the technical state of the art determines the confines within which the artist may work. As music is a language whose signs are continually changing, it must constantly enrich itself, however rich it may already be in the elements that form that language.

Orchestration is one of the most powerful means of expression for the composer, and can be what colors are to the painter. Haydn, Mozart, Beethoven, Cherubini, Rossini, and Meyerbeer brought orchestration to such a height of excellence that it does not seem to be surpassable with regard to the number, the nature, the combinations, or the proper use of the various instruments.

Verdi has certainly not enriched orchestration, but he has made discerning use of effects invented by his predecessors. Yet he has not maintained this valuable means of expression at the level to which it had been perfected; today, Italy cannot bask in glory on that point. That notwithstanding, we cannot but regret for art's sake that Verdi's orchestral scores are guarded so jealously by their owners.[26]

The benefit of art lies in a kind of public good, which must take precedence over every other concern. The right, or privilege, of literary property must therefore be placed under certain conditions that will profit art without harming the author.[27] What would we say if an author, taking advantage of property rights, published a foreign edition of a most useful work, and then, for personal reasons, forbade it being brought into the very country that accorded him those rights? Would that not be as though the vendors of bread, meat, vegetables, and so forth should one fine day agree to starve the city in which they sell their wares, taking advantage of their right to sell or not to sell? There is food for the spirit as there is food for the body; it is not legitimate to deprive society of one any more than the other, so long as society offers sufficient remuneration. In not publishing Verdi's [orchestral] scores,

26. This polemical remark refers to Ricordi's practice of printing and selling only vocal scores, while keeping full orchestral scores for hire only (as Basevi makes explicit toward the end of the following paragraph).

27. Throughout this passage Basevi writes of "literary" property: since his main concern is obviously music, the term is to be understood more broadly as "artistic" or (in today's terms) "intellectual" property.

the proprietors are within their rights; we therefore beg legislators to consider how far literary property should extend. If the stupendous scores of Mozart, Cherubini, and others had been hidden, would we be able today to glory in so many fine composers? Enough said.

The orchestra is useful to composers because it provides material for the imitation of nature that, though not the goal of music, aids in reaching that goal by enhancing expression and representing what stirs our emotions; Verdi took advantage of this in the storm scene of *Rigoletto*. But instruments are also an effective aid to the composer because of the qualities or timbres of their voices, which accord more or less with certain states of mind. Verdi showed understanding of this, too, in the scene preceding the *terzetto* of *I Lombardi*, where he made the sound of the violin dominate.[28] Consider too that the effect of a given instrument's sound is not always the same; not infrequently, it changes in relation to the impression produced by other, more perfect instruments. A case in point is that of the harpsichord, once so highly prized, now universally despised. In a letter of 1773 addressed to the *Journal de musique*, Canon Trouflaut, organist at Nevers, wrote thus of a harpsichord made by Taskin, who had substituted buffalo-leather for raven-quill plectra: "What prodigious variety in an instrument once so ungrateful! The magical sounds it produces today quickly draw the attention of the listener, touch his heart, enchant him, seduce him."[29] Although confident and secure in his handling of the orchestra, Verdi still has not focused on it enough to derive the greatest possible benefit from it.

In his second manner Verdi renounced certain sonority effects [*effetti di sonorità*] and certain abuses of some of the instruments, but his progress was not otherwise greatly notable. In *Les vêpres siciliennes* he lavished special care on the strings, but a composer must also be aware of all the other instruments and, making them strengthen each other, use them to a single end.

4

Like the sciences, the arts grow and improve by means of new discoveries, or of new applications of those discoveries. Verdi created new melodies, but that

---

28. See chapter 15 for Basevi's discussion of the storm in *Rigoletto*'s N. 13 as "objective correlative" of the scene's mood and chapter 2 for his view of the specific psychological effect of the violin (in relation to N. 13 of *I Lombardi*).

29. See *Journal de musique*, 1773, no. 5, 10–19, 14. Although Basevi uses the term *spinetta*, the passage he quotes clearly refers to the harpsichord, as does the article more generally.

kind of novelty pertains not to art proper, but rather, as noted above, to the changeable taste of the multitude. No significant novelty has been noted in the form and expression of the melodies, except in the *pezzi concertati*, which Verdi was almost always able to make into musical pictures; thus, through frequent use of what had rarely been done before, Verdi has acquired the right to be credited with their invention. There is much merit in the greater use of the good, even if it shows nothing but heightened judgment. With regard to the orchestra, not a single new instrument was used in Verdi's operas, nor were any of the old ones used differently or with greater effect. The science of harmony, too, is left as Verdi found it.

In the sixteen years during which Verdi's operas have reigned, it is curious to observe that no notable transformation of operatic music has taken place. If, on the other hand, we compare Rossini's *Tancredi* with the same composer's *Guillaume Tell*, or Meyerbeer's *Margherita d'Anjou* with his *Robert le diable*, we are forced to admire the giant steps those two composers took, not so much in the development of their imagination as in practical advances in the art of music.[30] True, Verdi has had several manners, but these cannot be considered as new steps forward, only as detours in the direction of various schools and various composers. With his first manner, Verdi grafted his plant onto the vigorous Rossinian tree; had he continued on the path of *Nabucodonosor*, who knows what heights he might have reached? With the second manner, he turned completely to Donizetti. With *La traviata* he approached the French school, and with *Simone* he tried to drink at the fountain of German music. In a certain sense, Verdi may be called eclectic — certainly not because he has tried to reconcile diverse styles, but rather because he has searched through them for a stable foundation for his own art.

Verdi was not wrong in *Simone* and *Aroldo* to try to instill into his music a fresh vigor, drawing new strength from German music. And we must not deny the importance of the attempt even if the result has not lived up to the intention. From time to time Italy has needed this marrying of the two schools: Jommelli, Paer, Mayr, Cherubini, and above all Rossini succeeded marvelously in that difficult undertaking. In my view, the music most suitable for the redirection of our own is that of Meyerbeer, especially as it is already somewhat tempered by Italian music.

---

30. Meyerbeer's *opera semiseria Margherita d'Anjou* was premiered at Milan's Teatro alla Scala in 1820; the later, French version, *Marguerite d'Anjou*, was first given at Paris's Théâtre de l'Odéon in 1826.

Not that we wish Italian music to lose what makes it so beautiful and so greatly enjoyed throughout the world; but neither should it go too far in becoming excessively sensual. Germanic music can be of use in remedying this fault: though not adorned by those gifts that make Italian music resplendent, it possesses others that, in a different way, make it most valuable and appealing.

Italy looks to Verdi for the greatest possible improvement in theatrical music, but it also demands from him a school that may protect it from the otherwise inevitable decadence of that art in which it has for so long retained primacy. Verdi must consider that the artist lives in posterity not only through the memory of the works he leaves to it, but also, and more nobly, through the generations of disciples who, in every age, gratefully perpetuate the glory of their master.

INDEX